CW01646835

The BRONICA MANUAL

The BRONICA MANUAL

William Cheung

R. Morgan Publishing

© 1989 William Cheung
All rights reserved

Published by:
R. Morgan Publishing
PO Box 11
Chislehurst
KENT BR7 5RH

British Library Cataloguing in Publication Data

Cheung, William
The Bronical Manual.
1. Bronica cameras
I. Title
771.3′1

ISBN 0-902979-07-8

Printed in the United Kingdom by:
Manor Park Press Ltd
Highfield Industrial Estate
Eastbourne, East Sussex

Contents

Introduction

Welcome to the world of Bronica: a world of flexibility, reliability, versatility and, of course, quality. Bronica medium-format cameras have been meeting the demands of the world's discerning photographers for more than 25 years and the current line-up comprises five models, each supported by an extensive system of lenses and accessories which make Bronica the ideal system for both amateur and professional users.

Although the name Bronica is world renowned few people are aware of the company's history.

Founded on profits from the manufacture of ladies' powder compacts and consumer novelties such as a wrist-watch type cigarette lighter, Bronica Camera Co. Ltd. was established in 1956. Its founder, Zenzaburo Yoshino, had first considered developing a camera some years earlier, but because his experience of optics and camera manufacture was limited the first venture ended in bankruptcy. Obviously, financial security was a prerequisite to further research and development, therefore ladies' compacts took precedence.

Backed by the capital accumulated from his business, Zenzaburo's study of his 'dream' camera began in earnest in the winter of 1952.

The decision to base his camera on 120 roll film was made early on, primarily because the 6 × 6cm format permitted sizeable enlargements with sparkling resolution, smooth tonal gradation and biting sharpness. The new camera had to be a single-lens-reflex (SLR) with an instant-return mirror mechanism so that it was possible to view the subject constantly except during the very instant when the photograph was exposed.

Handling had to be as simple, quick and all-encompassing as possible. He thought, for instance, that the film winding knob should handle several operations: advancing the film, cocking the shutter and focusing. An interchangeable film back system was high on the list of design priorities, enabling the freedom to use several film types with one camera body. Of course, interlocks would prevent any possibility of double exposing an already exposed frame, or of winding an unexposed frame to the next unintentionally. Finally, he wanted a long shutter speed range, from 10 seconds right up to 1/1300 sec.

These were the main features Zenzaburo envisaged and, considering the technical ability of the camera manufacturing industry at that time, his concept might never have become reality had it not been for his determination and patience, and the skill of his team.

The reflex mirror alone took a year's work. Because it was impractical for the new company to become embroiled in the intricacies of lens manufacture the decision was made to use available lenses. This, in turn, meant that it was essential to design a reflex mirror and camera body that would permit any make of lens to be used. Called the "Slide-down Instant Return Mirror Action", the development of this unique mechanism, in which the reflex mirror moved downward and forward simultaneously instead of swinging upwards, was the first of many brilliant triumphs for Zenzaburo and his engineering team.

Steady, rather than spectacular, progress supported with money generated by the continuing production of ladies' compacts and cigarette lighters meant it was not until 1956 that a hand-tooled metal body prototype camera was ready; for which Zenzaburo was awarded an Invention Gratuity from the Tokyo Metropolitan Office the same year. The following year he received an Invention Subsidy from the Japanese Patent Office for his endeavours.

Prior to going into full production in 1958 Zenzaburo approached Nippon Kogaku Kikai K.K. for cooperation in supplying their critically acclaimed Nikkor lenses for his camera. Nippon Kogaku scrutinised the new camera closely and, realising the originality and engineering quality of the product, agreed to supply Nikkor lenses.

The 1959 Philadelphia Camera Show in the United States was the venue for the camera's debut, but even at this stage no name had been decided upon. Finally, the name Zenza Bronica was chosen, which, in Japanese, means "the camera of Zenzaburo", in acknowledgement of the inventor. Public acclamation at the Philadelphia show was tremendous and the 'real' Zenza Bronica D immediately became the 'dream' camera of photographers the world over. Zenzaburo Yoshino died in November 1988.

Chronology of Zenza Bronica SLR cameras

1947 Zenzaburo Yoshino established a ladies' compact/cigarette lighter manufacturing business.

1952 Study of the original medium-format SLR commences.

1956 First Bronica camera prototype assembled.

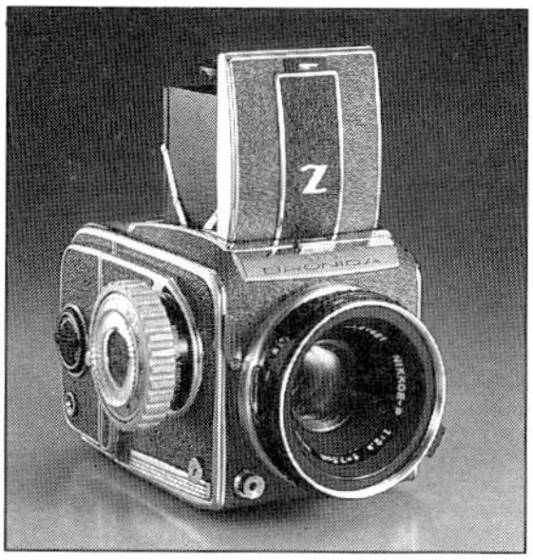

1959 Zenza Bronica D: This focal plane 6 × 6cm SLR was launched in March to the US market and introduced to Japan in December. It incorporated many features which were exciting and innovative in the field of medium-format camera design: automatic lens diaphragm, instant return mirror and a multiple purpose wind knob which controlled focusing and shutter selection as well as film transport.

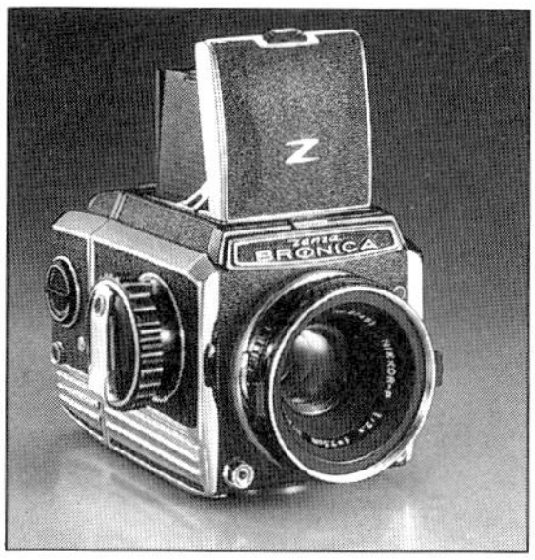

1961 Zenza Bronica S: Many of the outstanding features of the D were retained in this model, though several aspects of its operation were modified. The multi-function wind knob for example handled only shutter speed selection and film transport.

1964 Zenza Bronica C: A non-interchangeable film back 6 × 6cm format SLR with a focal plane shutter which had a top speed of 1/500 sec.

1965 Zenza Bronica C2: Basically the same as the model C but upgraded to accept the then recently introduced 220 size roll film. An improved shutter gave a top speed of 1/1000 sec.

1965 Zenza Bronica S2: Accepted either 120 or 220 film. The S2 had a host of practical features: a focal plane shutter with speeds from 1 second to 1/1000 sec plus B, and electronic X-flash sync at 1/40 sec; depth of field preview facility; instant-return reflex mirror; and accepted Nikkor lenses. The S2 had a dual-bayonet lens mechanism which also appeared on the S2A, EC, EC-TL and EC-TL II.

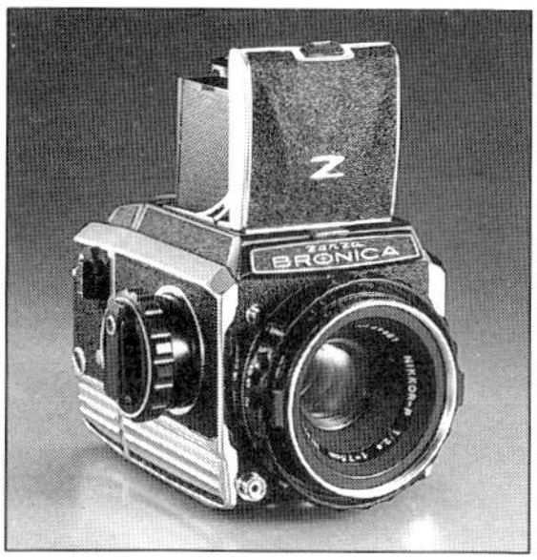

1969 Zenza Bronica S2A: Basically a black leather clad model of the S2 and much of its internal mechanism was nitrogenised for greater durability.

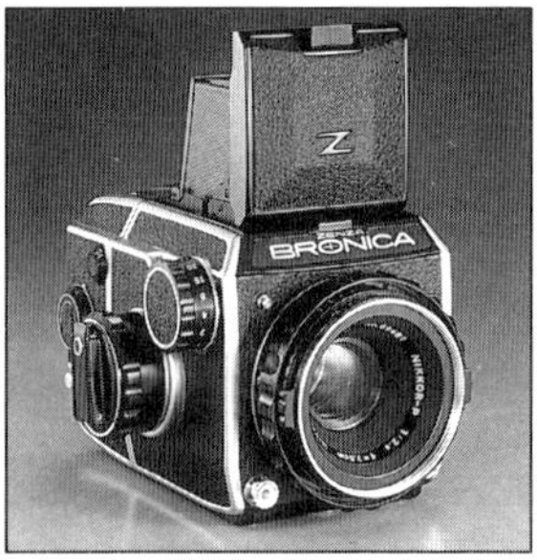

1972 Zenza Bronica EC: First medium-format SLR to incorporate an electronically controlled shutter; it was of the focal plane type with speeds from 4 seconds to 1/1000 sec plus B. Its system of accessories included the TTL Exposure Meter which coupled automatically to the camera's electronic control circuit when attached and provided open aperture metering.

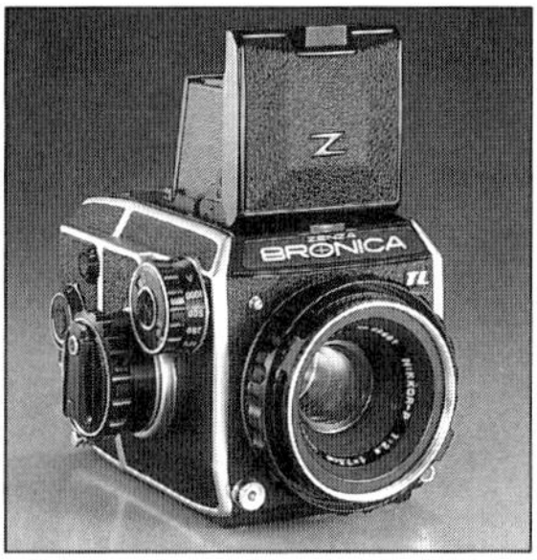

1975 Zenza Bronica EC-TL: The first 6 × 6cm SLR to feature an integral through-the-lens metering system with aperture-priority automatic exposure and manual modes based on fast response silicon blue cells. Focal plane shutter was electronically controlled with a range of 4 seconds to 1/1000 sec plus B.

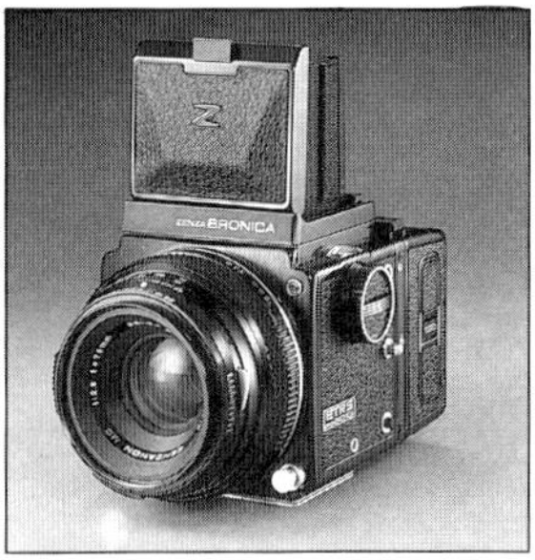

1976 Zenza Bronica ETR: The beginning of a dynasty which is still going strong today in the forms of the ETRS and ETRSi. It is a 6 × 4.5cm format system camera with electronic leaf shutter allowing flash synchronisation at all shutter speeds. Other noteworthy points include: an exclusive four-claw lens bayonet, interchangeable film backs and speed of handling; characteristics, of course, of the current ETR cameras.

1977 Zenza Bronica ETR-C: Identical in all respects to the ETR apart from the lack of the interchangeable film back facility though 120 or 220 film can be used with the appropriate insert.

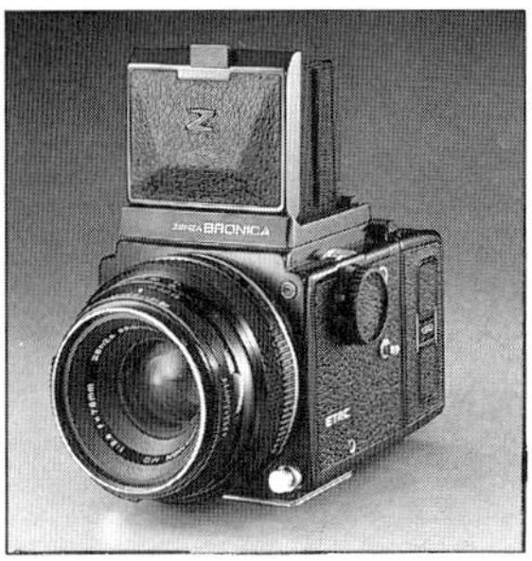

1978 Zenza Bronica ETRS: Principally an ETR with the same collection of sophisticated features plus a few minor improvements: modified lens release button, improved locking device on film backs and the AE-II Finder-E's viewfinder LED display switched on by touching the camera's shutter release.

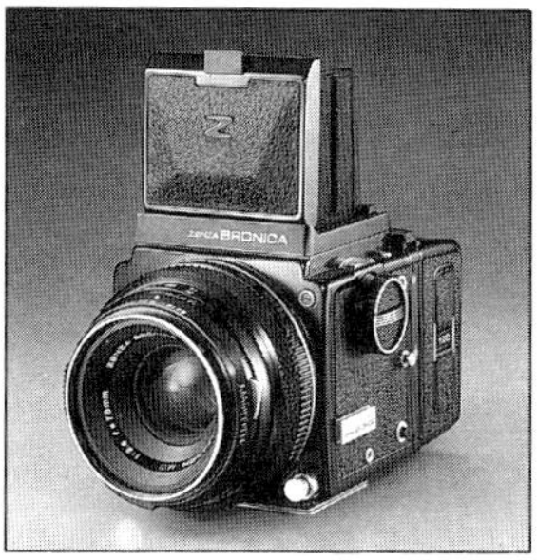

1980 Zenza Bronica SQ: Designed specifically with the professional photographer in mind the SQ was a leaf shutter 6 × 6cm SLR using an exclusive four-claw Bronica SQ lens mount. Had an interchangeable film back but no integral metering although exposure finders were featured in the SQ system.

1981 Zenza Bronica SQ-A: All the specification of the SQ plus a mirror lock-up mechanism and full film back interlock, ie the dark slide cannot be removed with back off the camera. Film backs are equipped with ISO film speed dial. Optional system accessories includes AE Prism Finder S for auto-exposure metering.

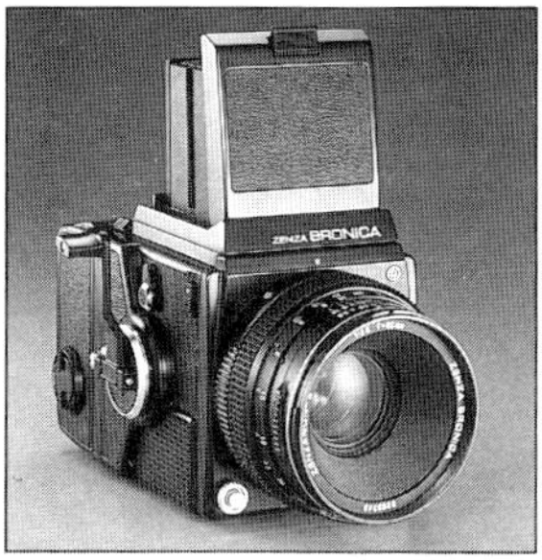

1982 Zenza Bronica SQ-Am: All the features of the highly successful SQ-A with the addition of an integral motor-drive.

1983 Zenza Bronica GS-1: Packed with sophisticated electronic circuitry the 6 × 7cm GS-1 represents Bronica's first involvement in this format; optional film backs give a multiple format capability.

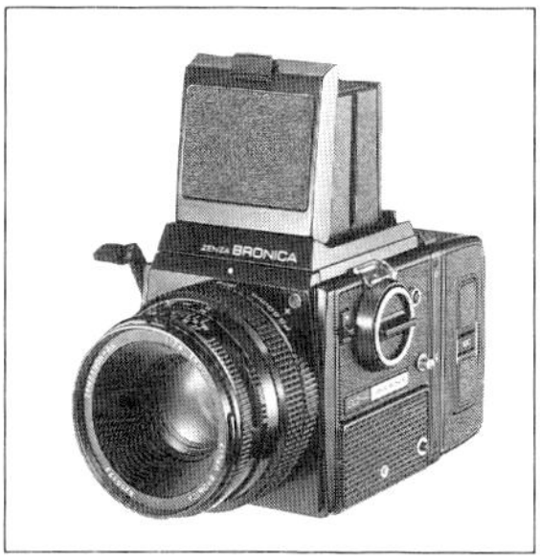

1988 Zenza Bronica ETRSi: Introduced at Photokina, the ETRSi is fundamentally an ETRS with the addition of several notable features: a mirror lock-up facility, viewfinder warning of multiple exposure operation and the option of dedicated through-the-lens flash metering. A fully interlocked film back and the compact Motor Winder Ei were also introduced.

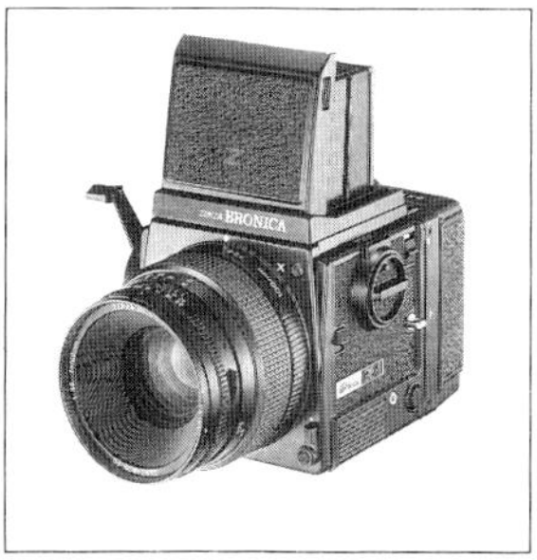

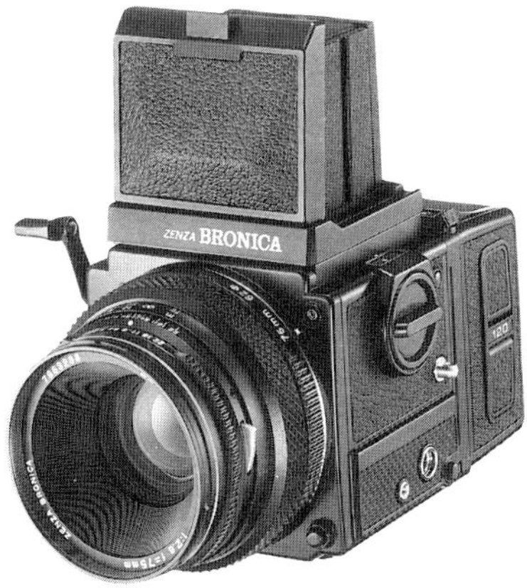

Chapter One

Why medium-format?

There are many reasons for shooting medium-format. Clearly, the greater image area of roll film compared with the 35mm format is a crucially important factor. Assuming identical films and technique, a medium-format photograph will exhibit finer grain, superior sharpness, smoother tonal gradation and better detail resolution.

Taking a slightly different viewpoint, a medium-format negative or transparency needs a lesser degree of magnification than 35mm to yield the same print size. To obtain a 10 × 8in print from a 35mm negative, for example, a magnification of ×8 is necessary; by comparison a 6 × 4.5cm negative needs only ×4.7 and a 6 × 7cm only ×3.7.

Camera considerations

Obviously, because of the larger image area medium-format cameras tend to be bulkier than 35mm equipment.

Both camera types have their pros and cons in the arena of system versatility. Generally, 35mm cameras are better catered for in terms of a wider selection of lenses; extending from the incredibly wide angle to extremely long telephoto.

For medium-format systems the range of focal lengths covered is usually not so extensive. Lenses are bulkier and maximum apertures slower but, what medium-format loses on the roundabouts it gains on the swings. With the exception of the modular designed Rolleiflex 3001 and 3003 models, 35mm single-lens-reflex cameras do not have an interchangeable film back capability; a feature considered essential by most professional users. An interchangeable film back facility makes it possible to switch from one film type to another, including Polaroid, with impunity. Moreover, with the flexibility proffered by Bronica it is possible to change from format to format simply by using the appropriate back.

The capability of changing films rapidly during a hectic photography session is another advantage; an important point because of the fewer exposures per loading available to roll film users compared with 35mm. A roll of 120 film gives 15, 12 and 10 exposures in 6 × 4.5cm, 6 × 6cm and 6 × 7cm formats respectively. 220 size film offers a way around this particular short-coming: it is twice the length of 120 film and therefore gives double the number of exposures, but unfortunately there is a relatively limited choice of emulsions in this size compared with 120.

The fewer exposures available with roll film and its relatively higher cost may, however, be factors in its favour since it is more probable that you will make every exposure count; the machine-gun approach of 35mm simply does not suit medium-format. A more deliberate, considered approach is good discipline for your photography in general.

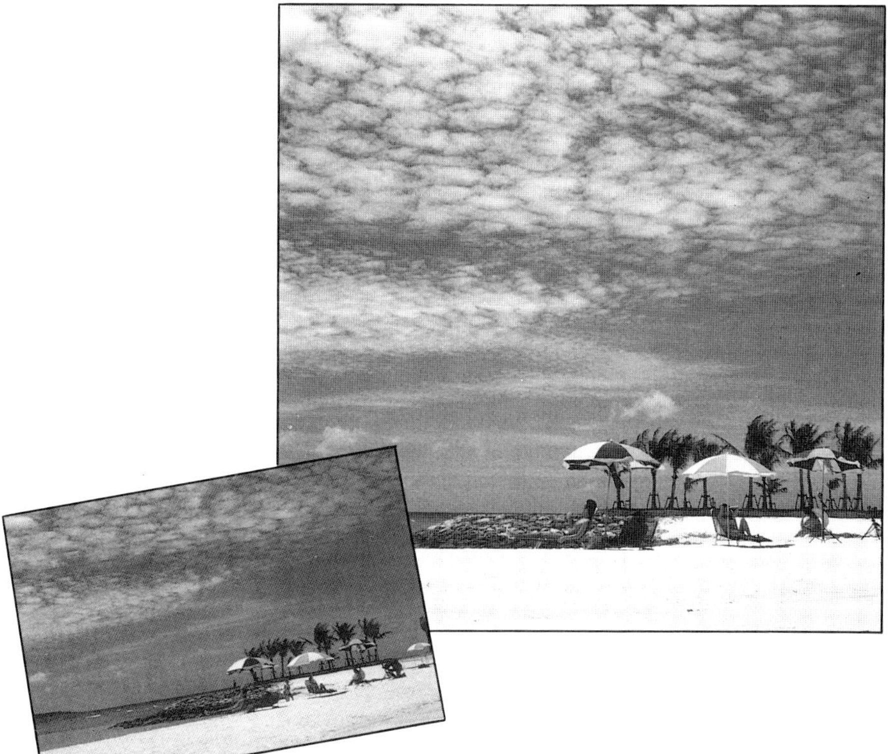

Which roll film format?

There are three commonly used roll film formats: 6 × 4.5cm, 6 × 6cm and 6 × 7cm. Bronica has an impressive presence in each camp: the ETRS and ETRSi are 6 × 4.5cm format, the SQ-A and SQ-Am are 6 × 6cm and the GS-1 is 6 × 7cm. That, however, is not the whole story because each Bronica model can cope with smaller formats. The GS-1, for example, can be used with the appropriate film back to give formats of 6 × 6cm and 6 × 4.5cm as well as 6 × 7cm.

The format you choose is obviously a subjective decision. Are you a studio specialist? If so, 6 × 7cm might be the most appealing format and the GS-1 the camera to have. On the other hand, the compactness of a 6 × 4.5cm SLR such as the Bronica ETRS is desirable if trekking around the countryside a great deal.

The shape of the format has to be considered. Despite its huge popularity the square shape of 6 × 6cm deters many photographers who say that it is a waste since most pictures sold commercially are reproduced rectangular, so why not start off with a rectangular format camera. Conversely, it is because of the square shape that others prefer 6 × 6cm.

Formats in detail

6 × 4.5cm

This deservedly popular format is frequently referred to as 'ideal'. Its shape is such that it can be enlarged to make the most of popular paper sizes with the minimum of wastage. With 15 exposures available from each roll of 120 film it is also comparatively economical yet provides significantly better picture quality than 35mm; not surprising since 6 × 4.5cm has 2.7 times more usable area than 35mm. The rectangular format means that a prism finder is advisable for maximum convenience when shooting upright photographs; with a waist level finder the process of taking vertical shots can be problematical.

6 × 6cm

Often known as 2¼inch square, this is probably the most widely known and accepted medium-format and gives 12 exposures from a roll of 120 film. The format's shape provides ample room for cropping and for this reason it is commercially highly successful. A prism finder is not essential and a simple waist level finder is perfectly suitable. Bronica has both types available in the SQ system.

6 × 7cm

The 6 × 7cm format is also often referred to as 'ideal' and it is the largest roll film format in widespread use. One roll of 120 film provides 10 6 × 7cm photographs. 6 × 7cm can be enlarged to give a 10 × 8in print with little wastage and in terms of quality it offers advantages over both the previously mentioned formats. A popular choice among commercial photographers.

There are several roll film formats which are less frequently used: 4 × 4cm Superslide, 6 × 8cm and 6 × 9cm are discussed below but others which turn up from time to time are specialist panorama formats such as 6 × 12cm and 6 × 17cm.

4 × 4cm

Known as the Superslide format, the 4 × 4cm is unusual in that neither a special camera nor film back is necessary to use it and appropriate size transparencies can be had simply by cutting down 6 × 4.5cm, 6 × 6cm or 6 × 7cm originals. Slides fit into special mounts which can be projected in conventional 35mm projectors. However, because the image area is roughly double that of 35mm Superslide, quality is noticeably superior.

6 × 8cm

A recent development on the medium-format scene and the choice of equipment employing this format is limited at present.

6 × 9cm

Few modern cameras adopt this format so it is now comparatively rare. This format has the same 3:2 aspect ratio as 35mm and is capable of stunning quality work if the image area is exploited to the full. One roll of 120 film gives only eight 6 × 9cm pictures so this format is relatively costly to maintain.

Bronica ETRS

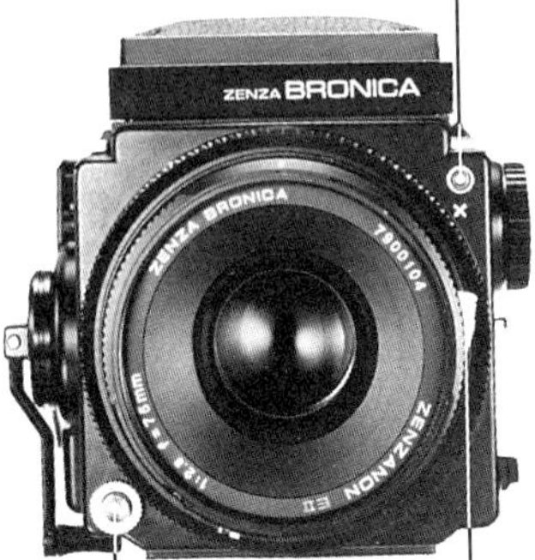

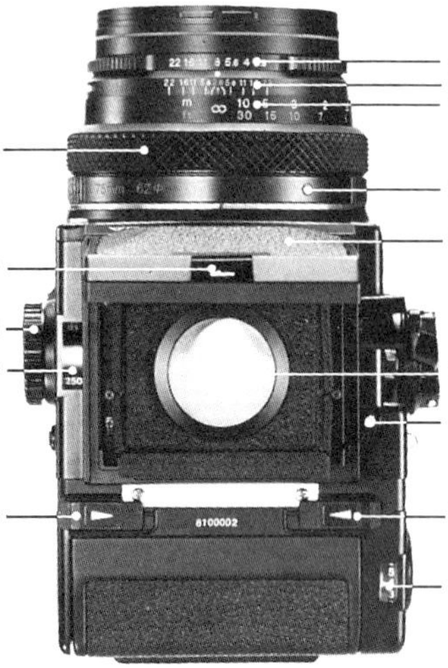

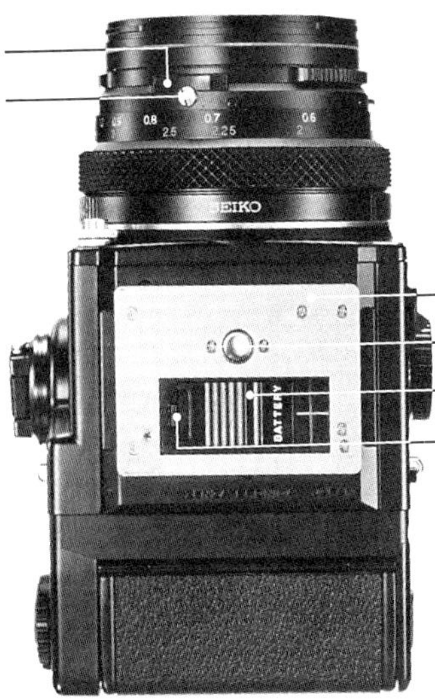

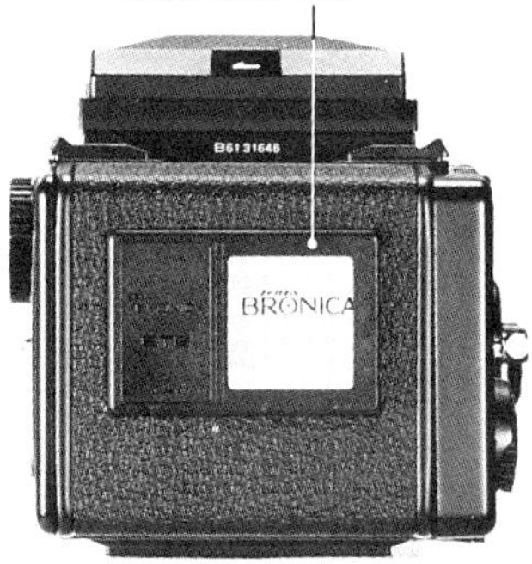

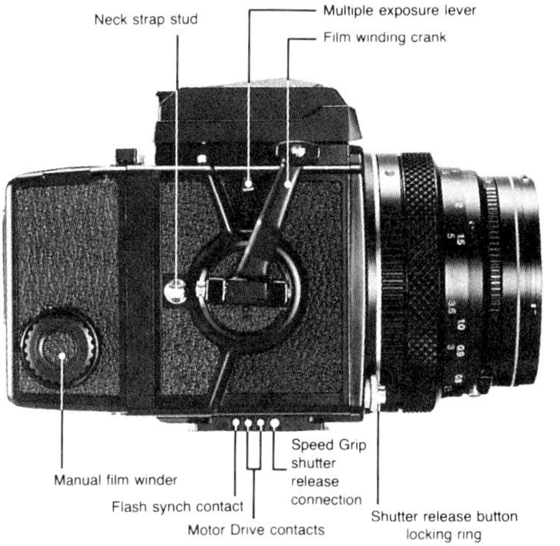
Neck strap stud
Multiple exposure lever
Film winding crank
Speed Grip shutter release connection
Manual film winder
Flash synch contact
Motor Drive contacts
Shutter release button locking ring

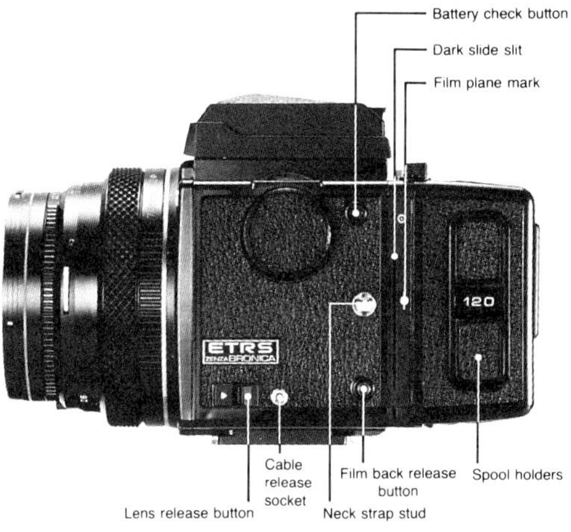
Battery check button
Dark slide slit
Film plane mark
ETRS
ZENZA BRONICA
120
Cable release socket
Film back release button
Spool holders
Lens release button
Neck strap stud

Chapter Two
Bronica ETRS

Encompassing the handling convenience of a 35mm SLR and the benefits of an image area which is almost three times as great, it is no surprise that the 6 × 4.5cm Bronica ETRS camera is the choice of discerning amateurs and professional photographers the world over.

When the 6 × 4.5cm Bronica ETR was introduced in 1976 it was the first full system SLR to embrace this format and was unique in offering all the attributes expected of a professional camera: an interchangeable film back capability, between the lens leaf shutter, and a comprehensive range of accessories and lenses.

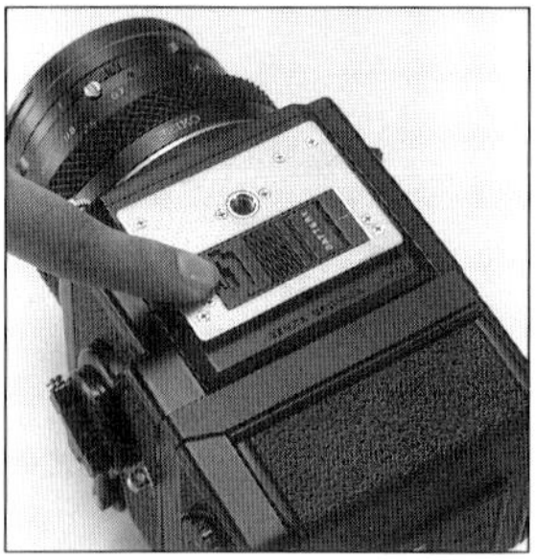

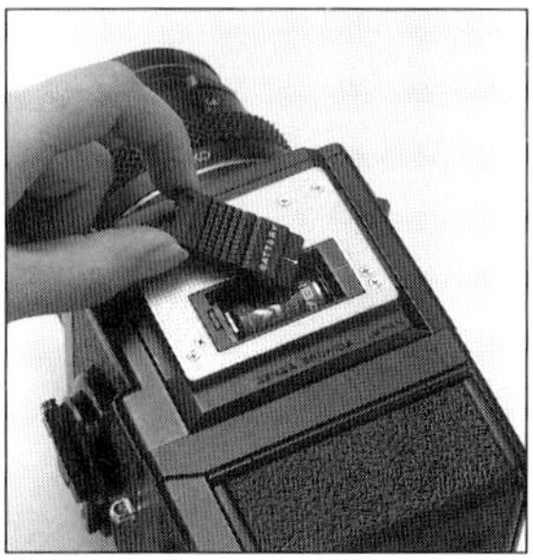

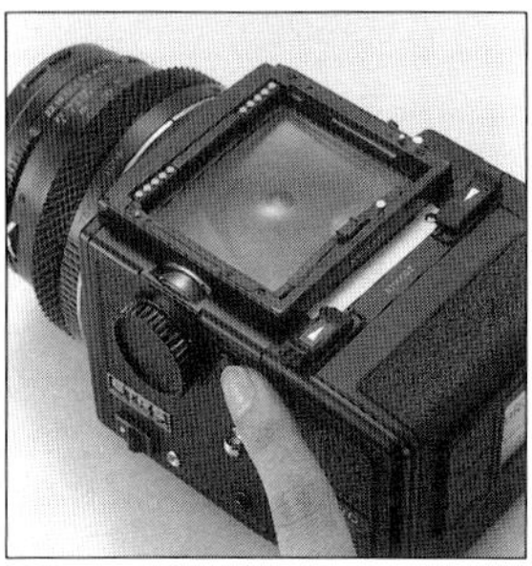

THE BATTERY

The camera body is a highly sophisticated chassis housing a reflex mirror mechanism and on to which the necessary components are attached and co-ordinated via electrical and mechanical linkages.

The ETRS's leaf shutter is electronically controlled except for two speeds, 1/500 sec and 'T' which are mechanical. For proper camera operation a six volt silver oxide PX-28 type battery or equivalent is essential; the battery also powers the AE-II Finder-E if it is fitted.

A fresh silver oxide battery will be good for up to one year's use. If an AE Prism Finder-E is used the battery should last between six and 12 months. Check the battery regularly. Pushing in the battery check button causes a red LED at the viewfinder's bottom left to light; if the LED does not light the battery is either flat or incorrectly loaded. When an AE Prism Finder-E is fitted it should be switched on before checking the battery; this ensures that the battery is tested under full load.

Loading the battery

Access to the battery chamber is via the base-plate. The chamber lid is clearly marked 'BATTERY' and is released by pushing in a catch and sliding it in the direction of the arrow until it is free. Insert the six volt cell observing the polarity indications in the chamber. Replace the lid and confirm correct loading by using the battery check button.

At low temperatures the battery works at reduced power and has less capacity. Use the accessory Remote Battery Pack E for maximum efficiency in freezing weather. This connects to the camera via a lead allowing the battery to be stored in a coat pocket.

ETRS LENSES

Lenses are the eyes of all camera systems so it is not surprising to find that Bronica has an extensive selection of high quality optics available in the ETR system. Eleven lenses are on offer covering focal lengths from 40mm wide angle to 500mm telephoto and including two superlative German-made zooms from Jos. Schneider GmbH & Co. and a perspective control optic, also from Schneider.

Each Zenzanon lens incorporates an electronic leaf shutter with settings from 8 sec to 1/500 sec plus 'T' (Time exposure) and is electronic flash synchronised at all speeds (except 'T'). Although each lens has its own shutter the selection of shutter speed is co-ordinated from the camera body. Intermediate settings are not possible except when the AE-II Finder-E is fitted and used in its aperture-priority auto-exposure mode during which shutter speeds are chosen by the finder itself in one-third stop intervals throughout the shutter range.

Examine the rear of the lens and you will notice six gold-plated contacts which, together with their counterparts in the lens throat, provide a reliable method of information interchange between camera and lens. Each lens is also equipped with its own depth of field preview facility; essential to assess the effects of a specific aperture or when creative filters are being used.

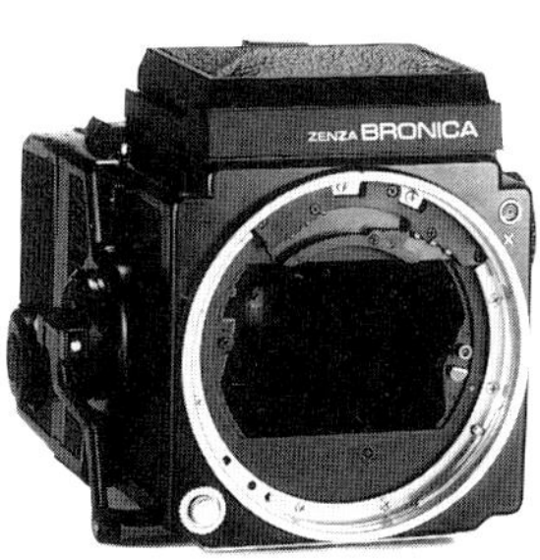

Lens mounting

The ETRS employs Bronica's exclusive four-claw ETR bayonet mount and because of its design it is not possible to mount or remove a lens incorrectly. Lenses cannot be fitted or detached without the shutter being cocked. Confirmation can be had by examining the camera's lens throat: if the shutter is cocked the two green dots towards the right of the throat will be immediately adjacent to one another. Also, the mirror will be in its 'down' position and providing a normal viewing image in the viewfinder. If the shutter is not cocked rotate the wind crank once.

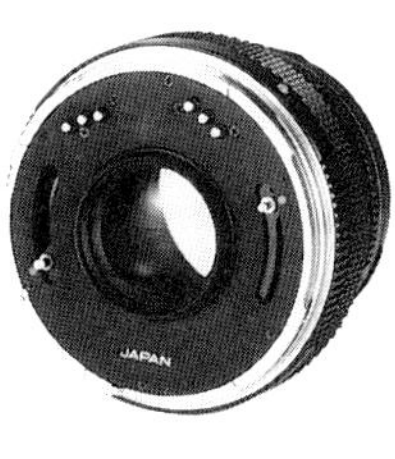

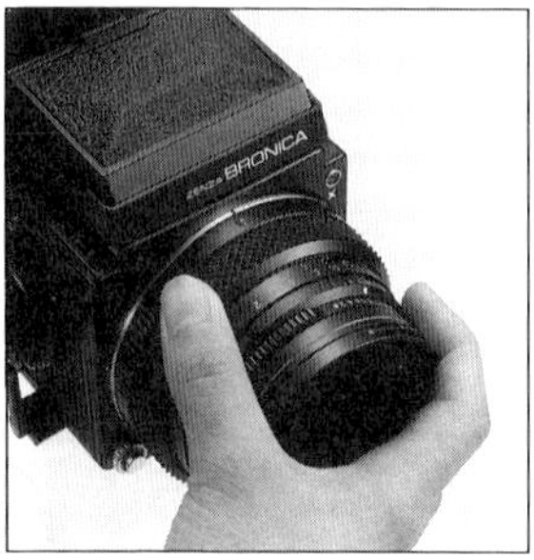

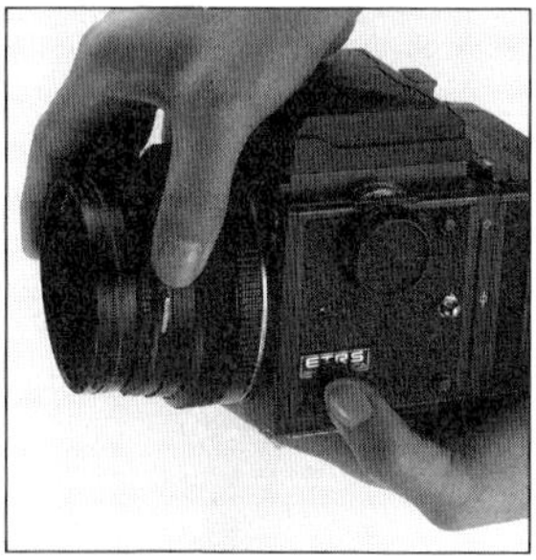

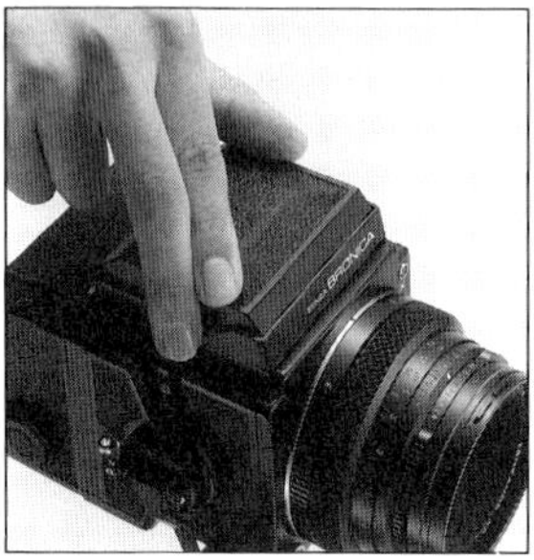

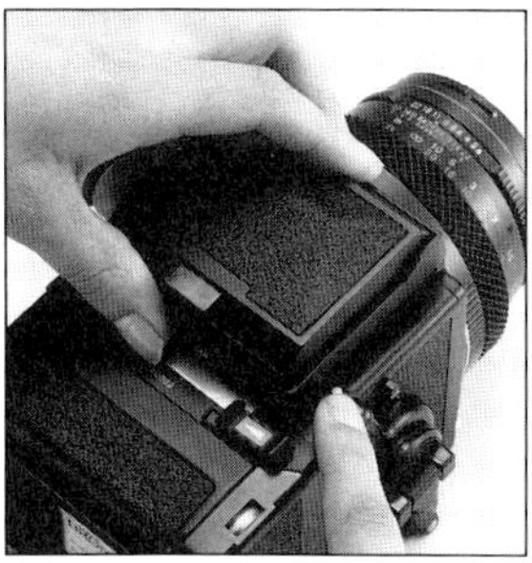

Similarly the lens must also be cocked before attachment can be successfully concluded. This can be confirmed by examining the rear of the lens panel: the two shutter cocking pins should be lying immediately adjacent to their respective green dots. If not, they can be set manually by turning the cocking pins counter-clockwise until they are aligned.

To fit the lens, match the red dot on the lens to red mark on the camera body, insert the lens into the mount and rotate firmly anti-clockwise 30 degrees until it clicks positively into position. The lens is now mounted and unintentional removal impossible. Releasing the lens can only be achieved by first pushing the lens mount release button and then rotating the lens clockwise. If the shutter is not cocked the lens release button cannot be depressed.

Safety features such as those built into the ETRS's lens mounting mechanism are essential. The camera does not have an instant return mirror nor does it have an auxiliary plate to protect the film from light; therefore, if the lens could be removed while the mirror was in an 'up' position the film would be exposed.

INTERCHANGEABLE FINDERS

No finder is supplied with the basic ETRS camera body but there are five to choose from. Finders are discussed in Chapter Six.

Attachment to the camera body is done by locating the four lugs on the unit's base in the finder frame so that the finder can be slid into position by pushing towards the front of the camera. A 'click' will be heard but proper fitting can also be confirmed by gripping the finder housing and wiggling it very gently. Once in place the finder can be removed only be depressing the finder release button which then permits the unit to be slid off.

FOCUS SCREENS

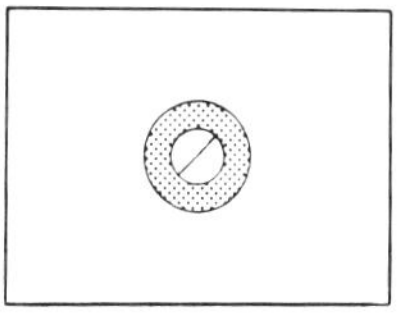

Microprism/Split-image

Focus screens are user-changeable and there are seven in the ETR system. The supplied standard screen has microprism and split-image rangefinder focusing aids. In addition, it is etched with the lines necessary for use with either of the two Bronica 35mm film backs available in the ETRS system, the normal 24 × 36mm format and the panoramic 24 × 54mm.

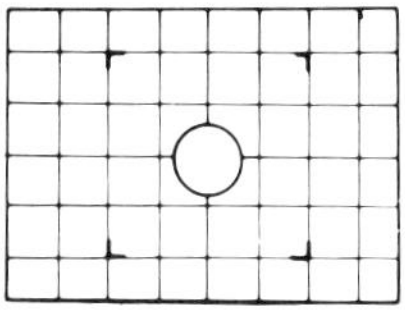

Grid-lines

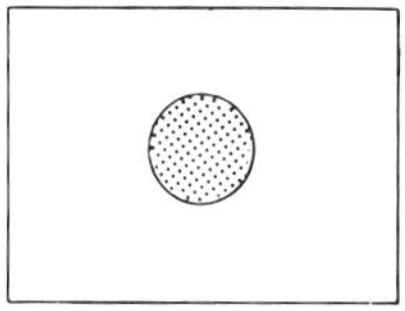

Microprism

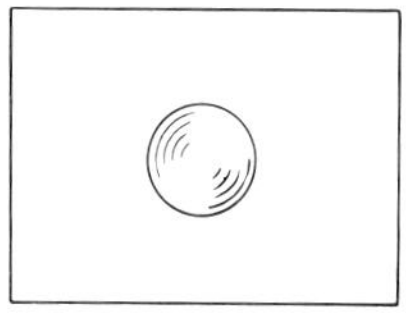

Matte

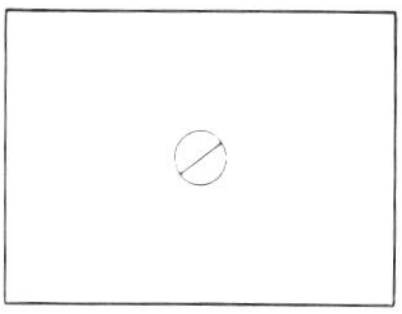

Split-image

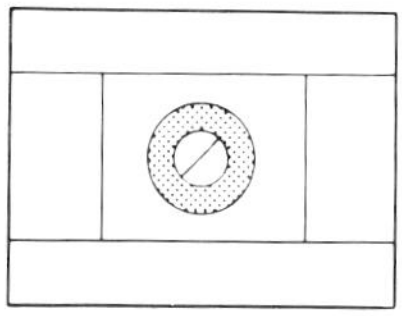

Microprism/Split-image (ETRS 135)

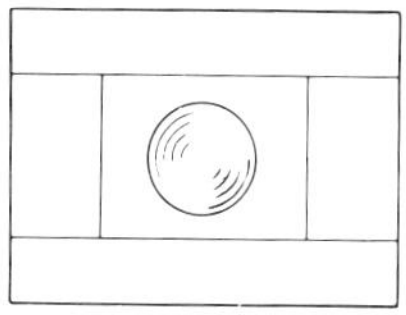

Matte (ETRS 135)

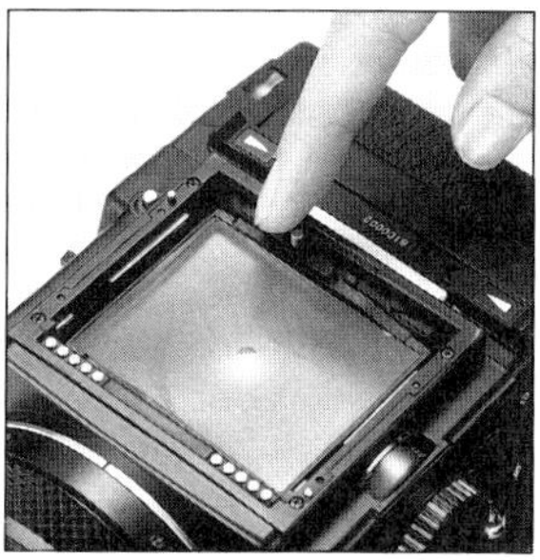

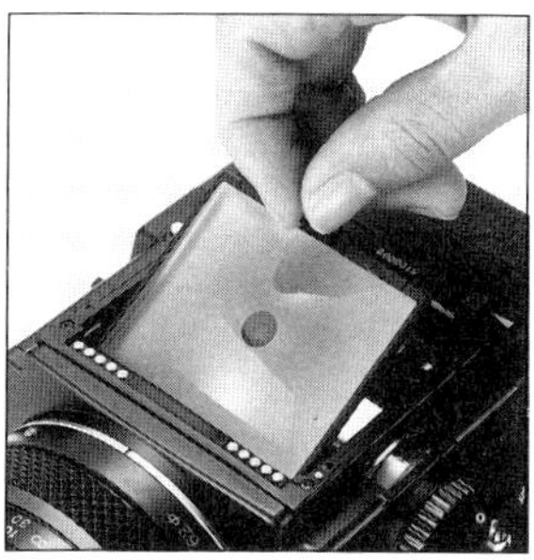

Changing focus screen

Remove the finder from the camera to allow access to the focus screen. Along the bottom of the screen's metal frame is a silver pin which when slid to the left permits the screen to be lifted out. When locating the replacement make sure that the screen's tab fits into the matching hole in the body before lowering into position. Sliding the silver pin to the right secures the screen in place. While exchanging screens be careful not to mark the sensitive surface otherwise irreparable damage might result.

INTERCHANGEABLE FILM BACKS

Film backs for 120, 220, 35mm and Polaroid are available for the Bronica ETR system. In this chapter we discuss loading and using backs for 120 and 220 film. The 35mm and Polaroid models are described in Chapter Fourteen.

ETRS film backs in operation

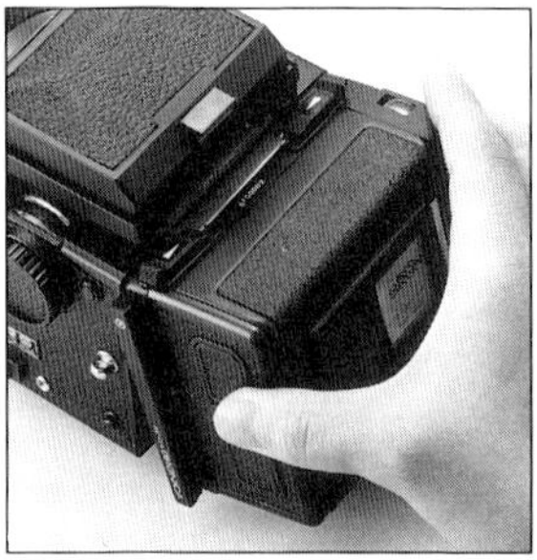

Interchangeable film backs must be able to be fitted and detached with rapidity yet be utterly secure; the ETRS's mechanism is particularly efficient in these respects. To attach a back, hold it so that the dark slide handle is on the left, matching the two protruding hinge lugs at the top of the back with the two holes on the camera's back-plate, and then push the back's lower half against the body until it locks solidly into place. Once mounted on the camera withdraw the dark slide immediately: this avoids any chance of the back release button being operated by accident when the camera is being carried around on the shoulder and the film back becoming detached as a consequence. Place the dark slide somewhere safe so that it will not get bent; there is no facility to store the slide on the camera.

Because film backs can be removed whether or not the camera is cocked, and whether or not an exposed or unexposed frame is in the film gate, upon attachment of a back and removing the dark slide always operate the wind crank. This guarantees that the camera and lens are fully prepared and that an unexposed frame is in position in readiness for photography. Rotating the crank when changing from back to back cannot waste film.

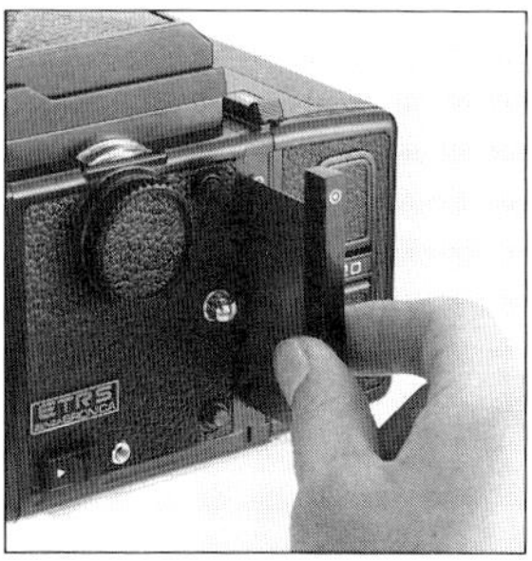

Film back removal is quick; insert the dark slide, push the back release button and the back's lower end can be disengaged and the unit separated from the body. Backs cannot be removed from the camera with the dark slide withdrawn. Nor can they be detached if the dark slide is incorrectly inserted.

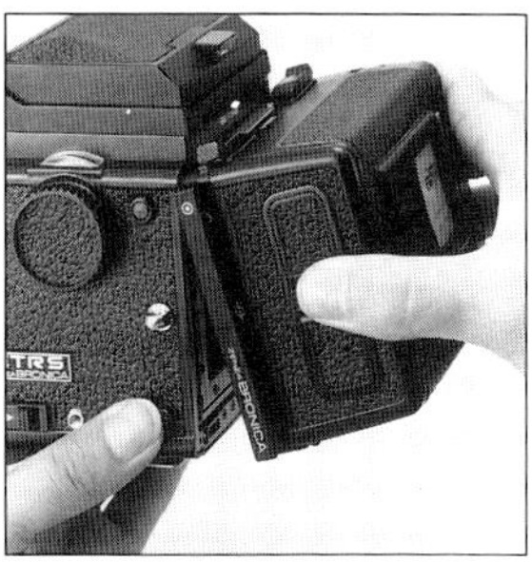

Two points of warning here; with the film back off the camera body the dark slide can be withdrawn, thereby exposing loaded film to light. This, however, applies only with ETR film backs with black handled dark slides. ETR film backs with grey handled dark slides are fully interlocked. Also, although the back cannot be taken off with the slide inserted the wrong way up, the shutter can be released.

It is possible to remove the film back minus its dark slide from the camera despite the various interlocks: push the lens release button at the same time as pressing the back release button. Obviously this procedure should be reserved for emergencies; when you have lost the dark slide, for example.

Specifications of the Bronica ETRS

Type	6 × 4.5cm format lens shutter single-lens-reflex system camera with interchangeable lens, film back, finder and focus screen.
Frame size	42.5mm × 55.1mm.
Film size	120 roll film (15 exposures); 220 roll film (30 exposures); 35mm cassette film; and Polaroid Land. Exclusive film backs available for each format.
Lens mount	Exclusive four-claw Bronica ETR bayonet.
Shutter	Electronically controlled SEIKO #0 between the lens leaf shutter with speeds from 8 seconds to 1/500 sec; 'T' (Time exposure) facility provided. Mechanical speeds of 1/500 sec and 'T' only.
Flash synchronisation	Electronic flash X-setting at all speeds.
Depth of field preview	All Zenzanon-E lenses have a depth of field preview lever built in.
Multiple exposure	Possible by operating lever on camera body.
Finder system	Interchangeable finder system with the choice of five: Waist Level Finder-E, AE-II Finder-E, Rotary Finder-E, Prism Finder-E and Action Finder-E.
Focus screen	Interchangeable type. Standard supplied screen has diagonally oriented split-image rangefinder surrounded by microprism ring and full area matte finish, and is etched with 24 × 36mm and 24 × 54mm frames.
Battery	Single six volt silver oxide (No 544, PX-28 or 4G13) or alkaline manganese battery (A544 or 4LR44). Battery check is provided; if sufficient power, red coloured LED lights up in the viewfinder when battery check button is depressed. Viewfinder LED also lights up to confirm correct shutter operation.
Dimensions	ETRS main body only: 91mm wide × 87mm high × 69mm long. Including Zenzanon-E 75mm f2.8, Film Back 120, Waist Level Finder-E: 91 wide × 107 high × 165 long mm.
Weight	1280 grams (with above accessories but no battery).

Chapter Three Bronica ETRSi

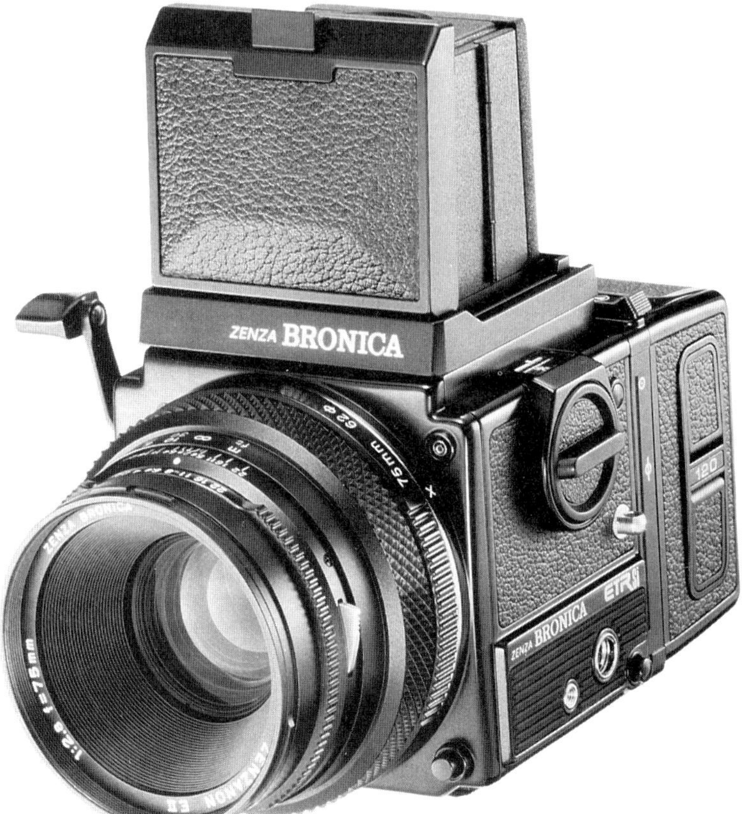

Photokina 1988 saw the introduction of the latest camera in the 6 × 4.5cm format ETR series. The ETRSi is based on the current ETRS model but, although several modifications have been made, the operational characteristics of both cameras are fundamentally identical. Furthermore, existing system accessories may be used on the new camera; meter finders, film backs, focus screens and so on are fully compatible. Consequently, in this chapter we concentrate on the differences between the two cameras.

The ETRSi camera body

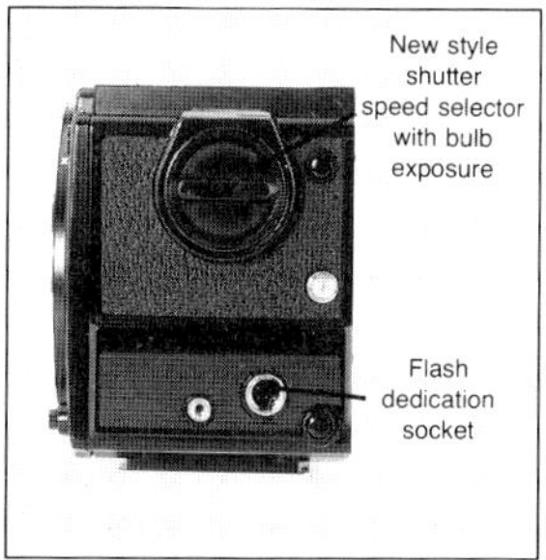

Viewed from the left.

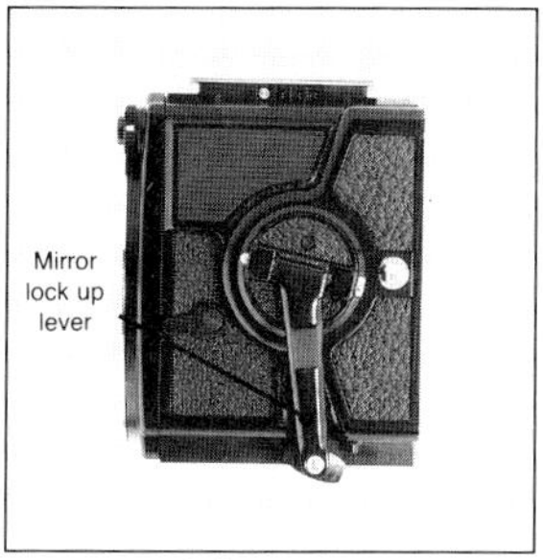

From the right.

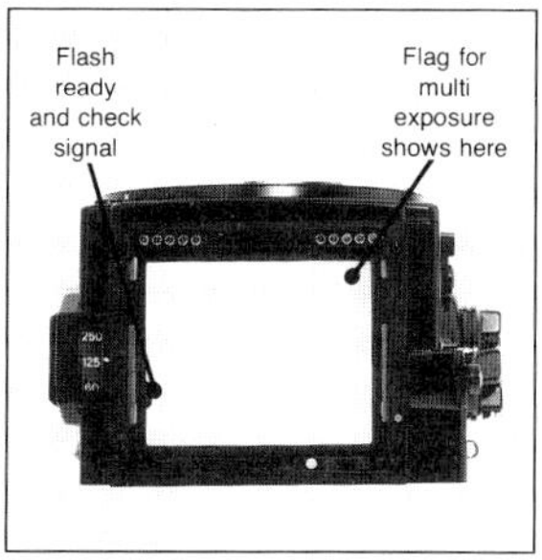

Looking down.

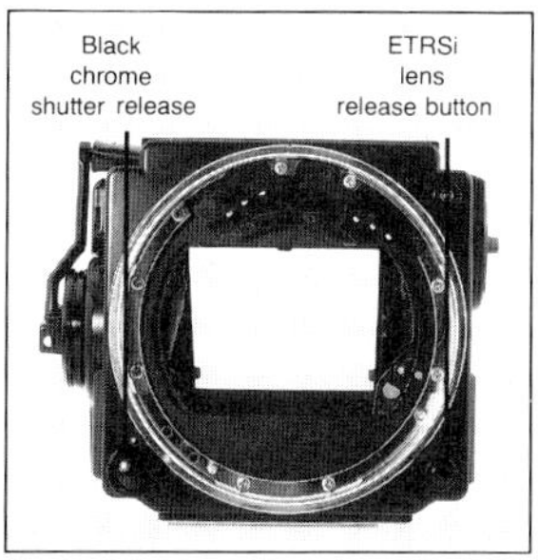

The view from the front.

The chief differences between the ETRS and the ETRSi are as follows:
*The ETRSi has an improved damping system to minimise the vibration generated by the reflex mirror's action during exposure.
*The provision of a mirror lock-up facility on the ETRSi.
*A red flag warning appears in the viewfinder during multiple exposure operation.
*The ETRSi has the option of through-the-lens, off the film flash metering based on the Metz Mecablitz SCA system.

Several cosmetic differences are also worth noting. The ETRSi's shutter release is black chrome, as is the finder release button. The lens release control has been moved to the front of the camera and this too is black chrome.

Introduced with the ETRSi camera is a modified film back which is fully interlocked so that the dark slide cannot be retracted while the film back is off the camera. In addition, to help speed up the film loading process, there is a manual film wind crank instead of a wind knob. The new film back is easily identified by its grey handled dark slide and its fold-out wind crank. Old backs, which have black handled dark slides, can be used on the ETRSi. Similarly, the new style backs may be employed with previous ETR cameras.

Using mirror lock-up

The mirror lock-up control can be found near the multiple exposure lever which lies horizontally during normal camera operation. Engage mirror lock-up operation by moving the lever to point vertically so that a small red dot is revealed.

When the lock-up lever is operated the reflex mirror swings up so that there is no viewing image. Obviously, exposure metering and picture composition should be completed before engaging lock-up. The shutter can now be triggered either by using the shutter release, a cable release or by returning the lock-up lever to its normal position.

Unless you require continuous mirror lock-up operation the last-given method is advised so that you are ready to resume normal photography as soon as the film has been advanced. If you require continuous mirror lock-up operation fire the shutter using the shutter release; the reflex mirror will flip up automatically as the film wind crank is rotated.

Cancelling mirror lock-up after the lever has been engaged is not possible without firing the shutter. The best method of avoiding wasting a frame is to insert the dark slide before returning the lock-up lever to its usual location. Then, prior to operating the film wind crank, engage the multiple exposure control so that the shutter is cocked but the film is not advanced. Now take the picture and return the multiple exposure lever to its normal position before winding on.

Flash operation

The ETRSi's C.C.C. (Current Control Centre) makes fully automatic flash operation with direct off the film plane metering possible. A Bronica exclusive SCA system adaptor connects to the camera via a six-pin connector. In addition to extremely accurate automatic flash metering, the dedication facilities provided include flash ready and confirmation of correct exposure signals in the viewfinder.

MOTOR WINDER Ei

The Motor Winder Ei is fully compatible with Bronica ETR, ETR-C, ETRS and ETRSi cameras. It provides single frame film advance at a speed of about 0.8 frames per second.

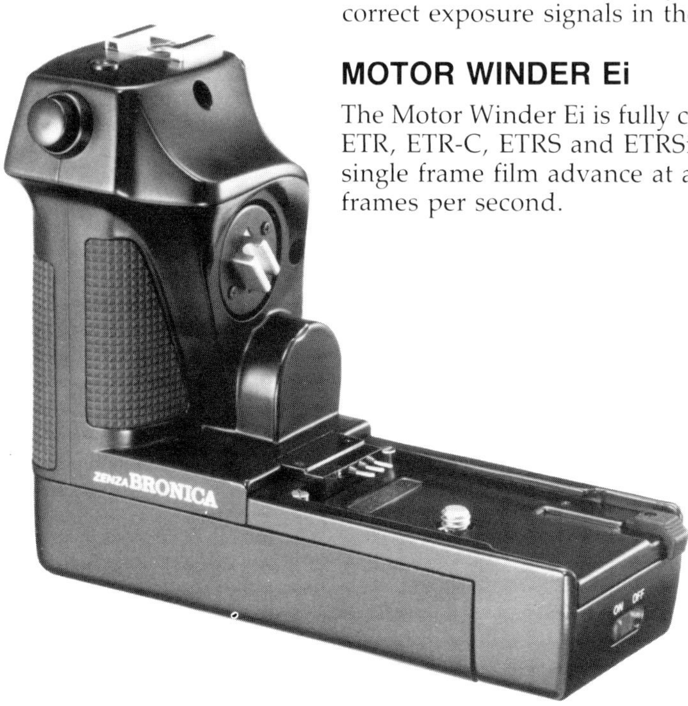

Six high quality alkaline AA batteries or the rechargeable nickel cadmium equivalent are required to power the unit. About 100 rolls of 120 film can be exposed with a fresh set of alkaline cells.

Loading the Motor Winder Ei

The battery compartment should be separated from the main body of the motor wind unit for battery loading and attaching to the camera. The battery compartment can be slid off when the locking button, located on the grip side of the winder, has been depressed. The battery holder clearly shows how the cells should be aligned. Replace the battery holder into the compartment but do not at this stage reunite it with the winder unit.

Attaching the Motor Winder Ei

Prior to attaching the unit, test the camera battery. Remove the camera's film wind crank by pulling out the attachment rod. Push the attachment rod back into place and rotate the crank base until it lies horizontal and there is no clockwise play.

Rotate the grooved drive connector on the winder unit until it too lies horizontally; this ensures that when the winder is pushed on to the camera the connector and the crank base attachment rod mate correctly.

Slide the unit on, taking care to hold the winder's locking screw clear of the camera's tripod base. If the locking screw is not held out of the way it could catch on the camera and prevent the winder being fitted. Push the winder as far as it will go making sure that the drive connector and the attachment rod engage correctly. When fully on the winder's locking catch will engage and this will prevent the two components being inadvertently separated. Tighten the locking screw to complete the attaching operation.

Relocate the battery pack until a 'click' confirms correct fitting and the unit is ready for use. The winder's on/off switch is located on the base, the opposite side of the hand grip.

Using the Motor Winder Ei

Whenever a film back is attached the drive button must be pressed to ensure that the camera and back are coupled. If an exposed frame is in position the motor winder will operate, cocking the shutter and advancing the film to the next frame. When the camera is fully prepared for photography the winder's red LED comes on briefly. Operating the drive button will also advance the film to the first frame if the film back has been freshly loaded.

Full depression of the shutter release will mean that a single picture is taken and the film advanced. Carefully depressing and releasing the winder's shutter release will enable the shooting of consecutive frames. Holding down the shutter release after an exposure has been made will prevent the winder advancing the film. Do not use the camera's shutter release when you require motorised film advance: the shutter fires as normal but the film is not advanced until the drive button is operated.

At the end of a film the winder continues to operate until the film leader is completely off the spool. After a few seconds the motor winder stops running and, at this point, the film back can be opened and reloaded.

Specifications of the Bronica ETRSi

Type	6 × 4.5cm format lens shutter single-lens-reflex system camera with interchangeable lens, film back, finder and focusing screen.
Frame size	42.5mm × 55.1mm.
Film size	120 size roll film; 220 size roll film; 35mm cassette film; and Polaroid Land. Exclusive film backs for each film type.
Lens mount	Exclusive four-claw Bronica ETR bayonet.
Shutter	Electronically controlled SEIKO #0 between the lens leaf shutter with speeds from 8 seconds to 1/500 sec; 'B' (Bulb); and 'T' (Time exposure). Mechanical speeds of 1/500 sec and 'T' only.
Flash synchronisation	Electronic X-flash setting at all shutter speeds. Auto-flash control, based on an off the film measurement system, possible with optional SCA 300 System Adaptor.
Depth of field preview	All Zenzanon-E lenses have preview lever built in.
Multiple exposure	Possible with lever on camera body. A warning shows in the viewfinder when multiple exposure control has been engaged.
Finder system	Five interchangeable finders available in the ETR system.
Focus screen	Interchangeable type.
Battery	Single six volt silver oxide (No 544, PX-28 or 4G13) or alkaline manganese battery. Battery check provided.
Dimensions	ETRSi body only 92mm wide × 87mm high × 69mm long. Including Zenzanon-E 75mm f2.8, Film Back 120, Waist Level Finder-E; 92mm wide × 107mm high × 165mm long.
Weight	1285 grams (with above accessories but no battery).

Chapter Four ETRS operation

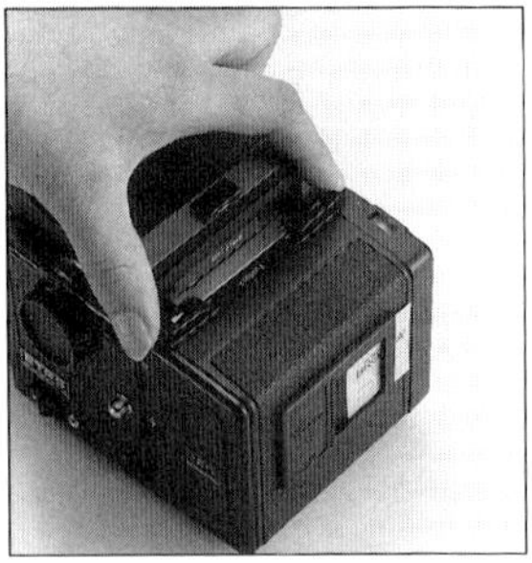

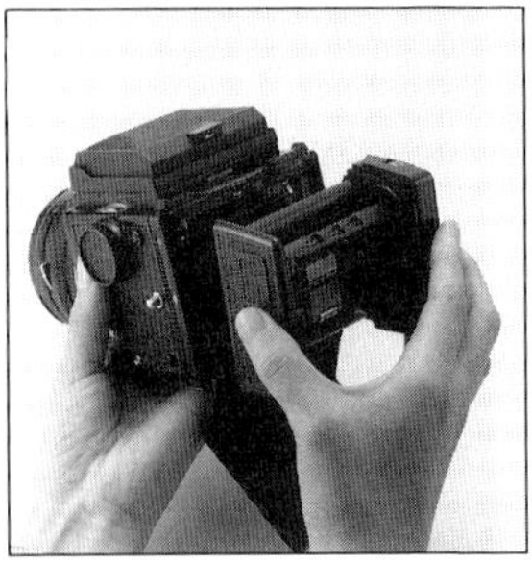

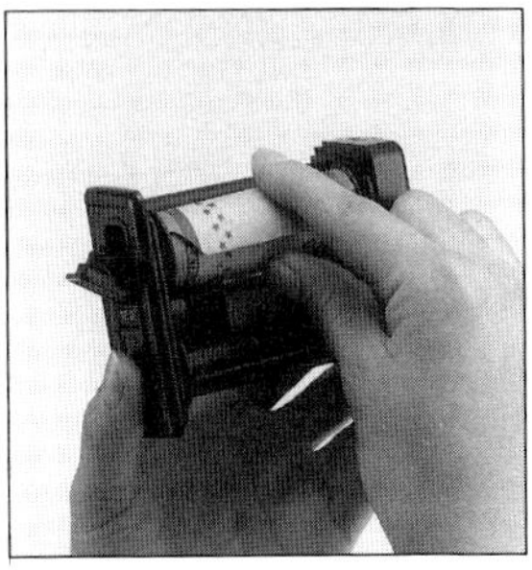

Film loading

Here we discuss the loading of 120 and 220 roll film backs. The basic procedure is identical but it should be noted that 120 film cannot be loaded into the 220 back, and vice versa. Loading of the two 35mm and the Polaroid models is discussed in Chapter Fourteen.

Each 120 and 220 film back comprises two main components: the back frame is a light-tight shield completely enclosing the film holder, and the film holder insert itself which holds the two film spools. Spring loaded spindle tabs keep the spools in place, and flipping them out from within the holder allows access.

Film loading is possible with the back on or off the camera. Simultaneously pressing the two film back locking buttons in the direction indicated releases the back cover. The film holder can then be pulled free from the back frame.

Always load film in subdued light. Fresh film goes into the top section of the holder. Remove the film's paper label entirely and draw out the leader across the pressure plate with its black side facing outwards and thread its tapered end into the take-up spool. Wind on slightly by turning the back's manual wind knob anti-clockwise to ensure that it is securely anchored. Continue winding until the film's start mark lies alongside the insert's red triangular start mark before closing the back.

Advance to the first frame can be accomplished by mounting the back on to the camera and operating the wind crank; it will stop automatically at the correct point after several revolutions. If the crank

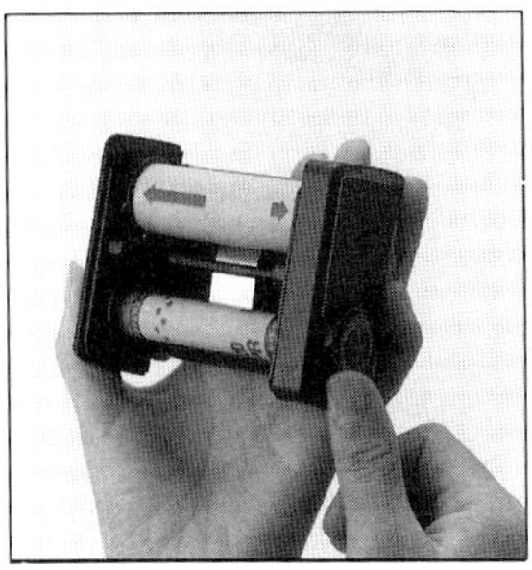

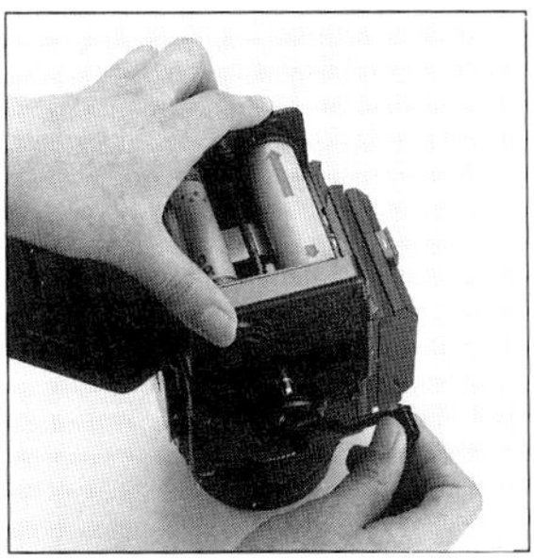

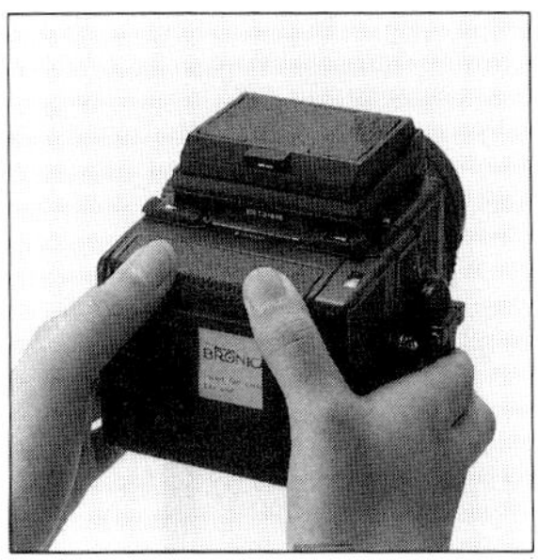

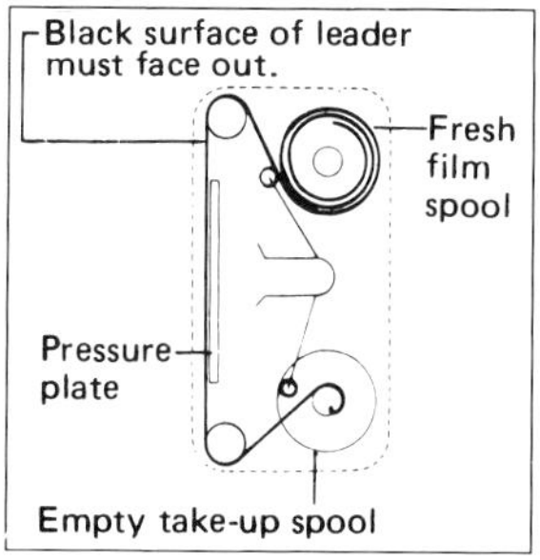

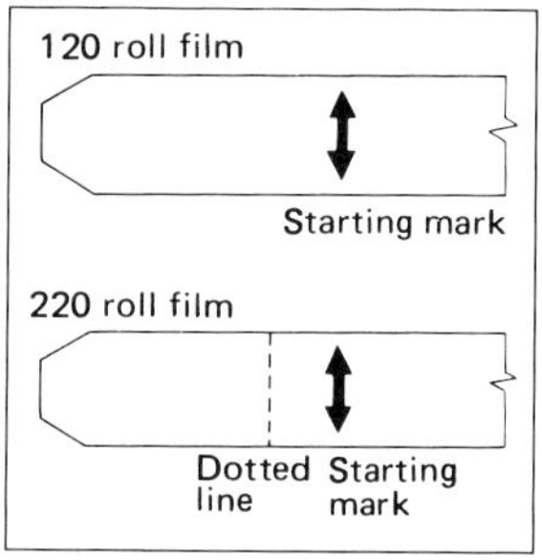

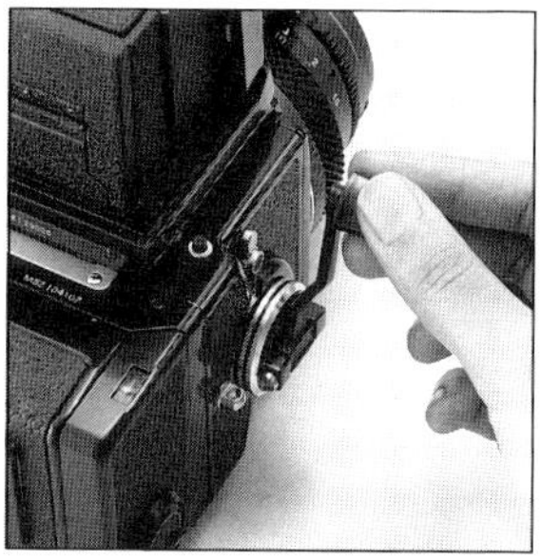

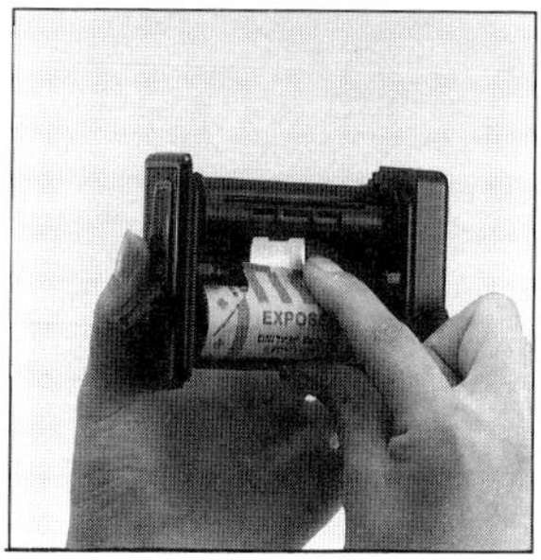

stops after one rotation the multiple exposure lever might be engaged; the lever should be in an upright position. Though slower, the first frame can be arrived at without fitting the back on to the camera by operating the manual wind knob until '1' shows in the frame counter.

Film unloading

At the end of a film the wind crank can still be rotated, but the shutter will not be cocked and an orange line will be visible in the frame counter instead of a number. Wind on until the film's leader has been transferred to the take-up spool; a significant lessening in the pressure required to operate the crank signifies that the back cover may now be opened and the exposed film retrieved. Place what was previously the film's spool on to the other spindle to become the take-up spool for the next roll.

ETRS in action

How you hold and manipulate the ETRS depends on personal preference as well as the accessories being used in conjunction with the camera. Since the shutter release is positioned on the bottom right of the camera body, the most convenient method, for both eye and waist-level photography, is to support the body in your left hand with the index finger poised over the shutter release. This frees the right hand for focusing, adjusting aperture and winding on. The shutter dial, positioned on the left side of the body, can be conveniently operated with either hand.

Shooting vertical format pictures with the Waist-Level Finder-E is possible but awkward and a prism finder is recommended for more convenient handling.

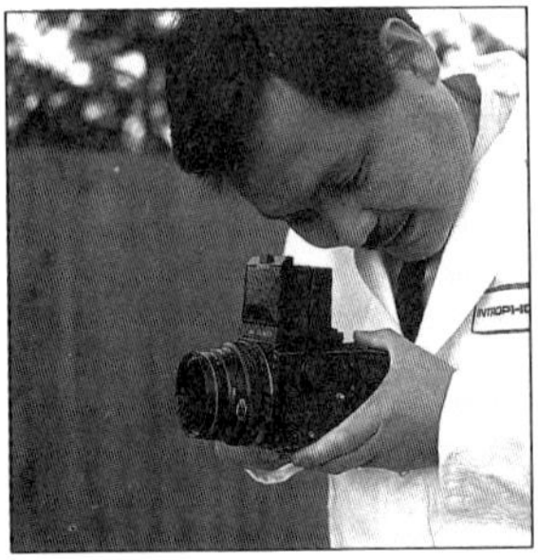

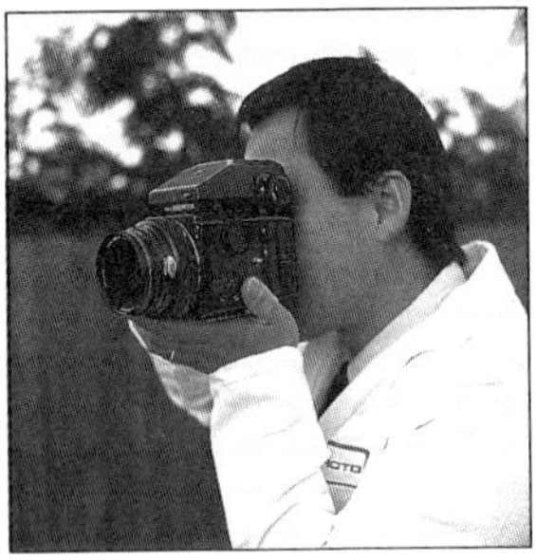

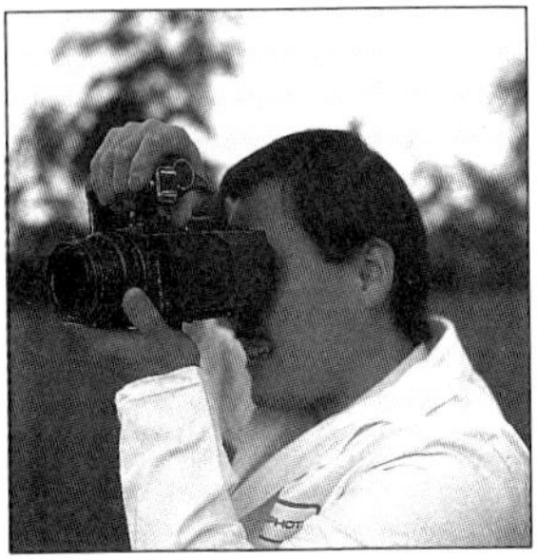

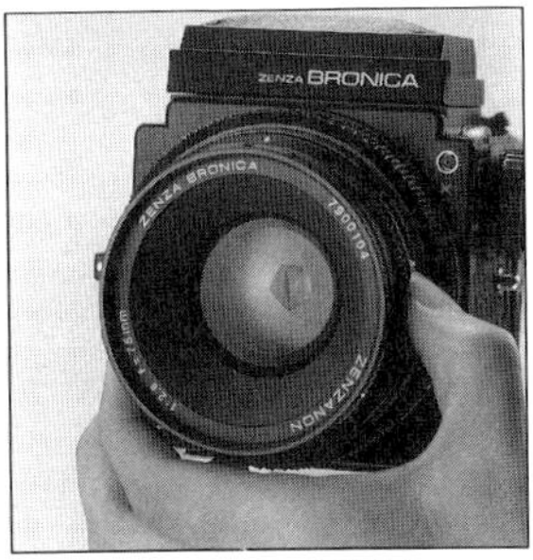

Using the depth of field preview control.

Operating the camera without film

You should become fully conversant with the ETRS's handling characteristics before tackling a photographic assignment. Practice the procedures for focusing, releasing the shutter, winding on to the next frame and so on. Normally the camera cannot be cocked and the shutter released unless a film is loaded. However, the multiple exposure facility (see page 34) offers a way round this obstacle: with it engaged the camera functions normally except for the frame counter which does not advance.

Exposing film

In its basic form the ETRS does not have an integral exposure metering system, and the accessory AE-II Prism Finder-E which provides both auto-exposure and manual metering is a useful extra. Alternatively, a separate hand meter can be employed and the exposure readings transferred manually to the camera.

Zenzanon-E lenses are click-stopped in one-stop increments. Intermediate aperture settings can be made except during use with the AE-II Finder-E when they may lead to inaccurate exposure metering. PE designated lenses are click-stopped in half-stop intervals.

Depth of field can be assessed by operating the lever on the left side of the lens: the lever cannot be locked in place and returns to its starting position when released. This control should not be operated during through-the-lens metering operation with the AE-II Prism Finder-E as an incorrect reading will be obtained and the photograph over-exposed by the difference between the lens's full aperture and the set aperture value.

The chosen shutter speed is displayed in a window above the shutter dial together with the speeds immediately either side of the one in use. Speeds are colour-coded: 1/2 to 1/500 sec are picked out in white, those from 1 to 8 seconds in orange. With three click-stopped positions the shutter release button can be locked to prevent unintentional operation. (See table opposite). Firing the shutter can also be conducted with a cable release.

Interior, Harry Lomax

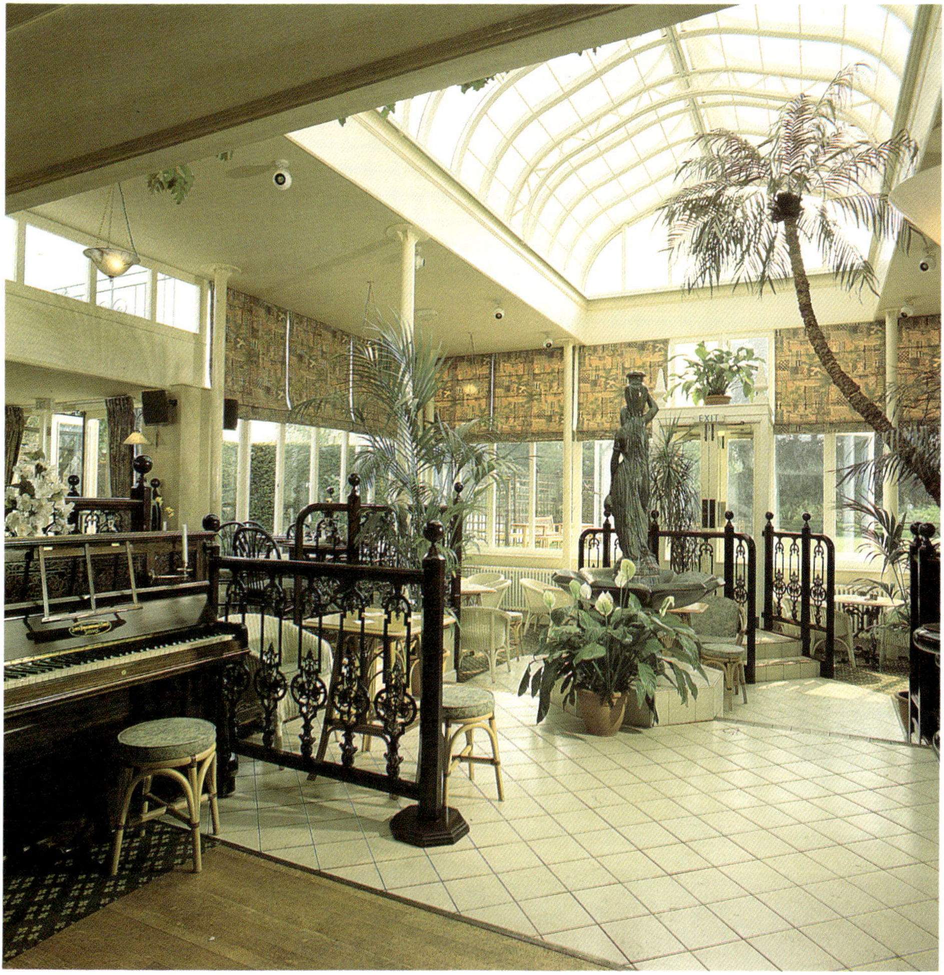

Masks, Andy Earl

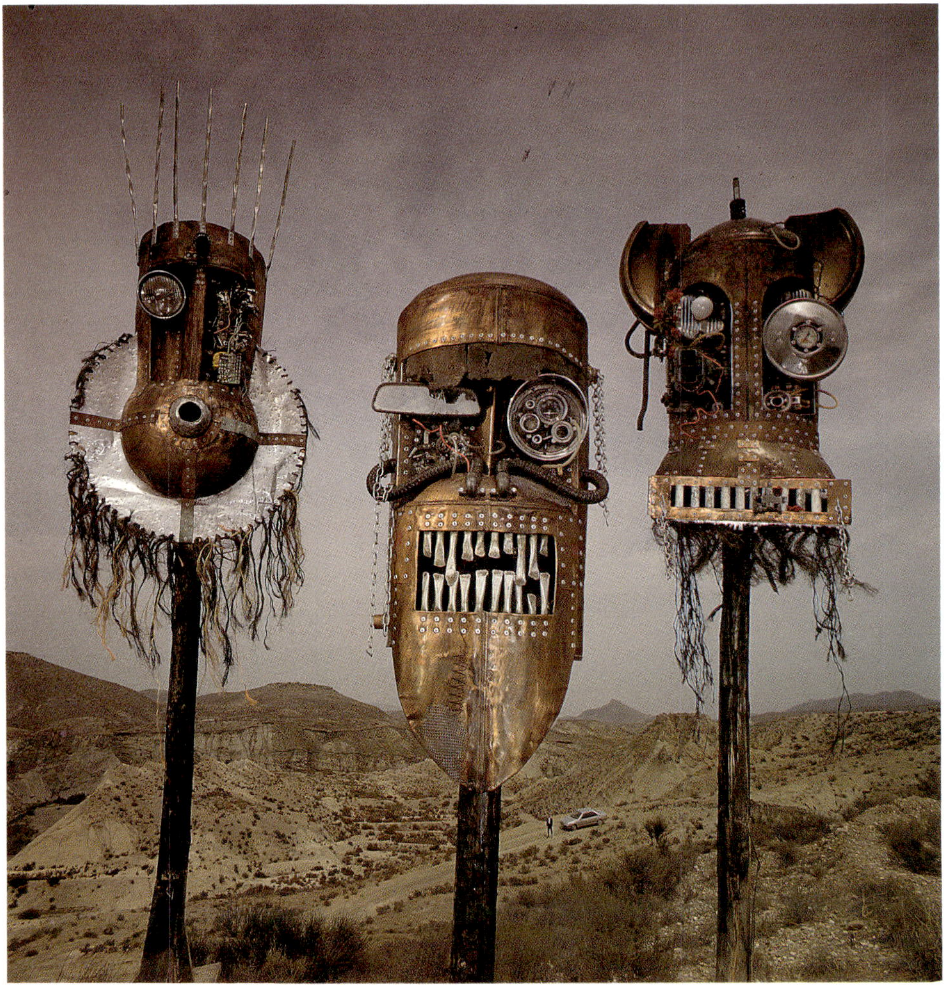

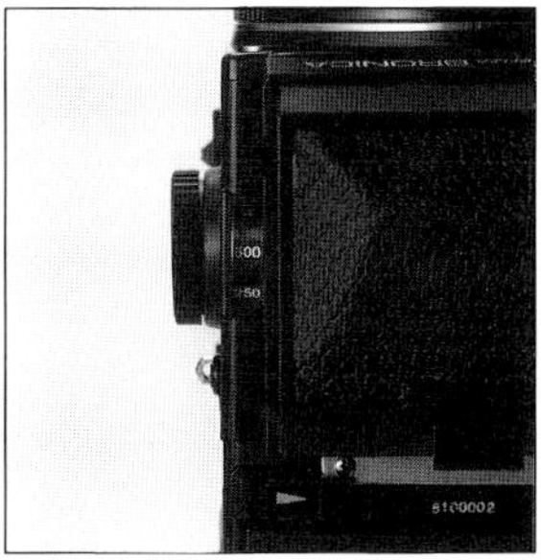

A number of actions take place virtually instantaneously when the shutter release is fully depressed: first the leaf shutter closes, then the lens diaphragm closes down to the selected aperture and the mirror swings out of the light path. At this point the shutter opens and closes after the predetermined time has elapsed and a red LED — the same one that serves as a battery check — in the viewfinder blinks briefly to confirm that the shutter has closed. If the LED fails to light the shutter has been released at the mechanical speed of 1/500 sec and the battery should be replaced.

After the shutter has closed, rotating the wind crank until it stops will advance the film to the next frame and return the reflex mirror to its working position. The crank can be operated in several short strokes if preferred. If the shutter release is held down while the wind crank is rotated the shutter will fire when the winding action is completed.

During a long exposure, if the crank is used before the shutter has closed the mirror will return to its viewing position, effectively and prematurely ending the exposure. Furthermore, the photograph you have just taken might be blurred and the following frame partially exposed. Also the next exposure will take place at 1/500 sec, regardless of what is set on the shutter dial. The viewfinder LED indicator is therefore more than a shutter okay signal; in noisy environments or during long exposures it is a valuable safety measure.

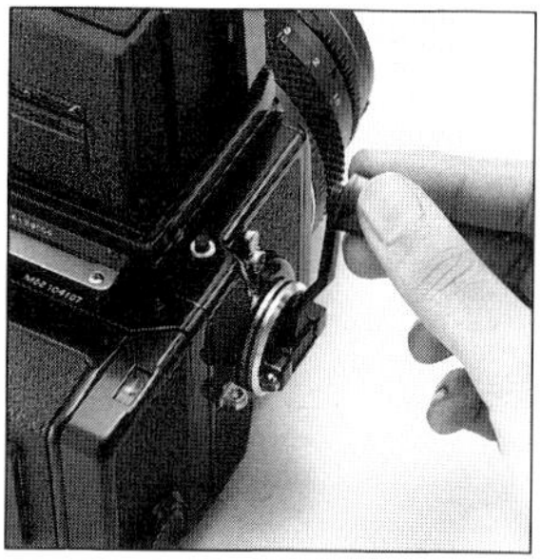

Do not close the shutter using the wind crank during a long exposure.

Release with / Shutter release button red dot position at:	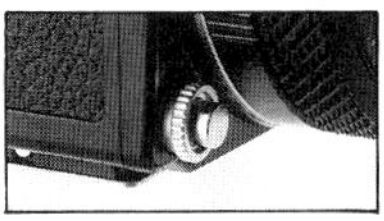 Shutter release button	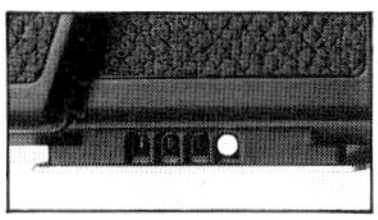 Motor Drive E & Speed Grip E release button	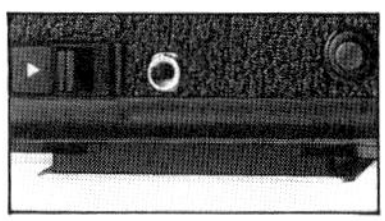 Cable release release button
Bottom	Releases	Releases	Releases
45° left	Locked	Releases	Releases
90° left	Locked	Locked	Locked

Remarks: Use Motor Drive E with red dot positioned at 45° left.

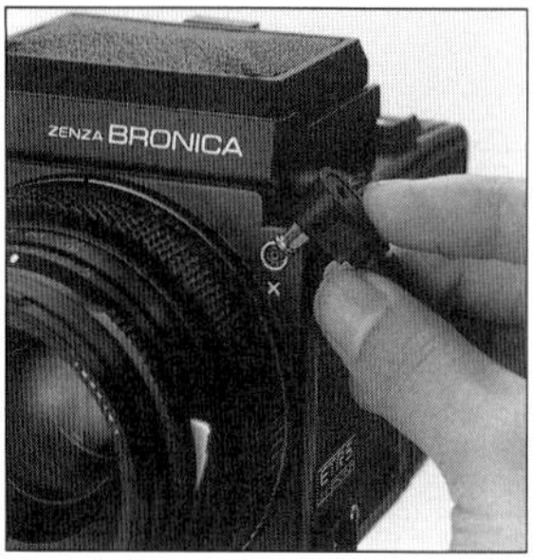

Flash photography

Electronic flash X-synchronisation is possible at all shutter speeds because of the leaf shutter built into every Zenzanon-E lens. The co-axial socket is on the upper right of the camera body (from a frontal view), and its safety cap should be left in place during normal photography. Synchronisation with F and M-type flash bulbs is possible, but over a smaller range of shutter speeds.

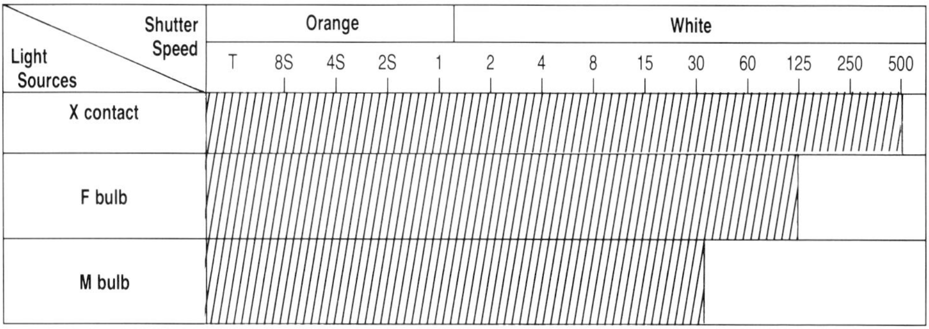

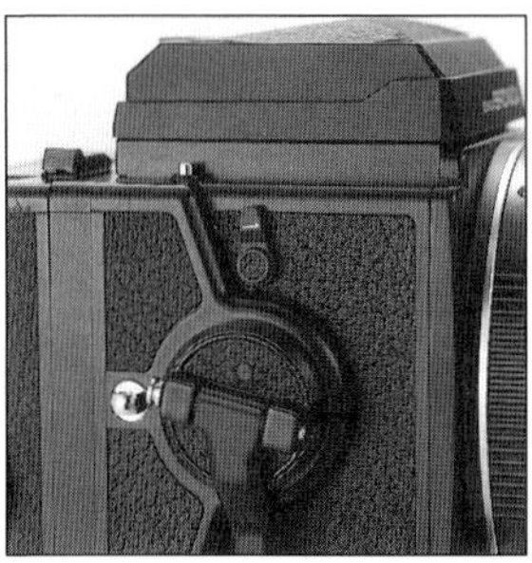

Making multiple exposures

The ETRS has interlock mechanisms to prevent unintentional double exposures and during standard operation the film is advanced automatically to the next frame as the wind crank is rotated. There is however a multiple exposure facility.

Before taking the first exposure engage the multiple exposure lever, positioned directly above the film wind crank, by moving the lever from its normal vertical position to lie horizontally, thereby revealing a red dot.

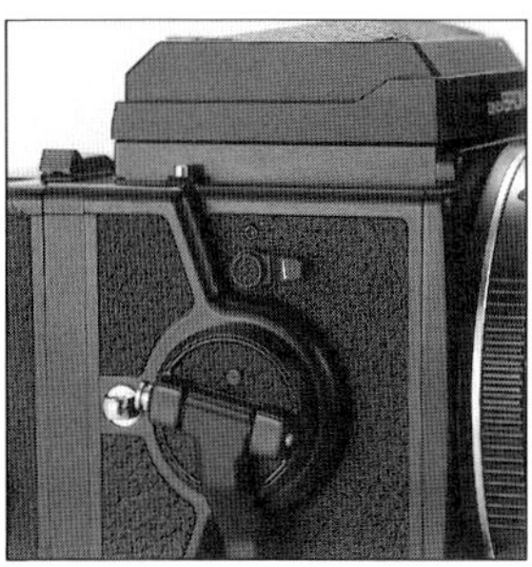

When the wind crank is revolved the shutter will be cocked but the film frame remains perfectly in position. This permits any number of exposures to be made on each frame; the frame counter does not advance during multiple exposure operation. Remember to reset the lever to an upright position immediately after the last exposure has been taken so that the next rotation of the wind crank will advance the film to the next frame and cock the shutter as normal.

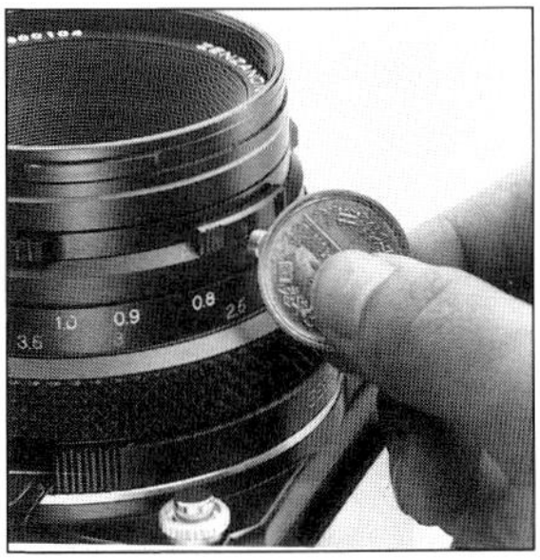

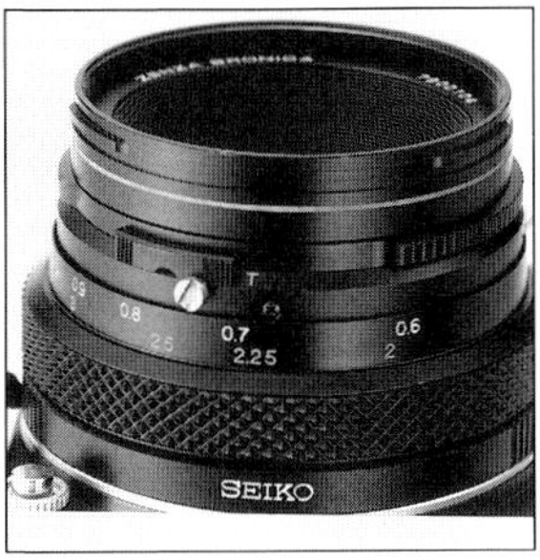

Using the 'T' setting

The 'T' (Time exposure) setting is the only shutter speed to be engaged from the lens itself and the camera shutter dial can be left at any speed. It is a mechanical setting and does not consume any battery power. With a small coin, undo the locking screw sufficiently to allow the switch to be moved from its normal 'A' position to expose a red letter 'T'; the locking screw need not be removed. The shutter is triggered in the normal way and will stay open as long as required. It is closed by returning the slider to reveal the green letter 'A'. Before closing the shutter, to avoid camera shake, it is best if the lens is covered using either your hand, a piece of black card or a lens cap.

A time exposure may also be ended by rotating the wind crank to re-position the reflex mirror in the light path, but this is not advised because the first exposure to be taken after returning to normal operation will take place at a speed of 1/500 sec. In addition, since the film is advanced slightly before the shutter is fully closed the picture might be blurred and the next frame partially exposed.

It is important that the slider control is locked back in place immediately after using 'T' and before reverting to normal photography to avoid any danger of inadvertently giving a time exposure; there is no indication to warn that 'T' is in use.

Chapter Five

Bronica ETR lenses

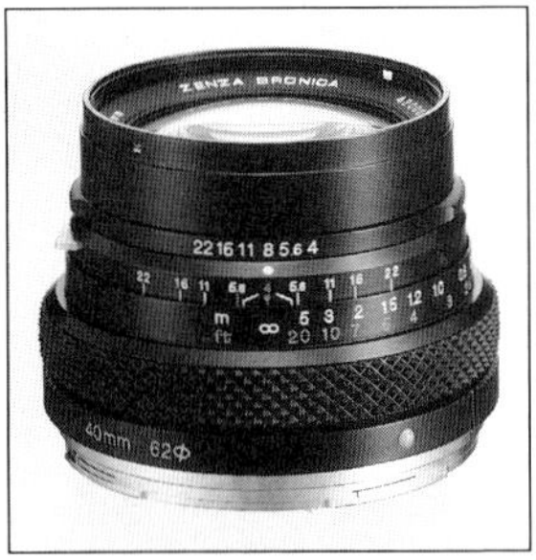

Zenzanon-E 40mm f4.0

Currently the widest wide angle lens in the ETR lens collection, equal to a 24mm focal length in 35mm format, the 40mm f4 has a construction of 10 elements in eight groups and is a compact, high performance optic with good handling characteristics. Its angle of view and very low distortion levels make it perfectly suited to photographing landscape, groups of people, interiors and any occasion where space is at a premium.

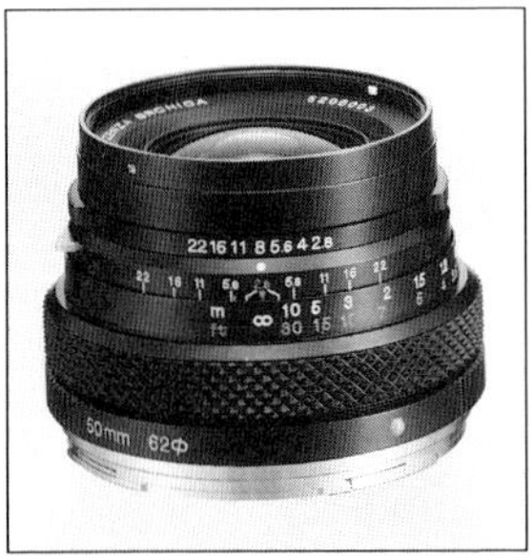

Zenzanon-E 50mm f2.8

Comprising nine elements in eight groups this lens, with its fast f2.8 aperture and moderately wide angle of view, is a capable photographic all-rounder and a perfect complement to the 75mm standard lens. In addition, it is a compact optic weighing in at 480 grams and measuring 51mm in length.

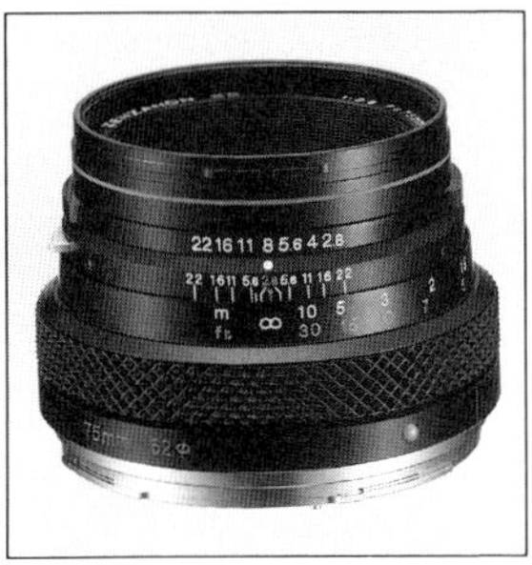

Zenzanon-E II 75mm f2.8

This is the standard lens for the Bronica ETR. Its angle of view is equivalent to a 45mm lens in the 35mm format and can be compared with that of a human eye. It combines well with the camera resulting in a smooth handling, well balanced package eminently suited to all types of photography.

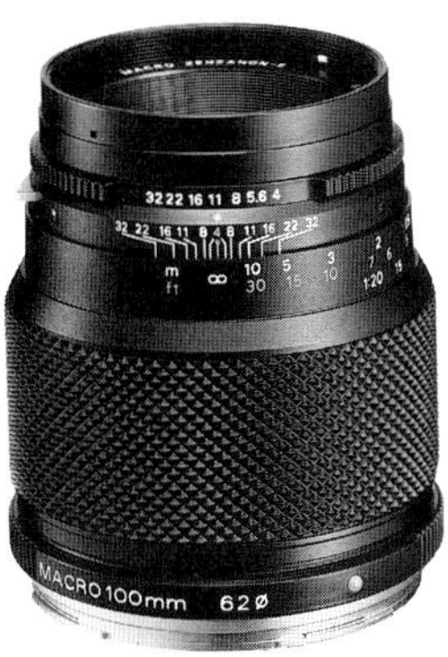

Macro Zenzanon-E 100mm f4

This lens is suitable for everyday photography but its macro capability is of particular interest. The closest focus distance of 0.61 metres from the film plane gives an image magnification of 1:4. It can be used in conjunction with Bronica Auto Extension Tubes-E or Auto Bellows-E for greater magnification without any deterioration in picture quality.

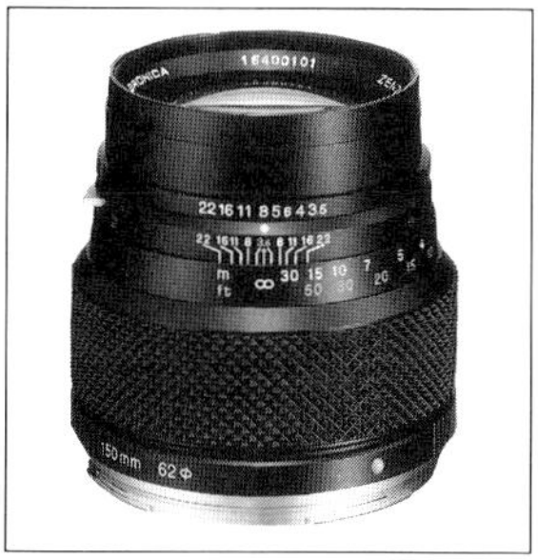

Zenzanon-E 150mm f3.5

A broad spectrum of subject matter can be tackled with this short-telephoto lens which is equivalent to the 90mm focal length in the 35mm format. It is in the sphere of portrait photography that this focal length excels, permitting a comfortable working distance from the subject without distorting the sitter's features. Optical competence and respectably fast maximum aperture are other noteworthy attributes of this popular lens.

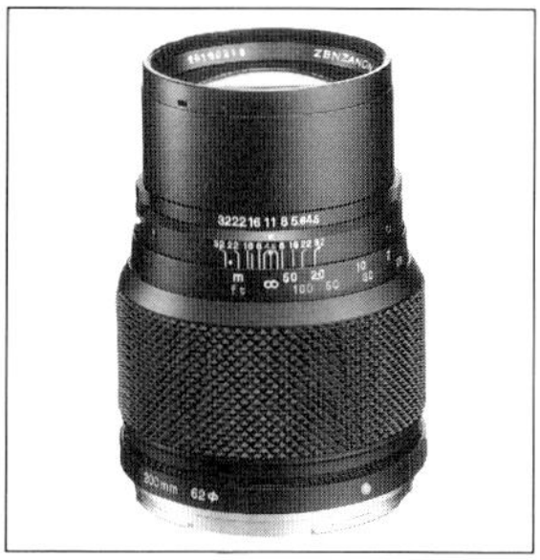

Zenzanon-E 200mm f4.5

This lens has an optical configuration of five elements in five groups and can be applied to a great many picture-taking situations from portrait work to sports and general photography. It is equivalent to a 120mm telephoto in the 35mm format. In addition to optical competence it is also compact which means that it can be hand-held at relatively slow shutter speeds.

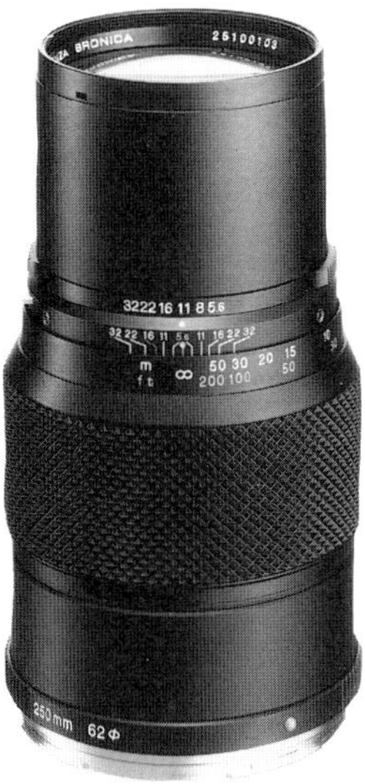

Zenzanon-E 250mm f5.6

Comprising an optical construction of five elements in five groups, this telephoto — equivalent to a 150mm lens in the 35mm format — is reasonably compact and nicely balanced. Its optical quality is well up to the exacting standards expected from a lens bearing the Zenzanon name. Suitable for many varied photographic subjects including sports and wildlife.

Zenzanon-E II 500mm f8

This long telephoto lens is the ideal partner for the discerning wildlife or sports photographer. It incorporates two special elements, of low refractivity and low dispersion respectively, to maximise resolution and minimise chromatic aberration. In addition to its optical charms it is uncompromisingly robust and should endure virtually anything asked of it.

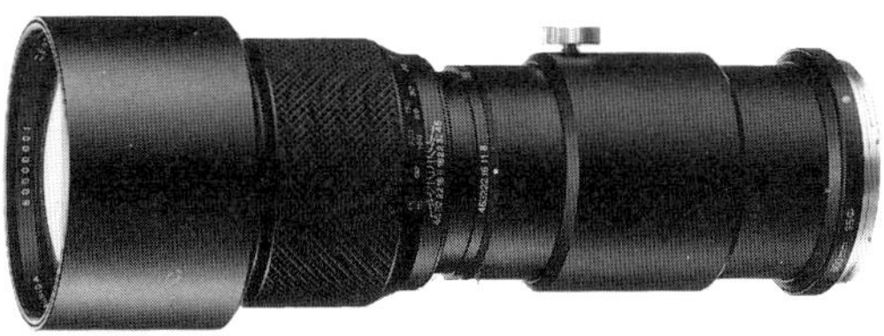

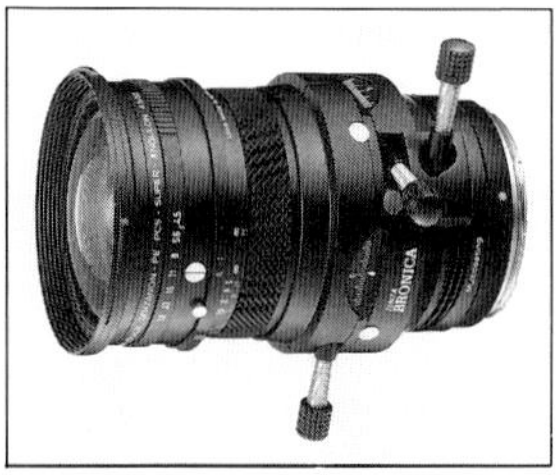

Zenzanon-PE Super Angulon 55mm f4.5 PCS lens

Architectural photographers will find much to admire and appreciate in this superb perspective control optic, manufactured by Jos. Schneider GmbH & Co. of West Germany to Bronica's specifications. This lens, with its gear driven shift and tilt movements, emulates large format cameras in its ability to correct converging verticals. Use of the tilt feature means that it is possible to obtain a greater depth of field than would normally be possible with a conventional lens of this focal length. Floating lens elements ensure that image quality is of a very high standard throughout the focusing range.

Zoom lenses

Although widely accepted and highly successful in the 35mm format, zoom lenses have only recently begun to make inroads into the world of medium-format photography. Bronica has two available for its ETR and two for the SQ system; all manufactured specially for them by world renowned German lens makers Schneider.

Specification of Bronica ETR lenses

Lens description	Lens construction (elements/groups)	Angle of view	Aperture range
Zenzanon-E 40mm f4	10/8	82°	f4-22
Zenzanon-E 50mm f2.8	9/8	70°	f2.8-22
Zenzanon-E 75mm f2.8	6/4	49°	f2.8-22
Macro Zenzanon-E 100mm f4	6/4	38°	f4-32
Zenzanon-E 150mm f3.5	5/5	26°	f3.5-22
Zenzanon-E 200mm f4.5	5/5	20°	f4.5-22
Zenzanon-E 250mm f5.6	5/5	16°	f5.6-32
Zenzanon-E 500mm f8	7/6	8°	f8-45
Zenzanon-PE Super-Angulon 55mm f4.5 PCS	10/8	64°	f4.5-32
Zenzanon-PE Variogon 70-140mm f4.5 zoom	15/13	51-28°	f4.5-32
Zenzanon-PE Variogon 125-250mm f5.6 zoom	17/14	31-16°	f5.6-32

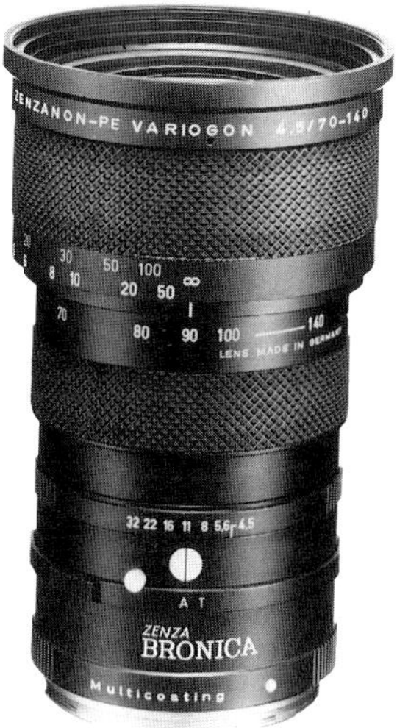

Zenzanon-PE Variogon 70-140mm f4.5

The Zenzanon 70-140mm lens with its 2× zoom ratio covers the most frequently used region of standard to short-telephoto focal lengths and does so in a compact package. Separate focus and zoom controls together with good balance ensure that handling is sound, and the provision of a macro close focusing mode opens up another dimension to be explored.

Zenzanon-PE Variogon 125-250mm f5.6

All the popularly used telephoto focal lengths are embraced by this weighty but well balanced 2× ratio zoom lens. A rotating tripod mount is provided to facilitate convenient vertical and horizontal shooting when the lens is mounted on to a tripod. Two-touch control, a macro mode and superb optical performance make it the ideal supplement to the standard 75mm lens.

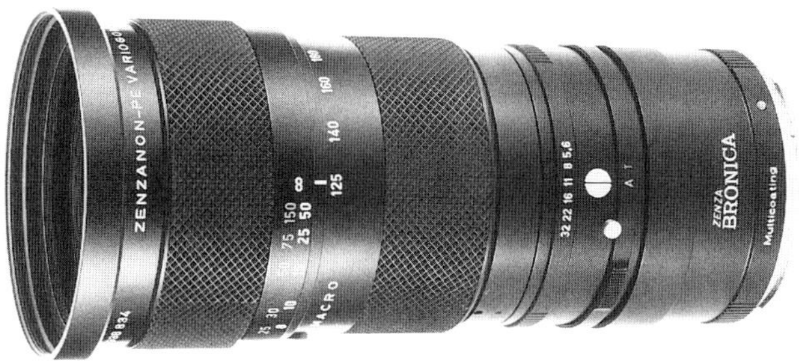

Shutter	Minimum focus distance	Macro magnification	Filter size	Size (length/ diameter)	Weight	Equivalent 35mm focal length
1/500, T	0.4m	N/A	62mm	53 × 80mm	515 grams	24mm
1/500, T	0.5m	N/A	62mm	51 × 80mm	480 grams	30mm
1/500, T	0.6m	N/A	62mm	51 × 80mm	450 grams	45mm
1/500, T	0.61m	1:4	62mm	87 × 82mm	650 grams	60mm
1/500, T	1.5m	N/A	62mm	73 × 80mm	625 grams	90mm
1/500, T	2.0m	N/A	62mm	103 × 80mm	700 grams	120mm
1/500, T	3.0m	N/A	62mm	141 × 80mm	840 grams	150mm
1/500, T	8.5m	N/A	95mm	267 × 100mm	1890 grams	300mm
1/500, T	0.5m	N/A	104mm	157 × 104mm	1650 grams	34mm
1/500, T	0.25m	1:4.8	93mm	152 × 100mm	1500 grams	43-86mm
1/500, T	0.76m	1·6.2	93mm	206 × 94mm	1650 grams	77-154mm

Lens accessories

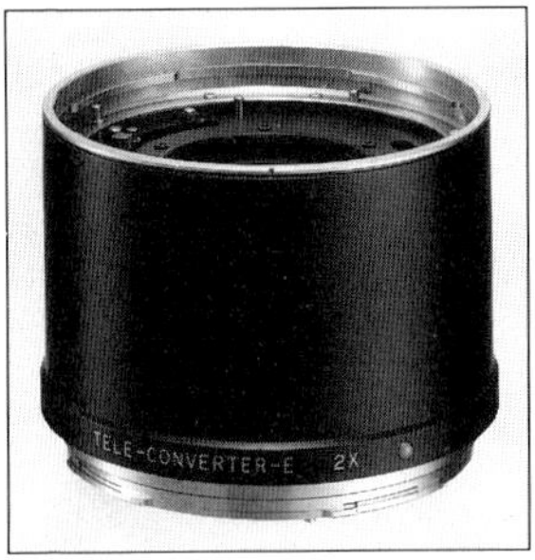

Zenzanon 2× Tele-converter E

A portable and comparatively inexpensive method of doubling lens focal length without altering its minimum focusing distance. Furthermore, this six element tele-converter has all the necessary internal couplings to retain fully automatic diaphragm operation. Therefore, if the AE-II Finder-E is fitted, through-the-lens metering in both automatic and manual metering modes is maintained with no exposure modification necessary. When using a non-metering finder allow an additional two stops exposure to compensate for the light loss caused by the converter.

Although it is not advised for use with wide angle lenses 40mm or 50mm, nor the 55mm perspective control lens, this tele-converter will deliver exceptional results with the following focal lengths: 75mm, 100mm, 150mm, 200mm, 250mm and 500mm.

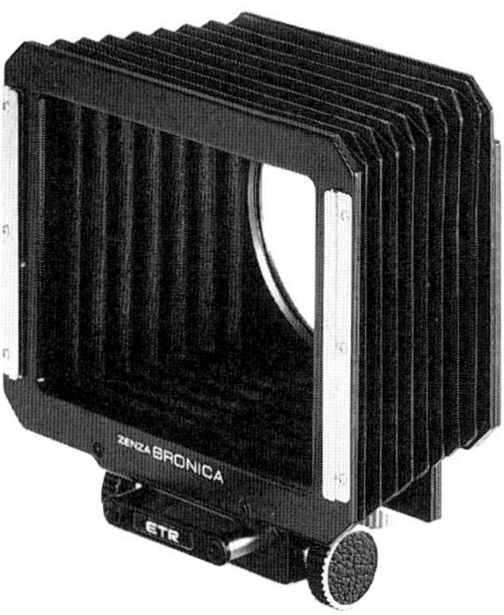

Professional Lens Hood-E

This extremely versatile lens hood has been designed to provide maximum flare protection for the following Zenzanon-E lenses: 40mm, 50mm, 75mm, 100mm, 150mm, 200mm and 250mm. The rail-mounted bellows can be adjusted to suit the focal length of the lens in use; a special mask insert is provided for focal lengths between 150mm and 250mm.

Adaptor rings of 58mm and 62mm size are supplied. Gelatin filters and masks of 75mm × 75mm size can be inserted in a slot at the rear of the unit. In addition, creative filters of the Hoyarex and Cokin type can be accommodated.

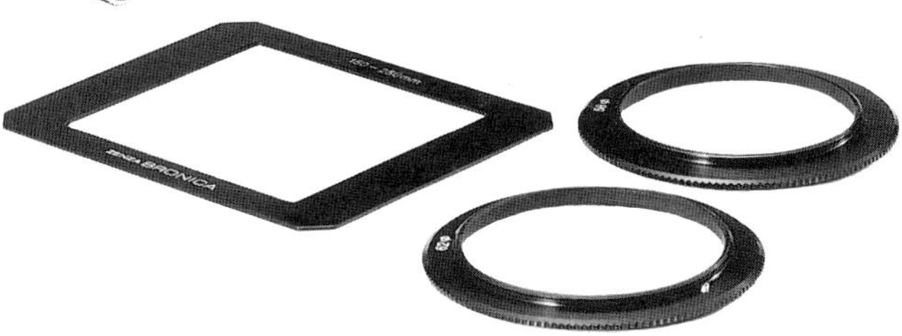

Lens hoods

Three non-extending, bayonet fit plastic lens hoods are available for Zenzanon lenses. The wide angle model is suitable for the 40mm and 50mm lenses; a standard version for the 75mm; and a longer one for focal lengths from 100mm to 250mm inclusive. The two zooms are supplied complete with built-in lens hoods.

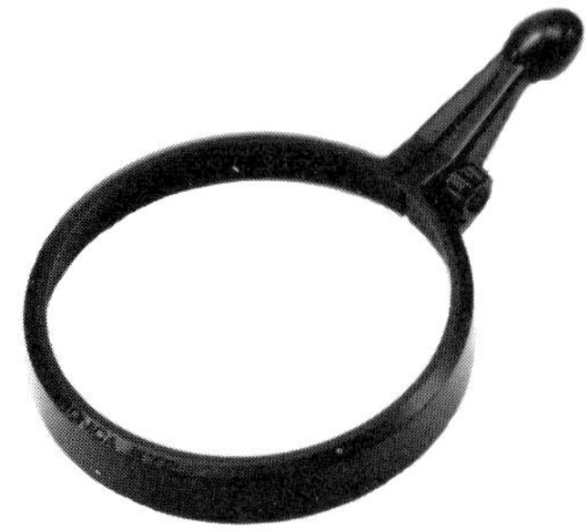

Rapid focus lever

This simple accessory fits around focus barrel of the lens and improves focusing speed and accuracy. It is compatible with the following Zenzanon-E lenses: 40mm, 50mm, 75mm, 100mm, 150mm, 200mm and 250mm.

Revolving camera adaptor

Although conceived originally for convenient switching from upright to horizontal picture taking, and vice versa, with the 6 × 7cm Bronica GS-1, this ingenious accessory may also be used in conjunction with any ETR camera provided that the Revolving Tripod Adaptor plate is purchased which has the necessary locating pins.

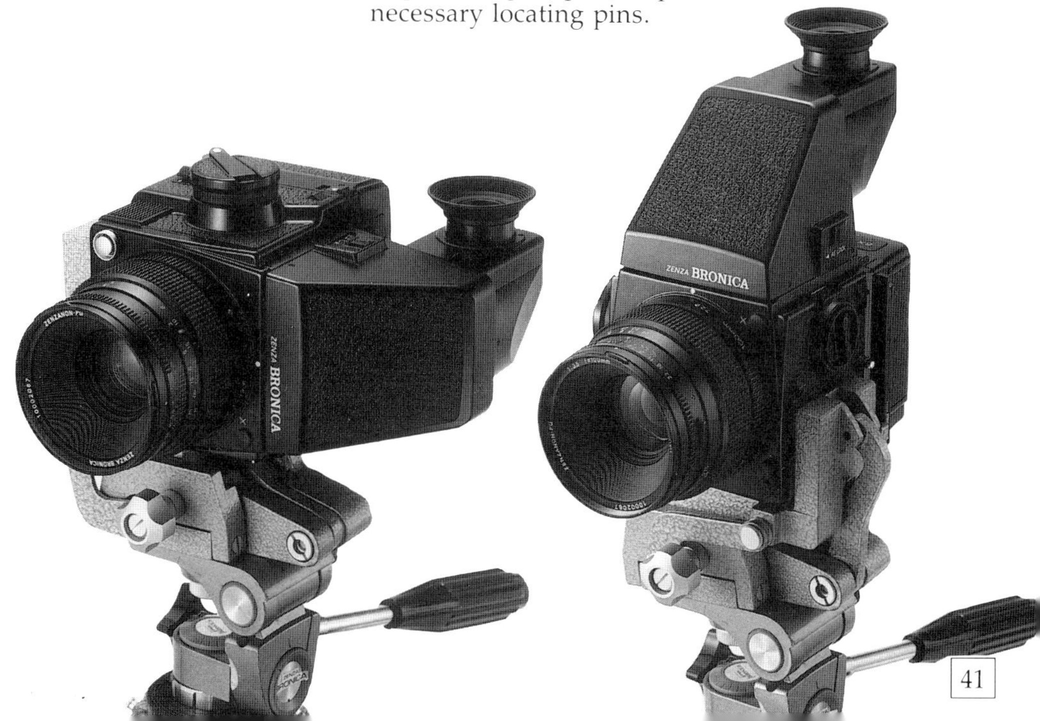

Chapter Six

Bronica ETR system accessories

FINDERS

Waist Level Finder-E

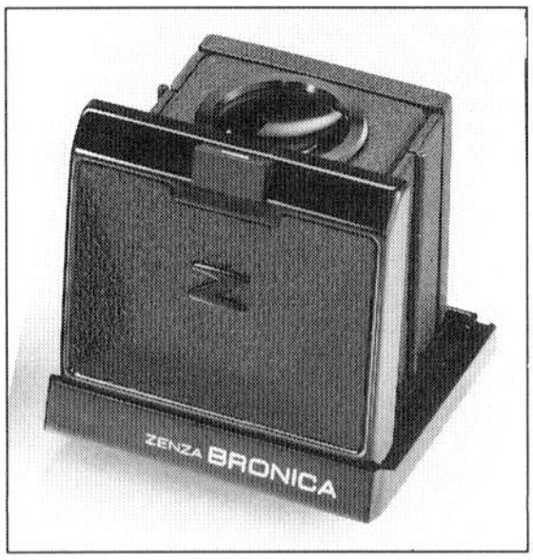

The non-metering Waist Level Finder-E provides a reversed, upright viewing image and, for operating ease, an integral flip-up magnifier is provided.

A spring loaded mechanism enables the finder to be ready for action in an instant. To close the hood first lock the magnifier into place (assuming it was in its working position). Then press in both sides of the finder while simultaneously pushing the front frame towards the rear end. At a particular point a spring will take over to close the finder fully.

The supplied magnifier eyepiece has a strength of − 1.5 diopters. Optional eyepieces are available in strengths of −4.50, −3.50, −2.50, −0.50, +0.50 and +1.50.

Prism Finder-E

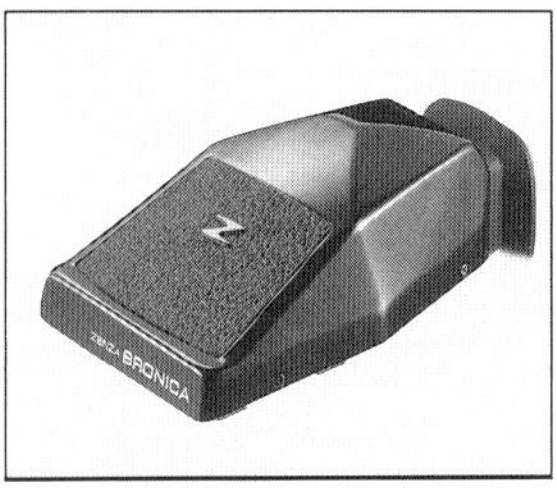

This compact, non-metering finder gives a bright laterally-correct, upright image and is ideally suited for both horizontal and vertical shooting. Used in conjunction with the optional Speed Grip-E handling is very fast indeed. A rubber eye-cap eliminates the problem of external reflections and the finder comes complete with a −1.50 diopters eyepiece. Optional eyepieces are available in strengths of −4.50, −3.50, −2.50, −0.50, +0.50 and +1.50.

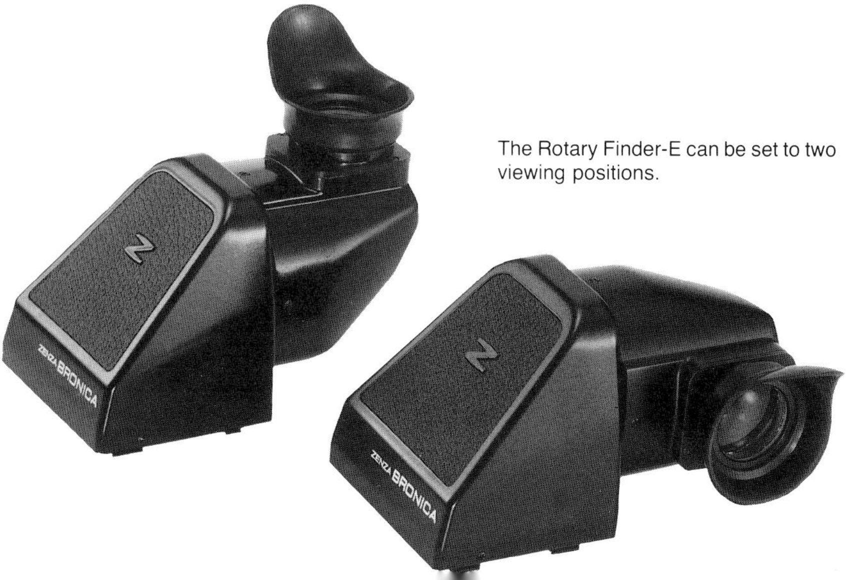

The Rotary Finder-E can be set to two viewing positions.

Rotary Finder-E

Designed to cope with photography in awkward situations such as extreme low-angle work the non-metering Rotary Finder-E gives a bright, laterally correct, upright viewing image. The rotating head can be adjusted either left or right and is located firmly into position by click-stops; it is also possible to use the finder at intermediate settings. The supplied eyepiece has a strength of −1.5 diopters. Others available are −4.5, −3.5, −2.5, −0.5, +0.5 and +1.5 diopters.

Action Prism Finder-E

The specialist photographer who needs to view his subject from some way from the finder eyepiece will be suited by the non-metering Action Prism Finder-E. Its low magnification permits the entire image area to be studied from up to 12cm from the eyepiece and it is possible, therefore, to continue to compose and take photographs even though the photographer may be wearing spectacles, a crash helmet or similar protective head garment, or is, for some reason, unable to get his eye up to the eyepiece.

This finder can be fitted on to the Bronica SQ-A and SQ-Am if the Action Prism Adaptor is used and it will perform as it does on the ETR.

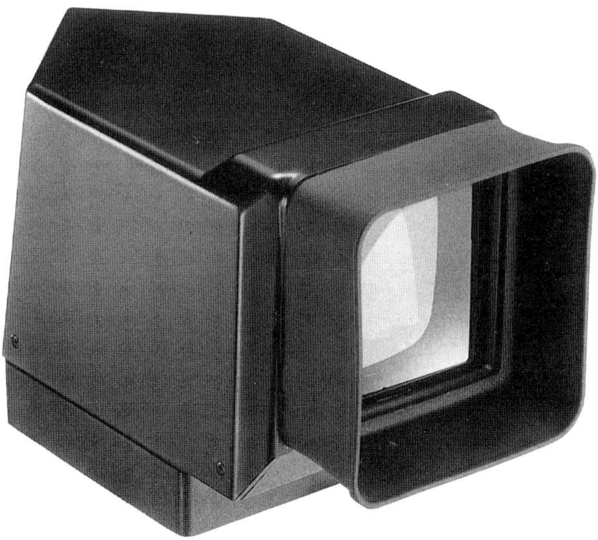

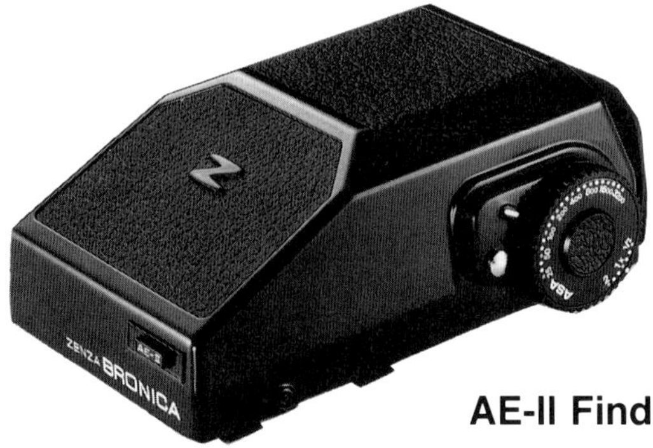

AE-II Finder-E

Of the five finders in the ETR system the sophisticated AE-II Finder-E is the only one to feature an integral through-the-lens open aperture metering system complete with two exposure modes: aperture-priority auto-exposure and manual. It gives a bright, laterally-correct, upright image. Power for the prism's metering functions is drawn from the camera's six volt battery. This finder shares the same system of diopter eyepieces as the Prism Finder-E and comes supplied with a −1.5 value lens as standard.

This finder may be used on Bronicas ETR and ETR-C with one minor operating modification: pressing the shutter button on either of these cameras will not bring on the LED display; the 'AE-II' display button on the front of the prism housing has to be used.

Exposure assessment is performed by two fast-reacting silicon blue cells, with a sensitivity of EV 4 to EV 17 (ISO 100 film and 75mm f2.8 lens), and are located to give centre-weighted measurement.

The unit's lockable mode switch has three settings: a red dot indicates off, 'M' stands for manual metering and 'A' for auto-exposure operation. To adjust the mode switch depress the centre button of the mode control and rotate the dial to the desired setting, making sure when you release it that the centre button returns flush with the dial.

Shutter speeds are indicated by an LED display which is actuated by pushing the button marked 'AE-II' on the pentaprism housing, or by partially depressing the shutter release. The display stays on for as long as one or the other is held down. Shutter speeds of 1/500 sec to 1/60 sec inclusive are shown by green LEDs; speeds of 1/30 sec and slower by orange LEDs. Over and under-exposure warnings are provided in the form of red triangular-shaped LEDs that indicate in which direction the aperture ring should be rotated for correct exposure.

In aperture-priority AE operation the prism transfers information regarding which shutter speed should be set directly to the camera via gold-plated contacts located on the base of the unit. Speeds within the range of 8 seconds to 1/500 sec are selected automatically by the finder in 1/3 stop increments. The nearest standard shutter speed lights up on the viewfinder LED readout to give an approximate guide to the actual speed. Altering the shutter speed selected by the camera is done by adjusting the aperture ring until the desired setting is shown. In AE mode the camera's shutter speed dial plays no part in the proceedings.

During metered manual, the required shutter value for correct exposure is shown in the viewfinder as a blinking LED and this speed must be transferred by hand to the camera's shutter speed dial, in which case any one of the 13 settings between 8 seconds and 1/500 sec can be selected. Intermediate settings must not be made.

If the metering prism is switched off the shutter will fire at the speed set on the camera's shutter dial and there are no LED readout or exposure indications.

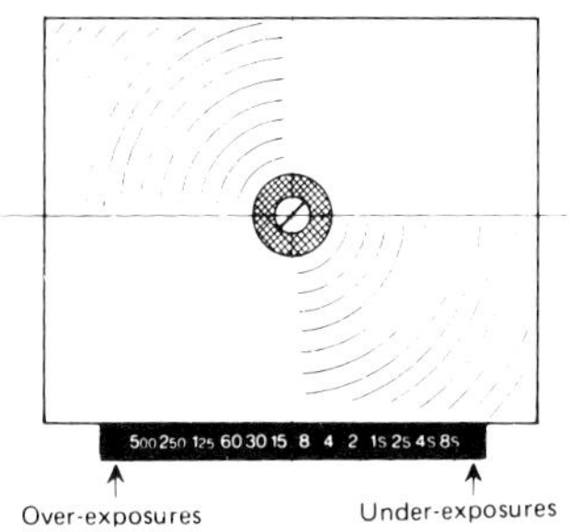

For over-riding the finder's AE system in unusual lighting situations a lockable exposure compensation dial is featured with a range from +2 to −2 stops in 1/3 stop increments; it should be set to '1X' during normal photography. Sharing the exposure compensation dial is the ISO film speed control which is marked from ISO 25 to ISO 3200 in 1/3 stop settings, though lack of space on the dial's face precludes every film speed being indicated.

Table of Film Speed

A S A	25	32	40	50	64	80	100	125	160	200	250	320	400	500	640	800	1000	1250	1600	2000	2500	3200
Film Speed Scale	25	·	·	50	·	·	100	·	·	200	·	·	400	·	·	800	·	·	1600	·	·	3200
D I N	15	16	17	18	19	20	21	22	23	24	25	26	27	28	29	30	31	32	33	34	35	36

Practical hints for AE-II Finder-E use

- With this finder attached battery check is best performed while the meter is on; this ensures that the battery is under full load during the test to give a true indication of its state.
- Clean the base and camera contacts with a soft, dry cloth before attaching finder. A poor connection might lead to inaccurate operation.
- Whenever the camera is not in use the finder should be switched off to conserve the battery.
- Battery consumption during long auto-exposures is considerable. Use the 'T' (Time exposure) setting to avoid excessive battery drain.
- The aperture ring should not be set at intermediate aperture values because erroneous exposure readings might result.
- When shooting several films of differing speeds it is imperative that each film's correct speed is set on the finder before commencing photography.
- If the displayed shutter speed is 1/30 sec or below use a camera support.
- Always return the compensation dial to '1×' immediately after use; the viewfinder does not display any warning that exposure compensation is in use.
- When the eye is away from the eyepiece, cover the eyepiece with some black cloth to prevent light entering and interfering with metering.
- When using long shutter speeds confirm that the shutter has closed — look out for the red LED blink in the viewfinder — before attempting to advance the film. If the wind crank is operated before the shutter has closed the picture you have just taken might exhibit streaking and the following frame partially exposed. In addition the next exposure will be made at 1/500 sec regardless of what is set on the shutter dial.
- Do not press the depth of field preview and take a meter reading simultaneously as incorrect exposures will result. The shot will be over-exposed by the difference between the selected aperture and the len's maximum aperture.
- Select 'M' for flash photography since there is the risk of slow shutter speeds being chosen during auto-exposure operation.

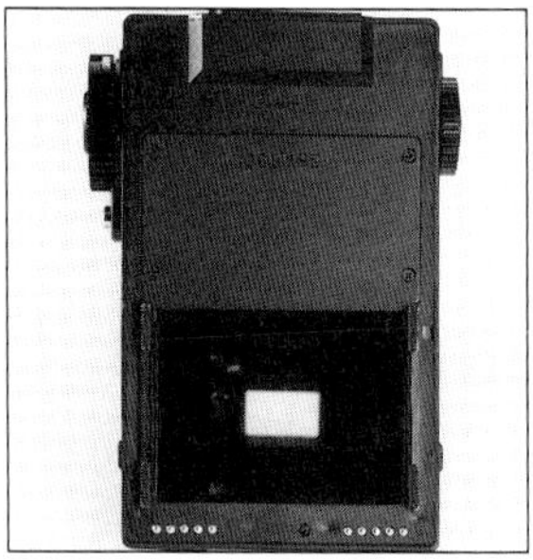

The contacts on the underside of the AE-II Finder-E should be cleaned regularly.

GRIPS AND MOTOR-DRIVE

Speed Grip-E

The Bronica ETRS on its own handles very nicely. Add the anatomically-shaped Speed Grip-E and handling improves further by making the shooting of horizontal and vertical shots straightforward and film advance rapid: the right hand holds the camera, fires the shutter and winds on film while the left focuses, changes aperture and shutter speed and assists in supporting the camera.

The grip's ratcheted lever wind is reminiscent of a 35mm SLR's though it needs two complete strokes to advance the film by one frame. It can also be operated in several short strokes. The first full stroke resets the mirror while shutter cocking and film advance are taken care of by the second stroke. Also incorporated is a flash hot shoe fitting, which when in use cancels the camera's co-axial socket.

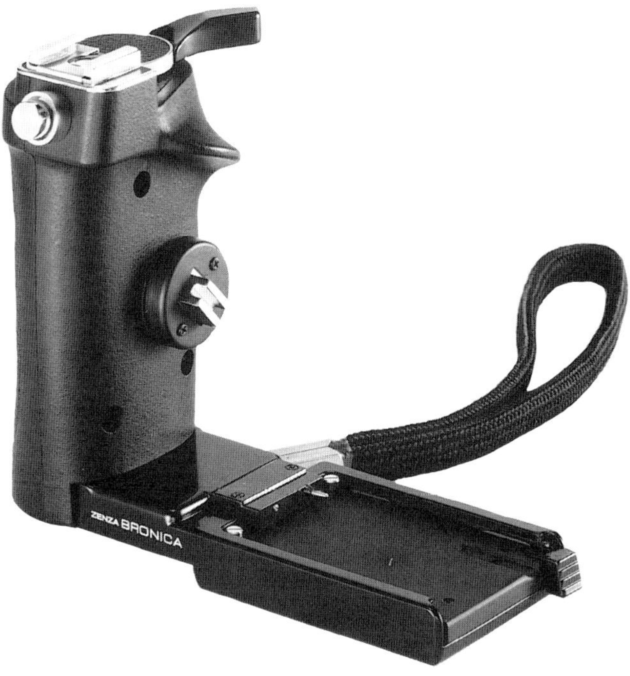

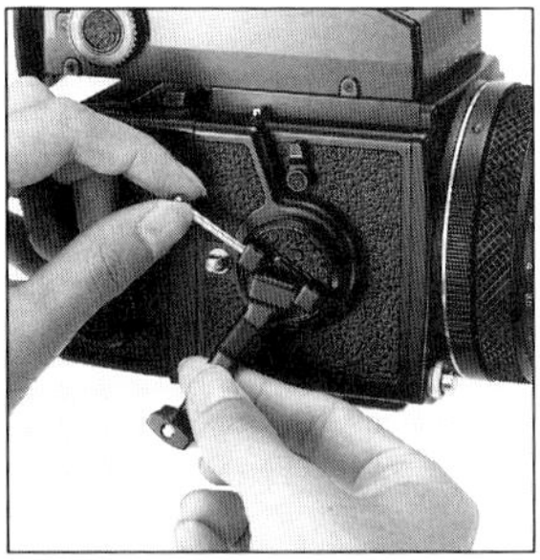

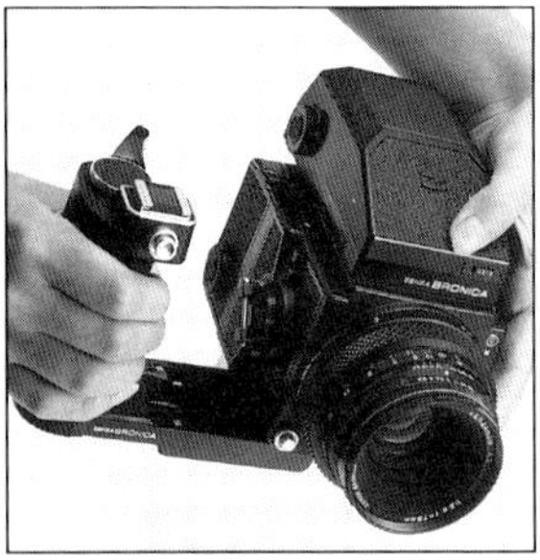

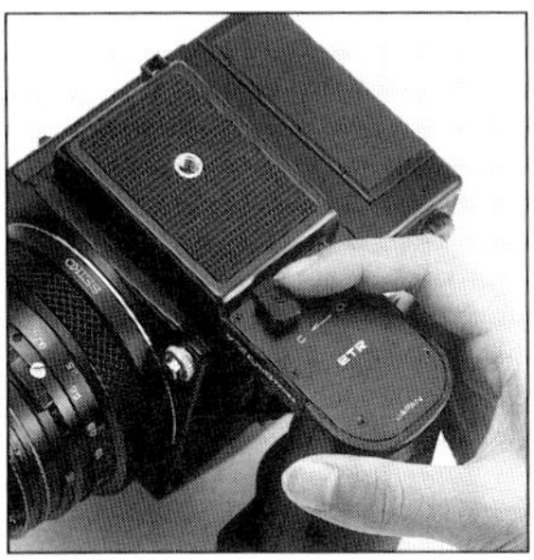

Attaching the Speed Grip-E

1. Remove the camera wind crank by pulling the rod attachment pin until the crank is free before pushing the rod back fully.
2. Engage the grip on to the camera's tripod mounting shoe taking care that the winder's grooved linkage mates correctly with the attachment rod. Operate the wind lever to obtain correct alignment if necessary. A spring-loaded safety lock engages once the grip is pushed fully home.
3. Once correctly positioned lock the grip into place by moving the locking lever situated on the base from '0' to 'C'.

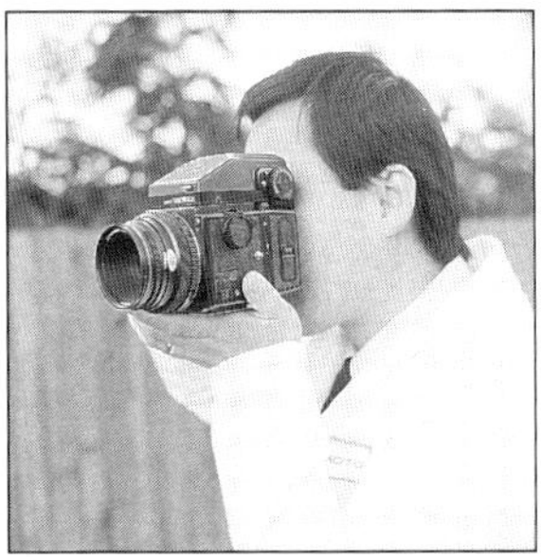

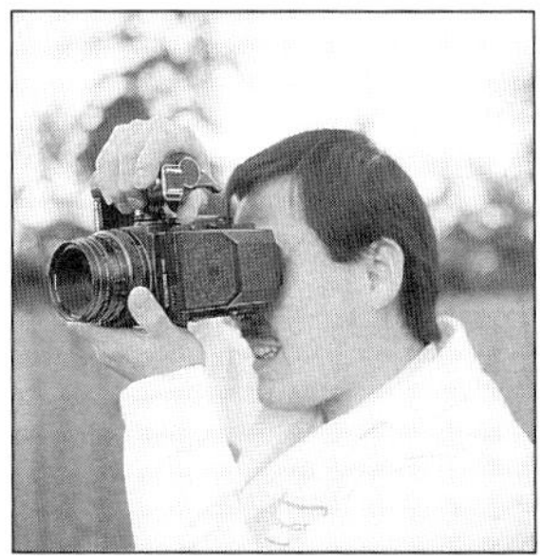

L-Grip E

The L-Grip E attaches to the camera by a bush which screws into the tripod socket. It does not provide any method of film transport — the camera's wind crank is used as normal — and the shutter is fired via a threaded cable release. A flash accessory shoe is fitted but this is not a hot-shoe.

The grip is mounted on the left of the camera which means that it can be used in combination with either the Speed Grip-E or the Motor-Drive E thus forming a very steady shooting platform. Coupled with the Speed Grip-E the shutter can be released by either hand and the film advanced by the right. Used in conjunction with the Motor Drive-E only the shutter release on the motor drive should be used.

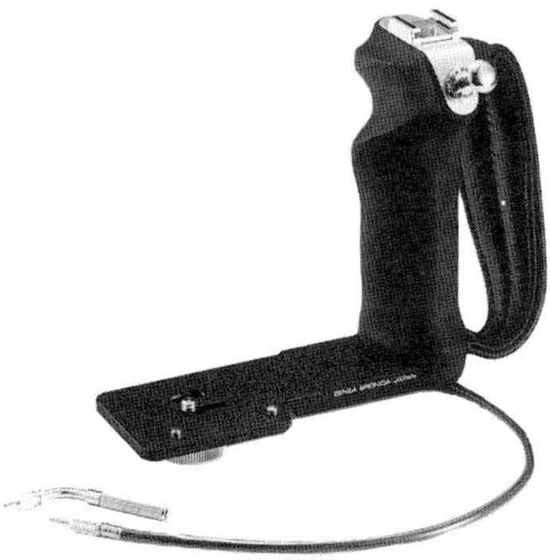

Behind Old Harry, Kos Photos

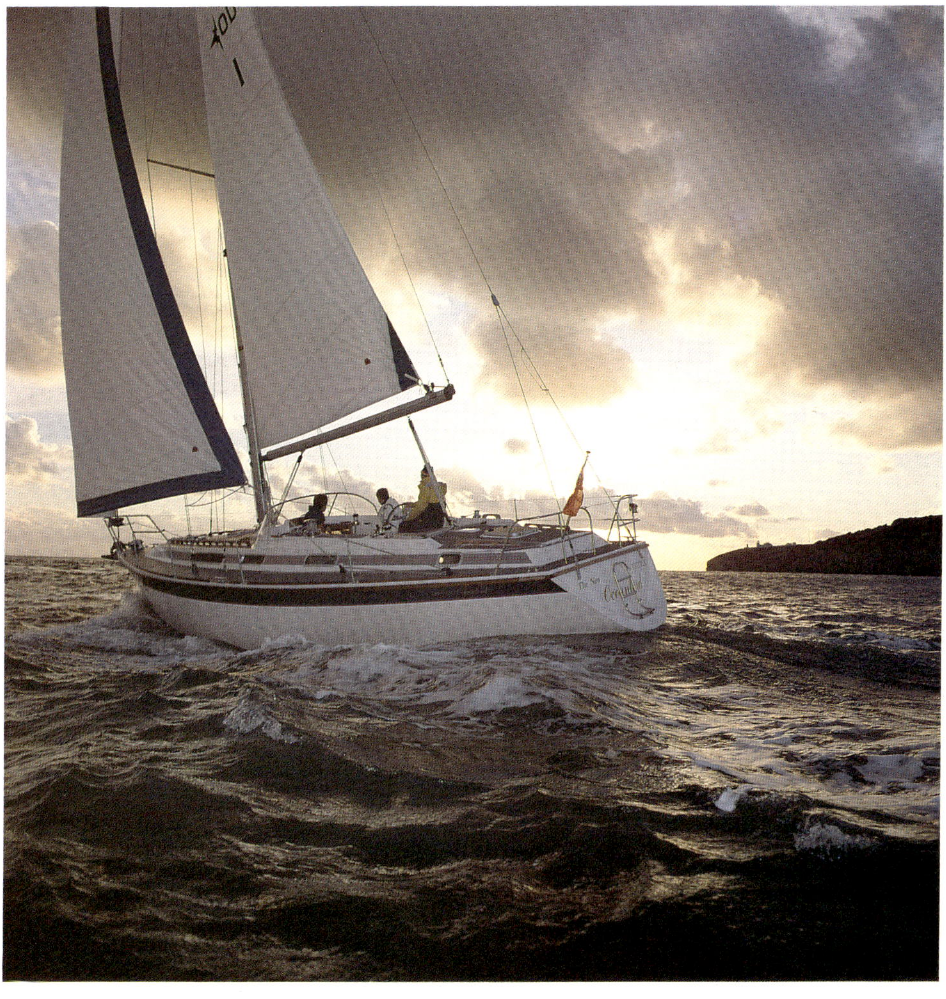

Glamour Shot, Nigel Holmes

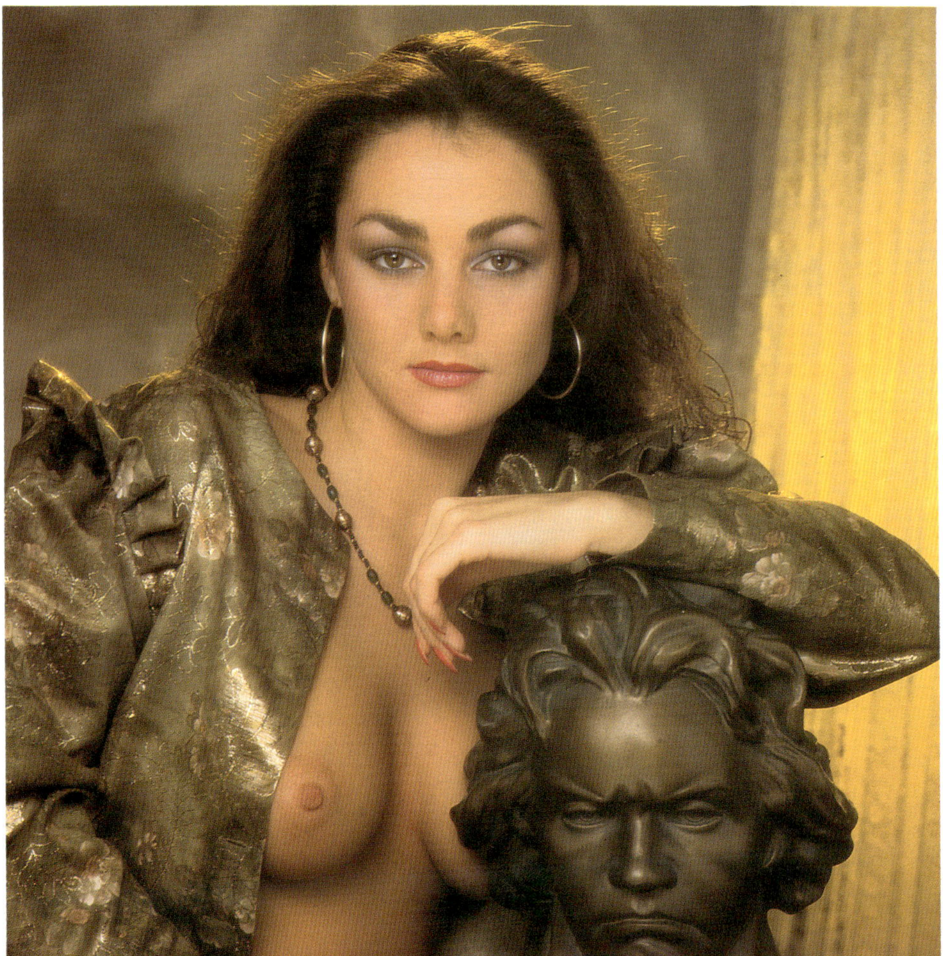

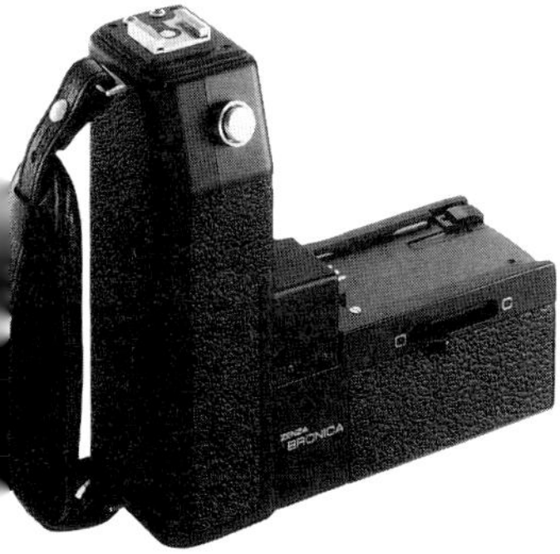

Motor-drive E

By offering unparalleled shooting convenience this motor-drive unit has much to commend it. It frees the photographer to concentrate on the subject while it looks after the job of transporting film and cocking the shutter.

Bronica ETR and ETR-C owners can also appreciate the Motor-drive E as it is fully compatible with these cameras.

Eight high quality AA batteries, or the rechargeable nickel cadmium equivalent, are necessary and these are stored in the unit's base. A fresh set of alkaline cells has a claimed life of 100 rolls of 120 roll film. The motor-drive can also be supplied via its external power input socket using a nine volt or 12 volt DC power pack. For remote control use a 2.5mm mini-jack socket is fitted. Prior to either plugging in or withdrawing the remote release connection switch the motor-drive off.

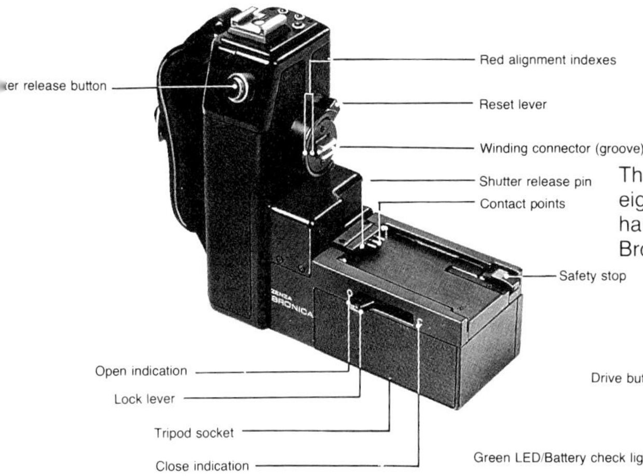

The Motor-drive E from all angles. It accepts eight AA size batteries and improves handling efficiency. It is compatible with all Bronica ETR cameras.

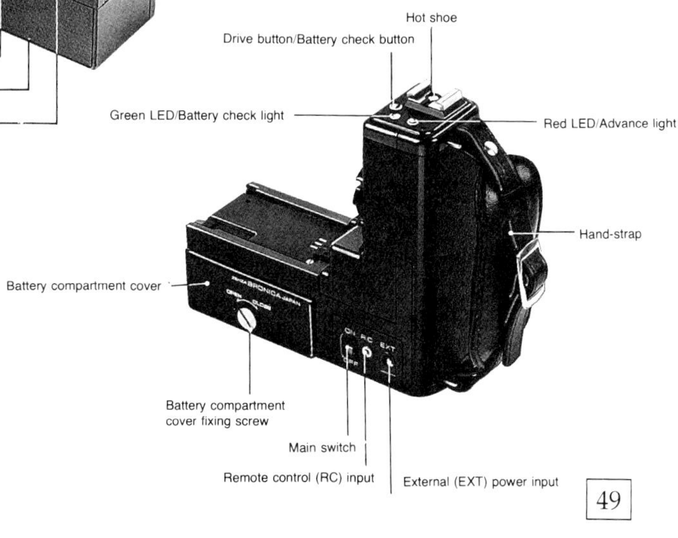

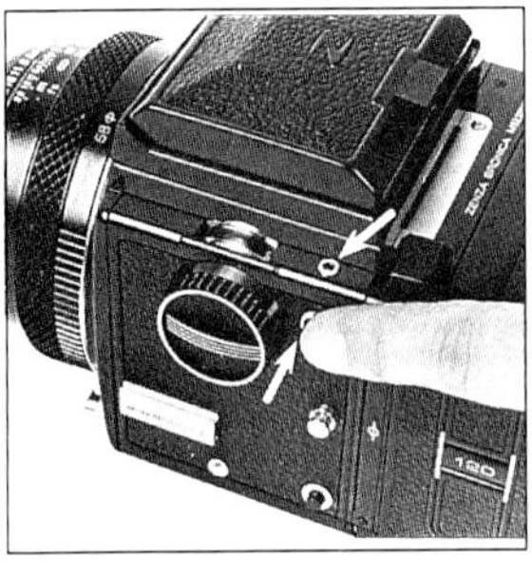

Test the camera battery before fitting Motor-drive E.

Loading and testing the Motor-drive E

1. With the unit switched to 'OFF', load the eight AA cells following the polarity markings in the battery chamber. Pressing the drive button will light the green LED, confirming that the batteries have been inserted correctly.
2. The motor-drive's correct operation should be confirmed before fitting it to the camera.

(a) Manually rotate the grooved winding connector anti-clockwise — you will feel some resistance and hear a 'click' — until the red dots match.

(b) Select 'ON' and press the winder's shutter button. The red LED on the hand-grip will blink and you should notice a small release pin, next to the motor-drive's electrical contacts, pop out for an instant. If not, operate the reset switch and try again.

(c) Press the drive button and the motor linkage will rotate freely. Switch off when correct operation has been confirmed.

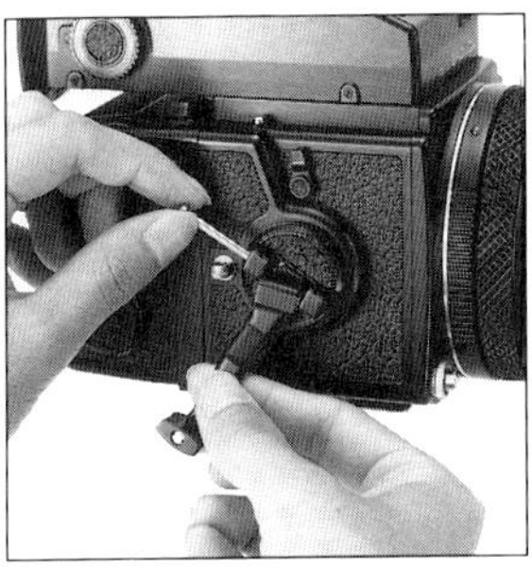

Slide out attachment rod to remove film wind crank.

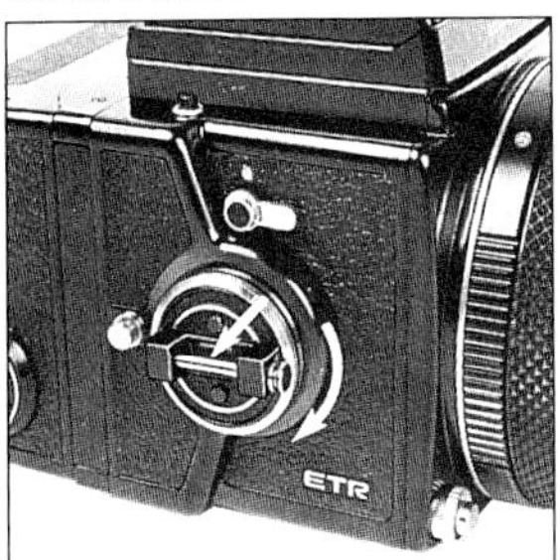

Rotate the crank case so that it is parallel with the camera base.

Attaching the Motor-drive E

1. Check the camera battery before proceeding. Set the multiple exposure lever to its horizontal position and any shutter speed except 'T'. Remove the wind crank by pulling out the attachment rod. This rod should then be pushed back and the crank base rotated anti-clockwise until the rod lies parallel with the camera's base, and there is no clockwise play, before moving on to the next step.
2. Reset the motor-drive's winding connector so that the two red dots face each other and there is no clockwise play. Then slide the motor-drive on to the tripod base ensuring that the attachment rod coincides with the grooved connector. Once in place a safety catch prevents the unit slipping off; moving the slide lock lever towards 'C' secures the unit.
3. At this point check that the motor-drive is connected properly. Without a film back attached return the multiple exposure lever to a vertical position, switch on and press the drive button. This will cause the film winding shaft mechanism to operate continuously but without firing the shutter. Switch off after a few seconds.

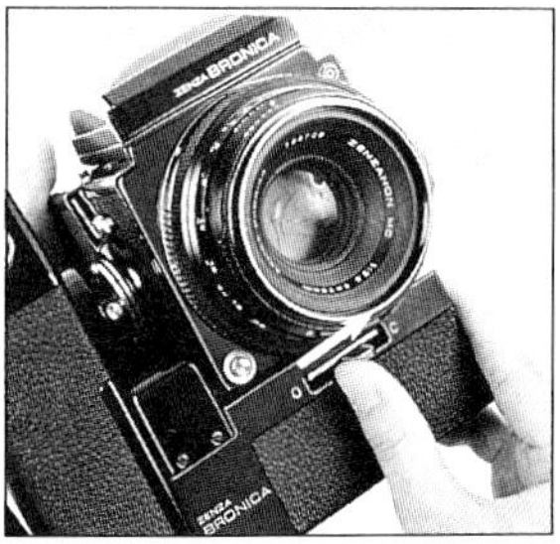

Attach Motor-drive E ensuring that the grooved drive connector mates with the attachment rod.

4. Correct shutter release and wind-on can be confirmed next. Set the multiple exposure switch to a horizontal position and, again without a film back, turn the unit back on and press the drive button. The film winding shaft will revolve once or so and stop, and the red LED will glow continuously. Press the shutter release and the shutter will fire, followed immediately by the motor winding on ready for the next frame. Familiarise yourself with the motor-drive's operation before actually taking photographs.

Using the Motor-drive E

The multiple exposure control should be in an upright position. A film back can be attached with either the first frame in position or with the film start mark aligned correctly. Pressing the drive button will ensure that the back is fully coupled in the former instance and will advance the film automatically to the first frame in the latter; the red LED will stay illuminated indicating that the motor-drive is fully prepared. Photography may now be performed as normal, or if you are not shooting immediately, switch the unit off to cancel the red LED.

Maximum continuous shooting rate is one frame-per-second with the fastest shutter speed. Single frame photography is achieved by the simple expedient of releasing the shutter button after one exposure has been taken.

After the last frame the motor will stop operating and the drive button should be pressed to wind up the remainder of the film and backing paper. A distinct change of tone will be noticed when the backing paper is off the film spool; the motor-drive should now be switched off and the exposed film removed.

Practical hints for Motor-drive E use

- When attaching the motor-drive to the camera, if the red dots on the winding linkage are not properly aligned the drive button must be depressed after every exposure to advance the film. For correct positioning revolve the linkage past the point where the two dots coincide and then turn the linkage back clockwise until it stops.
- Pressing the shutter button while the dark slide is inserted will trip the release pin but will neither make an exposure nor advance the film. Push the reset lever fully downwards, remove the dark slide and try again.

Trouble-shooting

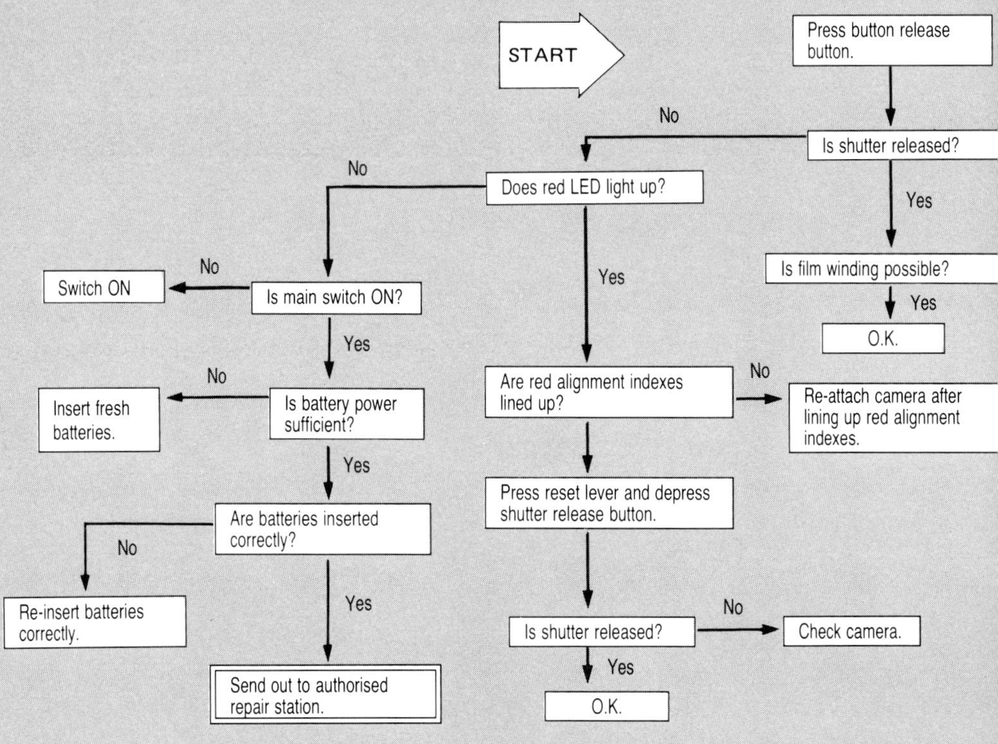

- Do not use the camera's shutter button or cable release socket during motor-drive operation. If you do, the camera will fire but the film will not advance until the drive button has been operated. Furthermore, there is the possibility of damaging the camera.
- When the film winding speed drops to about one frame every two seconds, replace the batteries.

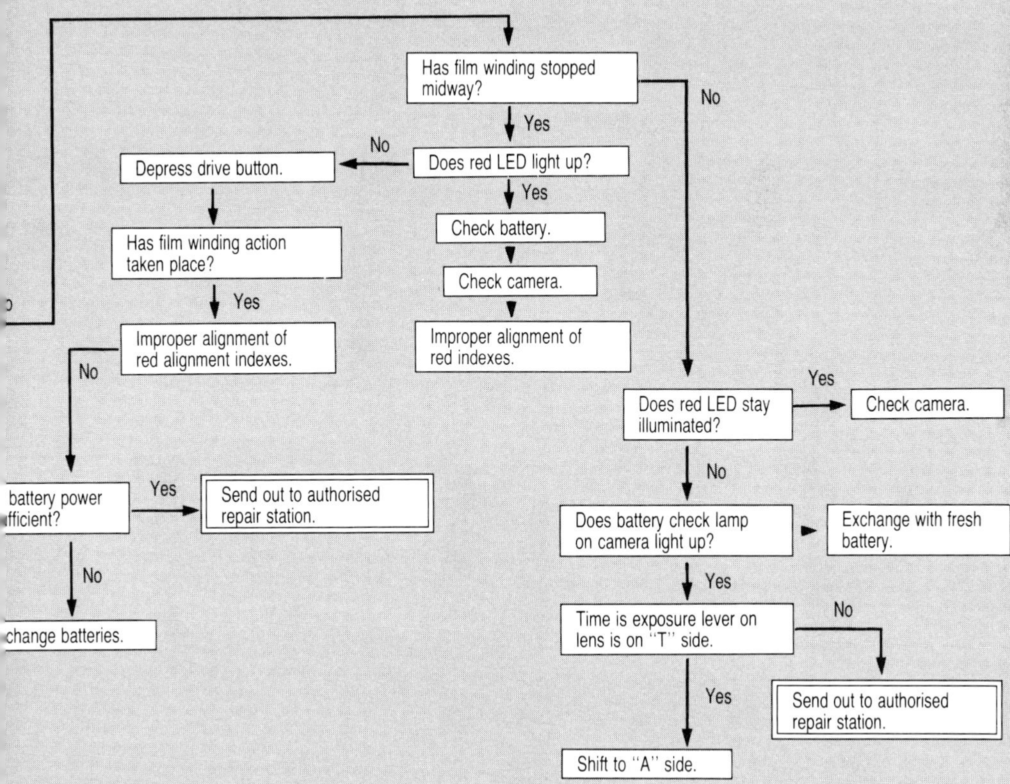

CLOSE-UP ACCESSORIES

Close-up filters

Two 62mm screw-fit close-up filters are featured in the ETR system. These provide a convenient, quick method of close-up photography and may be used in combination for even closer focusing. No exposure increase is necessary. If greater magnification is demanded extension tubes or the Automatic Bellows-E are advised.

CLOSE-UP ATTACHMENT LENS TABLE

	Focusing Scale Setting	Camera-to-Subject Distance	Magnification	Area Covered (cm)
C.U.L.-1 (f = 50)	∞	63.9	0.15×	27.8 × 36.0
	0.6m	38.6	0.34×	12.6 × 16.4
C.U.L.-2 (f = 25)	∞	38.1	0.31×	13.7 × 17.8
	0.6m	30.6	0.50×	8.5 × 11.0
C.U.L. + C.U.L.-2 (f = 17)	∞	30.4	0.46×	9.3 × 12.0
	0.6m	27.1	0.65×	6.5 × 8.4

(The camera-to-subject distance is the distance from the film plane to the subject with Zenzanon-EII 75mm F2.8 lens.)

Automatic Extension Tubes-E

Three automatic extension tubes are available for the ETR, with extensions of 14mm, 28mm and 42mm, and are fully compatible with all Zenzanon-E lenses. Housed in each tube are the necessary electrical and mechanical linkages for automatic diaphragm operation. Only one tube can be used at a time and if a greater lens extension than 42mm is required the Automatic Bellows Attachment E is recommended.

Extending the lens from the film plane causes a light loss and it is for this reason that, if a separate lightmeter is employed, exposure must be increased to compensate. See tables of exposure factors on page 56. With the AE-II Finder-E, open aperture through-the-lens metering is retained and any necessary exposure adjustment automatically accounted for. This finder is especially recommended for ease of operation.

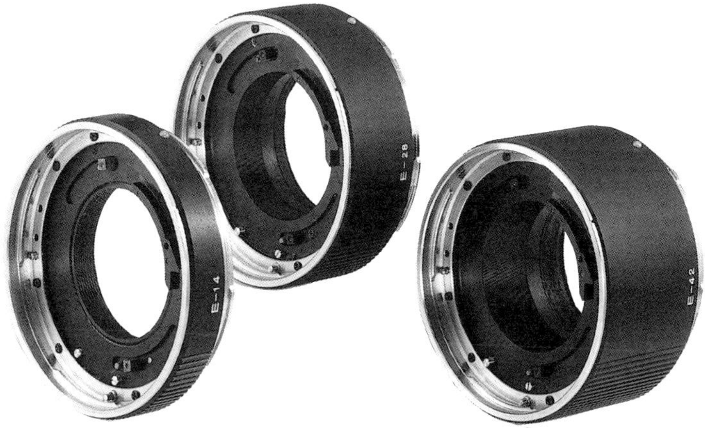

Using extension tubes

The procedure of mounting an extension tube is similar to that of using a lens. First cock the camera so that the lens can be removed and insert the cocked extension tube; the cocking pin should be aligned to the green dot. Rotate 30 degrees anti-clockwise to secure the tube in position. The lens can now be fitted to the tube. If you prefer, the tube and lens can be pre-assembled and the combination attached to the camera.

To dismantle the tube and lens assembly cock the shutter and slide the lens release button on the extension tube to allow the lens to be taken off. The tube may now be removed from the camera body by operating the latter's lens release button. The lens and tube may be taken off the camera while still adjoined and separated once off the camera.

With Automatic Extension Tube E-14

(Unit: cm)

Lens Used	Focusing Ring Setting	Magnification	Area Photographed	Object-to-Film Plane (Distance)	Object-to-Front Lens (Surface)	Exposure Factor
75 mm	∞ Infinity	0.18	23.5 x 30.5	59.2	46.2	1.5
	Max. Extension	0.36	11.8 x 15.3	39.1	24.7	2
150 mm	∞ Infinity	0.09	45.5 x 59.0	191.3	174.9	1.5
	Max. Extension	0.22	19.3 x 25.0	100.6	82.3	1.5
250 mm	∞ Infinity	0.06	75.9 x 98.4	502.9	480.3	1
	Max. Extension	0.14	30.4 x 39.4	236.2	211.5	1.5
40 mm	∞ Infinity	0.35	12.1 x 15.7	25.3	11.5	1.5
	Max. Extension	0.50	8.5 x 11.0	22.4	8	1.5
50 mm	∞ Infinity	0.28	15.2 x 19.7	32.7	18.9	1.5
	Max. Extension	0.42	10.1 x 13.1	27.3	12.8	1.5

With Automatic Extension Tube E-28

(Unit: cm)

Lens Used	Focusing Ring Setting	Magnification	Area Photographed	Object-to-Film Plane (Distance)	Object-to-Front Lens (Surface)	Exposure Factor
75 mm	∞ Infinity	0.36	11.8 x 15.3	39.1	24.7	2
	Max. Extension	0.54	7.84 x 10.2	33.4	17.6	2
150 mm	∞ Infinity	0.19	22.8 x 29.5	112.3	94.5	1.5
	Max. Extension	0.31	13.6 x 17.6	81.7	62	2
250 mm	∞ Infinity	0.11	37.9 x 49.2	280.3	256.3	1.5
	Max. Extension	0.20	21.7 x 28.1	186.4	160.3	2
40 mm	∞ Infinity	0.70	6.07 x 7.87	20.8	5.6	2
	Max. Extension	0.85	5.0 x 6.48	20.4	4.6	2
50 mm	∞ Infinity	0.56	7.59 x 9.84	24.9	9.7	2
	Max. Extension	0.7	6.07 x 7.87	23.8	7.9	2

With Automatic Extension Tube E-42

(Unit: cm)

Lens Used	Focusing Ring Setting	Magnification	Area Photographed	Object-to-Film Plane (Distance)	Object-to-Front Lens (Surface)	Exposure Factor
75 mm	∞ Infinity	0.54	7.84 x 10.2	33.4	17.6	2
	Max. Extension	0.72	5.88 x 7.63	31.2	14	3
150 mm	∞ Infinity	0.28	15.2 x 19.7	86.9	67.7	2
	Max. Extension	0.41	10.5 x 13.5	72.1	51	2.5
250 mm	∞ Infinity	0.17	25.3 x 32.8	207.0	181.6	1.5
	Max. Extension	0.25	16.9 x 21.9	159.4	131.9	2
40 mm	∞ Infinity	1.05	4.05 x 5.25	20.3	3.7	2.5
	Max. Extension	1.2	3.54 x 4.59	20.4	3.2	2.5
50 mm	∞ Infinity	0.84	5.06 x 6.56	23.2	6.6	2.5
	Max. Extension	0.98	4.34 x 5.62	23.1	5.8	2.5

AUTOMATIC EXTENSION TUBE TABLE

		Magnification	Area Photographed (mm)
75mm	E-14	0.18~.0.36×	23.5 × 30.5 ~ 11.7 × 15.1
	E-28	0.36 ~ 0.54×	11.8 × 15.2 ~ 7.8 × 10.1
	E-42	0.54 ~ 0.73×	7.8 × 10.2 ~ 5.9 × 7.6
40mm	E-14	0.34 ~ 0.51×	12.6 × 16.4 ~ 8.3 × 10.7
	E-28	0.67 ~ 0.85×	6.3 × 8.2 ~ 5.0 × 6.5
	E-42	1.01 ~ 1.19×	4.2 × 5.5 ~ 3.6 × 4.6
50mm	E-14	0.28 ~ 0.42×	15.4 × 20.0 ~ 10.1 × 13.1
	E-28	0.55 ~ 0.70×	7.7 × 10.0 ~ 6.1 × 7.9
	E-42	0.83 ~ 0.97×	5.1 × 6.7 ~ 4.4 × 5.7
105mm	E14	0.13 ~ 0.29×	31.7 × 41.1 ~ 14.5 × 18.8
	E-28	0.27 ~ 0.43×	15.8 × 20.5 ~ 10.0 × 12.9
	E-42	0.40 ~ 0.56×	10.6 × 13.7 ~ 7.6 × 9.8
150mm	E-14	0.10 ~ 0.23×	44.6 × 57.9 ~ 18.8 × 24.3
	E-28	0.19 ~ 0.32×	22.3 × 28.9 ~ 13.2 × 17.1
	E-42	0.29 ~ 0.42×	14.9 × 19.3 ~ 10.2 × 13.2
200mm	E-14	0.07 ~ 0.21×	59.2 × 76.7 ~ 20.6 × 26.7
	E-28	0.14 ~ 0.28×	29.6 × 38.4 ~ 15.3 × 19.8
	E-42	0.22 ~ 0.35×	19.7 × 25.6 ~ 12.1 × 15.8
250mm	E-14	0.06 ~ 0.16×	74.1 × 96.0 ~ 26.1 × 33.9
	E-28	0.11 ~ 0.22×	37.0 × 48.0 ~ 19.3 × 25.0
	E-42	0.17 ~ 0.28×	24.7 × 32.0 ~ 15.3 × 19.9

Auto Bellows Attachment-E

This bellows unit incorporates all the relevant linkages for fully automatic diaphragm operation and permits a maximum extension of 155mm. Furthermore, with the AE-II Finder-E the convenience of through-the-lens exposure metering is retained.

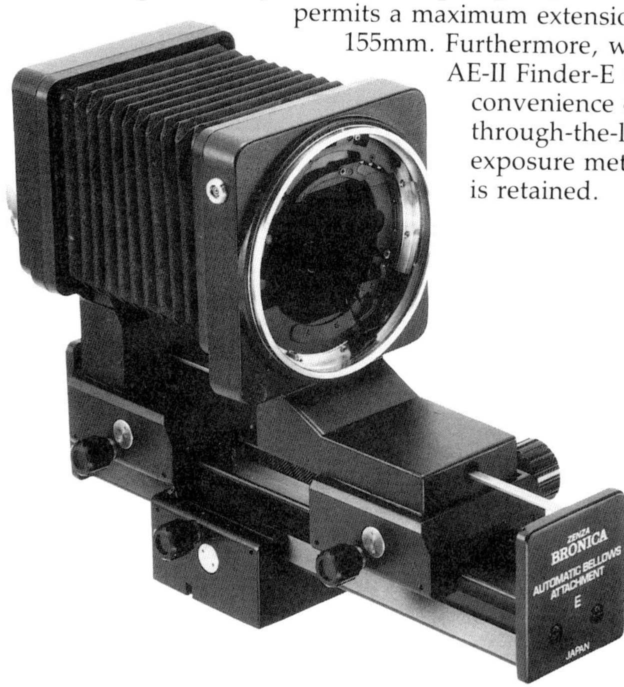

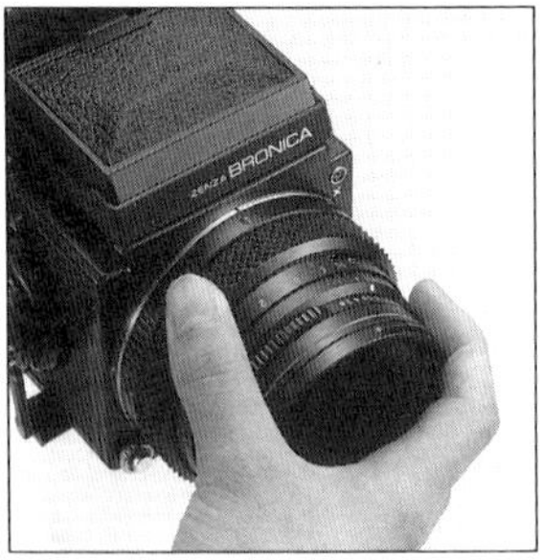

Attaching the bellows unit

Everything must be cocked before the camera, bellows and lens can be joined together. To cock the bellows unit revolve the pins on the back panel until they are aligned next to the green dots. Mounting bellows to camera body is achieved in the same manner as attaching a lens. The correct procedure is to fit the bellows on to the camera first and then fit the lens on to the bellows.

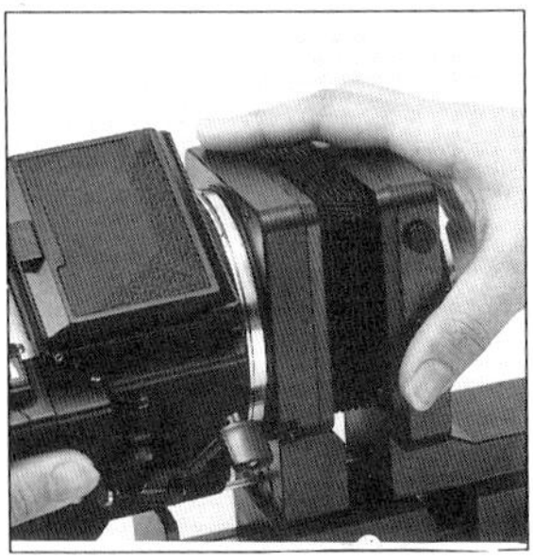

Detaching the bellows unit

Rotate the wind crank to cock the camera. The lens can now be removed by depressing the lens release button on the bellows unit and twisting in a clockwise direction. Separating the bellows from the camera is done by depressing the body's lens release button and rotating the accessory in a clockwise direction. As the bellows is detached from the camera its cocking pins will release.

The equipment can be dismantled either as described above or as follows: detach the complete assembly but before the lens can be released the cocking pins on the rear of the bellows unit must be manually cocked.

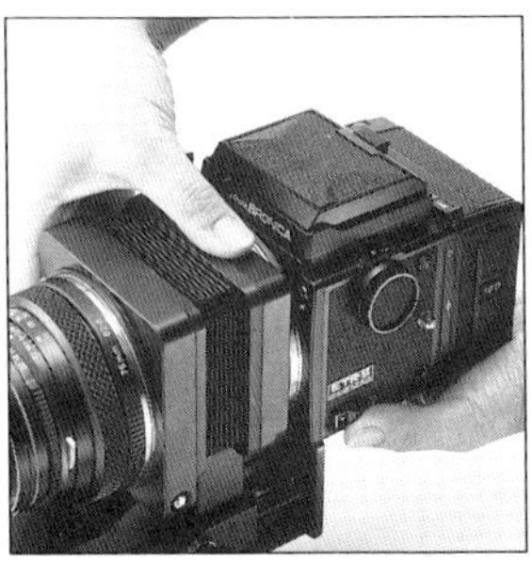

AUTOMATIC BELLOWS ATTACHMENT TABLE

Lens	Bellows Extension	Magnifi cation	Subject Area (cm)	Lens	Bellows Extension	Magnifi-cation	Subject Area (cm)
75mm	Min.	0.71×	5.99 × 7.76	150mm	Min.	0.37×	11.4 × 14.7
	Max.	2.18×	1.95 × 2.52		Max.	1.19×	3.59 × 4.65
40mm	Min.	1.32×	3.22 × 4.17	200mm	Min.	0.28×	15.0 × 19.5
	Max.	3.90×	1.09 × 1.41		Max.	0.92×	4.57 × 5.93
50mm	Min.	1.08×	3.92 × 5.08	250mm	Min.	0.23 ×	18.9 × 24.4
	Max.	3.20×	1.33 × 1.72		Max.	0.74×	5.74 × 7.44
105mm	Min.	0.53×	8.06 × 10.4				
	Max.	1.64×	2.58 × 3.35				

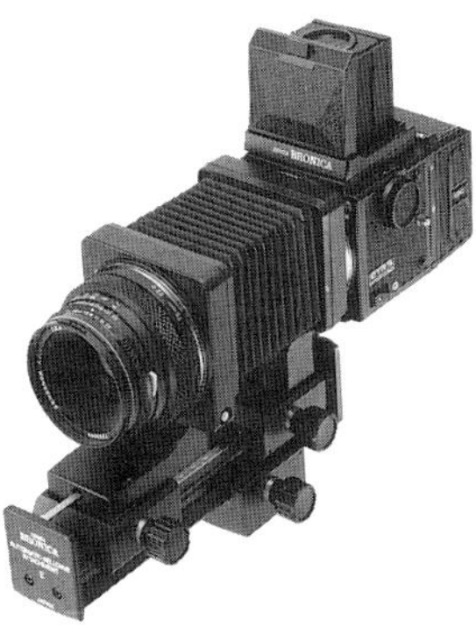

Using the bellows

Focusing is not quite as easy as when a conventional lens is attached because adding the bellows unit results in a slight loss of viewfinder brightness. It is best to use the matte area of the screen for focusing.

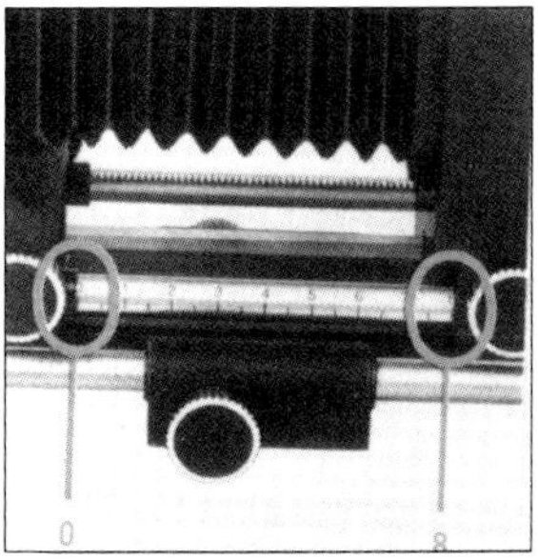

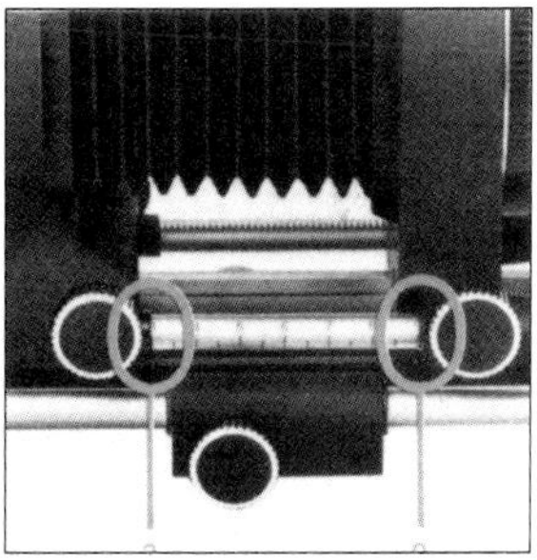

During close-up photography the amount of depth of field becomes more shallow as magnification increases. Therefore not only is accurate focusing critical but so too is the use of the smallest aperture possible to maximise depth of field. This in turn may necessitate the use of a slow shutter speed, so use a solid tripod and a cable release to minimise vibration.

If a flash unit is used it should be connected to the co-axial socket on the bellows unit. Do not use the socket on the camera body or that of the Speed Grip-E, if it is fitted. In either case the flash will not fire when the shutter is released. Apart from this aspect of camera operation all other functions remain normal.

The fully retracted bellows has an extension of 55mm; maximum extension is 155mm, which means that the bellows permit 100mm of extension. A scale is provided on the bellows rail unit.

If the AE-II Prism Finder-E is used in conjunction with the bellows unit fully automatic exposure operation and manual metering are possible. Exposure factors (supplied in the instruction manual for this unit) must be applied if a separate hand meter is employed.

Magnification and Exposure Factor Nomograph

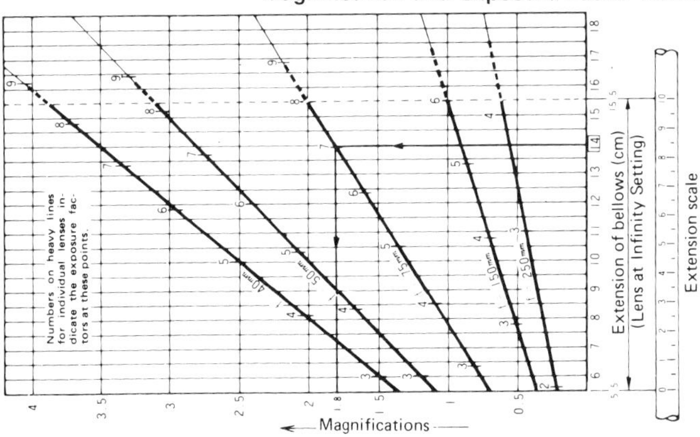

How to use the Nomograph
The extension of the bellows attachment is shown along the horizontal axis. Magnification factors are marked on the vertical axis.
The heavy lines slanting upwards indicate the lenses that can be used. The figures on these lines are the exposure factors at specific extensions. For example, with a 75mm lens used at an extension of 14cm. Read 14 off the horizontal scale and move upwards until you coincide with the 75mm lens line. This shows an exposure factor of 7. Lastly, by moving horizontally to the vertical axis a magnification of 1.8X can be read off. The total extension of the bellows as shown along the horizontal axis is for the lens at infinity focus. The broken line shows factors when the lens itself is extended with its helical focusing mechanism.

Bronica SQ-A

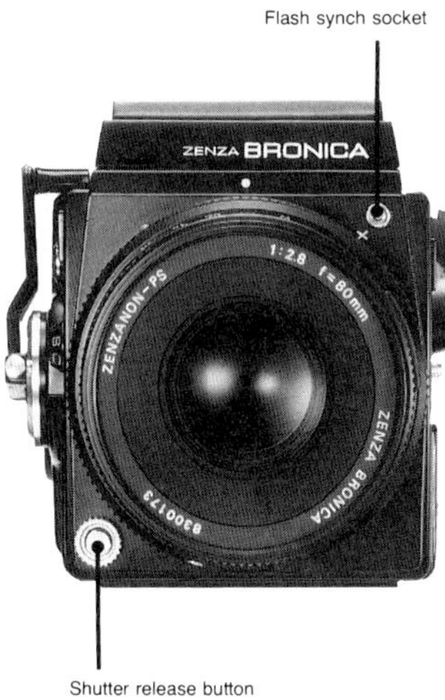
Flash synch socket
Shutter release button

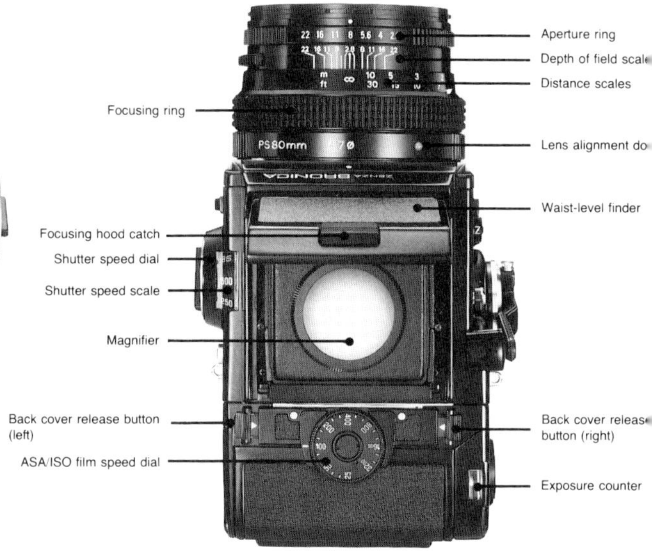
Aperture ring
Depth of field scal
Distance scales
Focusing ring
Lens alignment do
Waist-level finder
Focusing hood catch
Shutter speed dial
Shutter speed scale
Magnifier
Back cover release button (left)
Back cover releas button (right)
ASA/ISO film speed dial
Exposure counter

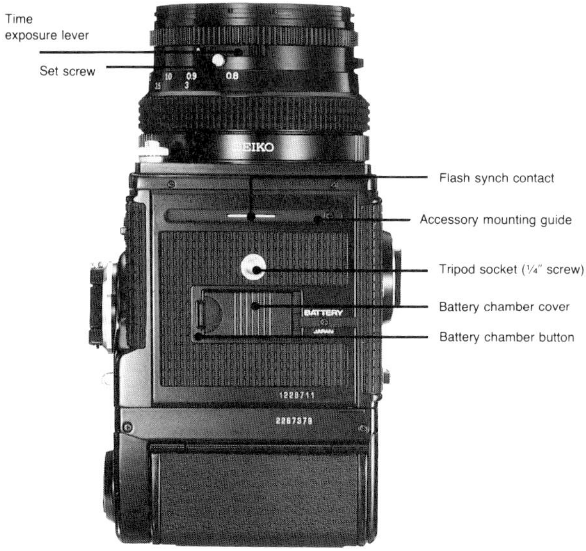
Time exposure lever
Set screw
Flash synch contact
Accessory mounting guide
Tripod socket (¼" screw)
Battery chamber cover
Battery chamber button

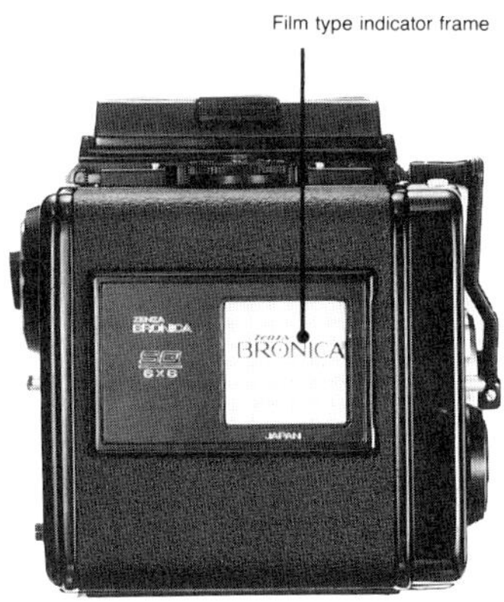
Film type indicator frame

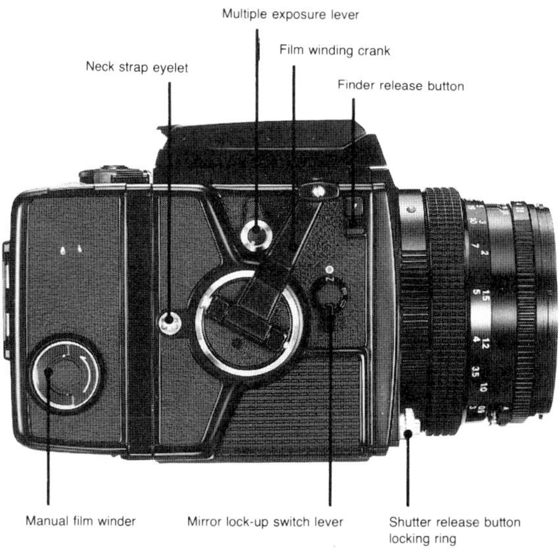
Multiple exposure lever
Film winding crank
Neck strap eyelet
Finder release button
Manual film winder
Mirror lock-up switch lever
Shutter release button locking ring

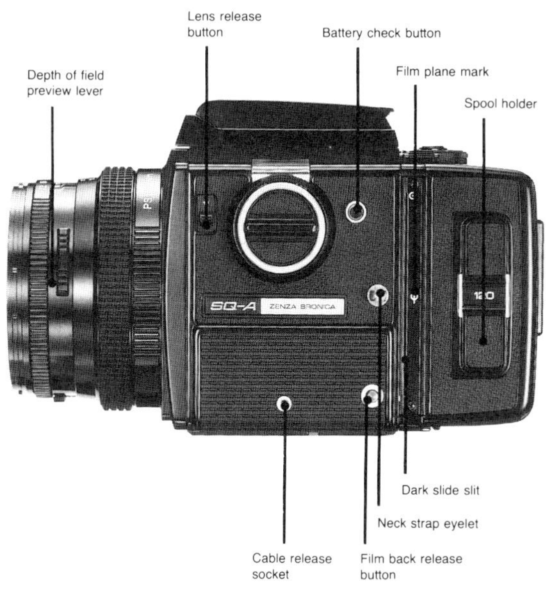
Lens release button
Battery check button
Depth of field preview lever
Film plane mark
Spool holder
SQ-A
ZENZA BRONICA
Dark slide slit
Neck strap eyelet
Cable release socket
Film back release button

Chapter Seven Bronica SQ-A

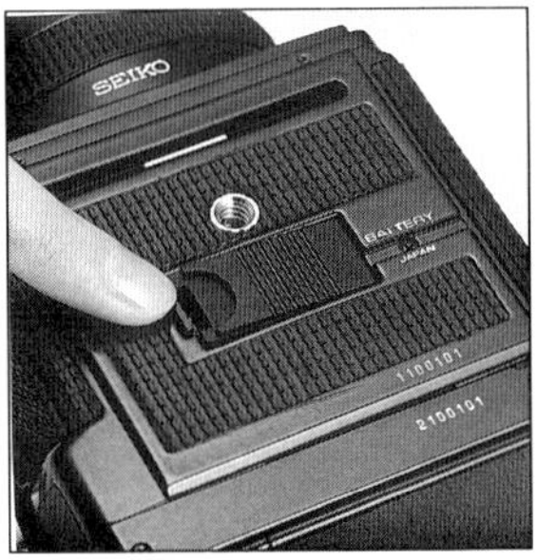

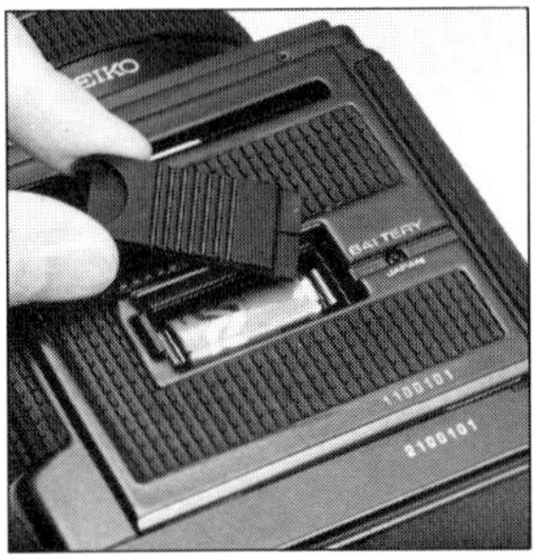

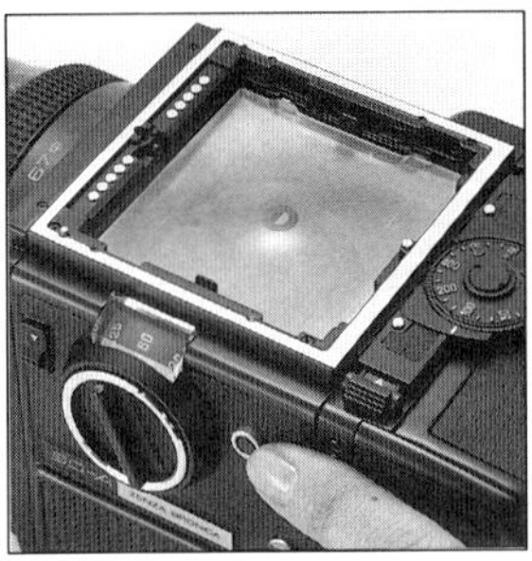

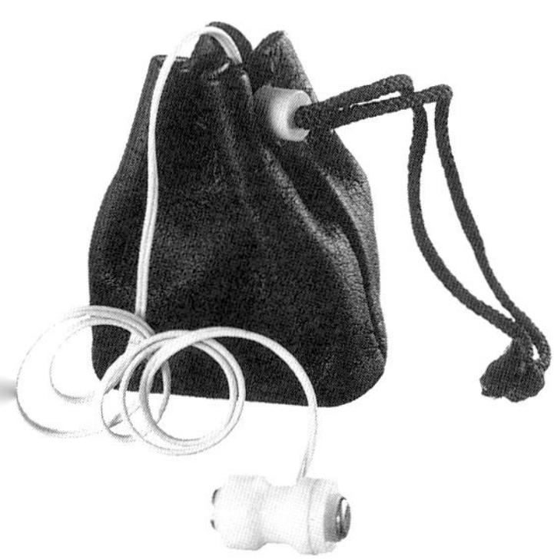

Superseding the SQ, the Bronica SQ-A was introduced in 1981 and has a specification similar to its predecessor but includes a couple of significant improvements: the provision of mirror lock-up and the option of accepting the AE Prism Finder S with its auto-exposure facility. The integral motor-drive Bronica SQ-Am is discussed in Chapter Nine.

THE BATTERY

The SQ-A body is a sophisticated shell incorporating the essential electrical and mechanical linkages that enable the system components to mesh and function together.

Power for the camera's electronic shutter is supplied by a PX-28 type, or equivalent, battery. A new six volt silver oxide cell should last for about a year if no meter finder is used. If a meter finder is in regular use the battery has a life of between six and 12 months. The SQ-A has only two mechanical shutter settings, 'T' and 1/500 sec, so check the battery regularly and have a spare available.

Loading the battery

Access to the battery chamber is via a slide-off panel on the base-plate which is removable by pressing its locking catch. Insert the battery according to the polarity markings, replace the cover and confirm that it is working properly by pushing the battery check button; a red LED at the top of the viewfinder lights up to indicate that all is satisfactory. Should the LED not light, the battery is either dead or incorrectly loaded but, because all functions apart from shutter control are mechanical, it is still possible to advance the film, cock and fire the shutter. The shutter, however, will be released at 1/500 sec regardless of what is set on the shutter dial.

Battery efficiency is liable to be affected by extreme cold and the optional Remote Camera Battery Pack E is recommended as this allows the cell to be stored in a warm pocket, ensuring continued camera operation despite adverse conditions.

SQ LENSES

Lenses suitable for the SQ system encompass focal lengths from 40mm wide angle to 500mm telephoto. In addition, two zoom lenses manufactured in West Germany to Bronica's requirements by Jos. Schneider GmbH & Co. are available. Every Zenzanon SQ lens has an integral leaf shutter with 13 speeds from 8 seconds to 1/500 sec plus 'T' (Time exposure). 'T' is the only shutter value to be engaged from the lens.

Shutter speeds are selected using the camera's shutter dial and intermediate speeds cannot be engaged except in certain circumstances. Namely, whenever one of the SQ's meter finders is fitted: the AE Prism Finder S can select speeds in 1/3 stop increments during auto-exposure operation; and both the CdS MF Finder S and the ME Prism Finder S allow speeds to be chosen from the finder itself at half-stop intervals throughout the 8 seconds to 1/500 sec range. Finders are discussed in greater detail in Chapter Ten.

Each Zenzanon SQ lens has a depth of field preview lever which enables the effect of specific apertures and creative filters to be judged. A depth of field, infra-red focus index and distance scales in feet and metres are marked on each lens.

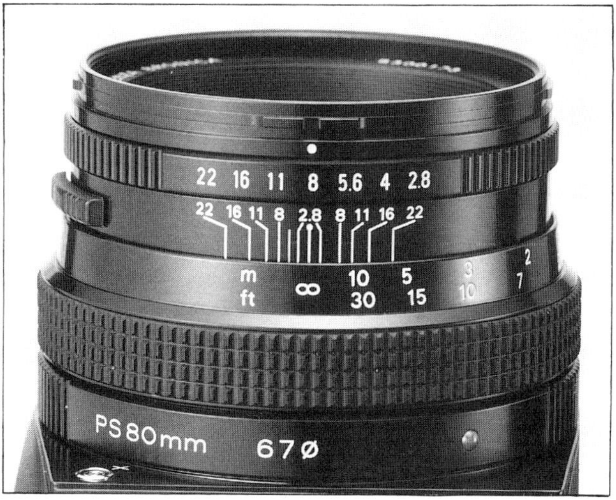

Lens mounting

The Bronica SQ-A and SQ-Am share an identical lens mount: an exclusive four-claw SQ bayonet. When the lens is fitted six gold-plated contacts on the camera body mate with six corresponding contacts on the lens to provide the method of information interchange. Clean these contacts periodically with a dry, soft cloth.

Exchanging lenses is a simple procedure. The mount's design makes it impossible to attach a lens unless both the shutter and lens are cocked. Therefore, before attempting to mount a lens complete a check of the camera and the rear of the lens. With the shutter cocked the mirror will be in its working position and the green coloured pin in the lens throat will be aligned with the green dot. If not, revolve the wind crank once to cock the shutter. On the lens rear plate the two cocking pins should lie at a point between the green dots and the red lines; the pins can be rotated manually if they are not in position.

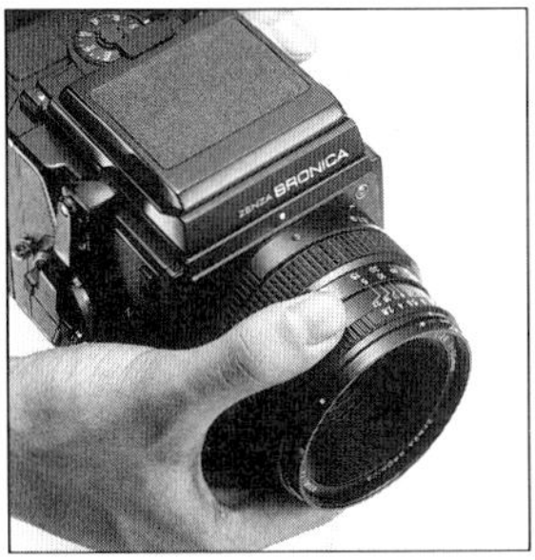

To mount the lens align the red dot on the lens flange with the orange dot on the body, insert the lens into the mount and twist firmly anti-clockwise about 30 degrees until it locks into position. It is now impossible to separate the lens from the body unless the lens release button is depressed.

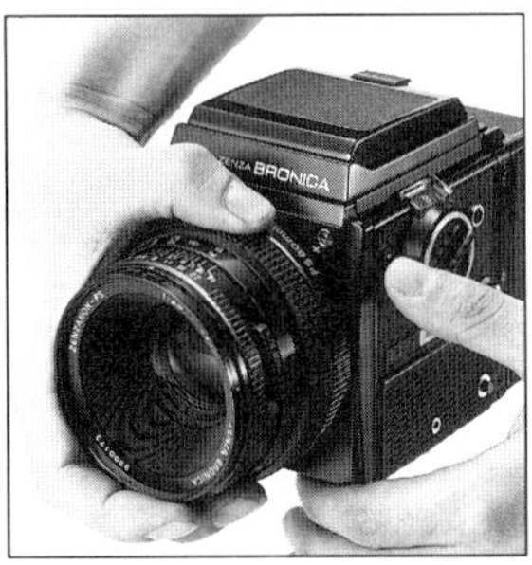

To detach a lens make sure the shutter is cocked and operate the lens mount release button, positioned forward of the shutter dial on the left side, while simultaneously twisting the lens clockwise until it can be separated from the body. The lens release button cannot be operated unless the shutter is cocked.

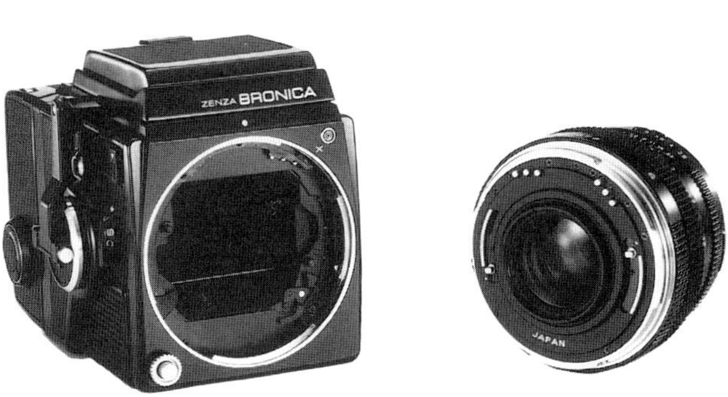

The exclusive SQ mount. Clean the lens contacts occasionally to ensure correct operation.

INTERCHANGEABLE FINDERS

The basic SQ body comes without a finder, giving you freedom to select the model most suitable for your particular requirements. There are five finders available in the Bronica SQ system. See Chapter Ten.

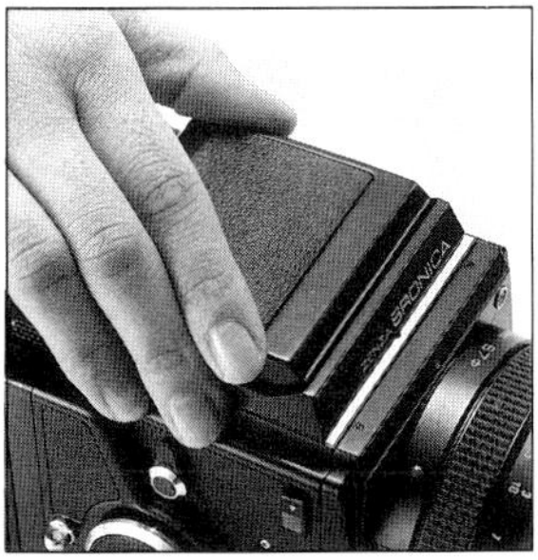

Fitting a finder

Finder fitting is a matter of lining up the unit's leading edge with the front end of the camera's finder frame so that it is flush to the body with its four lugs correctly seated. Then slide it home fully until a 'click' is heard. Prior to attaching an SQ meter finder the contacts on the base of the unit should be given a wipe with a dry, soft cloth to ensure good contact between finder and main body. Take care not to touch the finder's delicate glass surface. There is an arrowed slider switch on the wind crank side of the body. This is the release control which has to be pushed down before a finder can be removed from the body.

FOCUS SCREENS

Optional, user-changeable plastic focusing screens are available in a variety of patterns for different applications. The supplied screen incorporates split-image rangefinder and microprism focusing aids surrounded by a matte surface. It is also etched with guide lines which assist composition when photographing in 4 × 4cm Superslide format.

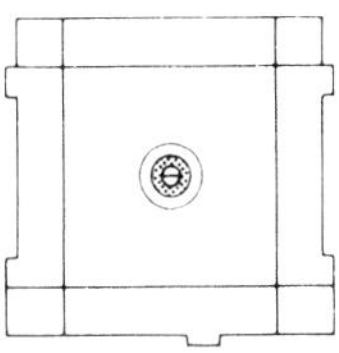

Microprism/split-image

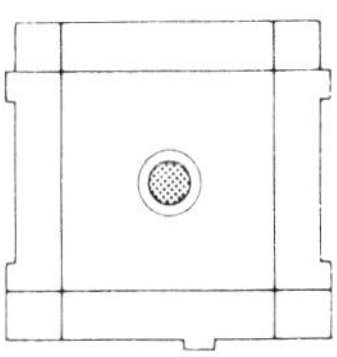

Microprism

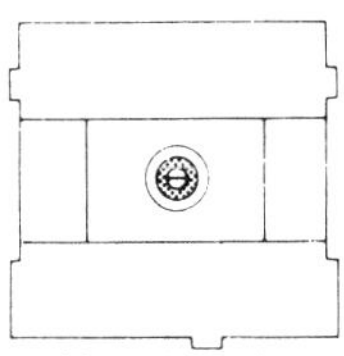

Microprism/split image (for 135 film)

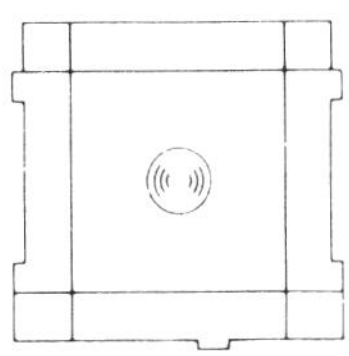

Matte

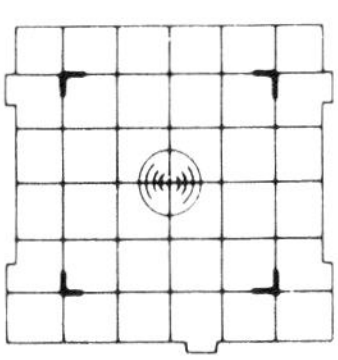

Grid-lines

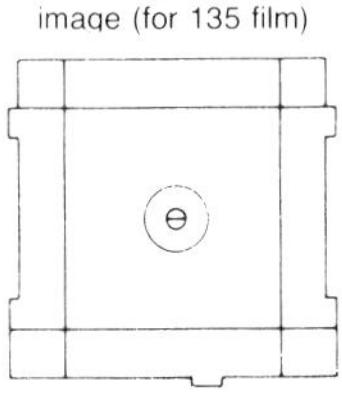

Split-image

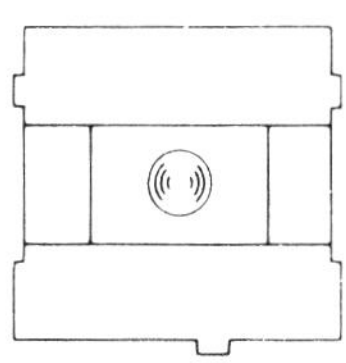

Matte (for 135 film)

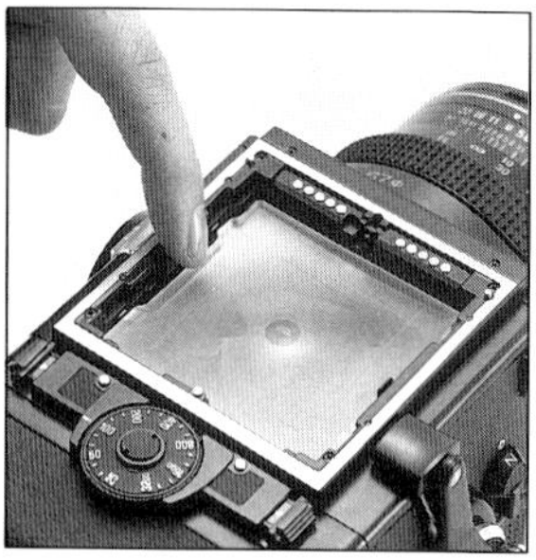

Changing focus screen

Remove the finder to allow access to the screen. To extract a focusing screen slide the two metal tabs on either side in the direction of the film back. Using tweezers, grip the tab along the screen's bottom edge so that it can be lifted out. The screen will also drop out if the camera is turned upside down. Carefully insert the replacement by lowering the front edge first, making sure that the rear tab is located correctly before sliding the retaining tabs back into place. If the tabs are not back in position the finder cannot be re-attached. Do not touch the screen's surface during the exchange procedure.

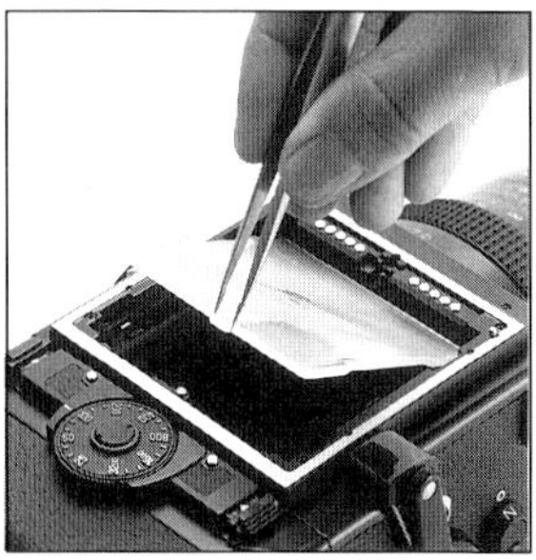

INTERCHANGEABLE FILM BACKS

Several formats are catered for by the SQ system: 35mm, 35 × 54mm panoramic, 6 × 6cm and 6 × 4.5cm. There is also a Polaroid Land film back.

Each SQ back is equipped with its own ISO speed dial. This dial has a lift-and-drop action that eliminates any chance of inadvertent operation and has a range of ISO 25 to 3200. When a non-metering finder is used the ISO dial is redundant except as a reminder of the speed of the film loaded.

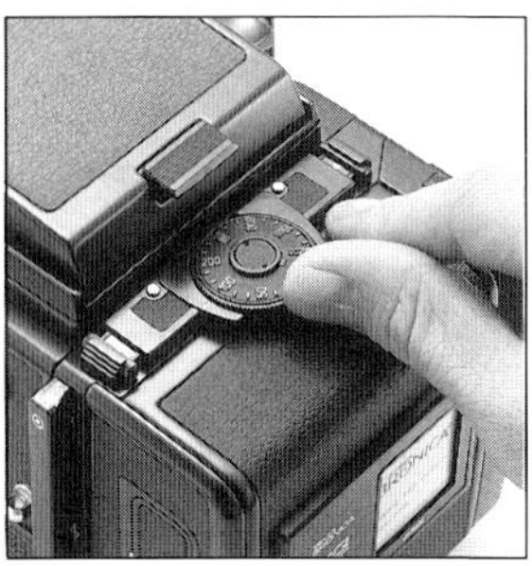

If, however, you are using one of the SQ metering finders it is imperative that this control is set to the film's correct speed as this information is automatically relayed to the meter and failure to do so might result in inaccurate exposures. Always check the film speed dial when loading a fresh film.

The advantage of having an ISO dial on each film back is that, if you are shooting with several backs, each loaded with a different film, you do not have to remember to alter ISO as you change from one back to another. The chances of error are therefore minimised.

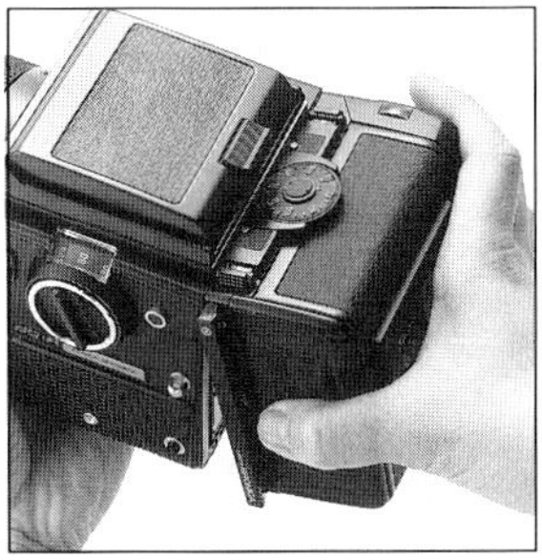

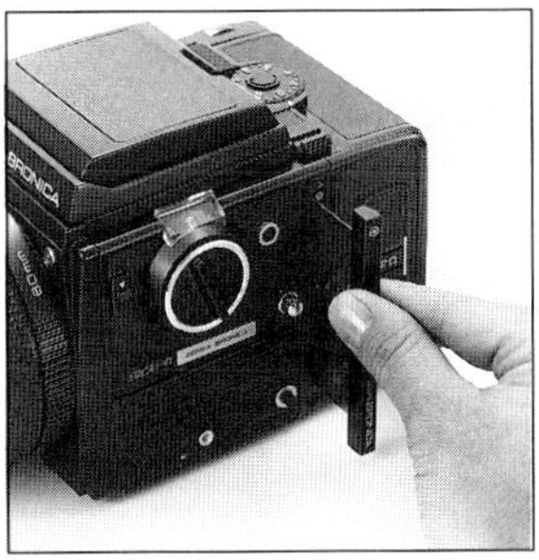

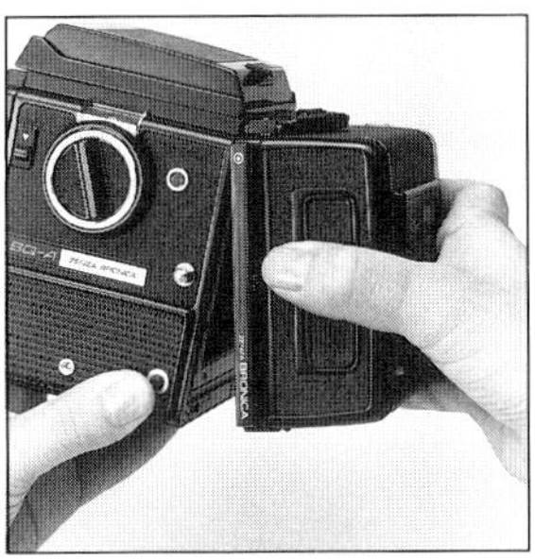

SQ film backs in operation

Mounting a film back to the camera body is straightforward. Position the two locating hinge lugs at the top of the back into the corresponding holes in the back plate. Then push the bottom of the back firmly against the body until it locks into place.

The dark slide has a right and wrong way of insertion so it is essential to match the circular symbols on the dark slide and camera body with each other.

When inserted, the dark slide prevents the shutter from being triggered. It is however a good idea to withdraw the dark slide as soon as the back is attached to avoid accidental operation of the back release button and the back being detached while the camera is being carried. Inserted incorrectly the dark slide cannot be pushed fully home, nor can the film back be detached; the shutter however can be released.

Keep the dark slide somewhere safe during photography so that it is not bent or lost; there is no storage place for it on the camera body.

After a back has been attached always operate the wind crank to ensure that it is fully coupled with the camera, that an unexposed frame is in place and that the shutter is cocked ready for photography. The film will only be advanced if an exposed frame is in the film gate so there is no wastage as the crank is rotated.

Backs are locked positively into position once attached to the camera and releasing them can only be achieved by pressing the back release button. Insert the dark slide and depress the release button to allow separation from the body.

The latest series of SQ film backs — identified by their grey handled dark slides — are fully interlocked and cannot have their dark slides accidentally pulled out when the back is off the camera body. Earlier SQ film backs — those with black handled dark slides — can have their dark slides removed with the back off the camera.

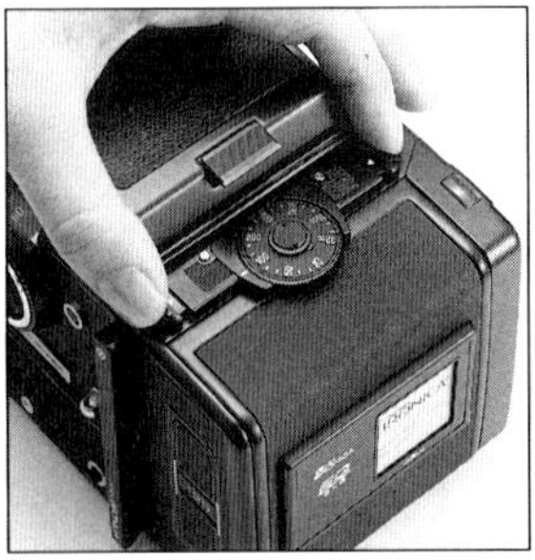

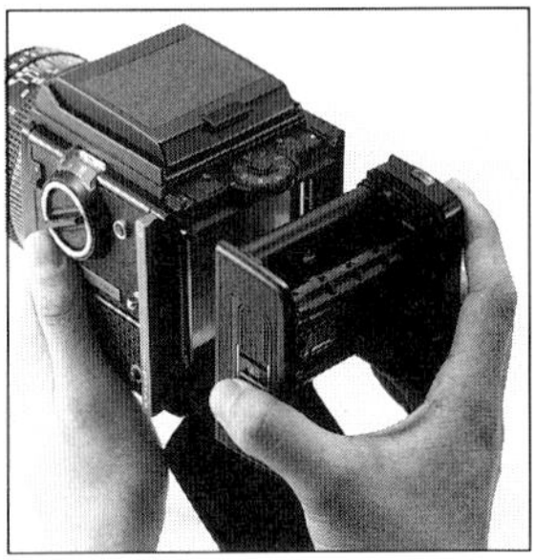

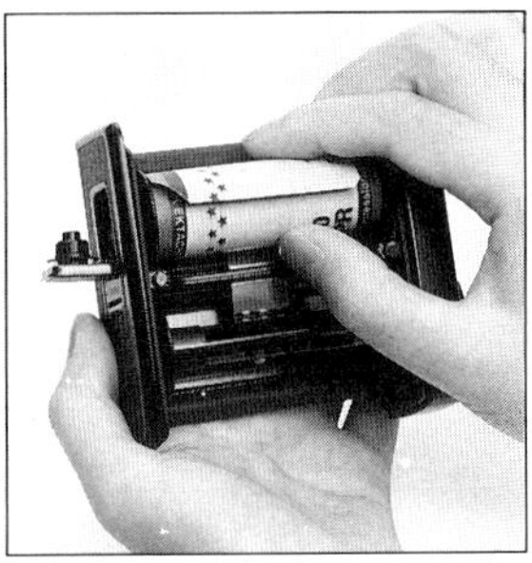

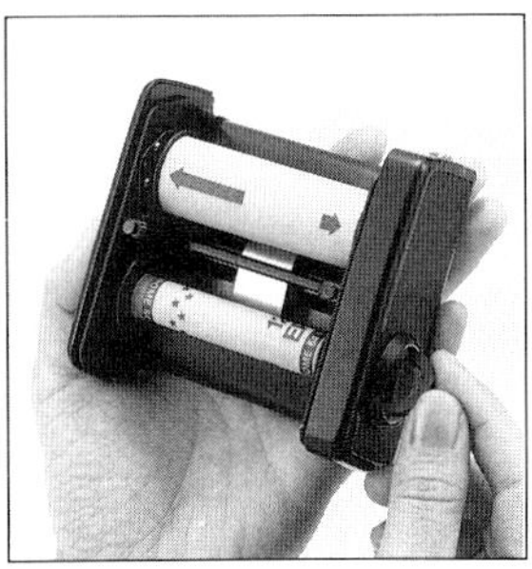

Film loading

Loading of the two 35mm format and the Polaroid backs is explained in Chapter Fourteen. Here we discuss the loading procedure for 120 and 220 roll film backs. Although the methods of loading 120 and 220 backs are very similar it is not possible to use 120 roll film in the 220 back, and vice versa.

Each back comprises two sections: the film back frame and the film holder. The former is equipped with the dark slide mechanism and is basically a light-tight shield which completely encloses the latter.

Opening the back is achieved by simultaneously pushing the two cover release buttons in the direction of the arrows. The rear flap will spring open to reveal the film holder which can now be removed and loaded. The film holder houses two spools — the top one for fresh film and the lower, the take-up spool. Both are held in place by spindle tabs which open outwards to allow spools to be inserted.

Always load film in subdued light. Completely remove the film's retaining label before threading the tapered leader into the take-up spool so that it faces away from the pressure plate. Ensure that it is securely in position by operating the back's manual wind knob. When the start mark lies opposite the red triangular mark on the film holder, close the cover.

Winding on to the first frame can be achieved either by continued operation of the manual wind knob or by mounting the back and using the camera's crank. Now set the film's ISO speed.

After the last frame has been exposed rotate the wind crank until there is a noticeable reduction in the pressure needed to operate it. A couple more rotations will make sure that the exposed film is fully wound off. The back cover can now be opened and the film removed. Transfer what was the film's spool to the lower compartment and this becomes the take-up spool for the next roll.

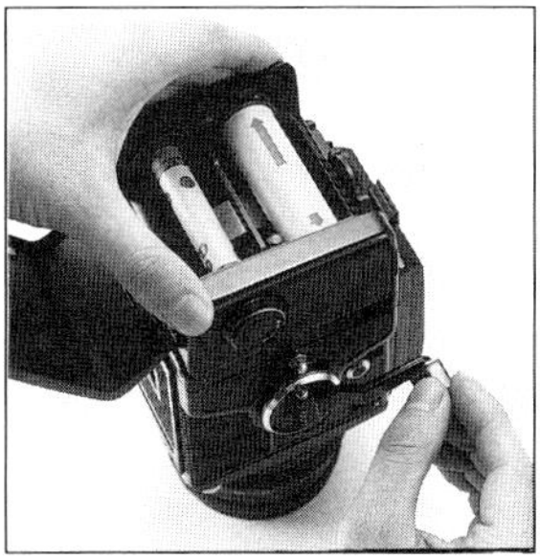

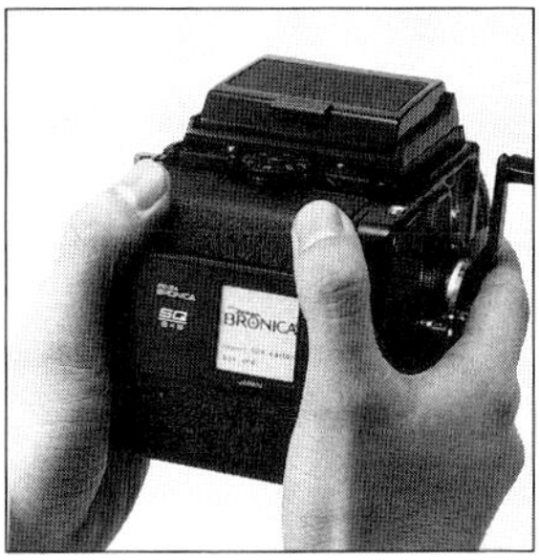

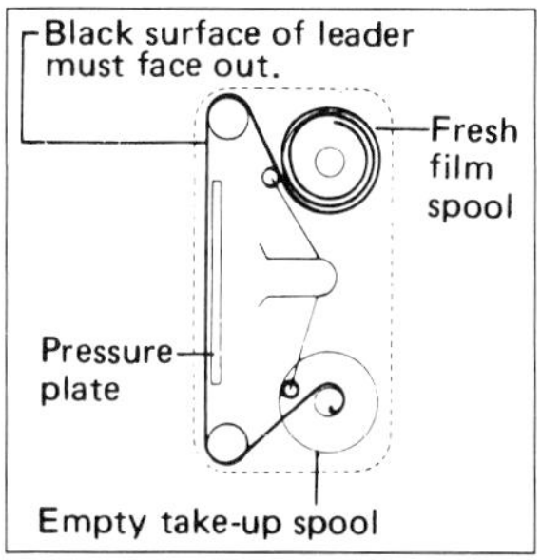

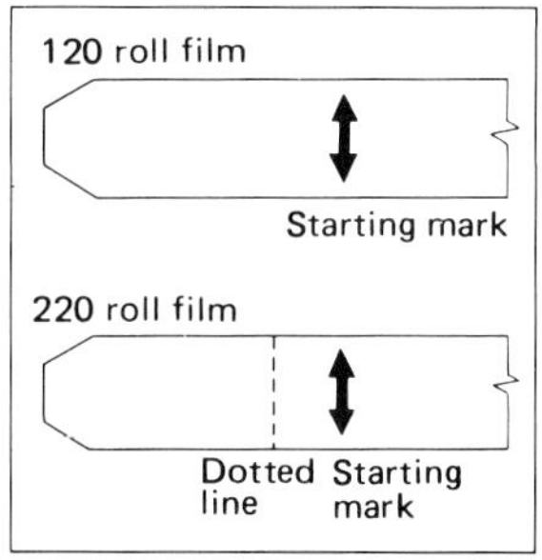

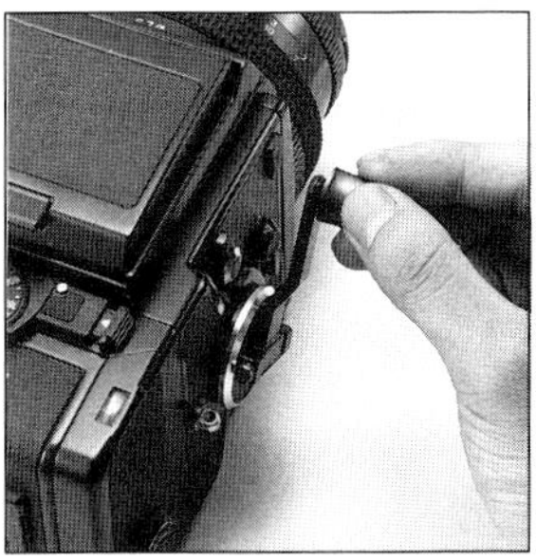

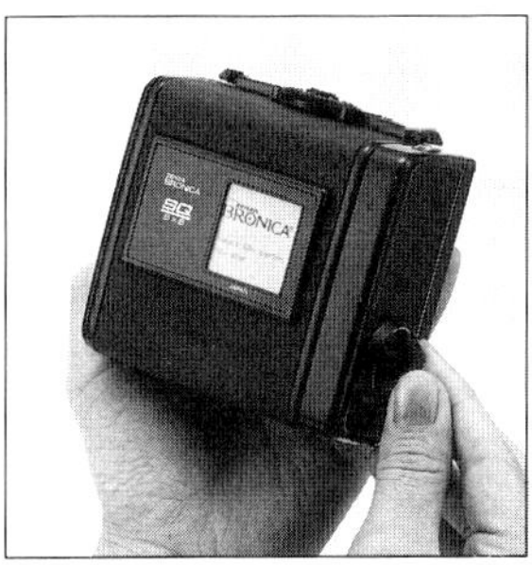

BRONICA SQ-A IN ACTION

One of the attractions of 6 × 6cm format is that it is not necessary for the camera to be tilted on to its side to take upright shots. Consequently, the square format admirably suits waist level operation as the camera can be cradled in the left hand with the index finger resting on the shutter release, leaving the right hand free to look after aperture selection, focusing, film advance and so on.

Operating the camera without film

Practising the many aspects of the SQ-A's operation is essential for fluent photography. Normally it is not possible to cock and release the shutter without a film loaded, but by setting the multiple exposure control to a horizontal position all camera functions, except the frame counter, behave as they would normally. Multiple exposure operation is discussed on page 72.

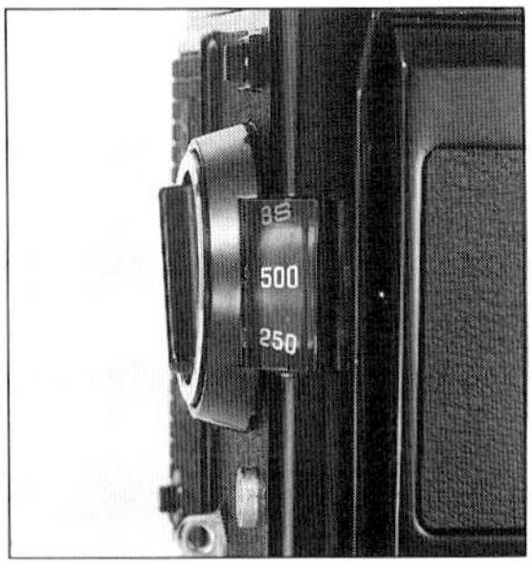

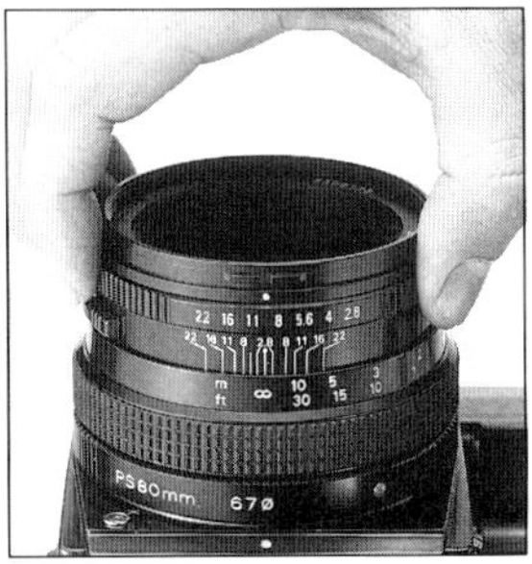

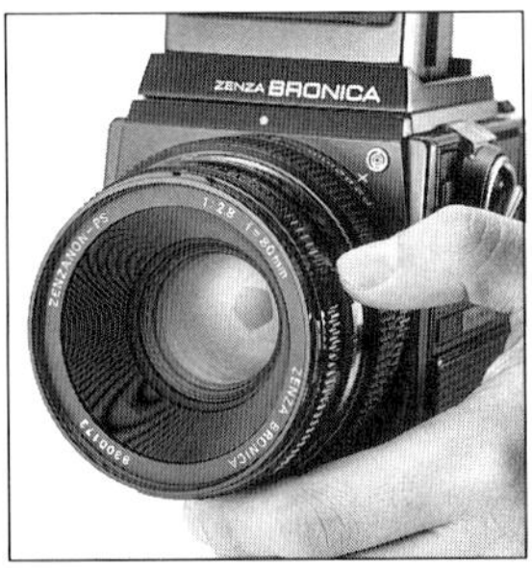

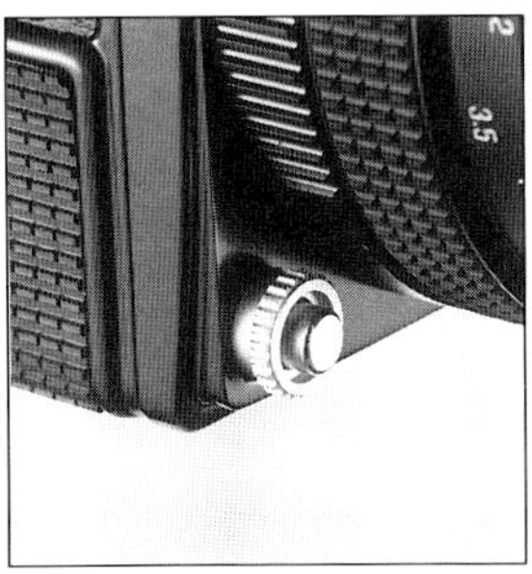

Exposing film

As the SQ-A does not have an integral exposure system a separate hand lightmeter or one of the meter finders available in the SQ system is needed for assessing exposure.

Without a metering finder, shutter speed selection is co-ordinated from the camera's shutter dial mounted on the left of the body. A window displays three shutter speeds: the middle is the one in use. Speeds from 1/2 second to 1/500 sec are colour-coded white, those from 1 to 8 seconds are orange.

When used in conjunction with an SQ meter finder the lens aperture should be set to click-stopped positions only: Zenzanon 'PS' designated lenses are stepped in half-stop increments; and 'S' lenses in one-stop intervals.

The effect of specific lens apertures on depth of field can be assessed by operating the depth of field preview control: a spring loaded switch on the lens which cannot be locked in place and returns to its normal position when released. The SQ's meter finders and lenses provide open aperture metering so using the depth of field control at the same time as taking a reading will interfere with correct meter functioning and cause over-exposure by the difference between the set aperture value and the lens's maximum aperture.

The shutter release has a safety lock built-in to avoid unintentional operation. This is brought into action by rotating the locking collar 60 degrees clockwise so that the red dot can be seen from the wind crank side of the camera. In this instance the cable release socket is also locked. Disengage the lock by revolving the collar so that the red dot faces diagonally downward. The cable release socket is situated on the left of the body and this will accept conventional screw thread releases; this too is locked if the shutter lock is engaged.

Pressing the shutter release fully triggers off a chain of events which take place almost instantaneously and culminate in the exposure being made: first the lens shutter closes and the diaphragm closes down to the set aperture followed by the mirror moving upwards out of the light path. The shutter now opens to make the exposure and closes

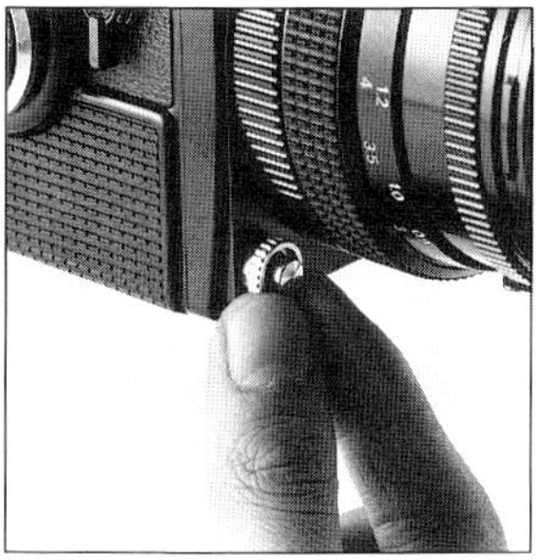

after the pre-selected time has elapsed. If you retain pressure on the shutter button while operating the wind crank the shutter will fire when the winding action is completed.

Provided that all is well the red LED at the top of the viewfinder frame will blink briefly. If this LED fails to blink after exposure the shutter has been released at the mechanical speed 1/500 sec and the battery should be replaced.

Once shutter closure has been confirmed the wind crank can be operated to advance the film to the next frame and cock the shutter. Turning the crank before the shutter closes during a long exposure, will mean that the exposure is brought to an abrupt end because the reflex mirror and baffle drop into the light path. More importantly, the next exposure will be made at a shutter speed of 1/500 sec and, because the film is moved slightly just prior to the shutter closing, there is a chance that the picture you have just taken will exhibit streaking and the following frame be partially exposed.

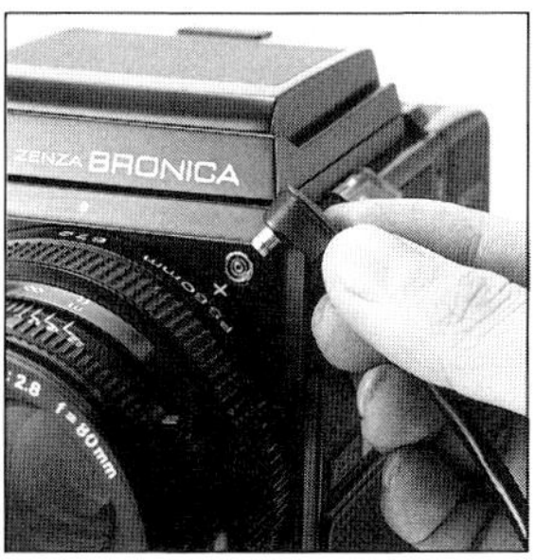

Flash photography

All SQ Zenzanon lenses with their leaf shutters are X-synchronised for electronic flash at all speeds. F and M bulbs are compatible but over a limited range. The flash socket is placed on the front camera panel close to the lens release button and the protective plastic cap should be left in place until flash is used.

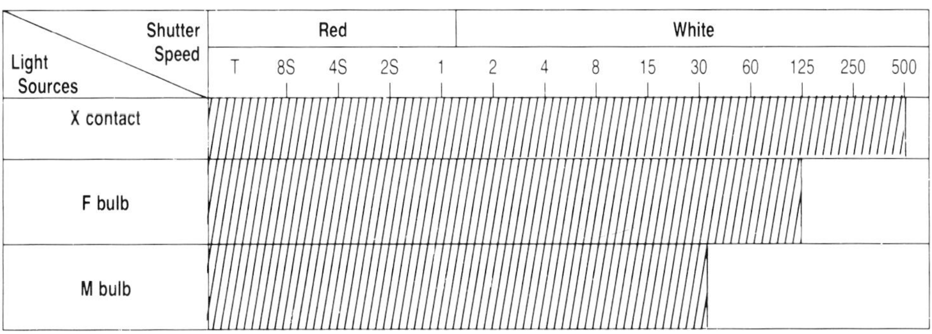

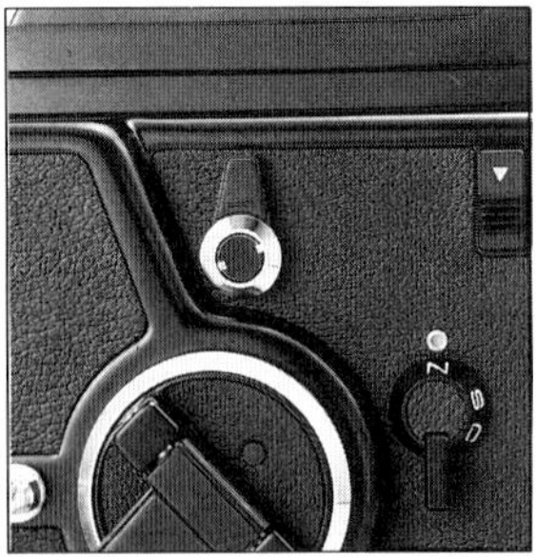

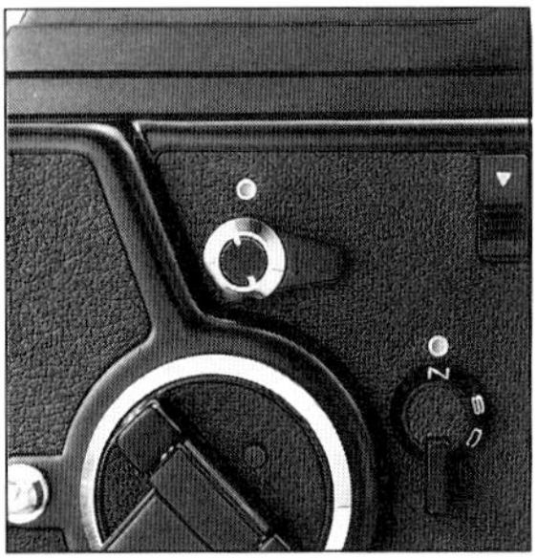

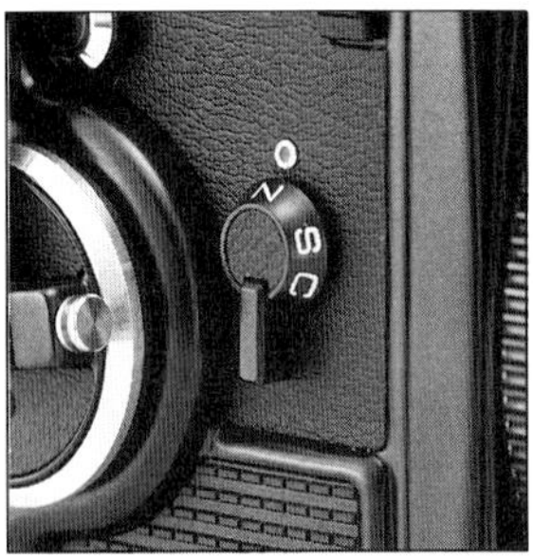

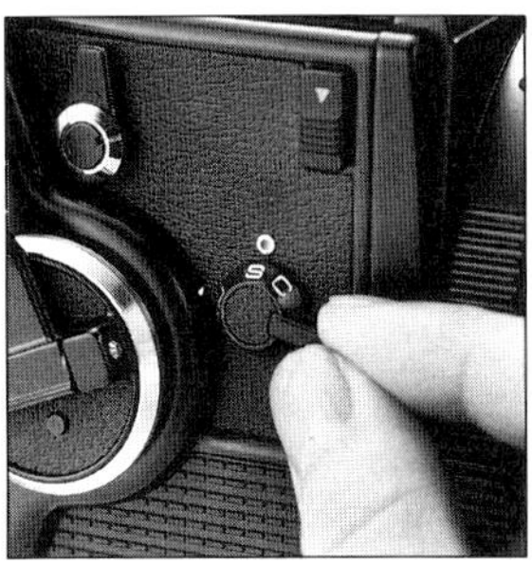

Shooting multiple exposures

The SQ-A has a number of interlocks to prevent double exposures but for creative effects a multiple exposure capability is provided. The control is located directly above the wind crank and during normal photography it should be in an upright position. Engage it by the following procedure: with the shutter cocked and an unexposed frame in position move the multiple exposure control from its normal vertical position to the horizontal, revealing a red dot. After making an exposure, rotating the wind crank will cock the shutter but not advance the film so that any number of exposures can be made on a single frame. The frame counter does not move during multiple exposure operation.

Remember to return the control to its usual upright position after the last exposure of the sequence has been made and the subsequent operation of the wind crank will advance the film to the next frame and cock the shutter as normal.

Mirror lock-up operation

A mirror lock-up feature has many practical applications including close-up photography, lengthy time exposures and when either the vibration or noise generated by the reflex mirror would be likely to spoil the shot or startle the subject.

The SQ-A's mirror lock-up control has three settings: 'N' (normal); 'S' (single-frame); and 'C' (continuous); 'N' is the position for conventional photography. Cock the shutter before engaging mirror lock-up; rotate the wind crank once if the shutter is not cocked. If you are using the AE Prism Finder-S always select manual metering mode and take an exposure reading before locking the mirror up.

Select 'S' and the reflex mirror and light baffle will flip up immediately. The shutter can now be released as normal using either the shutter button or a cable release. During 'S' operation the lever will automatically return to 'N' as the shutter is cocked for the next exposure. Subsequent operation will be perfectly conventional.

Continuous mirror lock-up is facilitated by 'C' which operates in a similar manner to 'S'. However, after an exposure has been made the mirror returns to

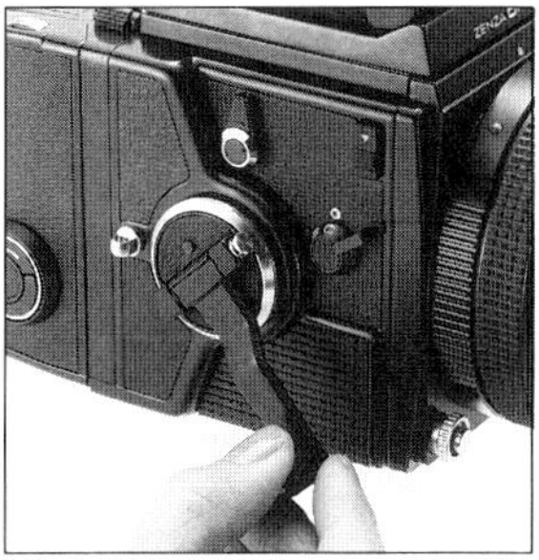

a locked up position as the wind crank is operated.

Once you have finished shooting in 'C' mode move the mirror lock-up lever to either 'N' or 'S' before cocking the shutter ready for the next frame and this will reset the mirror in its usual working position as the wind crank is operated.

Should you change your mind after mirror lock-up has been engaged the shutter will fire as the lever is returned to 'N'. The most convenient method of avoiding the loss of an exposure is to insert the dark slide before resetting the mirror lock-up lever so that when the shutter opens no light reaches the film. Then set the multiple exposure switch to its horizontal position and operate the wind crank to cock the shutter without the film being advanced. Take your picture before resetting the multiple exposure control to its upright position prior to winding on for the next exposure.

Using 'T'

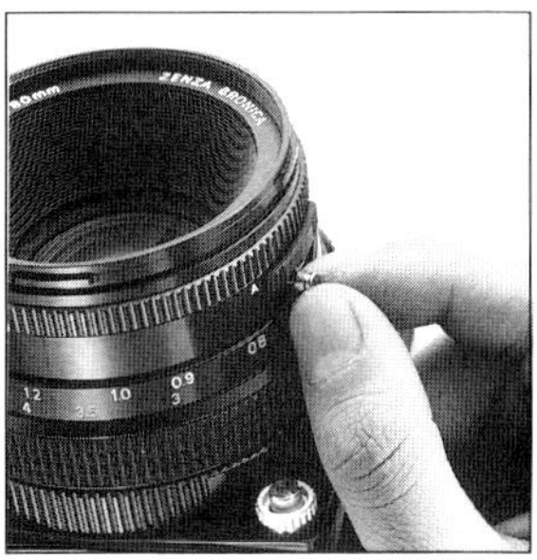

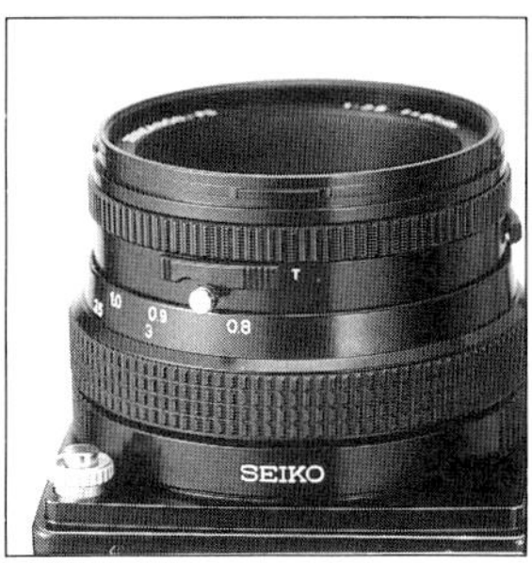

Although the SQ-A has a range of shutter speeds which extends to 8 seconds, longer exposures are sometimes required and the mechanical 'T' (Time exposure) facility satisfies this need.

The selection of the 'T' setting is performed from the lens itself: lift up the locking button so that it is possible to slide the control to reveal the red letter 'T'. When the shutter button is depressed the leaf shutter will stay open until the control is slid back to cover the red 'T'. Before closing the shutter, and in order to eliminate camera shake, it is good technique to place a lens cap, a sheet of black card, or your hand over the lens because, even with the greatest care, it is possible to rock the camera.

The shutter can be closed by revolving the wind crank to cause the reflex mirror and safety baffle to drop in the light path. This however has three side-effects. Firstly, the 'T' slider is still engaged and unless reset the next exposure will again be at this setting. Secondly, and of more relevance, the next exposure in normal photography will be exposed at 1/500 sec regardless of what is set on the shutter dial. Finally, because the film is moved as the crank is operated, the picture you have just taken might be blurred and the following frame partially exposed.

Prior to returning to normal photography, return

the 'T' lever to reveal the white letter 'A' and push the silver locking button in so that you do not make time exposures unintentionally. There is no reminder to tell you that 'T' is in operation.

Specifications of the Bronica SQ-A

Type	6 × 6cm format lens shutter single-lens-reflex, with interchangeable lens, film back, finder and focusing screen.
Frame size	55.6mm × 55.6mm.
Film size	120 roll film (12 exposures); 220 roll film (24 exposures); 35mm cassette film; and Polaroid Land. Exclusive film backs for each type.
Lens mount	Exclusive four-claw Bronica SQ mount.
Shutter	Electronically controlled SEIKO #0 between-the-lens leaf shutter with speeds from 8 seconds to 1/500 sec; 'T' (Time exposure) facility provided. Mechanical speeds 1/500 sec and 'T' only.
Flash synchronisation	Electronic X-flash synchronisation at all speeds.
Depth of field preview	Every Zenzanon S lens has a depth of field preview lever.
Multiple exposure	Multiple exposure possible with lever on camera body.
Mirror lock-up	Single and continuous mirror lock-up capability.
Finder system	Interchangeable finder system with the choice of five: Waist Level Finder S; CdS MF Finder S; Prism Finder S; AE Prism Finder S; and ME Prism Finder S.
Focus screen	Interchangeable type with seven options. Supplied screen has microprism and split-image rangefinder focusing aids on a matte background. The screen is marked with lines for the 4 × 4cm Superslide format.
Battery	One six volt silver oxide battery (No 544, PX-28 or 4G13) or alkaline-manganese battery (A544 or 4LR44).
Battery check	Red coloured LED in viewfinder lights up when battery button is depressed to confirm battery is good. This red LED also acts as shutter closing signal.
Dimensions	92mm wide × 109mm high × 179mm long. (SQ-A main body with 80mm f2.8 lens, Film Back SQ 120 and Waist Level Finder S.
Weight	1500 grams (with the above accessories but no battery).

Chapter Eight

Bronica SQ lenses

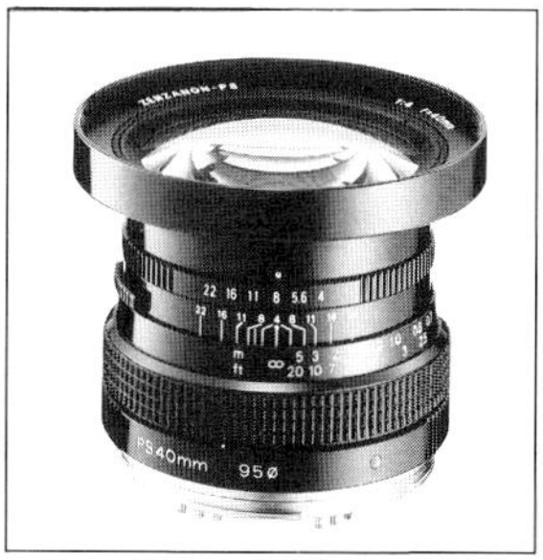

Zenzanon-PS 40mm f4

Interior, landscape and industrial photography are just three subject areas that this wide angle lens can be employed to tackle. Optical quality is of a very high level throughout its aperture and focusing ranges and distortion is minimal. Its optical construction comprises 11 elements in 8 groups and a vestigal lens shade is built-in.

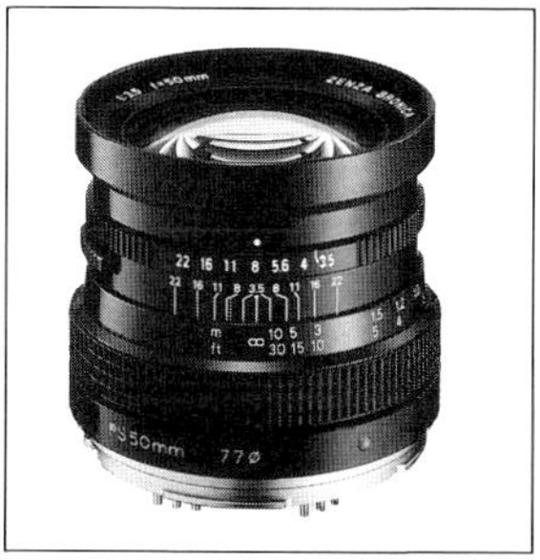

Zenzanon-PS 50mm f3.5

Ideal as a general purpose wide angle this lens is endowed with many practical properties: it is compact, focuses as close as 0.5 metres and delivers an impressive optical performance. Equating to an angle of view of 28mm in the 35mm format this lens can satisfy a multitude of photographic needs and do so comfortably. Candids, groups, landscape, environmental portraiture, interiors and so on are potential subjects for this capable lens.

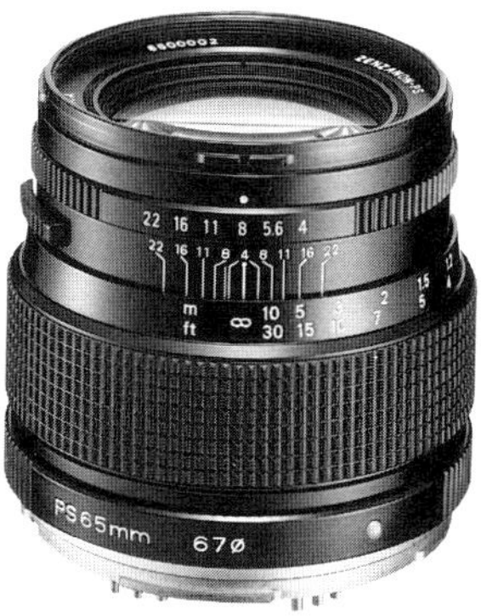

Zenzanon-PS 65mm f4

This moderate wide angle lens has almost universal appeal. It has a focal length equivalent to a 35mm wide angle in the 35mm format and it can be considered as an alternative to the 80mm standard focal length, particularly if you prefer a slightly wide approach to your photography without it appearing obvious that a wide angle lens has been used.

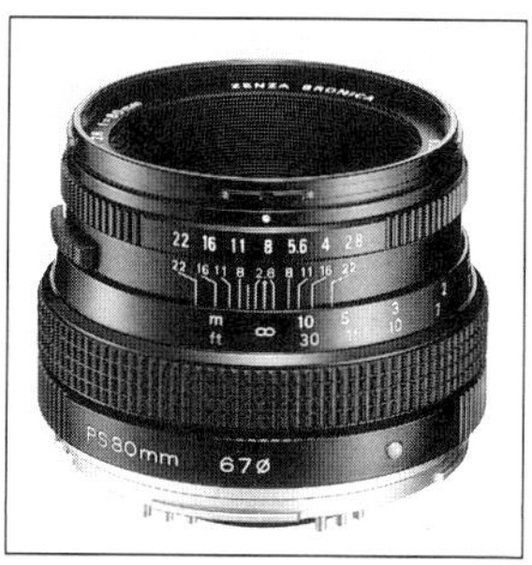

Zenzanon-PS 80mm f2.8

With a fast maximum aperture and an angle of view approximating that of the human eye this compact lens is perfectly suited to the myriad difficult tasks demanded of a standard lens, and if you were to purchase just one lens for your Bronica SQ camera, then this is the one to have.

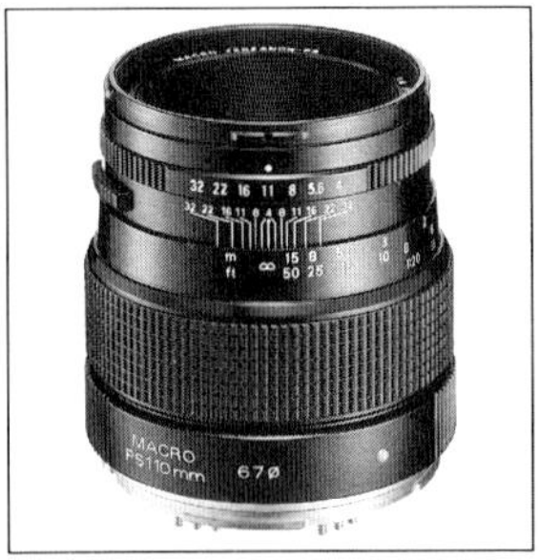

Zenzanon-PS 110mm f4 Macro

Though formulated specifically to give a faultless performance at close distances this lens gives such a good account of itself throughout its focusing range that it is suitable as an all-round lens.

Its unaided minimum focus distance of 0.66 metres allows a maximum reproduction ratio of 1:4, and it can be combined with Auto Extension Tubes S or Auto Bellows Attachment-S for greater magnification.

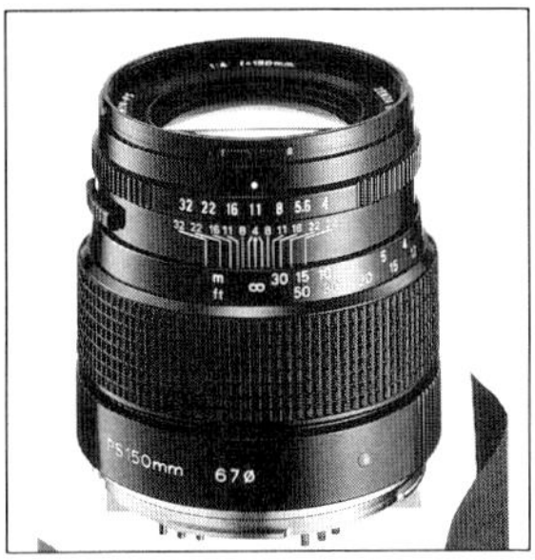

Zenzanon-PS 150mm f4

This respectably fast, short telephoto lens has an optical construction comprising six elements in four groups. The 150mm focal length is without equal in the field of people photography, permitting a comfortable working distance from the subject and delivering a flattering perspective.

Zenzanon 200mm f4.5

Having the capacity to cope with a wide selection of pictorial subjects this compact telephoto lens, giving an equivalent focal length of 105mm in the 35mm format, has much to commend it; not least its competent optical ability and good handling characteristics.

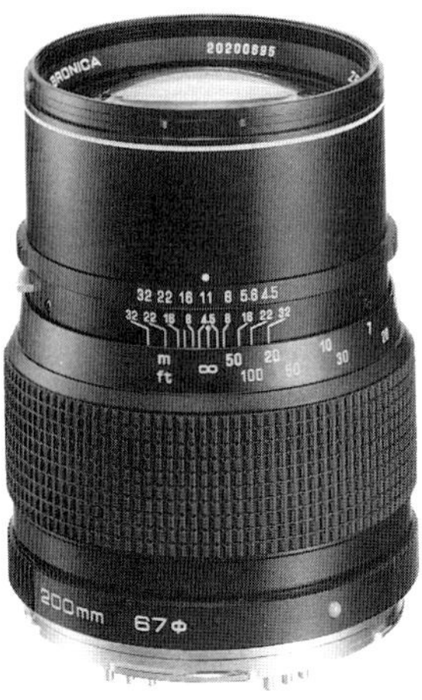

Specification of Bronica SQ lenses

Lens description	Lens construction (elements/groups)	Angle of view	Apertu rang
Zenzanon-PS 40mm f4	11/8	87°	f4-2
Zenzanon-PS 50mm f3.5	10/8	76°	f3.5-2
Zenzanon-PS 65mm f4	9/7	62°	f4-2
Zenzanon-PS 80mm f2.8	6/5	50°	f2.8-2
Macro Zenzanon-PS 110mm f4	6/4	40°	f4-3
Zenzanon-PS 150mm f4	6/4	29°	f4-3
Zenzanon-S 200mm f4.5	5/5	22°	f4.5-3
Zenzanon-S 250mm f5.6	5/5	18°	f5.6-3
Zenzanon-PS 500mm f8	11/10	9°	f8-6
Zenzanon-PS Variogon 75-150mm f4.5 zoom	15/13	53-30°	f4.5-3
Zenzanon-PS Variogon 140-280mm f5.6 zoom	17/14	30-16°	f5.6-3

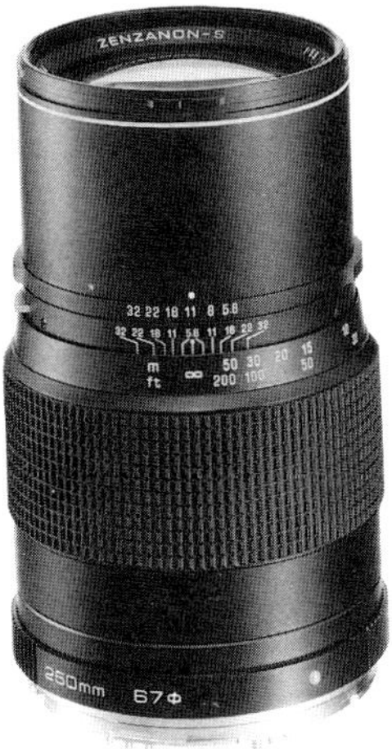

Zenzanon 250mm f5.6

Ideal for pulling in distant detail this is the longest of the general purpose telephoto lenses currently available for the Bronica SQ system. It handles deftly for its focal length and its capable optical performance means that it can be confidently applied to the most critical assignments. As much at home for portraiture as it is for sports and wildlife.

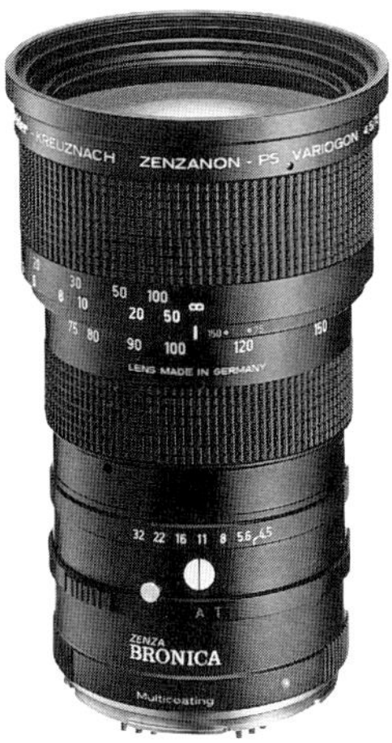

Zenzanon-PS Variogon 75-150mm f4.5 zoom lens

Encompassing a very popular region of focal lengths this 2× zoom offers considerable compositional freedom in the framing of subjects. Suitable for any aspect of photography from portraiture to commercial and landscape this solidly made two touch zoom should satisfy the most critical user. A macro mode is provided.

Zenzanon-PS Variogon 140-280mm f5.6 zoom lens

This 2× telephoto zoom lens boasts similar outstanding levels of optical competence to the previous lens. It features two touch operation and has a macro mode which, at closest focus, permits a magnification ratio of 1:5.8 without any additional aids; it can be used in conjunction with bellows or extension tubes for greater magnification. A rotating tripod mount is built-in.

tter	Minimum focus distance	Macro magnification	Filter size	Size (length/ diameter)	Weight	Equivalent 35mm focal length
00, T	0.4m	N/A	95mm	67 × 98mm	650 grams	23mm
00, T	0.5m	N/A	77mm	61 × 82mm	590 grams	28mm
00, T	0.6m	N/A	67mm	69 × 82mm	665 grams	35mm
00, T	0.8m	N/A	67mm	52 × 82mm	490 grams	45mm
00, T	0.66m	1:4	67mm	79 × 83mm	685 grams	60mm
00, T	1.5m	N/A	67mm	74 × 83mm	750 grams	85mm
00, T	2.5m	N/A	67mm	97 × 82mm	740 grams	105mm
00, T	3.0m	N/A	67mm	129 × 82mm	870 grams	135mm
00, T	8.0m	N/A	122mm	307 × 139mm	3760 grams	270mm
00, T	0.25m	1:4.4	93mm	152 × 100mm	1800 grams	41-82mm
00, T	0.76m	1:5.8	93mm	221 × 94mm	2000 grams	77-154mm

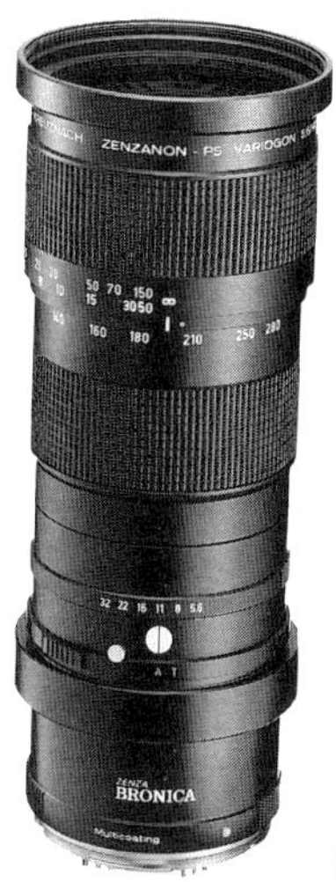

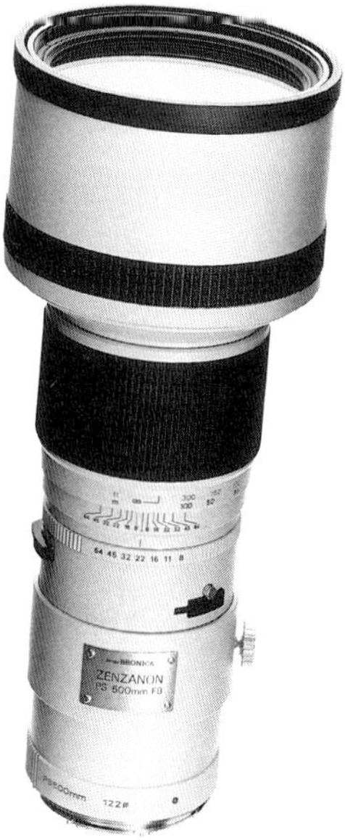

Zenzanon-PS 500mm f8

This lens is perfect for wildlife and sports photography, though it is no lightweight and a tripod mount is fitted. It boasts superb performance at all apertures and, because of the use of two special lens elements, it exhibits extremely low levels of chromatic aberration and its colour reproduction is faithfully accurate. Furthermore, high performance is maintained at close focusing distances thanks to the use of a floating lens element system.

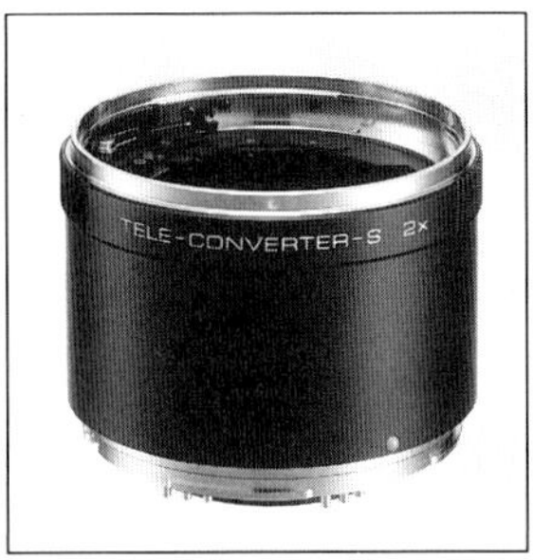

Tele-converter S 2X

A practical and lightweight method by which you can expand your lens armoury, effectively doubling the focal length of the prime lens to which it is attached while maintaining its minimum focusing distance. It does so with the minimal deterioration of picture quality and without any loss of automatic diaphragm operation so that it can be used with SQ metering finders without any exposure modification. However, a two stop increase in exposure must be allowed for when a separate lightmeter is used.

It is recommended for the following Zenzanon SQ lenses: 80mm, 110mm, 150mm, 200mm, 250mm and 500mm.

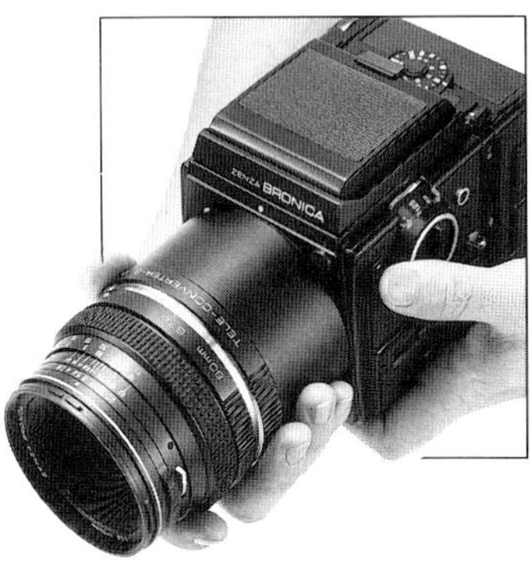

Rapid Focus Lever

An invaluable aid, which fits around the barrel of the lens, to improve focusing accuracy and speed. Suitable for the following Zenzanon SQ lenses: 50mm, 80mm, 100mm, 150mm, 200mm and 250mm. Fits around the focus barrel of each lens.

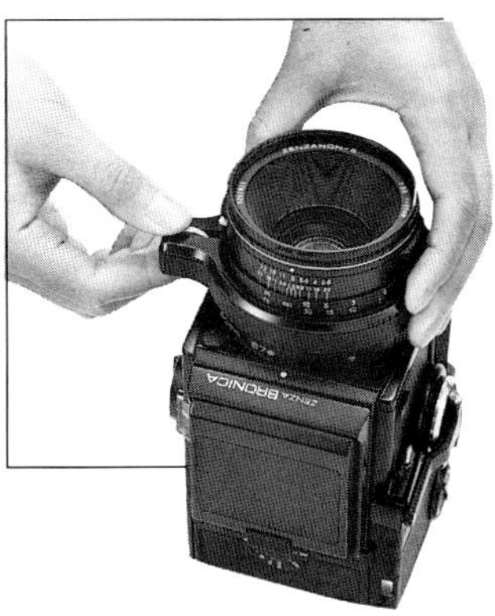

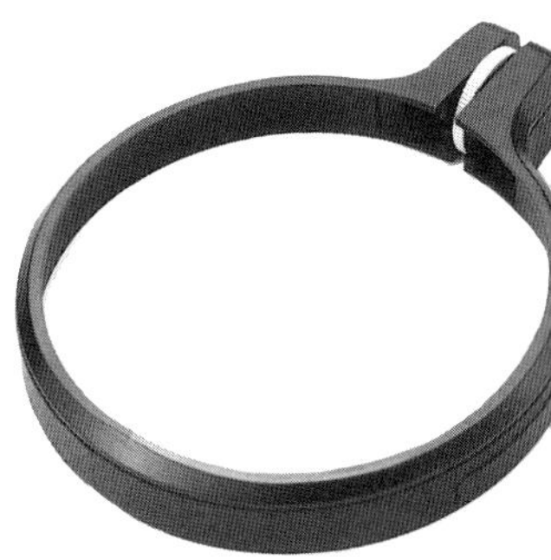

Professional Lens Shade S

This bellows unit has been developed for the efficient elimination of image degrading flare and ghosting and, as a consequence, promotes optimum image quality. Suitable for focal length lenses 50mm, 80mm, 100mm, 150mm, 200mm and 250mm.

It is attached via the 67mm adaptor ring supplied. The bellows are mounted on a pair of rails and can be racked out to suit the focal length of the lens in use. A slot is provided behind the bellows to accommodate 75mm square gelatin filters or one of the many creative filters of the Cokin-type. Screw-in filters can be used and should be attached to the lens prior to fitting the adaptor ring.

Lens shades

The ingenious design of the Professional Lens Shade S provides maximum flare protection although it is not the most convenient accessory to use in fast-moving situations. Under such circumstances a rigid plastic lens hood might be preferred. Bronica has four bayonet-fit models on offer to suit focal lengths from 50mm to 250mm.

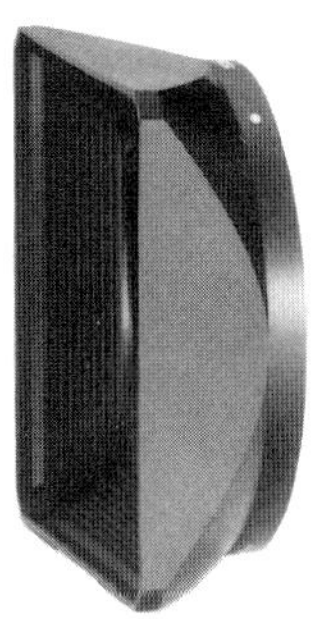
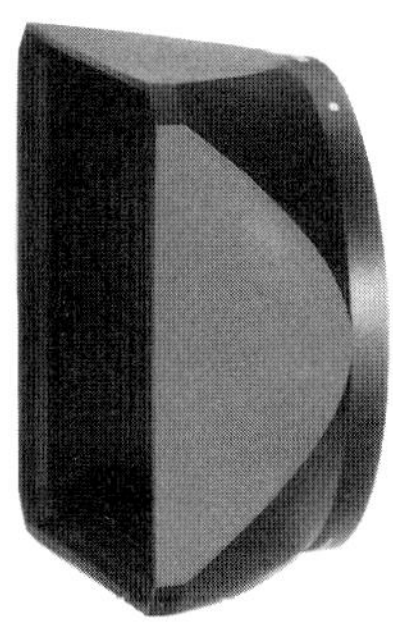
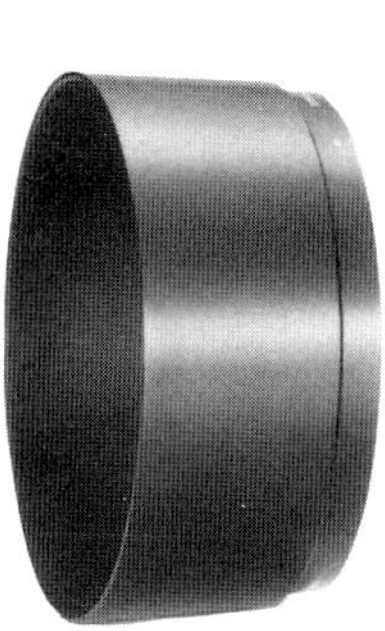
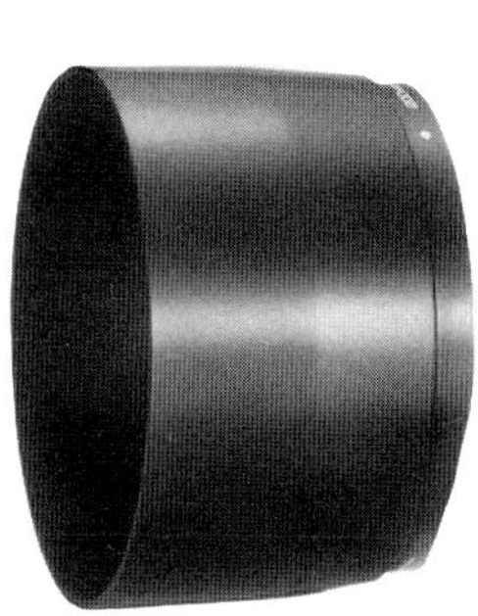

Bronica SQ-Am

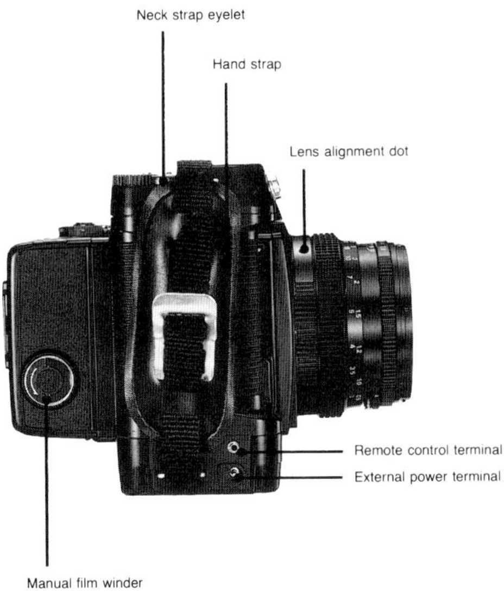

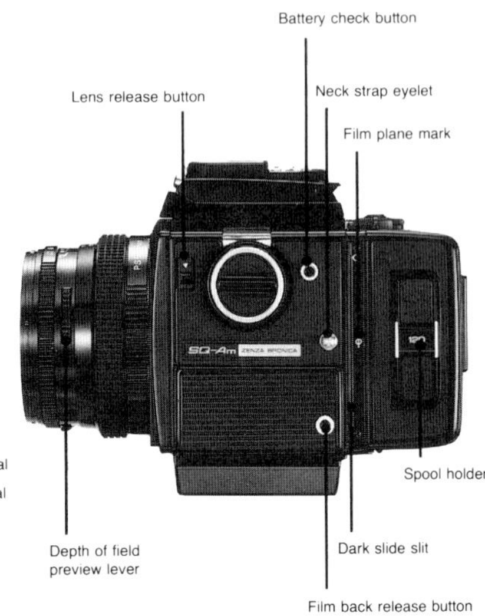

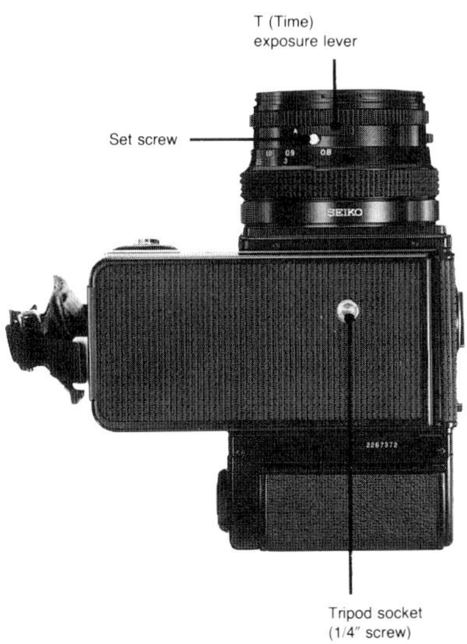

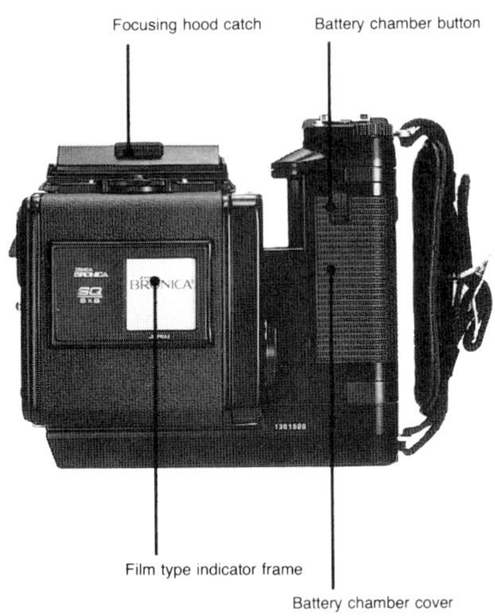

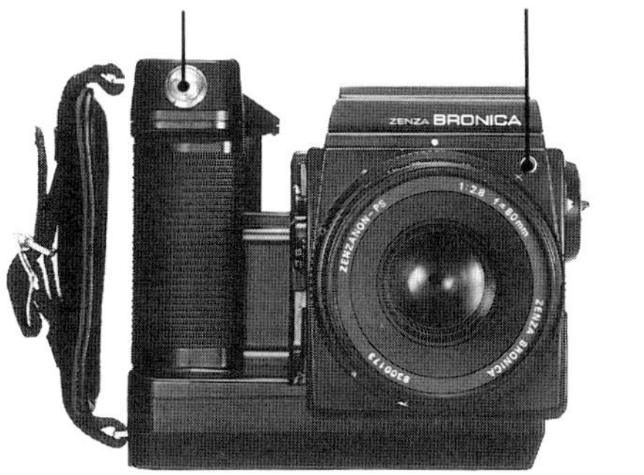
Shutter release button
Flash synch socket
ZENZA BRONICA

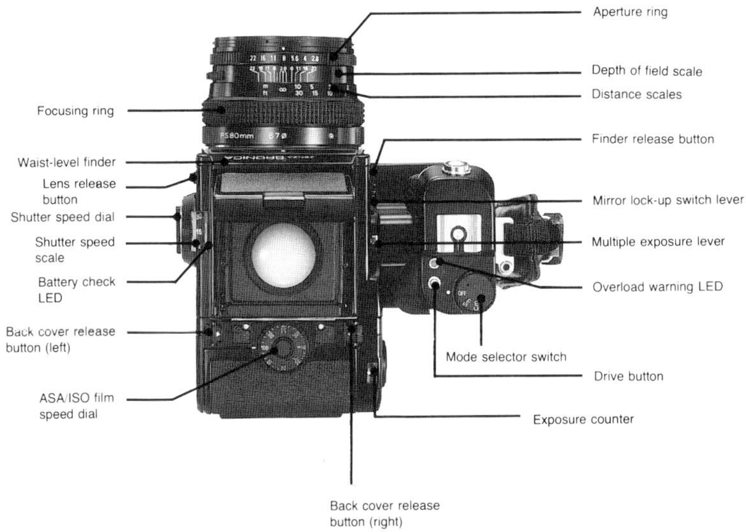
Aperture ring
Depth of field scale
Distance scales
Focusing ring
Finder release button
Waist-level finder
Lens release button
Shutter speed dial
Mirror lock-up switch lever
Shutter speed scale
Multiple exposure lever
Battery check LED
Overload warning LED
Back cover release button (left)
Mode selector switch
Drive button
ASA/ISO film speed dial
Exposure counter
Back cover release button (right)

Chapter Nine

Bronica SQ-Am

The Bronica SQ-Am is a motor-driven version of the SQ-A. It is the ideal camera for photographers who appreciate the superb operational qualities and system versatility offered by the SQ-A but demand even smoother handling in the form of motorised film transport.

The SQ-A and the SQ-Am have much in common and can be used in tandem without any handling difficulties. Most of the features and procedures outlined in Chapter Seven on the SQ-A apply equally to the SQ-Am, so here we concentrate on their differences, in particular, the integral motor-drive.

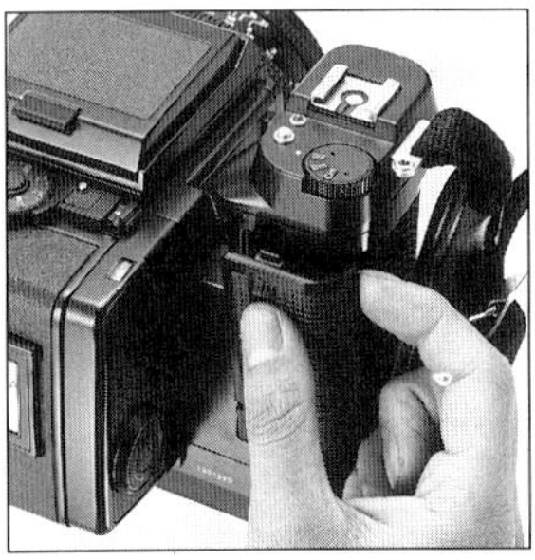

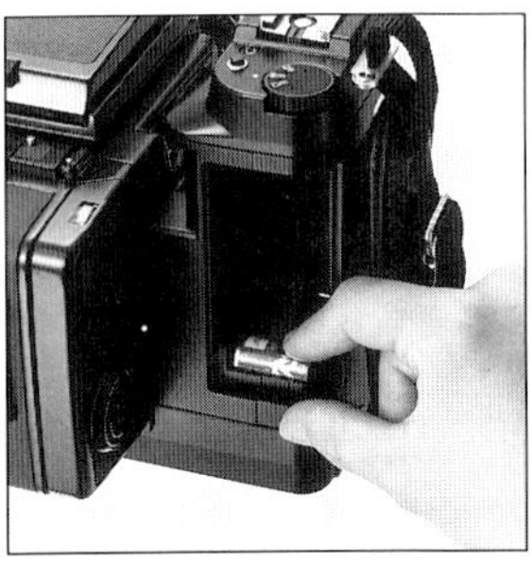

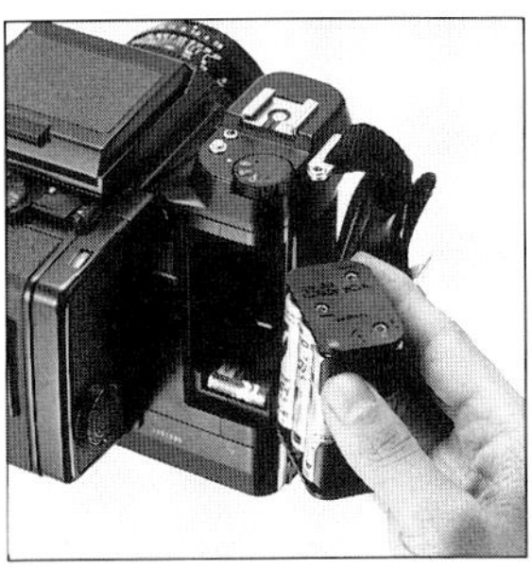

THE BATTERY

The SQ-Am's battery requirements differ significantly from those of the SQ-A. In addition to the six volt camera battery an extra six high quality AA-size alkaline or rechargeable nickel cadmium cells are necessary to power the motor-drive.

Loading the batteries

The battery chamber is an integral part of the hand-grip and is revealed by releasing the cover. Pull out the plastic battery holder, which accepts the six AA-cells, and insert the six volt camera battery obeying the polarity indications. Failure to load the battery correctly will mean that the electronic shutter will fire at its mechanical speed of 1/500 sec.

Load the battery holder, carefully following the polarity indications, before sliding it back into the hand-grip, ensuring that it is inserted so that the words "Zenza Bronica, Japan" are visible from above and according to the arrow indicator.

The shutter and motor-drive circuits are independent of each other as far as their power supplies are concerned, consequently two battery checks have to be performed.

Checking the camera battery

Set 'Sm' or 'Cm' on the control panel and depress the camera battery check button which, if the battery has been loaded properly, will cause a red LED to light in the shutter speed window on the left of the body. If not, check that the battery has been installed correctly.

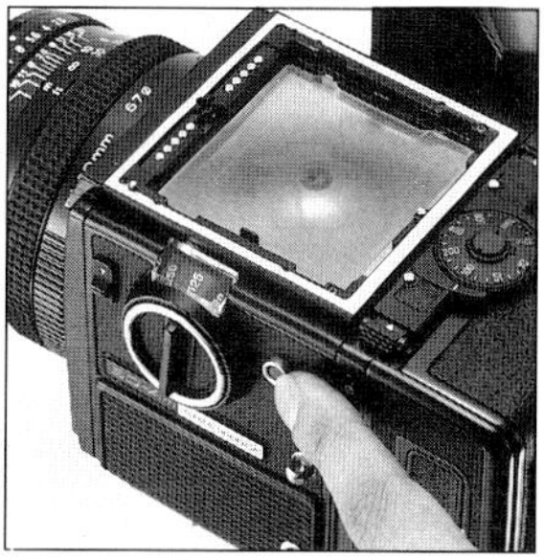

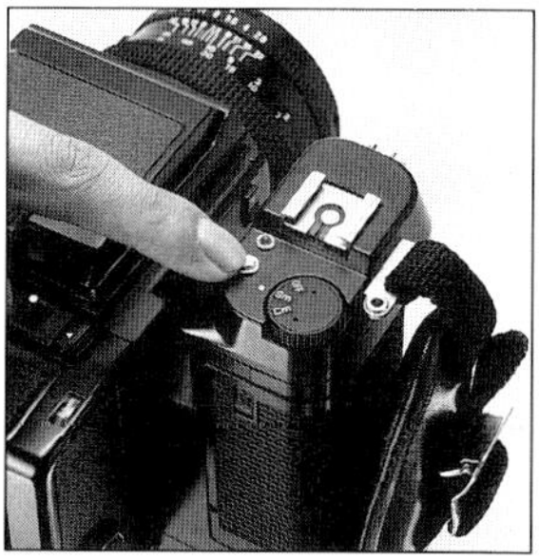

Checking the motor-drive batteries

The motor-drive batteries can be tested by setting the camera to 'Sm' or 'Cm' and the multiple exposure control to a vertical position. Press the drive button located on the hand-grip which, if the batteries are correctly loaded, will bring the motor to life. Switch off once correct functioning has been confirmed. One point to note is that even if the motor-drive's batteries are functioning correctly the shutter will fire at 1/500 sec if the camera's battery is not working; the former will not supply the latter.

Battery efficiency can be adversely affected by freezing conditions and it is best to store batteries somewhere warm and load them just prior to the session. Keep a spare set on hand or alternatively, use the optional Remote Battery Pack E and the External Battery Pack S.

Using an external power source

The External Battery Pack S holds six AA cells and is plugged into the camera's external power socket at the base of the hand-grip. Plugging in this unit automatically switches from the internal battery pack to the external one; a loaded battery holder must be left in position. The Remote Battery Pack E houses a camera battery and is connected to the body via an extension lead.

MOTOR-DRIVE OPERATION

In addition to containing the camera's batteries the hand-grip has other functions; it provides a comfortable grip which means that the camera can be held extremely securely and is also home for the motor-drive controls, described as follows:

(1) **Overload red LED warning.** Whenever this warning appears switch the camera off. After the fault has been found and rectified photography may be resumed.

(2) **Drive button.** Pressing this cocks the shutter and advances the film to the next frame and so satisfies a number of important functions:

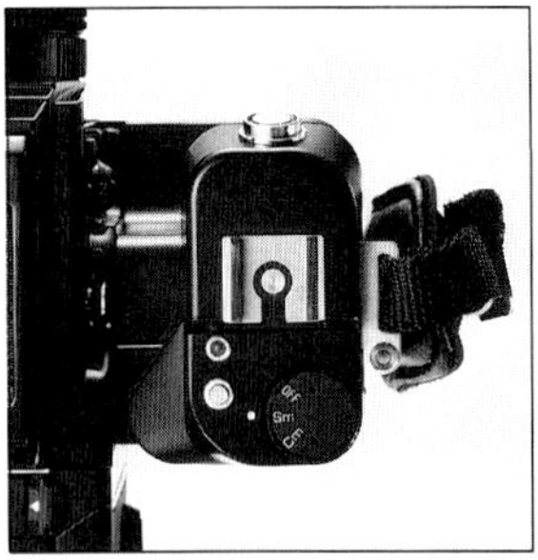

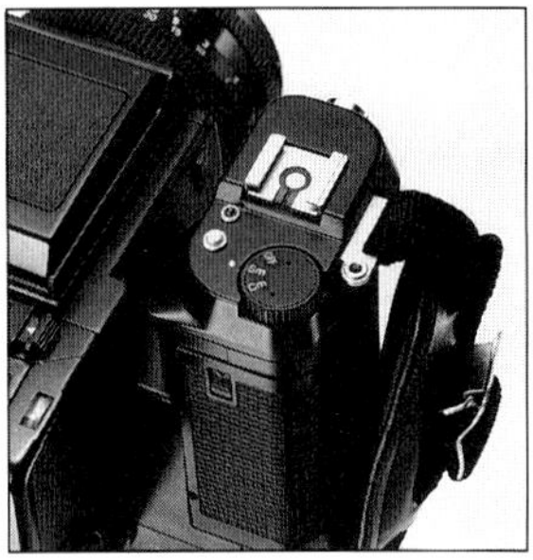

(a) to advance to the first frame after the film has been aligned to the start mark and the film back attached.
(b) to complete coupling with the body when a film back is attached. If the viewfinder LED lights up but the shutter cannot be released, operate the drive button and the film will be advanced so that an unexposed frame is in position.
(c) to wind on to the next frame after a multiple exposure sequence has been completed. Return the multiple exposure lever to an upright position before operating the drive button.
(d) to advance the film and cock the shutter after an exposure using the 'T' setting has been made.

(3) **Motor-drive selector switch.** Three positions are marked on this control: 'OFF' which immobilises all the camera's functions as well as those of any attached meter finder; 'Sm' in which the camera is in complete readiness and the film advanced by one frame after an exposure has been made; and 'Cm' which gives continuous shooting if the shutter release is held down, working at about one frame-per-second.
(4) **Shutter release button.** Self-explanatory. Also activates viewfinder LED display with the various SQ meter finders.
(5) **Flash hot-shoe.** This allows electronic flash operation without the need for connecting cables. The flash hot-shoe and the co-axial socket may be used at the same time.

The Bronica SQ-Am in action

Many aspects of the SQ-Am, such as attaching film backs and exchanging lenses, are identical to the SQ-A although several noteworthy differences do manifest themselves.

Holding the SQ-Am

Most of the supporting work is done by the right hand. The well designed grip and hand strap permit a secure grasp with the right index finger resting on the shutter button while the thumb can be used to operate the drive button and mode selector dial.

The left hand looks after shutter speed selection, focusing, aperture setting and, if a meter finder is attached, initiating metering procedure. This handling approach applies almost equally whether the SQ-Am is being used at a waist-level or as an eye-level camera.

There are various safety measures that the SQ-Am has incorporated and these are described as follows:

- For lenses to be attached or detached both the camera and the lens must be cocked. Switching the motor-drive on and pressing the drive button will advance the film and cock the shutter provided that a lens is attached.
- The viewfinder shutter confirmation LED will light if the shutter release is depressed but the shutter cannot be fired in the following situations.
  - (a) The film back's dark slide is in position.
  - (b) The lens is not attached properly.
  - (c) The lens release button is being depressed.
  - (d) The film is not advanced to an unexposed frame.
  - (e) The motor-drive batteries do not have sufficient power for correct functioning.
- If the red viewfinder LED does not light up during exposure the shutter will have fired at 1/500 sec and the battery needs replacing. Note the following important difference between the SQ-A and the SQ-Am: whereas the SQ-A's viewfinder LED flashes immediately after the shutter has closed and the exposure completed, the SQ-Am LED lights up during the exposure.

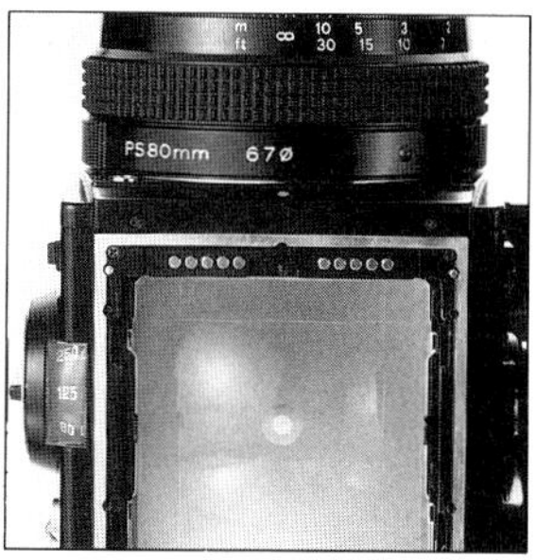

A red LED at the top of the viewfinder blinks to confirm correct shutter operation.

Operating the camera without film

Normally the shutter cannot be fired or the motor-drive operated unless there is a loaded film back in place, but by setting the multiple exposure control to the horizontal position, so that a red dot is visible, the shutter can be fired as many times as you desire. The exposure counter does not advance during this procedure.

Attaching a film back

Since the SQ-A and SQ-Am share the same system of film backs the method of attaching, detaching and loading them is identical. Preparing the camera for action is however slightly different. When a freshly loaded film back is attached pressing the drive button will advance the film to the first frame automatically.

When exchanging film backs press the drive button to ensure full coupling. This, if an exposed frame is in position, will automatically advance the film to the next frame. If an unexposed frame is in position the film will not be advanced.

After the last frame has been exposed (the 12th on 120 film, the 24th on 220 film) the motor-drive will continue to operate, winding off the exposed film before stopping automatically. The back cover can now be opened and the exposed film removed.

The motor-drive in use

During 'Sm' mode each time the shutter button is depressed the shutter will be released, the film advanced by one frame, the reflex mirror returned to give a viewing image and the shutter re-cocked. Keeping the button held down will not give sequential shooting; to take more than one shot consecutively the finger must be lifted from the shutter release before being pushed down again. In 'Cm' mode, holding down the shutter button will give continuous shooting at a rate of about one frame-per-second.

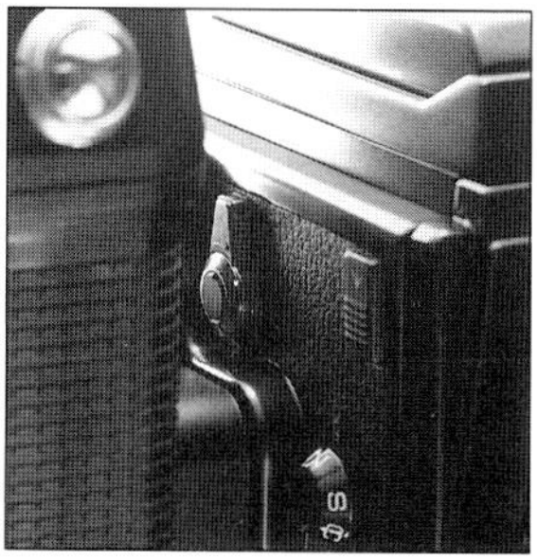

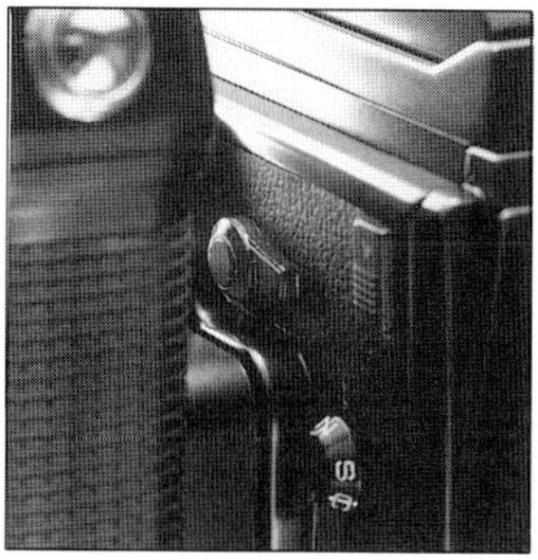

Making multiple exposures

Move the multiple exposure lever from its vertical position to the horizontal, revealing a red dot, prior to taking the first exposure in the sequence. When the shutter button is depressed the shutter will release normally before being cocked by the motor-drive. The film winding mechanism however will be uncoupled so that the film does not advance.

Upon completing the sequence of exposures you must not only remember to return the lever to its vertical position but also to press the drive button to advance the film by one frame. Failure to do this will mean that the next frame will also be double exposed.

Using a remote release

Triggering the SQ-Am remotely is possible via an electronic remote release socket. This is located at the base of the hand grip, accepts a 2.5mm mini jack-plug and enables the camera to be fired using a remote release lead, intervalometer or wireless remote release equipment. The camera should be switched off before a remote release is plugged in otherwise the shutter will fire.

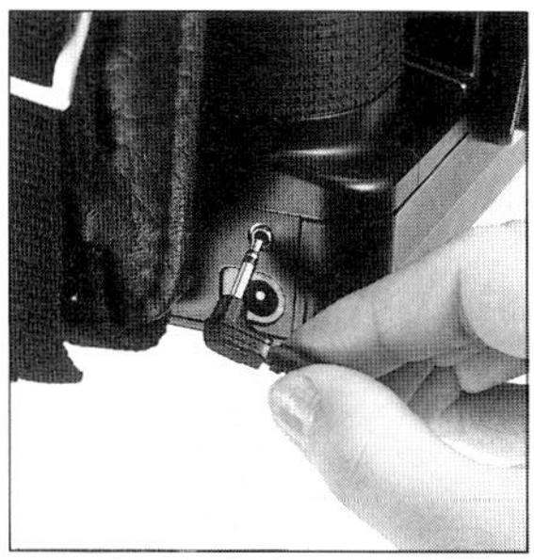

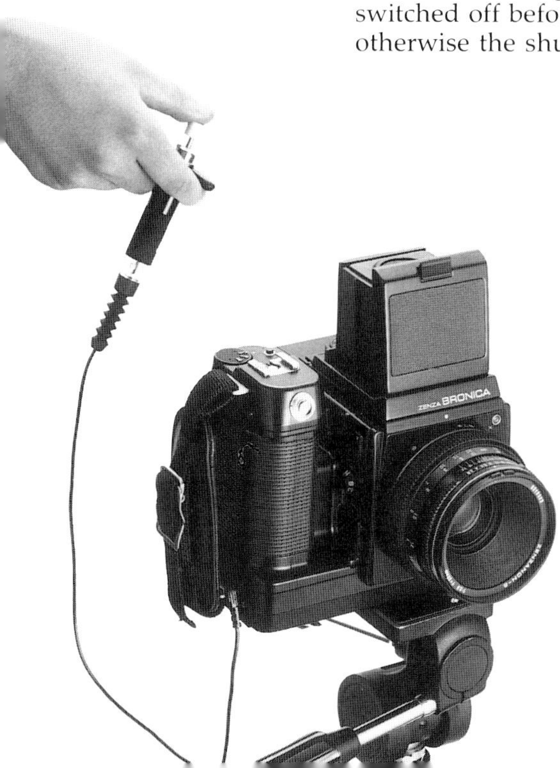

Mirror lock operation

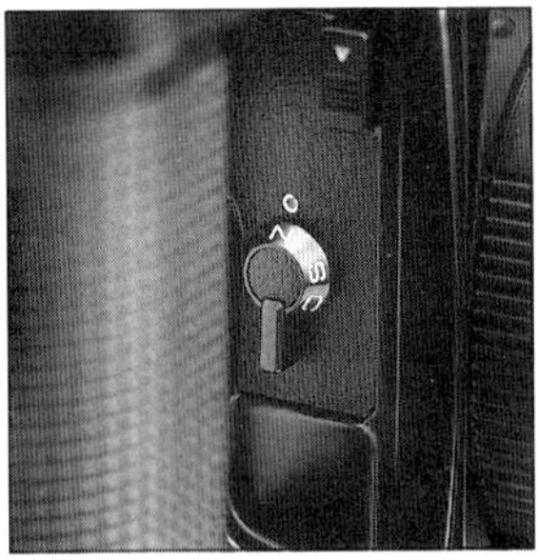

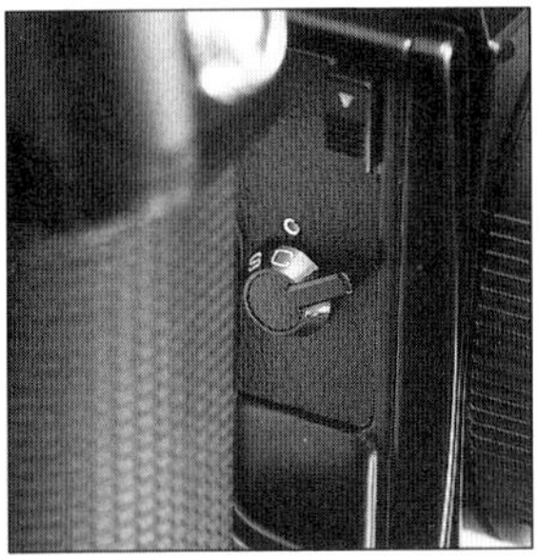

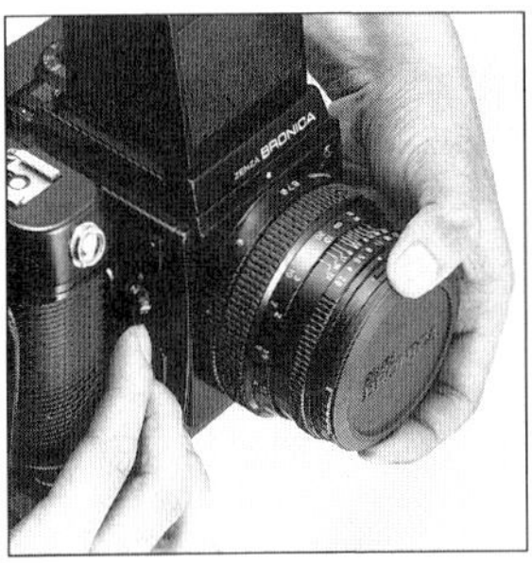

The SQ-Am's mirror lock-up operation is similar to that of the SQ-A. There are three settings: 'N' for normal photography; 'S' for single shot mirror lock-up when the switch is reset to normal after one mirror up operation; and 'C' for continuous mirror lock-up operation. In 'S' mode the mirror lock-up lever will reset automatically when the motor-drive winds on and cocks the shutter ready for the next exposure. The shutter can be triggered either normally by using the shutter button or by remote release.

One difference will be noticed if mirror lock-up operation is initiated and then subsequently revoked. As the lever is moved from 'S' or 'C' back to 'N' the shutter will fire and the motor-drive will operate to return the mirror to its working position but the film will not advance. Therefore, while the shutter is prepared for the next exposure, the film is not and a double exposure will be the result. This can be prevented by fitting a lens cap before resetting the lock-up switch from 'S' or 'C' back to 'N' so that the film is not exposed when the shutter is opened. Photography may now be continued.

An alternative to this method is to detach the film back before returning the lock-up lever to 'N' and then re-attach the back after the motor-drive has cocked the shutter.

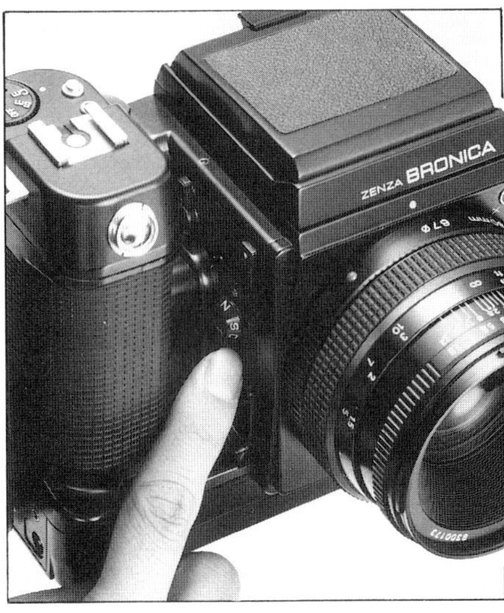

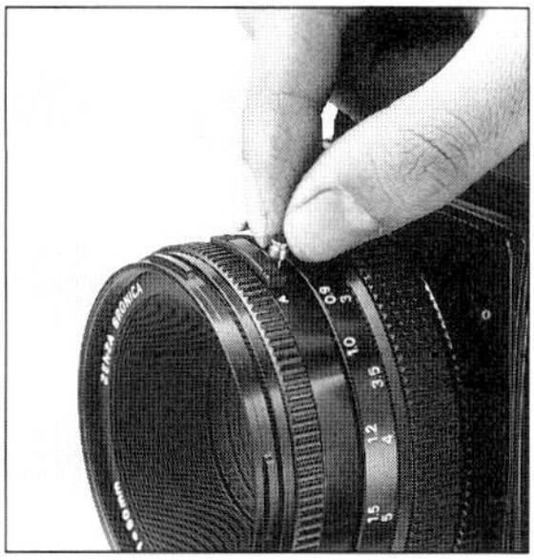

Using the 'T' setting

Engaging 'T' (Time exposure) mode is achieved by operating the control mounted on the lens; it does not matter what the camera's shutter dial is set to. Pull up the locking button so that the lever can be moved from the 'A' setting to show a red-coloured letter 'T'. The shutter may be triggered as usual by depressing the shutter button and it can be held open indefinitely. The mirror lock-up can be used in conjunction with the 'T' setting to minimise vibration. To close the shutter slide the 'T' lever back to its original location. The film is not advanced when the shutter is closed so you must remember to depress the drive button to wind the film to the next frame.

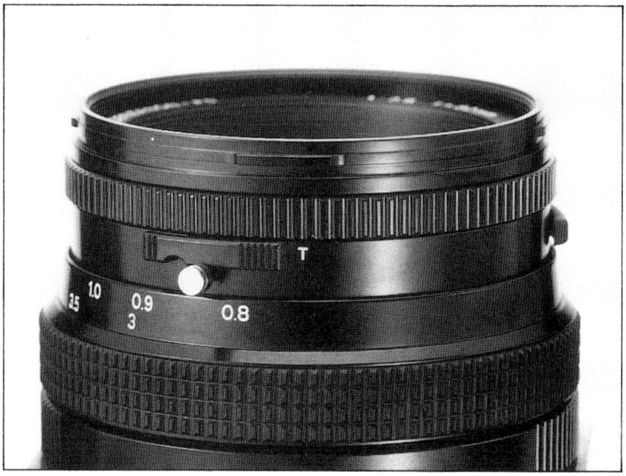

The shutter should not be closed by pressing the drive button. If you do close the shutter by this method you risk blurring the picture you have just exposed as well as partially exposing the next frame. Furthermore, the first exposure taken after normal camera operation has been resumed will take place at 1/500 sec.

Specifications of the Bronica SQ-Am

Type	6 × 6cm format lens shutter single-lens-reflex, with interchangeable lens, film backs, finder and focusing screen.
Frame size	55.6mm × 55.6mm.
Film size	120 roll film (12 exposures); 220 roll film (24 exposures); 35mm cassette film; and Polaroid Land. Exclusive film backs for each type.
Lens mount	Exclusive four-claw Bronica SQ mount.
Shutter	Electronically controlled SEIKO #0 between-the-lens leaf shutter with speeds from 8 seconds to 1/500 sec; 'T' (Time exposure) facility provided. Mechanical speeds 1/500 sec and 'T' only.
Film winding	Integral motor-drive.
Firing speed	Single frame or continuous shooting. Maximum shooting speed of three frames every two seconds with fast shutter speed. A fresh set of alkaline-manganese batteries will give approximately 500 exposures.
Flash synchronisation	Electronic X-flash setting at all shutter speeds.
Depth of field preview	Every Zenzanon S lens has a depth of field preview lever.
Multiple exposure	Possible with lever on camera body.
Finder system	Interchangeable type with five options: Waist Level Finder S; CdS MF Finder S; Prism Finder S; AE Prism Finder S; and ME Prism Finder S.
Focus screen	Interchangeable type with seven options. Supplied screen has microprism and split-image rangefinder focusing aids on a matte background. The screen is marked with lines for the Superslide 4 × 4cm format.
Battery	One six volt silver oxide (No 544, PX-28 or 4G13) or alkaline-manganese (A544 or 4LR44) for the camera's electronic shutter. Battery check provided. Six AA-size alkaline-manganese or nickel cadmium batteries for the motor-drive system.
Dimensions	144.5mm wide × 125mm high × 179mm long (SQ-Am main body, 80mm f2.8 lens and Waist Level Finder S).
Weight	1925 grams (with above accessories but no batteries).

Chapter Ten

Bronica SQ System Accessories

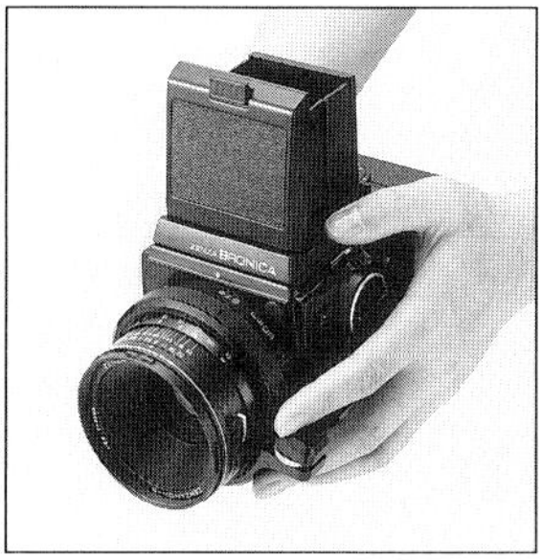

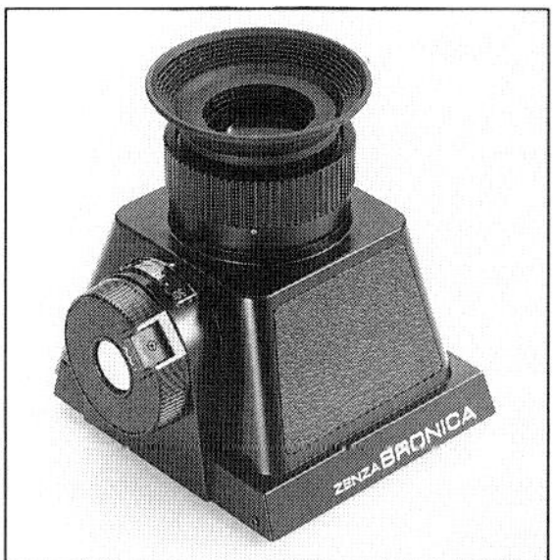

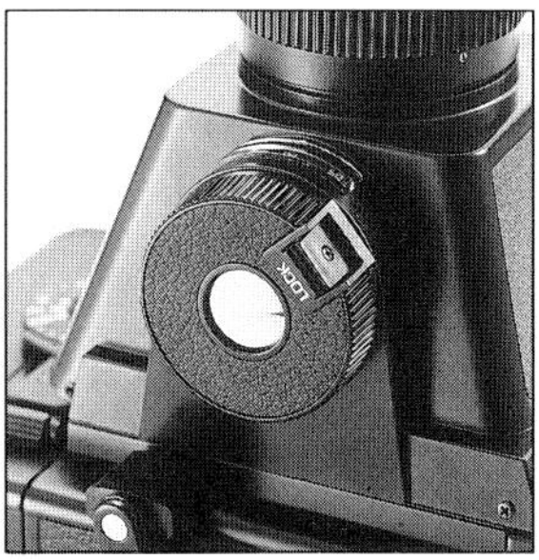

Waist Level Finder-S

This, the simplest and most compact finder in the Bronica SQ system, gives an upright, reversed image. It has an integral magnifier and the option of user-changeable diopter eyepieces. The one supplied has a strength of −1.5 diopters; optional eyepieces of −4.5, −3.5, −2.5, −0.5, +0.5 and +1.5 are available.

CdS MF Finder S

Offering the benefits of through-the-lens manual metering while preserving the viewfinder's inherent high brightness level, this finder produces an upright, reversed image and is ideal for photographers who demand waist level operation at its most convenient. An adjustable eyepiece with a range of −3 to +2 diopters is built-in.

When fitted to the SQ-A or SQ-Am body this finder completely overrides the camera's shutter dial which can be left in any position without it affecting proper functioning. Shutter speed selection is achieved using the finder's own dial which is click-stopped in half-stop steps and functions over the full 8 seconds to 1/500 sec range; steps other than those click-stopped should not be chosen. Using two CdS photocells this finder has a metering range of EV 4 to EV 16 (ISO 100, f2.8 lens).

The SQ-A does not have an on/off control and the meter finder is ready for use as soon as it is mounted on to the body. In the case of the Bronica SQ-Am the camera has to be set to 'Sm' or 'Cm' mode. With both the SQ-A and SQ-Am power for the finder's metering system is provided by the camera battery. This is the case with all SQ meter finders.

Pressing the chrome display button mounted at the centre of the finder's shutter dial turns the meter on for 30 seconds. The meter switches itself off automatically after this period; if the exposure is made before 30 seconds has elapsed the meter also switches itself off. A lock button is provided and this should be engaged if, for example, the camera is being stored.

Three LEDs in the viewfinder indicate exposure level: a red '+' or '−' for over and under-exposure respectively and a green circle for correct exposure. Determining exposure is a straightforward matter of

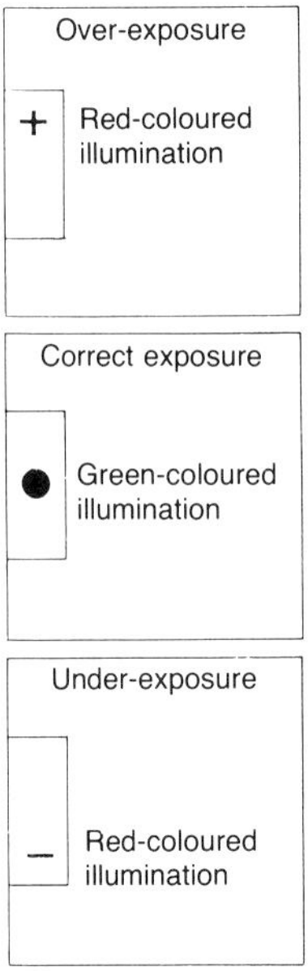

adjusting either the shutter dial or the lens aperture, or a combination of the two, until the green circle LED lights up.

This finder is designed to give an exposure reading with the lens at full aperture, therefore do not operate the depth of field preview facility at the same time as taking a reading otherwise over-exposure will result. Before commencing photography check that the film's correct ISO has been selected on the film back.

Prism Finder S

This non-metering finder offers the convenience of eye-level viewing in a portable package and supplies a bright, upright, laterally-correct finder image. The standard eyepiece lens is −1.5 diopters with optional lenses of −4.5, −3.5, 2.5, −0.5, +0.5 and +1.5 available.

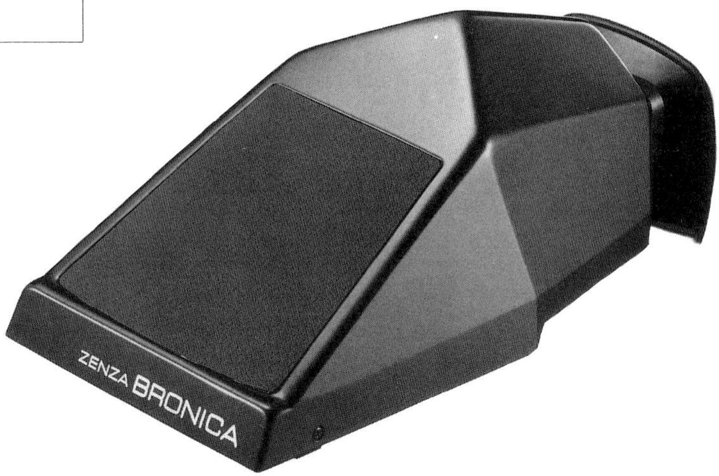

ME Prism Finder S

This finder is essentially a prism version of the CdS MF Finder S giving a crisp upright image which is laterally correct. The camera's battery powers the unit. Fitted to the SQ-Am the finder does not function unless the camera is set to 'Sm' or 'Cm'. With the SQ-A the meter is ready for use.

Upon attachment of this finder the camera's shutter circuit is bypassed and the selection of shutter speed is controlled by the finder's own dial which is click-stopped in half-stop settings throughout the 8 seconds to 1/500 sec range. The camera's dial may be left in any position without it affecting the finder's operation.

Pushing the chrome central display button actuates the meter for 30 seconds. Should exposure assessment be incomplete within that time push the display button again. In the event of the picture being taken within 30 seconds the meter switches itself off.

If the camera is being stored for any length of time the display button should be locked by moving the lock button outwards; this will prevent unintentional metering and the subsequent draining of the battery.

With the meter switched on, the lens aperture or the shutter speed, or both, should be adjusted until the correct exposure is indicated on the viewfinder LED display situated above the picture area: a red '+' LED indicates over-exposure, a green spot LED correct exposure and a red '−' symbol warns of under-exposure. The meter's sensitivity range is EV 4 to EV 16 (with ISO 100 film).

Equipped with a standard −1.5 diopter eyepiece, this finder accepts the same optional eyepieces as for the Prism Finder S and the AE Prism Finder S.

Relationship between aperture, exposure and shutter speed

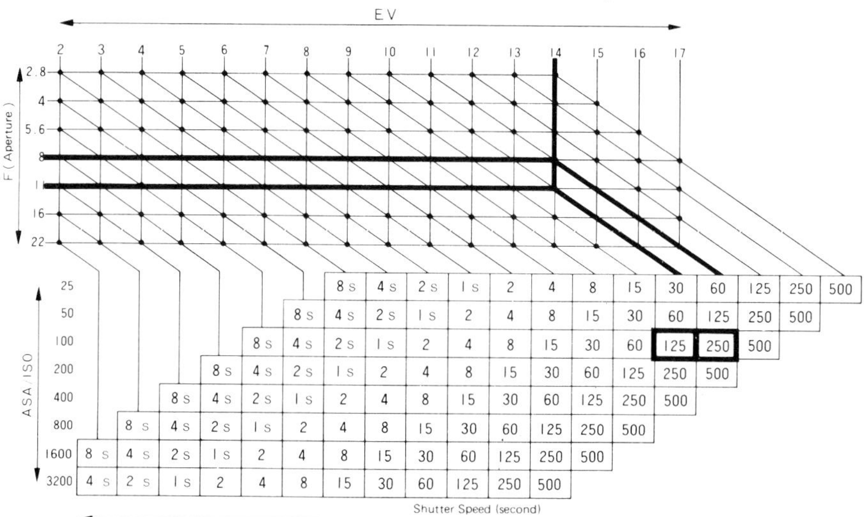

Take an Exposure Value of 14 with ISO 100 film as an example. Reading off the top scale you get an exposure of 1/250sec at f8. By setting an aperture of f11 and reading off the scale you can see that a shutter speed of 1/125sec needed to maintain the same exposure.

AE Prism Finder S

This model is the most versatile of the finders available for the SQ system and incorporates automatic exposure and manual metering modes. It is compatible only with SQ-A and SQ-Am cameras. Two silicon photocells endow the meter with a sensitivity of EV 4 to 17 (ISO 100 film). It is a streamlined, compact unit enabling eye-level use and projecting an upright, laterally-correct image. In common with other SQ finders power for the meter is provided by the camera battery.

This finder has two selector switches: the 'ON/OFF' control isolates the finder from the camera and there is no LED readout; the 'AUTO/MANUAL' gives the option of automatic or manual exposure measurement.

The finder gives aperture-priority auto-exposure when set to 'AUTO' and chooses the appropriate shutter speed to give correct exposure with the selected lens aperture, the shutter operating in 1/3 stop steps throughout its 8 seconds to 1/500 sec range. Partially depressing the shutter button brings on the viewfinder LED display which stays on only for as long as it is held down. During automatic exposure operation the nearest standard shutter speed to the actual speed selected by the finder lights up the display. In auto-exposure mode the camera's shutter control plays no part.

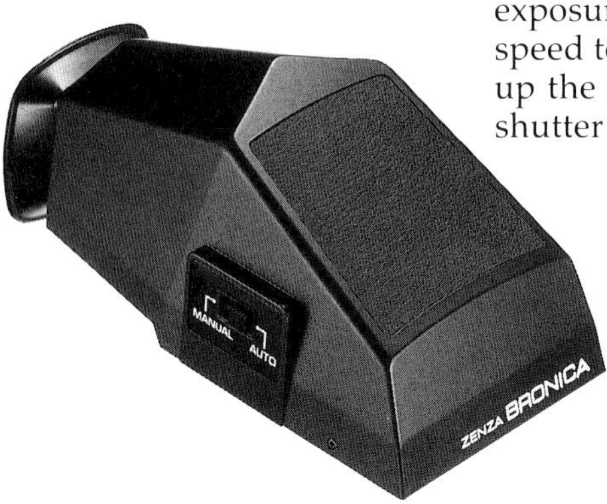

AUTO/MANUAL switch / Power source switch		AUTO	MANUAL
ON	Shutter	Automatic control	Shutter speed operates by shutter speed dial on camera body
	Finder indication	LED illumination	Flickering LED
OFF	Shutter	Shutter speed operates by shutter speed dial on camera body.	
	Finder indication	No indication	No indication

In manual mode, however, the camera's shutter dial is used. Partial depression of the shutter button causes the shutter speed needed for correct exposure with the selected lens aperture to blink, and this setting has to be transferred to the camera's shutter dial manually.

The supplied eyepiece has a diopter strength of −1.5. The range of optional eyepieces available is the same as for the Prism Finder S and the ME Prism Finder S.

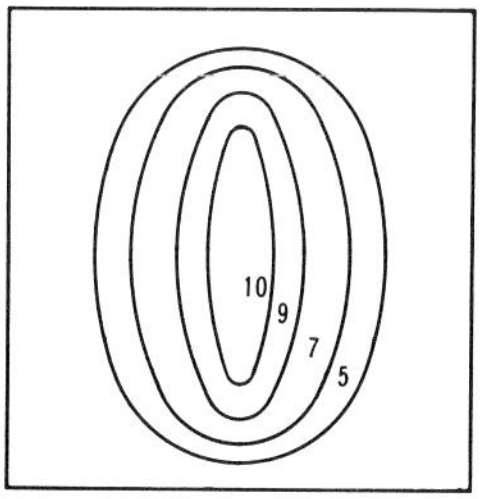

Meter Sensitivity Pattern

Practical hints for AE Prism Finder S use

- Clean the finder and camera contacts from time to time with a soft cloth. Poor connection can cause incorrect operation.
- Conserve battery power by switching the finder off when it is not in use.
- Do not set either the aperture or shutter to values other than those click-stopped because it might interfere with correct operation.
- Always check that the correct film speed has been selected on the film back before commencing photography.
- Use a tripod if the shutter speed is slow; with an 80mm lens beware of speeds of 1/30 sec or slower.
- There is no exposure memory lock nor is there a purpose-designed exposure compensation facility. However exposure compensation is possible by adjusting film speed on the film back. Always remember to reset the film's correct speed after compensating for exposure.
- Cover the finder eyepiece with a piece of black cloth if your eye is not up to the eyepiece during automatic exposure operation. This will prevent extraneous light entering the finder and affecting the exposure.
- Do not operate the depth of field preview control at the same time as taking a meter reading because this will cause over-exposed pictures.
- Confirm that the shutter has closed during long exposure operation by watching for the red confirmation LED in the viewfinder. Operating the wind crank before the exposure has ended can result in streaking of the picture because the film is advanced slightly just prior to the shutter closing;

the next frame may also be partially exposed. Also, the next photograph will be exposed at 1/500sec. This is not a problem with the SQ-Am because its motor-drive will operate only when the shutter has closed.

- Manual mode should be used for mirror lock-up operation. During flash photography the meter should be switched off.

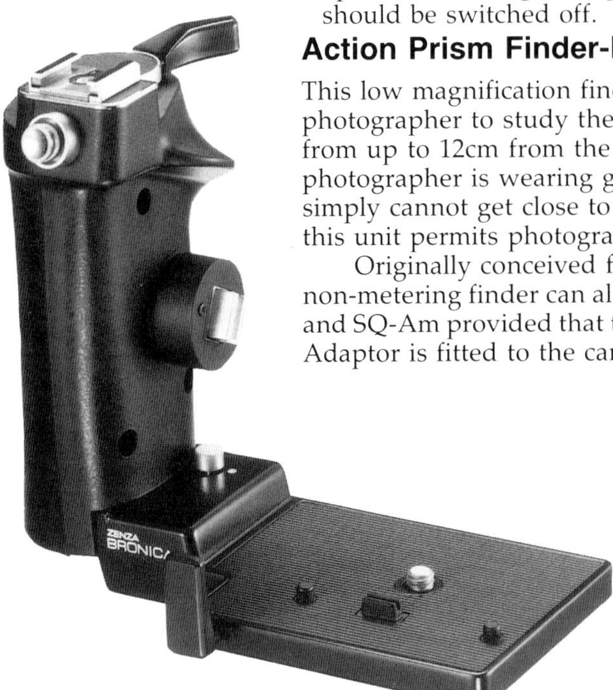

Action Prism Finder-E

This low magnification finder enables the photographer to study the entire viewfinder image from up to 12cm from the eyepiece. Therefore if the photographer is wearing glasses, a crash helmet or simply cannot get close to the viewfinder eyepiece this unit permits photography to be performed.

Originally conceived for the Bronica ETRS this non-metering finder can also be attached to the SQ-A and SQ-Am provided that the necessary Action Prism Adaptor is fitted to the camera body.

GRIPS

Speed Grip S

The Speed Grip S provides a significant improvement in camera handling. Obviously it is unsuitable for the motor-drive Bronica SQ-Am which already has a hand-grip incorporated.

When attached the grip permits fast film advance with two strokes of the thumb operated lever and convenient shutter release using the button available. The grip is located on the right side of the camera, freeing the left hand to look after the remainder of the camera's functions. A hot-shoe flash fitting and shutter lock control are provided.

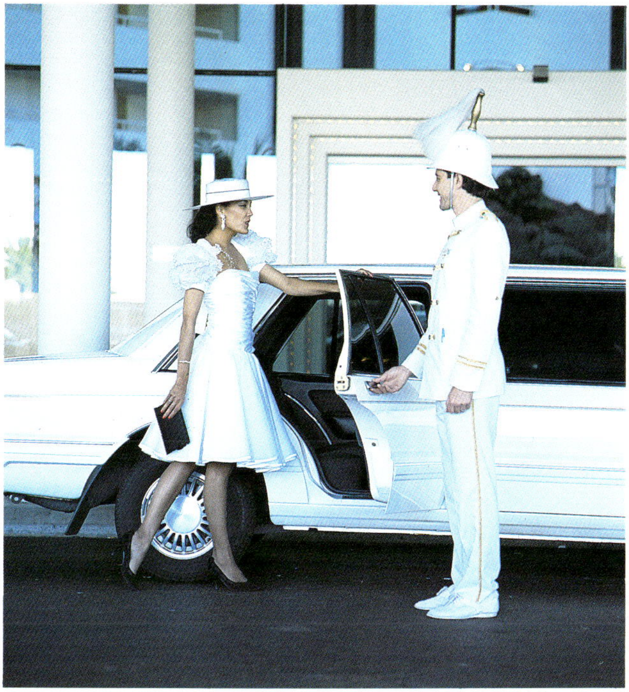

Fashion Shots,
Ashley Smith & Duncan Roe

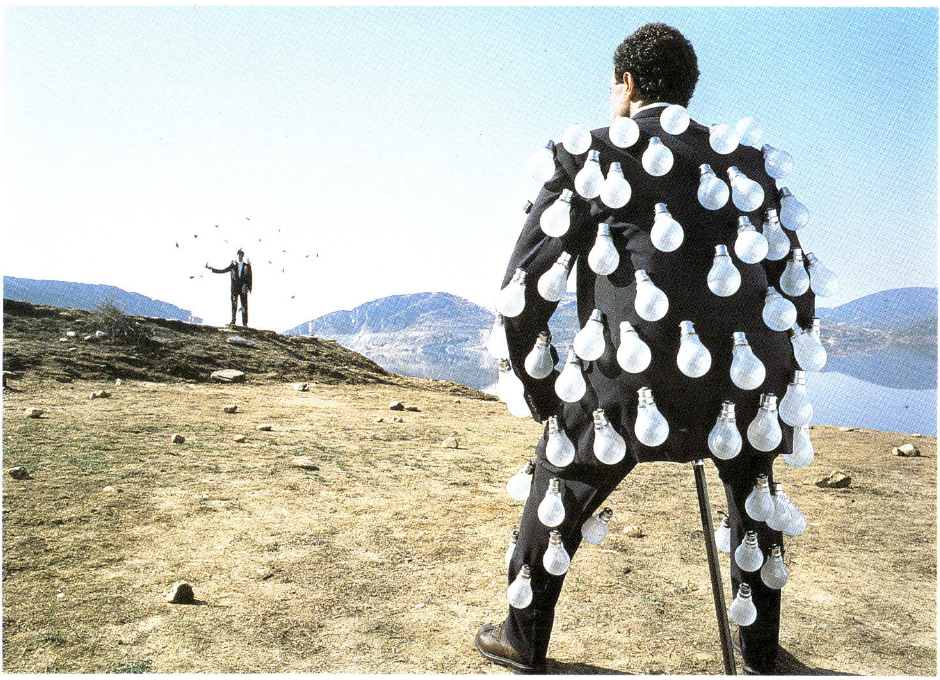

Pink Floyd Record Cover, Andy Earl

Co Galway, John Freeman

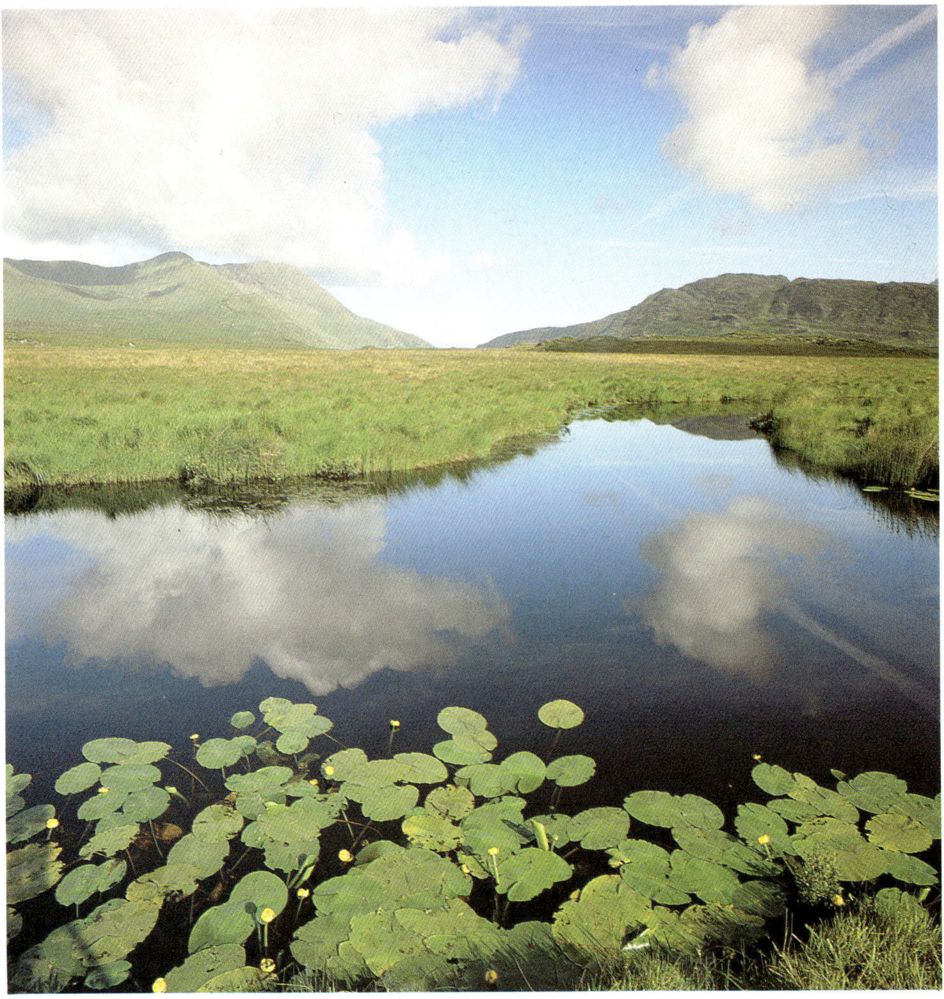

Attaching the Speed Grip S

1. Remove the camera wind crank by withdrawing the rod attachment pin until the crank is released.
2. Take off the flash sync cover on the camera's base-plate. The detached cover should be stored on the holding pins on the base of the grip.
3. Align the guide pins on the front end of the grip's base with the guide on the base of the camera.
4. When correctly located, stroke the film lever so that the winding connector mates with the attachment rod of the camera body.
5. When aligned push the grip fully into place and tighten the base screw.

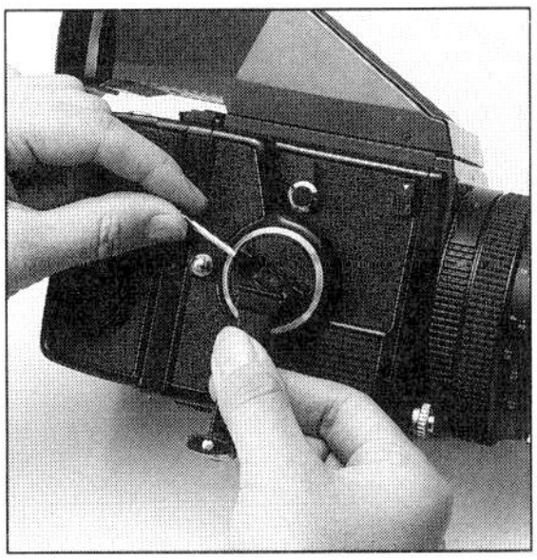

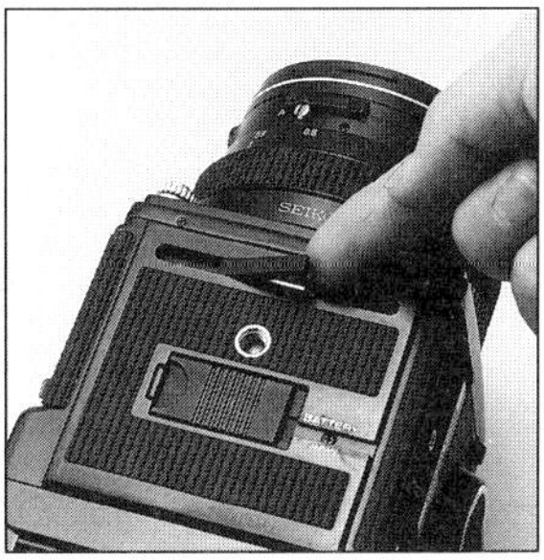

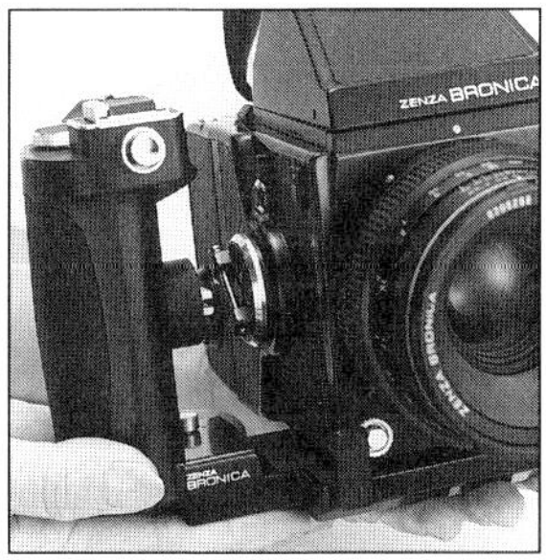

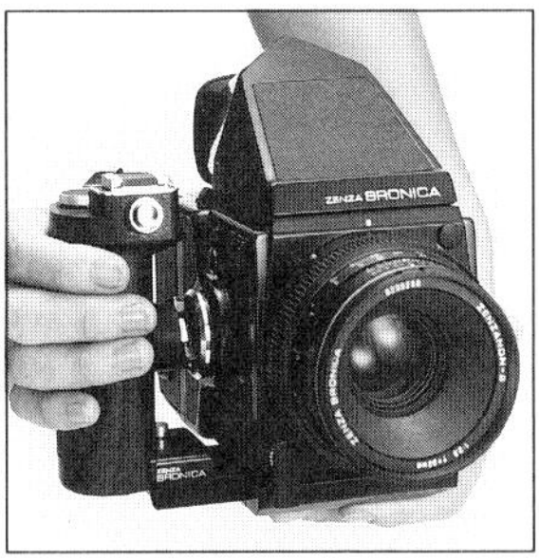

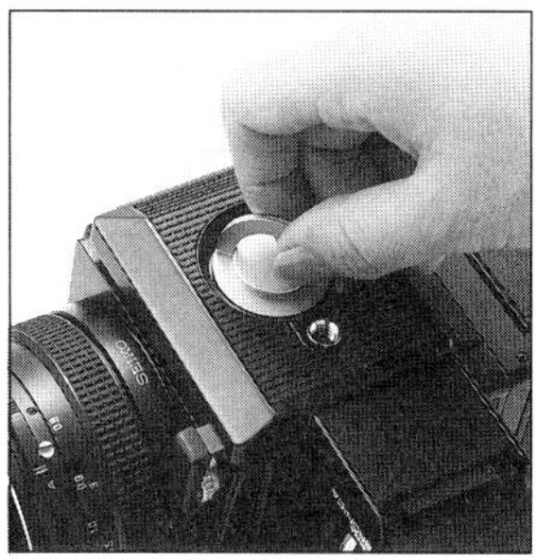

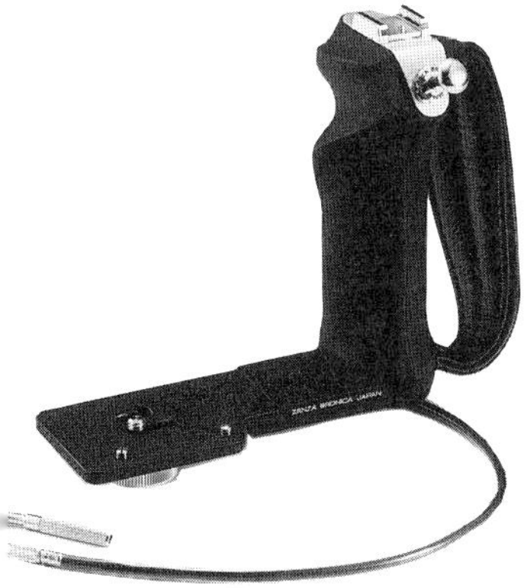

L-Grip E

This is the same grip as that for the Bronica ETRS. Although suitable for the SQ-A it should not be used on the SQ-Am because it lacks a conventional screw-in cable release. The grip attaches via a screw-in bush which locates in the camera's tripod socket. Film advance is conducted in the usual manner but the shutter is released using a cable release which screws into the camera's threaded socket. A flash shoe fitting is provided but this is not a hot-shoe.

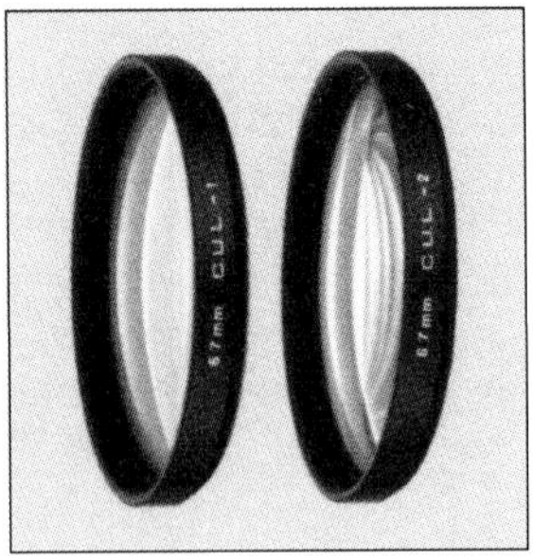

CLOSE-UP ACCESSORIES

Close-up filters

Two 67mm screw-in close-up filters are available to fit Zenzanon-S lenses from 65mm to 250mm. Used singly or in combination, these filters allow a closer minimum focusing distance than normal. No exposure compensation is necessary. Extension tubes or the Automatic Bellows Attachment-S are recommended if greater magnification is required.

Zenzanon-S \ C.U.L.	No. 1		No. 2		No. 1 + No. 2	
	Magnification	Area Covered (cm)	Magnification	Area Covered (cm)	Magnification	Area Covered (cm)
80mm	0.12 ~ 0.26	44.8 ~ 21.4	0.25 ~ 0.39	22.3 ~ 14.3	0.37 ~ 0.51	15.0 ~ 10.9
50mm	0.08 ~ 0.21	73.7 ~ 25.9	0.15 ~ 0.29	36.7 ~ 19.3	0.22 ~ 0.36	24.7 ~ 15.6
105mm	0.16 ~ 0.33	35.7 ~ 16.8	0.31 ~ 0.50	17.8 ~ 11.1	0.46 ~ 0.66	12.0 ~ 8.4
150mm	0.22 ~ 0.37	25.3 ~ 15.1	0.44 ~ 0.62	12.6 ~ 9.0	0.65 ~ 0.85	8.5 ~ 6.5
200mm	0.29 ~ 0.42	19.0 ~ 13.2	0.59 ~ 0.75	9.4 ~ 7.4	0.87 ~ 1.07	6.4 ~ 5.2
250mm	0.36 ~ 0.51	15.3 ~ 10.8	0.73 ~ 0.93	7.6 ~ 6.0	1.09 ~ 1.33	5.1 ~ 4.2

Automatic Extension Tubes S

Two fully coupled automatic extension tubes of 18mm and 36mm respectively are available for the SQ system, and are fully compatible with all Zenzanon-S lenses. Contained in each tube are the mechanical and electrical linkages that enable automatic diaphragm operation and through-the-lens metering when a meter finder is in use. Only one tube can be used at any one time; they cannot be used in tandem for greater magnification. The Automatic Bellows Attachment-S is advised for greater magnification.

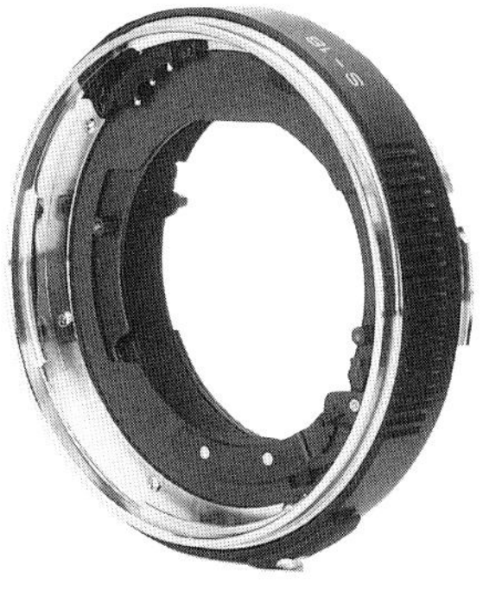

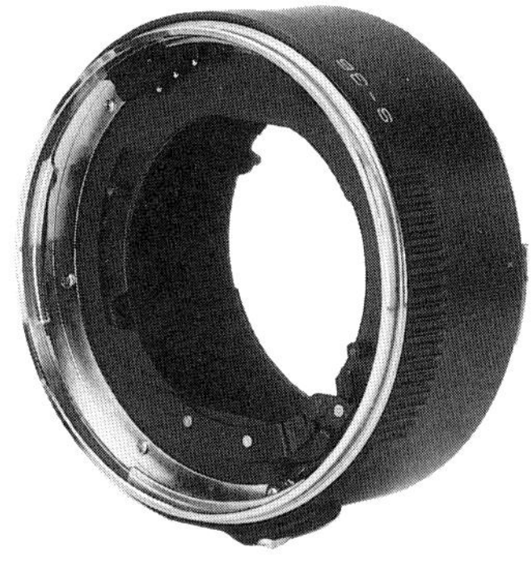

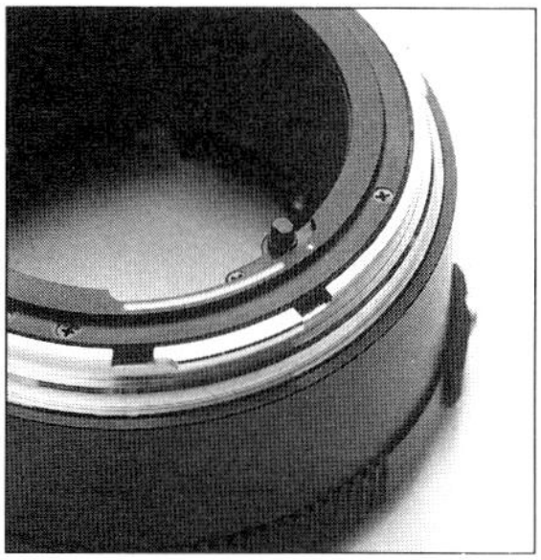

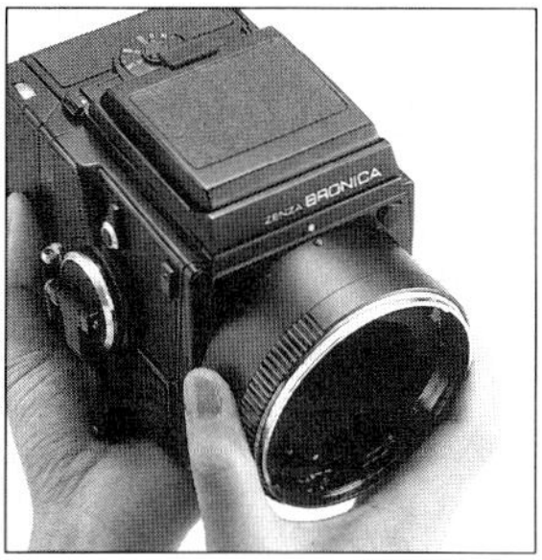

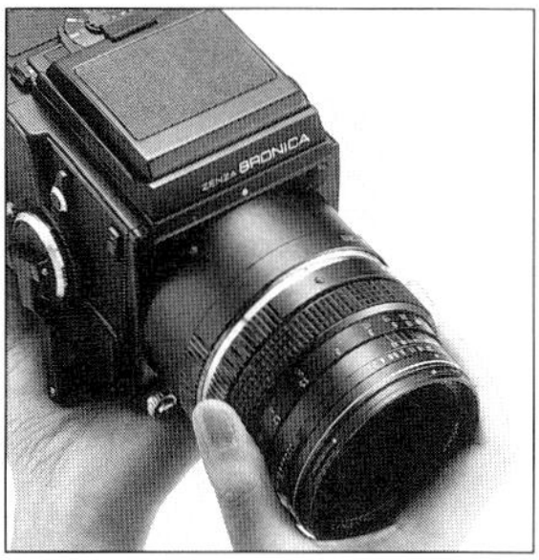

Using extension tubes

A light loss is caused by fitting an extension tube and this has to be accounted for when calculating exposure. With a separate lightmeter the meter reading has to be multiplied by the exposure factor (see table below). For operational convenience, and because both tubes are fully coupled, if a meter finder can be used exposure calculation is straightforward and no correction is necessary.

There are two methods of assembling the camera, lens and tube. You can either assemble the lens and tube and then fit the combination on the body, or the tube can be fitted to the body and then the lens mounted. The important thing to remember is that all three components have to be fully cocked. On the tube, the cocking pins on its rear-plate should be aligned opposite their respective green dots. If not they can be cocked by revolving them by hand. The process of attaching a tube is the same as that of fitting a lens directly on to the body.

As with fitting there are two methods of detaching the tube and lens assembly and the process itself is similar to removing a lens: first cock the camera, then slide the tube's lens release button and rotate the lens 30 degrees clockwise. The tube can now be detached by operating the camera's lens release button. Alternatively detach the lens and tube combination and divide them off the camera.

	S-18				S-36			
Lenses	Magnification	Area Covered (cm)	Focusing Distance (cm)	Exposure Factor	Magnification	Area Covered (cm)	Focusing Distance (cm)	Exposure Factor
80mm	0.22	25.7 × 25.7	56.4	1.4	0.43	12.8 × 12.8	39.0	1.9
	0.36	15.6 × 15.6	42.5	1.7	0.57	9.7 × 9.7	35.4	2.3
40mm	0.43	12.8 × 12.8	25.1	1.4	0.87	6.4 × 6.4	22.1	2.0
	0.62	8.9 × 8.9	23.0	1.7	1.06	5.3 × 5.3	22.0	2.2
50mm	0.36	15.6 × 15.6	30.0	1.4	0.71	7.8 × 7.8	24.7	1.9
	0.51	10.9 × 10.9	26.5	1.6	0.87	6.4 × 6.4	24.2	2.2
105mm	0.17	32.2 × 32.2	82.0	1.4	0.35	16.1 × 16.1	53.6	1.8
	0.35	15.8 × 15.8	53.1	1.8	0.52	10.6 × 10.6	45.1	2.3
150mm	0.12	45.4 × 45.4	151.0	1.4	0.24	22.7 × 22.7	92.8	1.9
	0.25	22.3 × 22.3	91.8	1.9	0.37	14.9 × 14.9	74.2	2.4
200mm	0.09	60.7 × 60.7	259.0	1.4	0.18	30.4 × 30.4	154.0	1.9
	0.19	29.0 × 29.0	149.0	1.9	0.28	19.6 × 19.6	118.0	2.5
250mm	0.07	75.4 × 75.4	388.0	1.3	0.15	37.7 × 37.7	224.0	1.7
	0.18	31.0 × 31.0	196.0	1.9	0.25	22.0 × 22.0	158.0	2.3

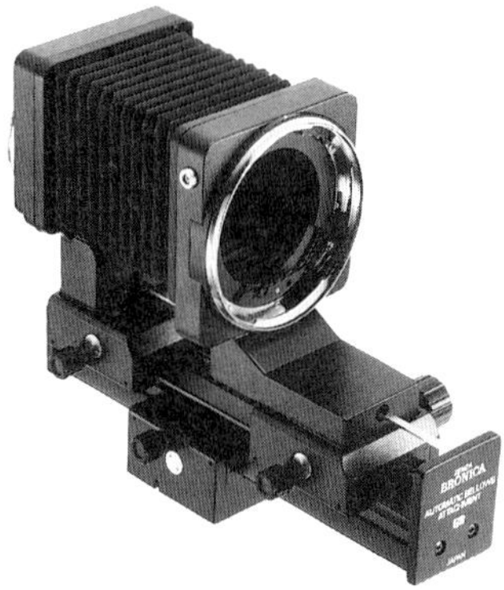

AUTOMATIC BELLOWS ATTACHMENT-S

Extreme close-up photography is possible with this unit; it has a maximum extension of 155mm and a minimum of 55mm. Like the extension tubes, this bellows unit has the appropriate electrical and mechanical connections necessary for automatic diaphragm coupling. Therefore through-the-lens metering capability is retained if an SQ meter finder is fitted.

Attaching the bellows unit

The lens, camera shutter and bellows must be fully cocked before they can be fitted together. The cocking pins of the bellows may be cocked by rotating them until the pins align with the green dots. Attach the bellows to the camera first using the same method as mounting a lens and then fit the lens on to the bellows unit.

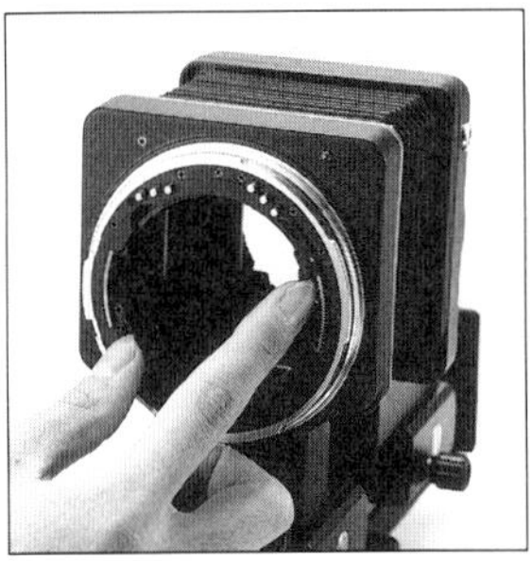

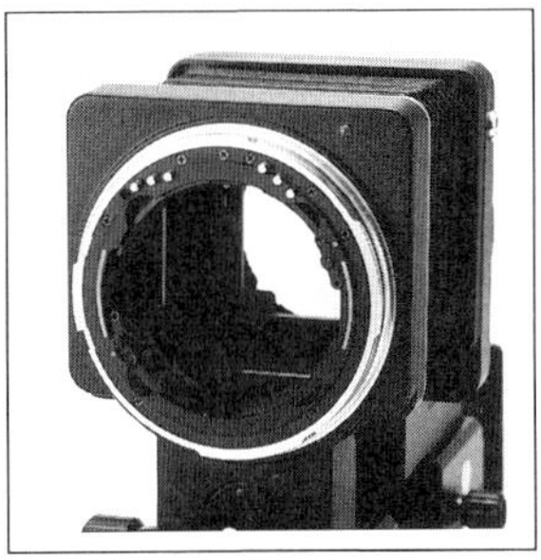

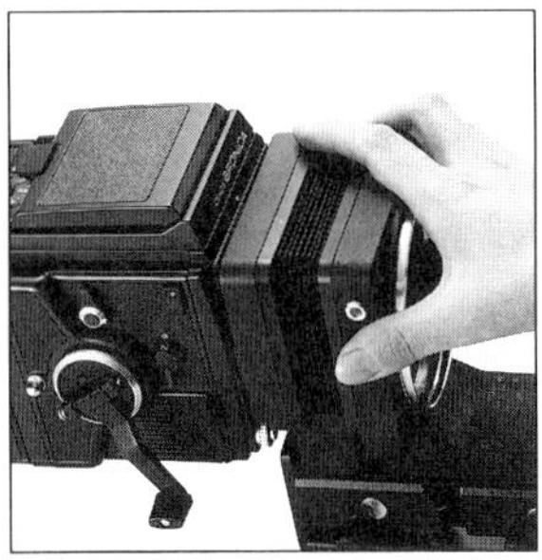

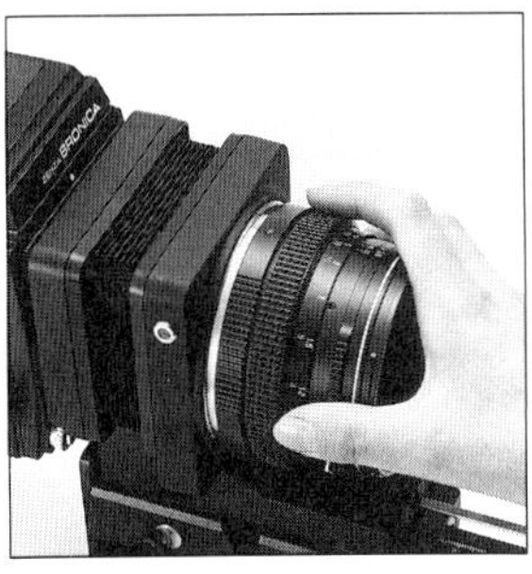

Detaching the bellows unit

Operate the wind crank to ensure that the camera is cocked. The lens can be removed by depressing the lens release button and rotating it in a clockwise direction. The bellows can now be detached employing a similar method. As the bellows unit is separated from the camera body its cocking pins will release; these pins can be recocked manually.

Using the bellows unit

At its minimum the bellows unit gives an extension of 55mm; with the bellows fully racked out the maximum is 155mm. To determine the amount of extension being used a scale is provided on the bellows rail; the difference between the two readings gives the total extension.

Focusing should be performed with great care. Not only is the viewfinder image relatively dim when the bellows unit is in use, there is also strictly limited depth of field. To make the most of the depth of field select the smallest aperture possible. A tripod and cable release should be used for the optimum picture quality.

If flash lighting is used the flash unit's cable must be plugged into the co-axial socket on the bellows; if the camera's terminal is used the flash will not fire.

The meter finders available in the SQ system are especially recommended for metering convenience as obtained meter readings can be used without modification. When using a separate hand-meter, compensation must be applied according to the exposure factor listed in the table below.

Zenzanon-S	Magnification	Area Covered Length of One Side (cm)	Focusing Distance (cm)	Exposure Factor
80mm	0.64 ~ 1.98	8.72 ~ 2.81	34.5 ~ 36.8	2.4 ~ 7.6
50mm	1.05 ~ 3.18	5.30 ~ 1.75	24.1 ~ 31.7	2.5 ~ 7.5
105mm	0.51 ~ 1.65	10.9 ~ 3.38	45.6 ~ 43.3	2.3 ~ 7.1
150mm	0.36 ~ 1.17	15.4 ~ 4.76	7.53 ~ 58.9	2.4 ~ 7.6
200mm	0.27 ~ 0.88	20.6 ~ 6.33	120.9 ~ 82.3	2.4 ~ 7.6
250mm	0.22 ~ 0.73	25.6 ~ 7.59	172.7 ~ 106.3	2.1 ~ 6.4

Bronica GS-1

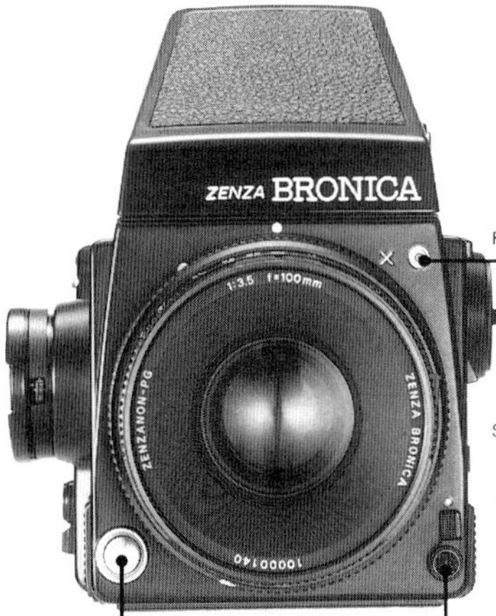

Flash synch socket
AE finder contacts
Shutter speed dial
Shutter speed scale window
Screen removal lever (left)
Shutter release button
Mirror lock-up lever

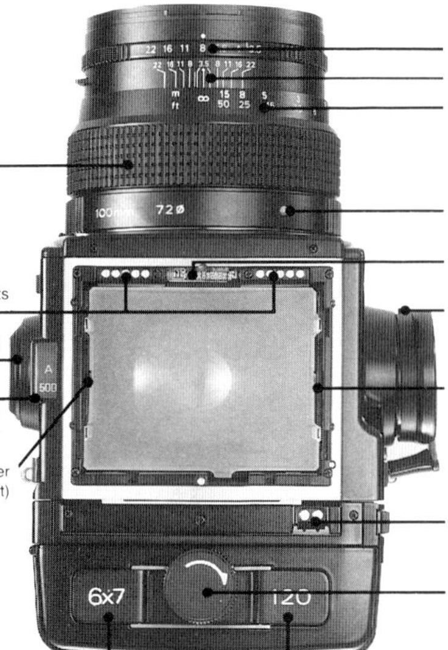

Aperture ring
Depth of field sca
Distance scales
Focusing ring
Lens alignment d
LED display plate
Film winding cran
assembly release
Screen removal le
(right)
ASA/ISO film spe
contacts
Manual film winde
Spool holder

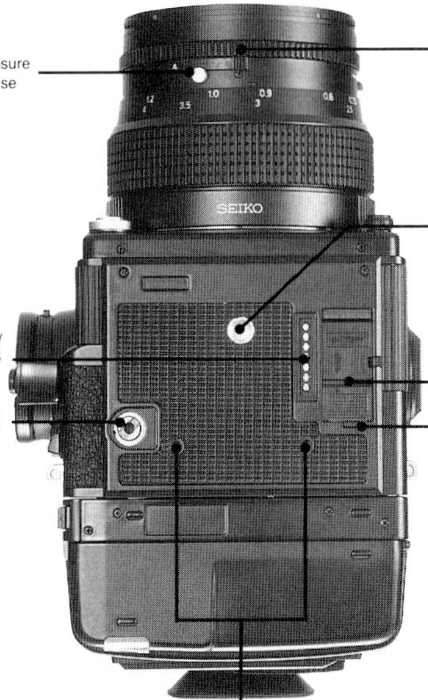

Time exposure lever release
Time exposure lever
Tripod socket
Accessory contacts
Film winding coupler
Battery chamber cover
Battery chamber button
ASA/ISO film speed scale
ASA/ISO film speed dial lock button
Accessory guide sockets

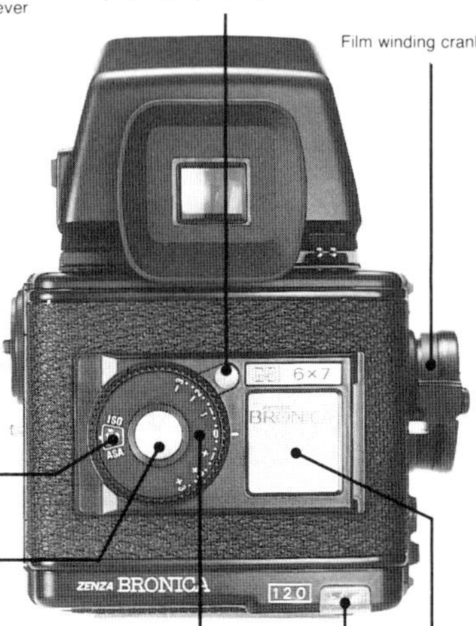

Exposure compensation dial lock button
Film winding crank assembly
Exposure compensation dial
Exposure counter window
Film type indicator frame

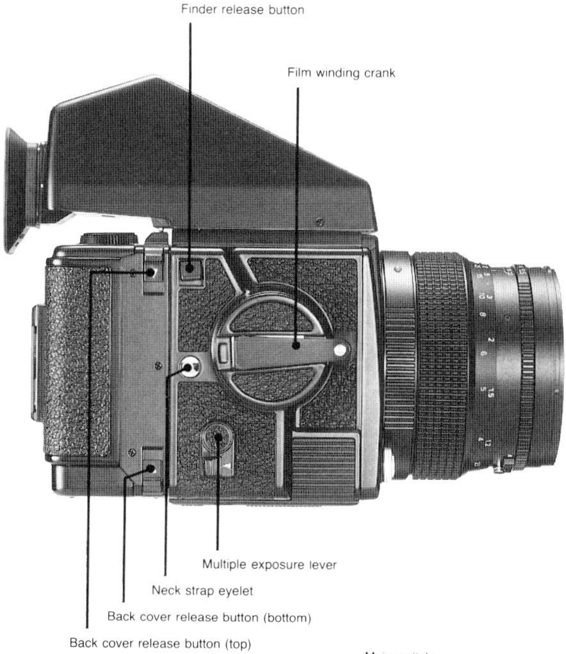
Finder release button
Film winding crank
Multiple exposure lever
Neck strap eyelet
Back cover release button (bottom)
Back cover release button (top)

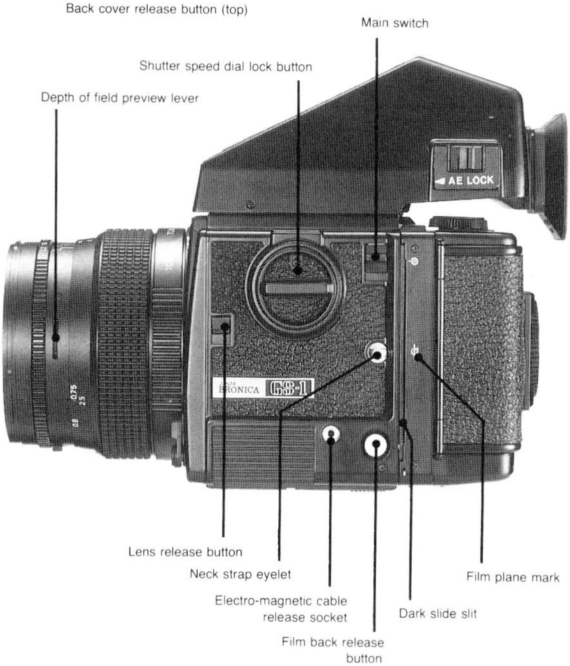
Main switch
Shutter speed dial lock button
Depth of field preview lever
AE LOCK
BRONICA
GS-1
Lens release button
Neck strap eyelet
Electro-magnetic cable
release socket
Film back release
button
Dark slide slit
Film plane mark

Chapter Eleven Bronica GS-1

The Bronica GS-1 was introduced in 1983 and although designed primarily for 6 × 7cm photography, it has multiple format capability and 6 × 4.5cm and 6 × 6cm formats may be utilised. The GS-1 also incorporates a host of high technology features including the option of through-the-lens flash metering with the Speed-Light G1.

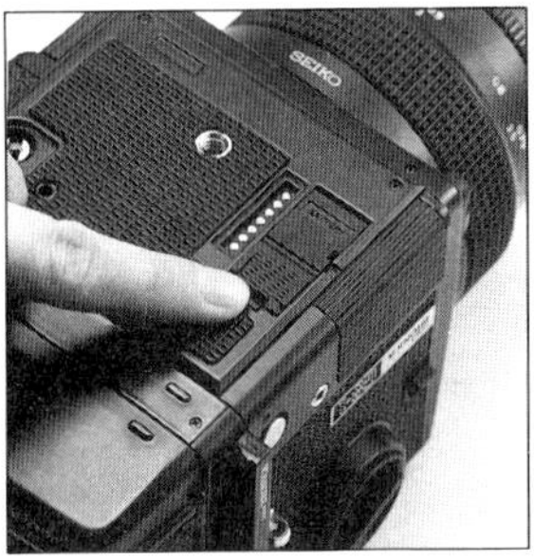

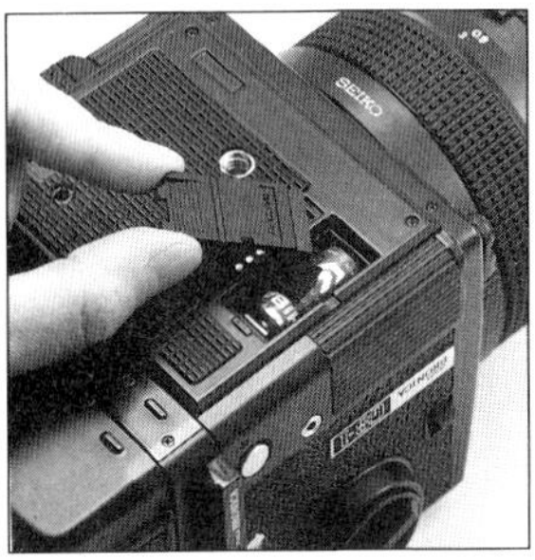

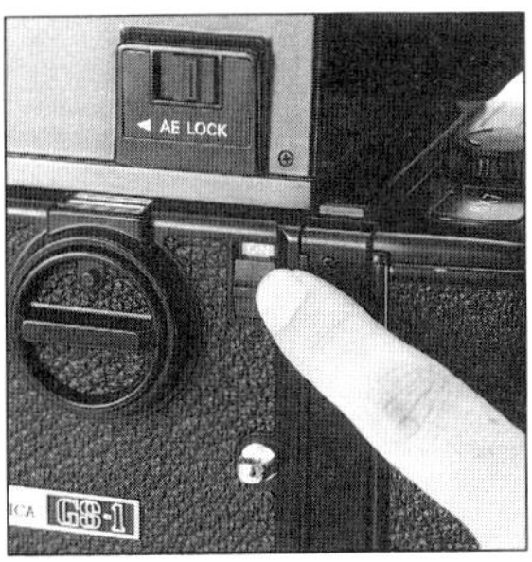

THE BATTERY

The GS-1 has an electronically controlled shutter linked to an electro-magnetic release system. The camera needs a six volt PX-28 type battery to function fully. Check the battery regularly and keep spares available. A fresh battery should last for about a year if no meter finder is used, but if one is employed life expectancy drops to between six and 12 months.

If the battery does fail two mechanical shutter settings of 'T' (Time exposure) and 1/500 sec are available; in both instances the shutter has to be fired by operating the mirror lock-up lever, not the camera's shutter release.

Loading the battery

To gain access to the battery chamber depress the cover's release catch while simultaneously sliding it in the direction of the lens. This will free the cover which can now be pulled from the body. Insert the battery according to the polarity markings in the chamber before replacing the cover.

Located on the upper left of the camera body is its main on/off switch which has a red-coloured indicator to show that the camera is on. Nothing functions until the camera is switched on though no power is consumed until the shutter release is partially depressed. Switch the camera off if it is not to be used for some time.

Partially depressing the shutter button will cause a red LED in the viewfinder to glow steadily or flicker, according to which finder is attached; thus confirming that the battery is working. When using Waist Level Finder G the battery check LED will not light when the shutter button is semi-depressed

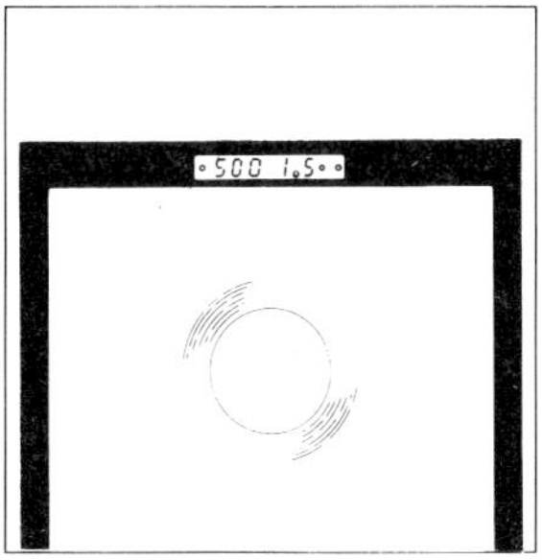

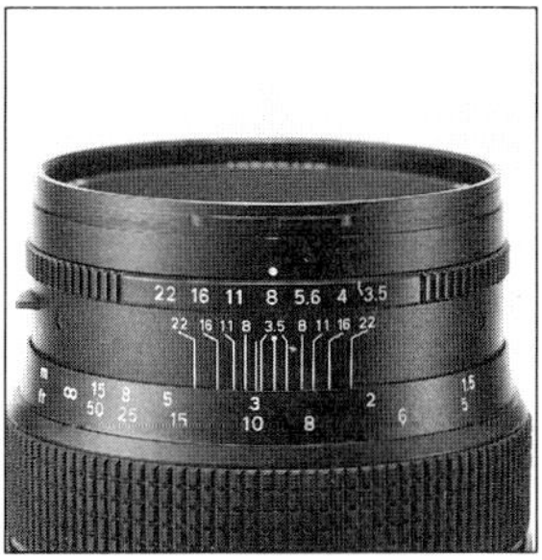

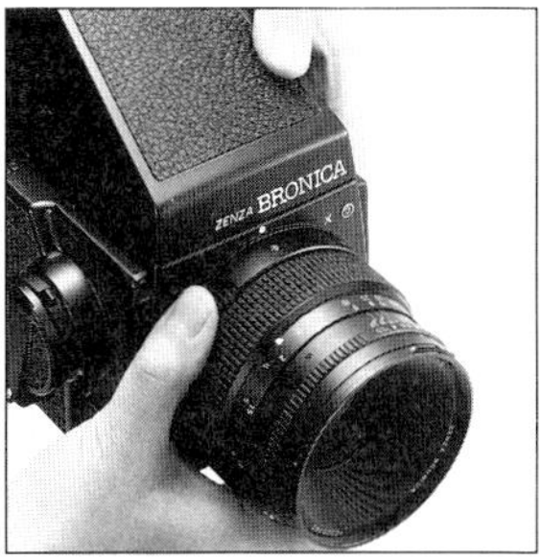

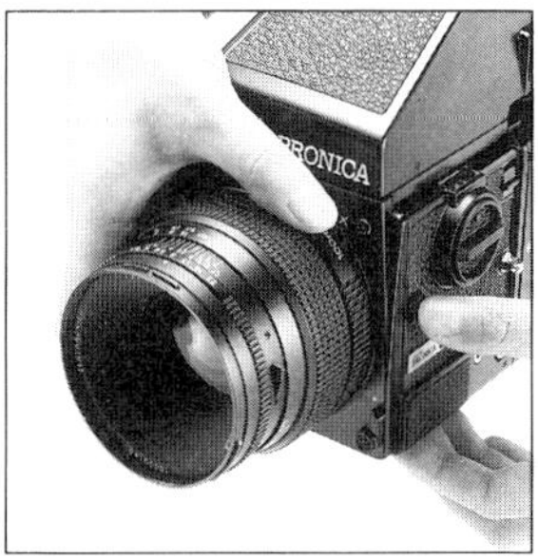

unless the dark slide is inserted. Attach the Prism Finder G and the shutter speed LED will blink and the battery check LED glow steadily if the dark slide is in. If there is no confirmation signal change the battery or check its loading.

Battery performance can be adversely affected by freezing temperatures and the Remote Camera Battery Pack E is recommended in such conditions. This unit connects to the camera via an extension lead and the compartment containing the battery can be stored in a warm pocket.

GS-1 LENSES

Every Zenzanon-PG lens incorporates a between-the-lens leaf shutter with a speed range of 16 seconds to 1/500 sec plus 'T' (Time exposure), 'B' (Bulb) and 'A'. The last-mentioned setting is employed when one of the GS-1's metering finders is fitted and used in aperture-priority auto-exposure mode; if 'A' is engaged with a non-metering finder fitted an exposure of 16 seconds is given. Settings other than those click-stopped should not be selected.

The aperture ring on PG-lenses is click-stopped in half-stop intervals. Each lens is equipped with a spring loaded depth of field control; this is useful for examining the effects of a creative filter or a specific aperture. During use with a meter finder the depth of field control must not be operated at the same time as taking a meter reading otherwise over-exposure will result.

Depth of field indications, infrared focusing index, and distance scales in both feet and metres are marked on the lens barrel.

Lens mounting

For lenses to be attached or detached the shutter and lens must be cocked. The shutter is cocked if the reflex mirror is in a 'down' position and providing a normal viewing image. If not, rotate the wind crank once to cock the shutter. A quick glance at the len's rear panel will tell you whether the lens is cocked: the single cocking pin should be at a point between the red line and the green dot. The lens may be cocked manually.

To mount the lens match the red dot on the lens with the white dot on the body flange. Insert and rotate the lens 30 degrees in an anti-clockwise direction until a 'click' confirms correct fitting.

Detaching a lens requires that the lens release button be operated at the same time as twisting the lens in a clockwise direction until it can be pulled clear of the body. If the shutter is not cocked the release button cannot be depressed.

There is a reason why the lens cannot be detached while the shutter is uncocked: the mirror and light baffle would be in an 'up' position and if the lens were to be removed at this point the film would be fogged.

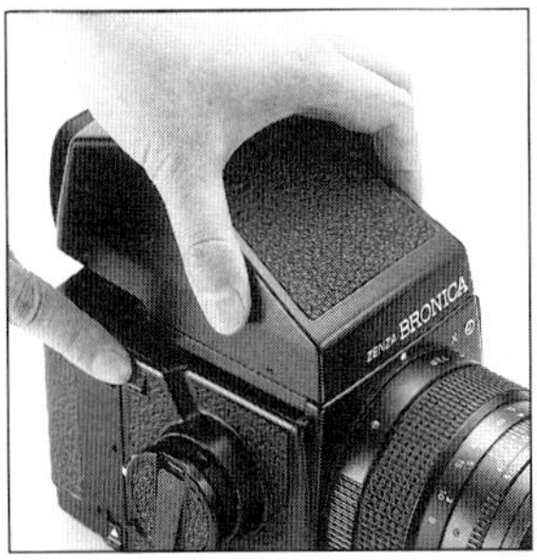

INTERCHANGEABLE FINDERS

The GS-1 system is endowed with four interchangeable finders and since one is not supplied as standard you have the choice. Specifications are discussed in Chapter Thirteen.

Fitting a finder

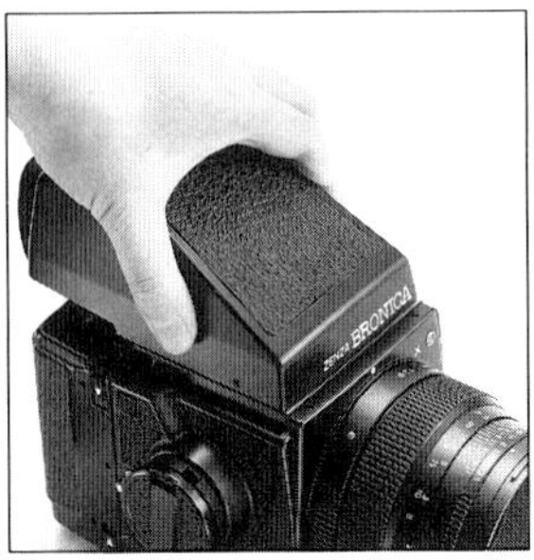

Align the front end of the unit with the leading edge of the finder frame, seating it so that its four lugs are located in their corresponding holes. At this point the finder should be flush with the body and pushing it forward will secure finder attachment. The finder can be removed only by first pressing the finder release button.

Before attaching a metering finder carefully wipe the gold-plated contacts visible on the unit's base and camera body with a soft, dry cloth. Dirty contacts can interfere with correct metering operation.

FOCUS SCREENS

Seven user-changeable focus screen designs are offered in the GS-1 system. The supplied screen has a plain matte finish; it should be noted that if you are using the GS-1's AE Rotary Finder G the spot meter function operates only with this screen.

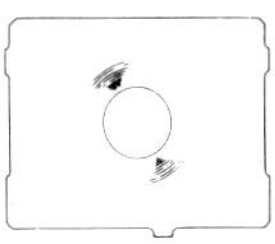

Matte (Standard type)

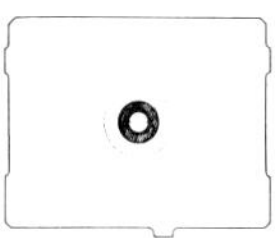

Microprism/Split-Image

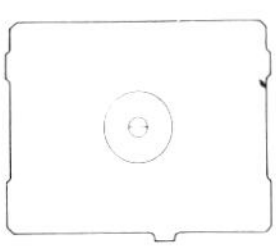

Split-Image

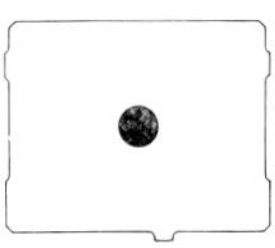

Microprism

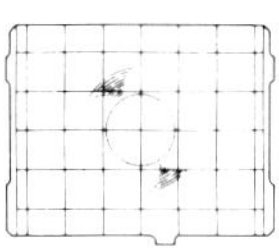

Grid-lines

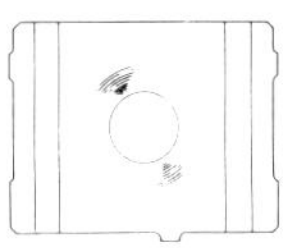

Matte (for 6×6 & 6×4.5 formats)

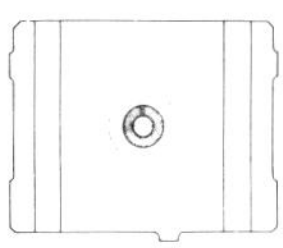

Microprism/Split-image (for 6×6 & 6×4.5 formats)

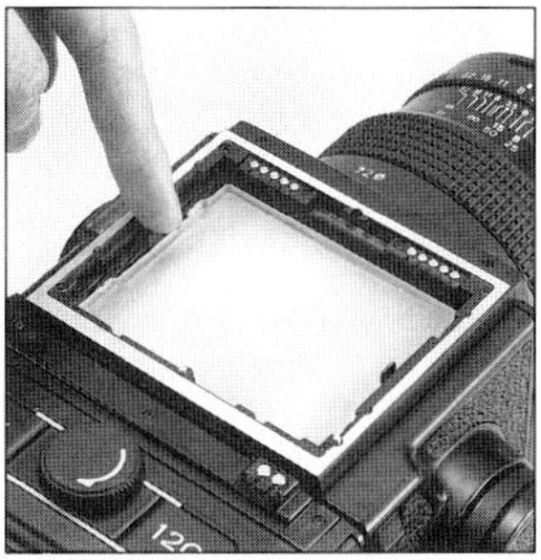

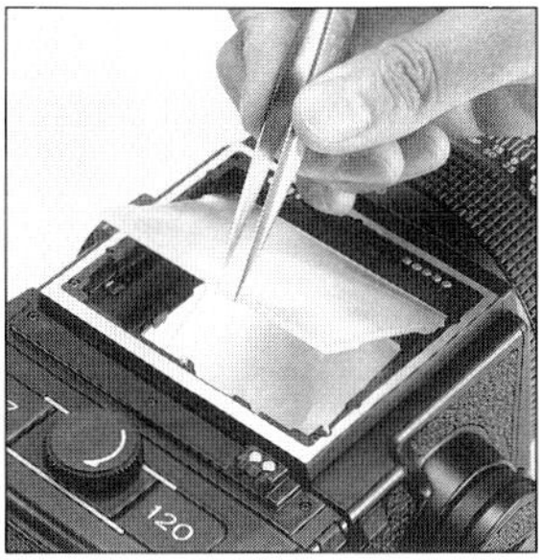

Changing focus screen

First remove the finder following the procedure outlined previously. Two sliding catches, one on each side, hold the focus screen in position. Slide these catches towards the rear of the camera and you will be able to lift the screen out using tweezers to grip the lug along its bottom edge. Alternatively, tip the camera upside-down and the screen will drop out.

Insert the replacement carefully so that its lug corresponds with the gap in the camera body. It is important to return the holding levers to their original positions for two reasons; firstly to hold the screen in place and secondly, if the levers are not back in position the finder cannot be re-attached.

INTERCHANGEABLE FILM BACKS

The Bronica GS-1 has a fully interchangeable film back facility making it possible to change from film to film in mid-roll. Furthermore, with the variety of backs featured in the GS-1 system it is possible to change from format to format. In addition to 6 × 7cm, the formats on offer are 6 × 6cm and 6 × 4.5cm; film backs are available for all three formats in both 120 and 220 roll film sizes. A Polaroid Land film back is also available and its operation is discussed in Chapter Fourteen.

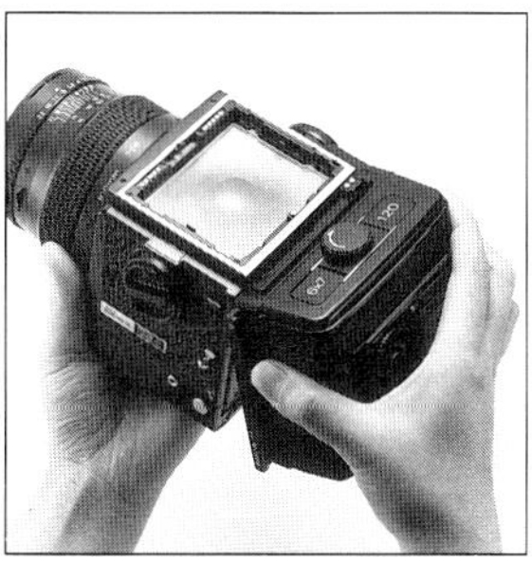

GS-1 film backs in operation

To fit a film back marry up the back's two hinge lugs with the matching holes at the top of the camera back-plate. Then, firmly press the lower end of the film back against the body until it clicks into place. To avoid any risk of the back becoming detached by accidental operation of the film back release button while the camera is being carried around it is best to pull out the dark slide as soon as a back is fitted. As no storage space is provided for the dark slide take care to keep it somewhere safe so that it does not get bent.

The wind crank should be operated every time a film back is attached so that the camera and back are fully coupled. If the crank does not move then the camera and back are prepared for photography. If winding is possible rotate the wind crank until it stops and this will ensure that the shutter is cocked and an unexposed film frame in position.

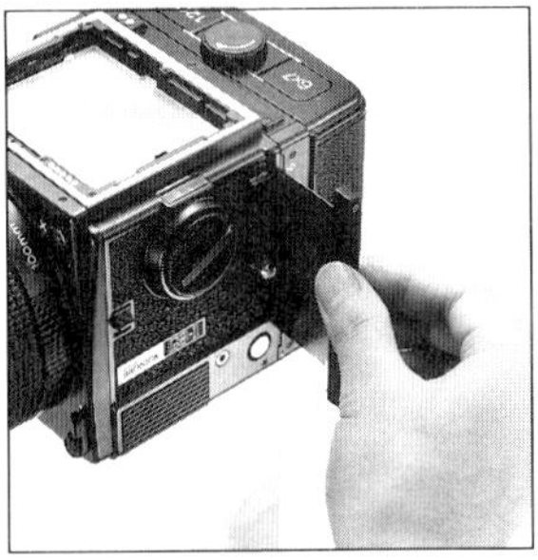

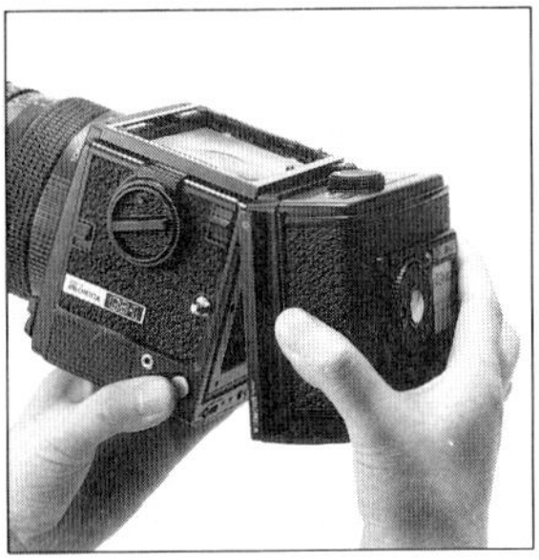

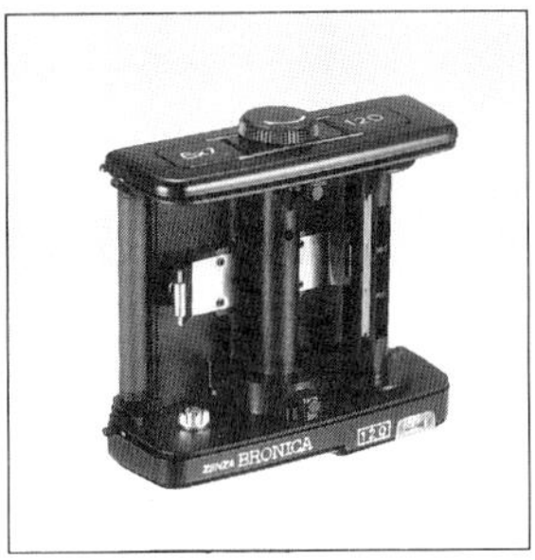

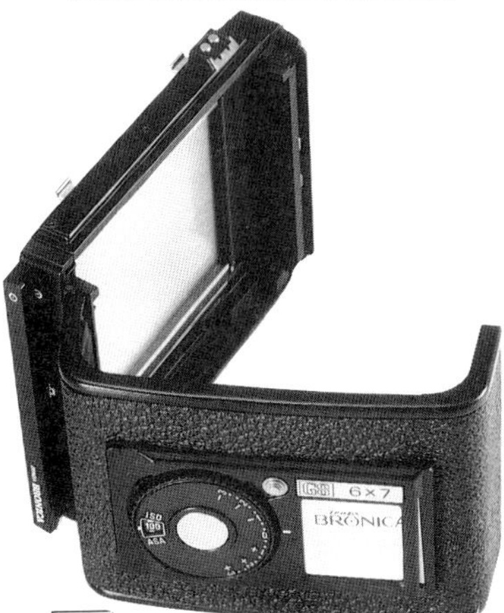

The dark slide has a right and wrong way of insertion: match the dots on the dark slide grip and film back for correct insertion. If it is inserted incorrectly the back cannot be detached but the shutter can be released.

A number of interlock mechanisms concern the dark slide. With the dark slide in place the shutter cannot be fired and a red LED in the viewfinder will light up to warn you when the shutter release is semi-depressed. The dark slide has to be in position before the film back can be detached. When the back is off the body the slide cannot be withdrawn.

To detach a film back first replace the dark slide ensuring that it is the correct way round and pushed fully home. Depress the film back release button and, by pulling its lower end first, the back can be lifted clear of the body.

Film loading

Each film back comprises two components: the film holder containing the spindles for the film spools and a manual film advance mechanism; and the film back frame which houses the dark slide and a combined ISO and exposure compensation dial. This last-named section completely encloses the former.

Pressing the film back's upper and lower buttons on the right side towards one another will make the rear cover spring open and allow the film holder to be pulled free of the back frame.

The film holder has two spindles: the one on the right is for the fresh film, the left is the take-up spool. Film loading should always be conducted in subdued light. Insert a film, remove its securing label entirely and draw the film leader across the pressure plate with its black side facing outwards. Thread the tapered end of the leader into the take-up spool using the manual wind knob to help secure it in position. Continue to rotate the wind knob until the film's start mark lies opposite the red triangular mark on the holder.

Advance to the start mark can also be achieved by using the camera's wind crank: hold the film holder in the film back frame so that it is coupled to the body.

When the start mark has been arrived at close the back cover and operate the wind crank until the number '1' appears in the frame counter window. If you find that operating the crank has no effect on the exposure counter, check that film back is correctly loaded. If it cannot be rotated after one turn, check the multiple exposure lever; it should be pointing downwards, ie not engaged. The manual wind knob can be used to advance the film to the first frame.

After making an exposure, the film wind crank will stop automatically when rotated completely one full turn. This will advance the film to the following frame and cock the shutter ready for the next photograph. If preferred, because of a ratchet mechanism, several short rapid strokes will do the same job.

Each film back has its own combined exposure compensation/ISO control with two contacts which relay information to the metering finder, if one is in use. When a non-metering finder is in operation this dual control has no influence on exposure proceedings.

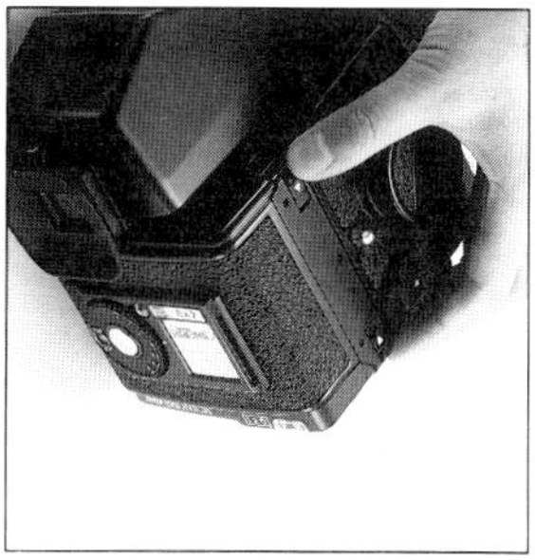

The ISO dial incorporates a locking button which prevents unintentional operation. Adjust speeds by pressing in the central, chrome lock button to release the dial, it can then be set to the desired setting. Film speeds are click-stopped in 1/3 stop increments and a range of ISO 3 to 6400 is featured.

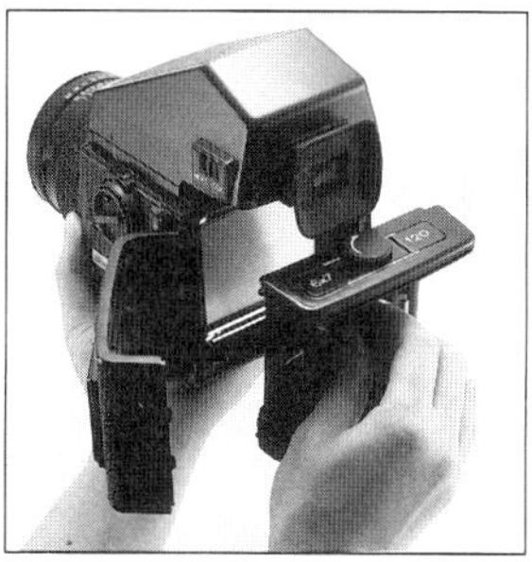

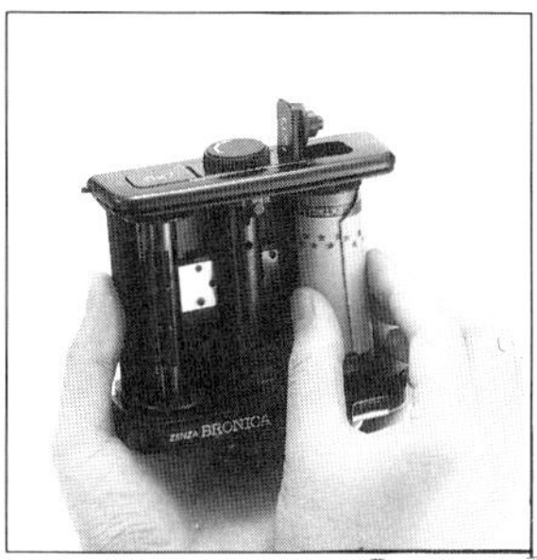

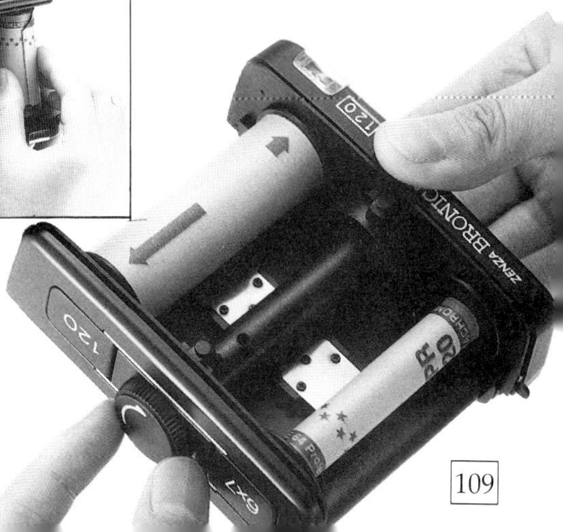

The exposure compensation dial also has a built in lock. To set exposure compensation slide the locking button in the arrow-indicated direction and rotate the dial to the desired setting. Zero the dial and it will automatically stop at the click-stopped '0' value.

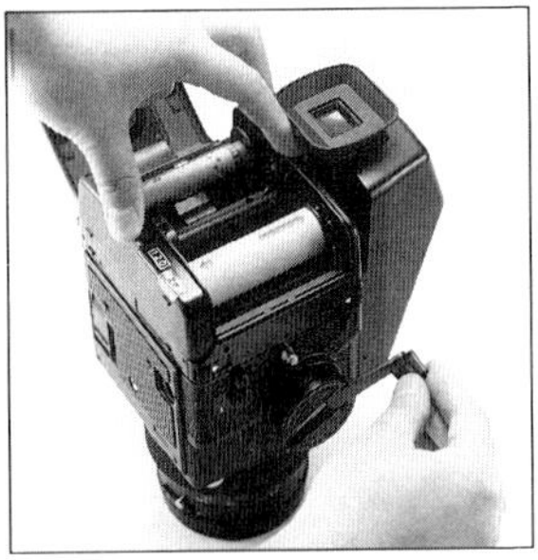

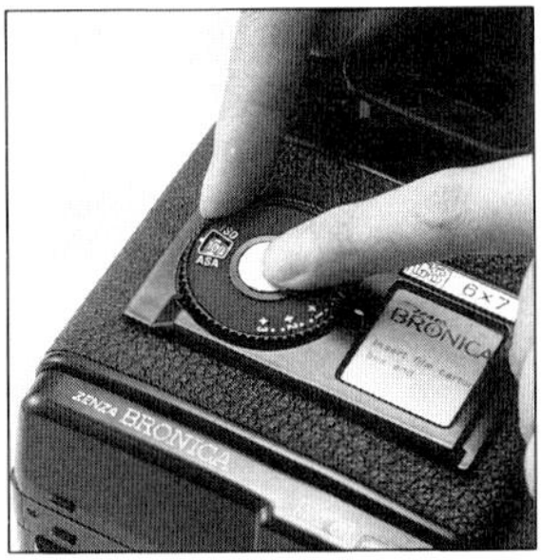

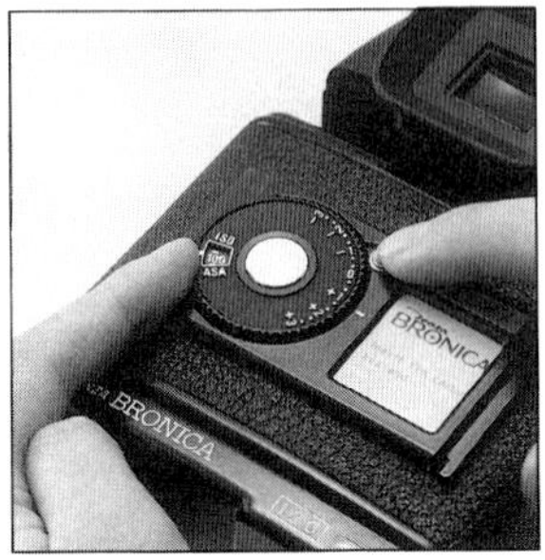

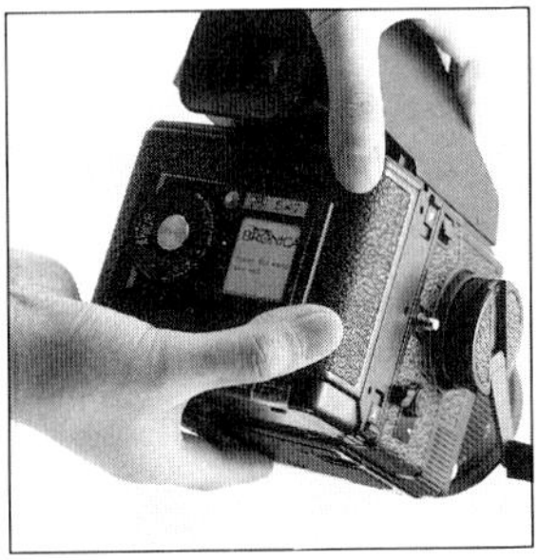

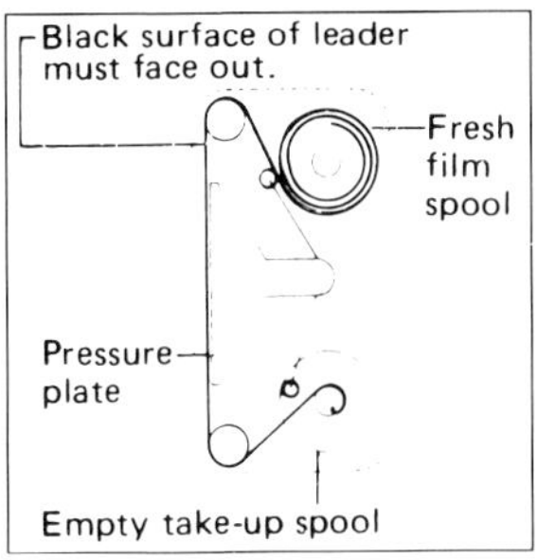

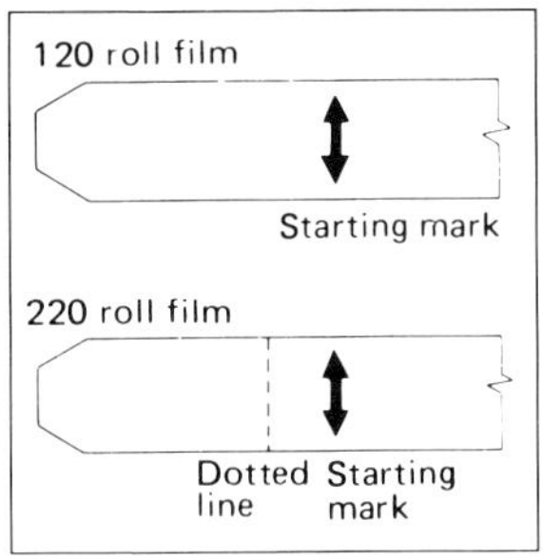

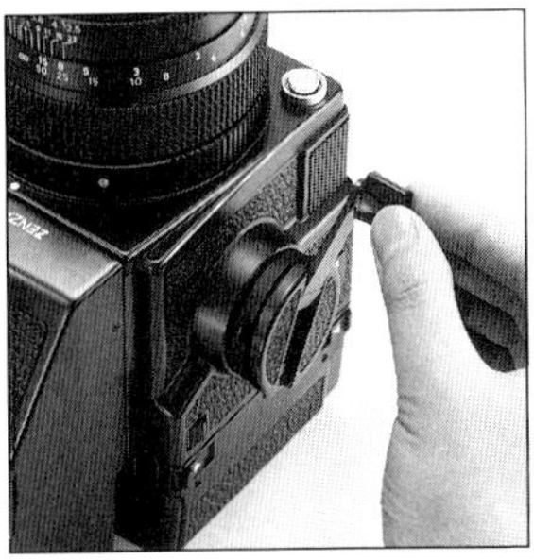

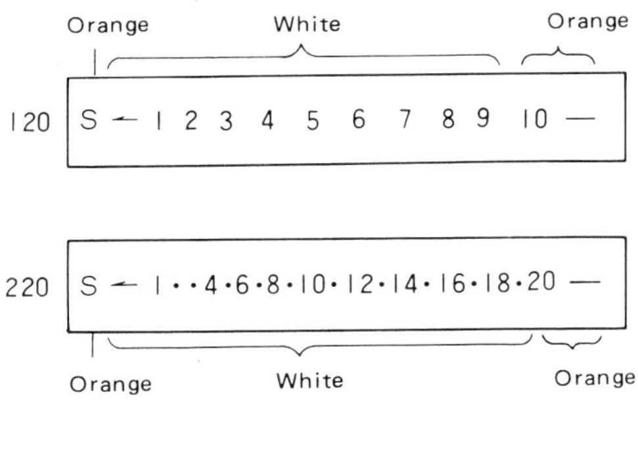

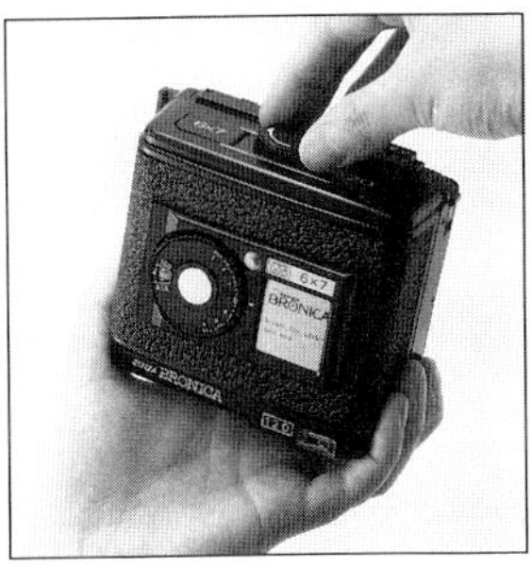

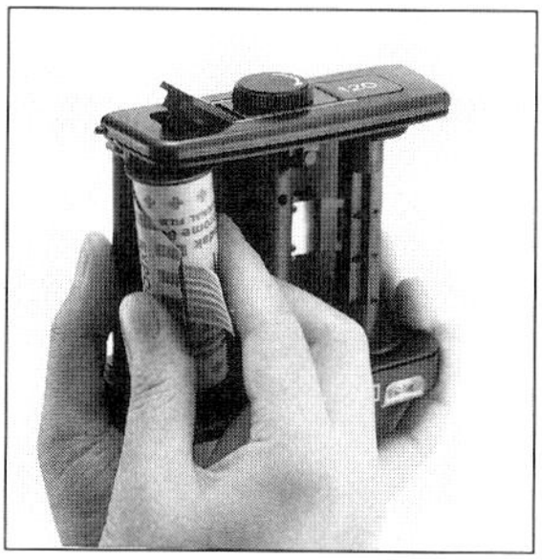

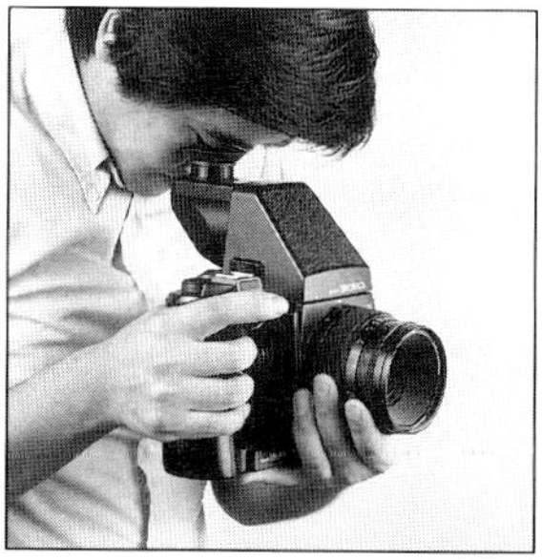

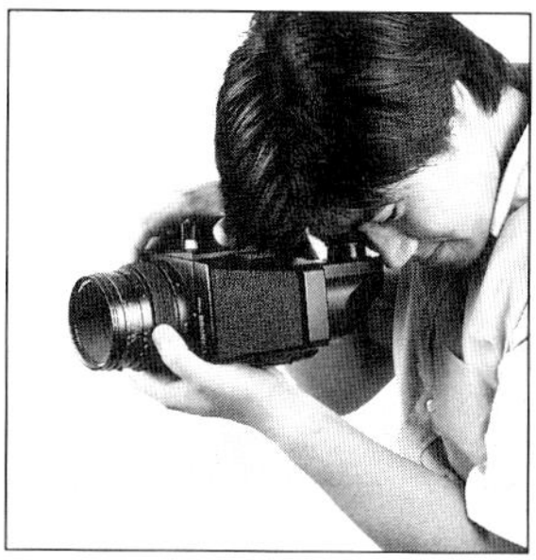

Film unloading

Each roll of 120 film gives 10 exposures on the 6 × 7cm format (20 on 220 film). After the last exposure has been made the wind crank can still be rotated. Operate the crank until a reduction in the effort necessary is noticed. Give a couple more turns to make sure that the film leader has been completely wound off and the back cover may then be opened and the exposed film retrieved. Transfer what was the film's spool to the empty spindle and this will be the take-up spool for the next film.

GS-1 IN ACTION

How you hold and use the GS-1 depends on which system components you own. Typically, for waist level operation, the left hand cradles the camera and the left index finger fires the shutter. This frees the right hand to focus, adjust aperture and wind on. To adjust shutter speed it is best to transfer the camera to the right hand so that this operation can be performed with the left hand.

Shooting horizontal format pictures using the waist level finder is straightforward but, although possible, shooting vertical shots is less convenient because the camera has to be tilted 90 degrees. A waist level finder simply does not lend itself to this and a more practical alternative would be a prism finder. Another option would be to use the Revolving Tripod Adaptor G.

When shooting horizontal pictures with an eye-level prism finder a similar hand-grip to that adopted for waist level operation is desirable, though you might prefer to release the shutter using the right index finger purely because that is more comfortable. Swivel the camera 90 degrees to take a vertical picture and your grip will have to be modified. Again, it is probably most comfortable for the left hand to support the camera leaving shutter firing, focus adjustment and so on to the right.

For optimum handling comfort a combination of the GS-1, a prism finder and the Speed Grip G is difficult to beat. In this instance the right hand takes camera's weight and the right forefinger releases the shutter. The left hand is utilised to change shutter speed, aperture and to focus.

Operating the camera without film

Normally it is not possible to operate the camera unless it is loaded with film. However, by engaging the multiple exposure control it is possible to revolve the wind crank to cock the shutter and release it in usual fashion. All camera functions, apart from the frame exposure counter, behave as normal. Familiarising yourself with the GS-1 is, therefore, possible without loading a film.

Exposing film

The GS-1 as supplied does not have any form of integral metering system. The optional units AE Prism Finder G and the AE Rotary Finder G both have through-the-lens metering and provide aperture-priority auto-exposure and metered manual. See Chapter Thirteen.

Selection of shutter speed is performed using the shutter dial, except during auto-exposure operation, with either of the two above mentioned finders. A window shows three speeds at any one time but it is the middle setting which is the one in use. Shutter speeds are colour-coded: speeds from 1/2 to 1/500 sec plus 'A' and 'B' are white and those from 1 to 16 seconds orange. Depending on the finder and the mode it is in the selected shutter speed can also be seen in the viewfinder. The LED shutter readout disappears as the shutter release is pressed fully home to fire the shutter. If the dark slide has not been withdrawn the shutter is locked and a red LED shows in the viewfinder.

Remote release is possible via the 2.5mm mini-jack plug socket fitted on the shutter dial side of the body. Switch off the camera before plugging in a remote release otherwise the shutter will fire.

Immediately after the shutter has closed a red LED in the viewfinder will blink to indicate successful firing; this LED is the same one that lights up during battery checking. If the LED fails to light up the shutter has been released at its 1/500 sec mechanical speed and the battery needs replacing.

Rotating the wind crank will advance the film to the next frame. During long exposures take care not to operate the crank before the shutter has closed. If

Blue Nude, Nigel Holmes

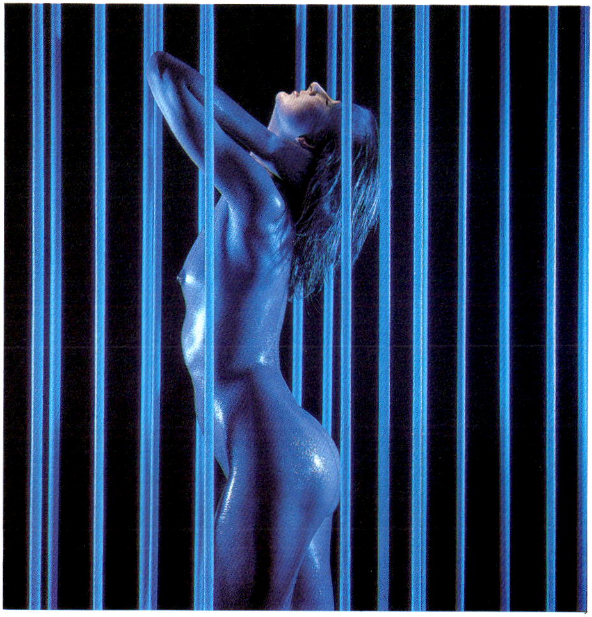

Ski Calendar Shot, John Shire

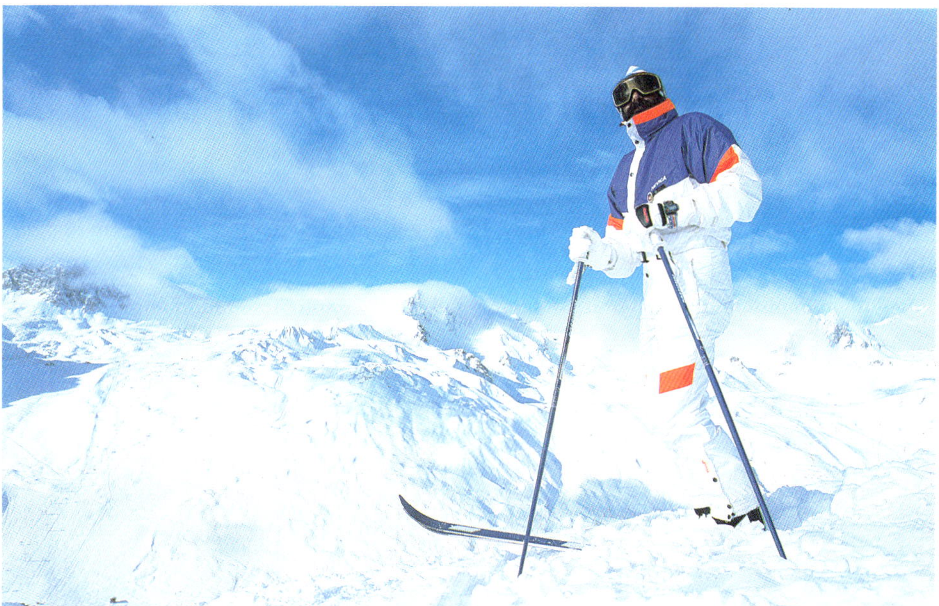

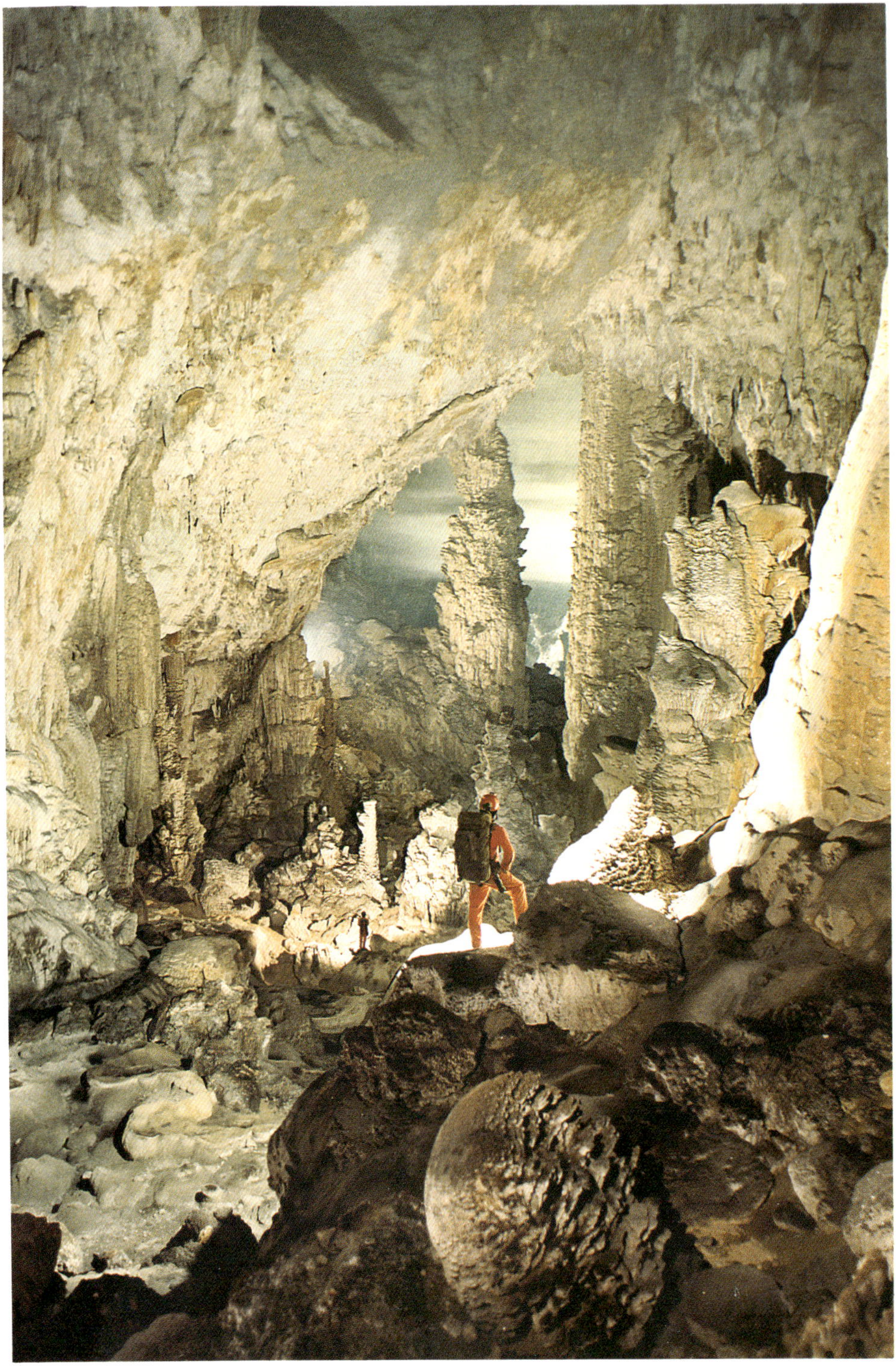

Beimo Cave, Jerry Wooldridge

you do, the shutter will close with the result that the exposure is terminated prematurely. In addition there are side-effects. There is the risk that, because the film is advanced slightly before the shutter closes, the shot you have just taken will be blurred and the following frame partially exposed. Also you will notice that the shutter cannot be released until after the original set shutter time has elapsed. Finally, the following exposure will be made at a shutter speed of 1/500 sec. Therefore, while shooting long exposures always keep an eye on the confirmation LED before proceeding to wind on the film.

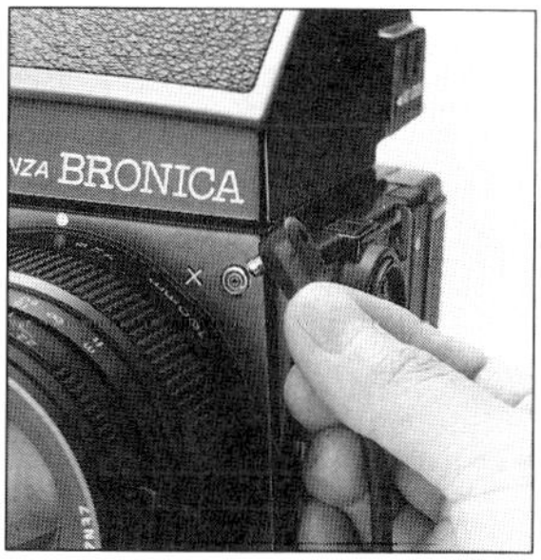

Flash photography

Electronic X-flash synchronisation at all shutter speeds is possible with the between-the-lens leaf shutters incorporated into Zenzanon-PG lenses. M and F flash bulb synchronisation are also possible but with a limited range of shutter speeds, as outlined in the table below.

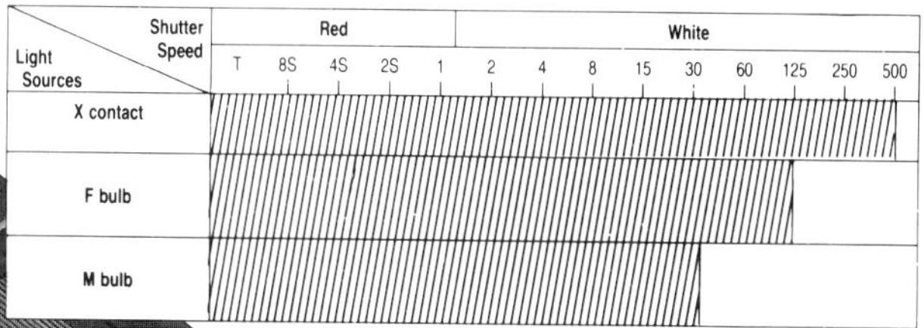

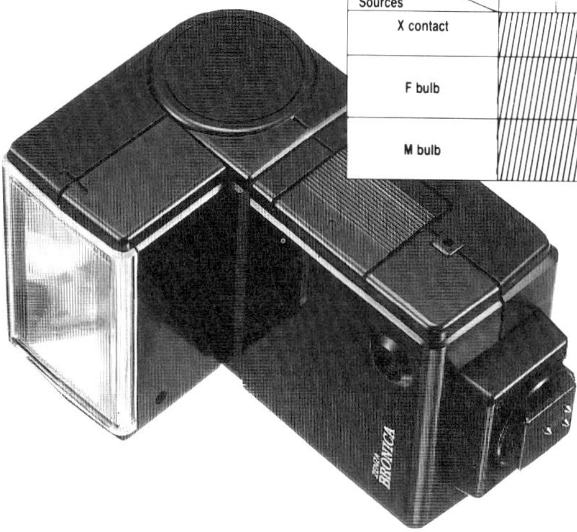

The accessory Speed-Light G1 flashgun meshes with the Bronica GS-1 and Speed Grip G to provide automatic through-the-lens flash metering. This accessory is described in greater detail in Chapter Thirteen on the GS-1's system accessories.

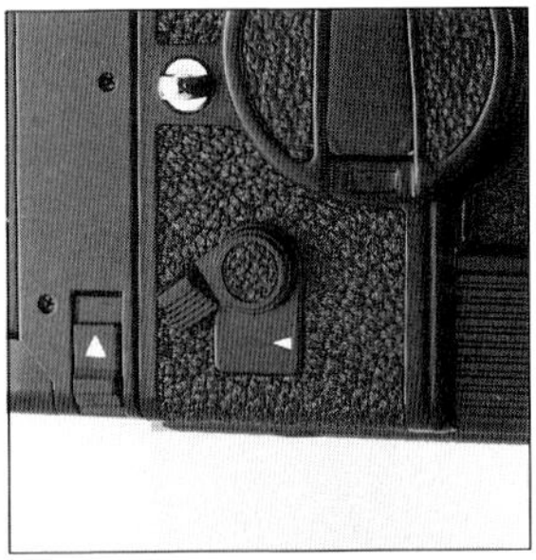

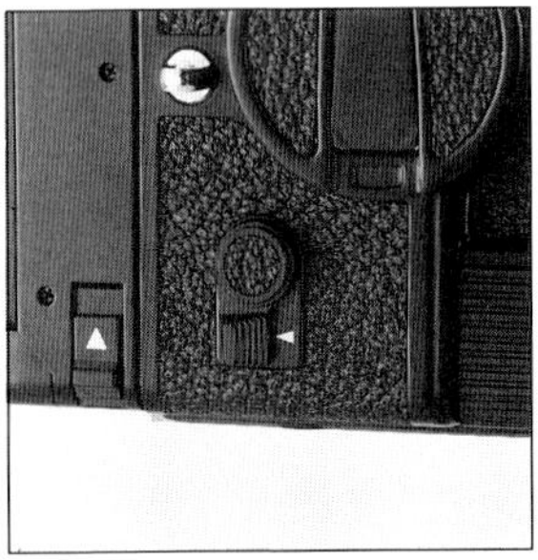

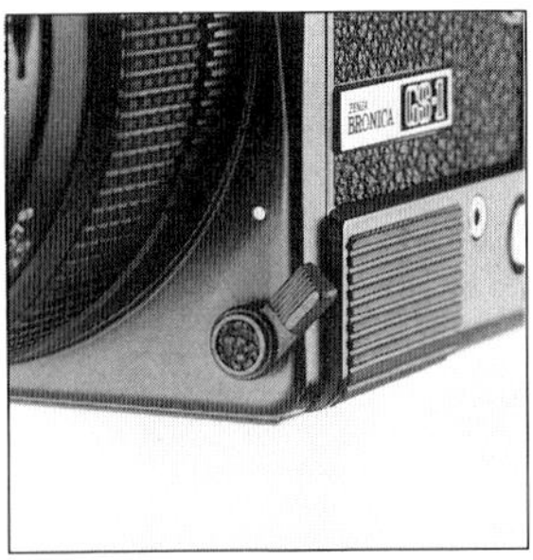

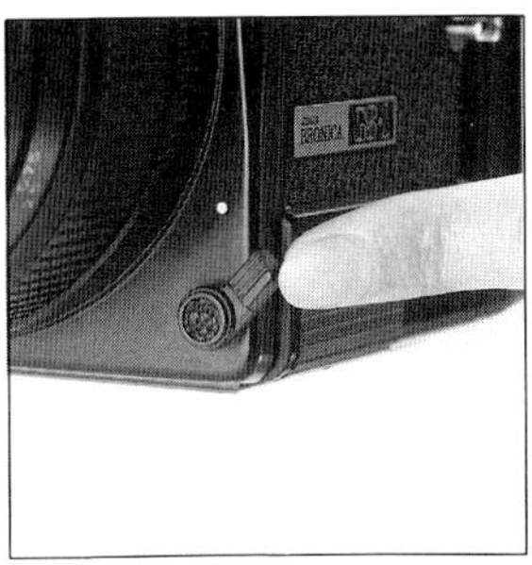

Making multiple exposures

The GS-1 has a multiple exposure capability. Before engaging the multiple exposure control, which is mounted on the right hand side of the camera, operate the wind crank so that the shutter is cocked and the film advanced.

When engaged, as many exposures as you desire can be taken and the film will remain in perfect register as the wind crank is operated to cock the shutter in readiness for each exposure. The frame counter does not advance during multiple exposure photography.

It is important to return the lever to its normal position as soon as the last picture in the sequence has been completed. Winding on will advance the film to the next frame and cock the shutter.

Mirror lock up

For photography when noise or vibration might be distracting the GS-1's mirror lock-up facility should be used. Moving the lock-up lever in the direction indicated will flip the mirror and the film baffle out of the light path. The shutter can then be released using either the camera's shutter button or the GS-1's electro-magnetic cable release socket.

Unless the mirror lock-up button is returned to its original setting after an exposure has been made the mirror will swing up as the wind crank is operated. Remember to reset the control lever before operating the wind crank unless you want continued mirror-lock operation.

If you set the mirror lock-up lever but then change your mind resetting it will release the shutter. There are two methods of avoiding the waste of a frame:

(1) Cover the lens with a lens cap before returning the lock-up lever to its normal position. Once the shutter has been released engage the multiple exposure facility before winding on. This will mean that the shutter will be cocked but the film does not advance as you wind on. Take your picture before returning the multiple exposure control to its normal position and winding on as normal.

(2) Insert the dark slide and detach the film back. Reset the mirror lock-up lever to release the shutter and then re-attach the film back. Continue photography as normal.

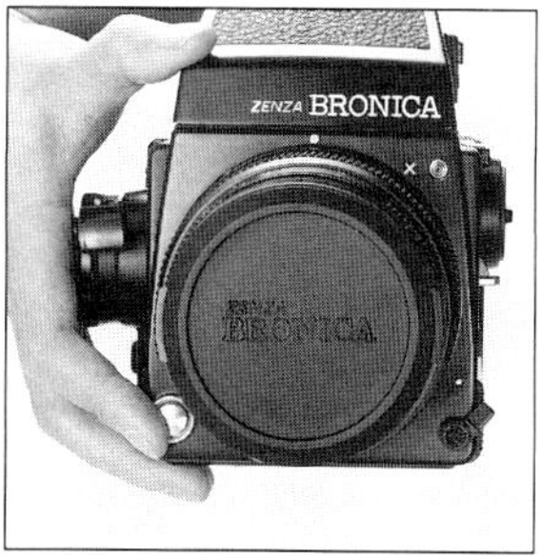

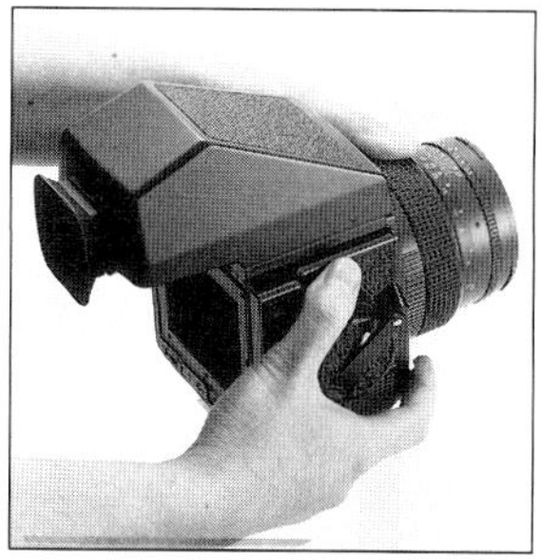

Using the 'B' (Bulb) setting

This is an electronically governed setting selected using the shutter speed dial. During 'B' operation the shutter remains open only as long as the shutter release is depressed. The camera's remote release facility can also be used to hold the shutter open.

With one of the GS-1's prism finders fitted the warning letters 'bul' appear in the viewfinder indicating that 'B' has been selected. As usual, shutter closure is confirmed in the viewfinder by the red LED blinking. During 'B' operation with either of the two metering finders the exposure system is inoperative.

Using the 'T' (Time exposure) setting

While 'B' (Bulb) consumes battery power 'T' is a wholly mechanical setting and therefore does not. Consequently 'T' is preferable for extremely long exposures. This is the only shutter setting to be chosen from the lens and works regardless of what is shown on the shutter speed dial. Pulling out the silver locking button enables the slider to be moved to reveal a red letter 'T'. Releasing the shutter can be done using the shutter release as normal. Closing the shutter is achieved by moving the locking slider back to conceal the red 'T' and unveil a white 'A'. Before closing the shutter cover the lens with a lens cap. This is the procedure if the battery is working correctly.

If, however, the battery is dead the shutter has to be opened by operating the mirror lock-up lever and then returning it to its original position; it is at this point that the shutter opens. Shutter closure is effected in the manner previously described.

The shutter can also be closed by turning the wind crank which will swing the mirror and safety baffle into the light path and so terminate exposure. However this procedure is not recommended for two reasons. Firstly, the time exposure slider on the lens remains engaged and a long exposure might be made in error. Secondly, as the crank is operated the film is advanced slightly before the shutter closes and so blurring of the picture might result as well as partial exposure of the next frame.

After the 'T' setting has been finished with remember to push the locking button back into place to avoid unintentional operation.

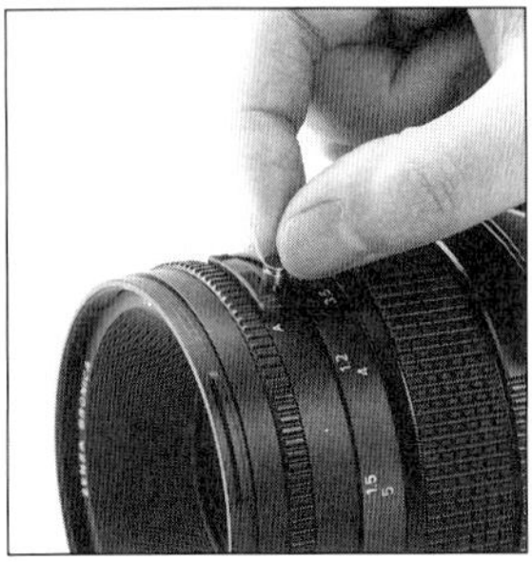

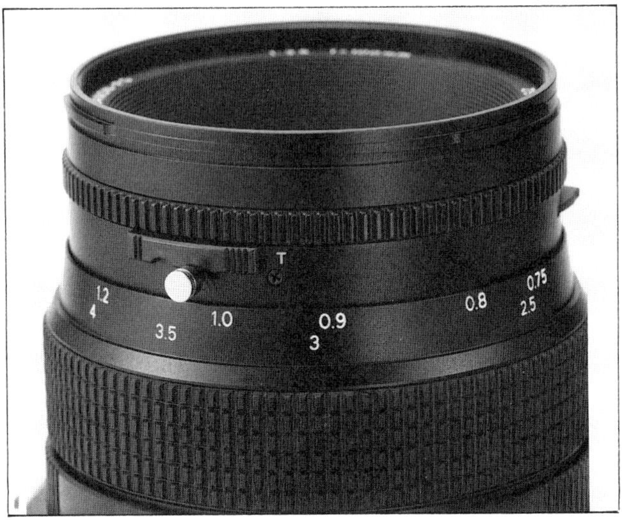

Chapter Twelve Bronica GS-1 Lenses

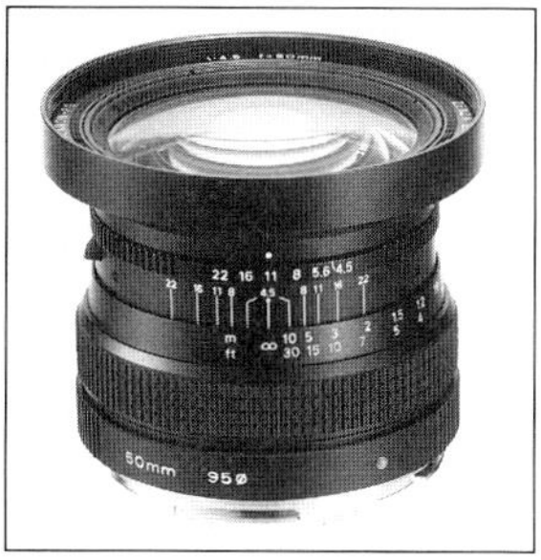

Zenzanon PG 50mm f4.5

This wide angle, with its 83 degrees angle of view (equivalent to 25mm in the 35mm format), can be employed in all manner of photographic situations but it is particularly at home in cramped situations and whenever you want to record wide sweeping vistas. Its optical construction of 11 elements in eight groups ensures that distortion is extremely low while image quality remains high throughout both aperture and focusing ranges.

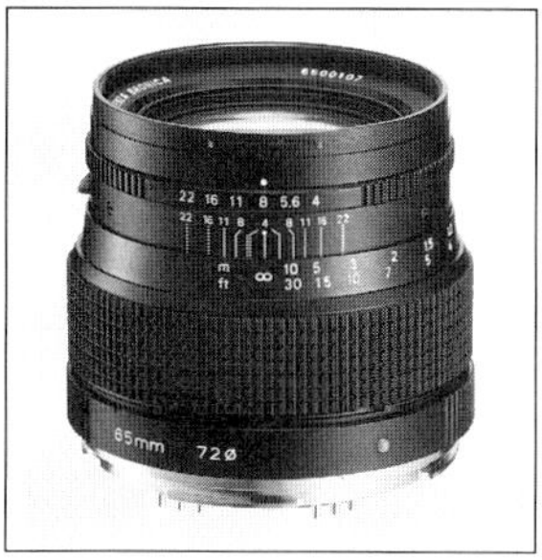

Zenzanon PG 65mm f4

If the Zenzanon PG 50mm is too wide for you then this might be the lens to have. Its 68 degrees angle of view is sufficient to be noticeably different from that of a standard lens and wide enough to cope in most situations without being so wide that perspectives are exaggerated. The PG 65mm shares the same 72mm filter size as several of its brothers and this point is worth serious consideration if you are a keen filter user.

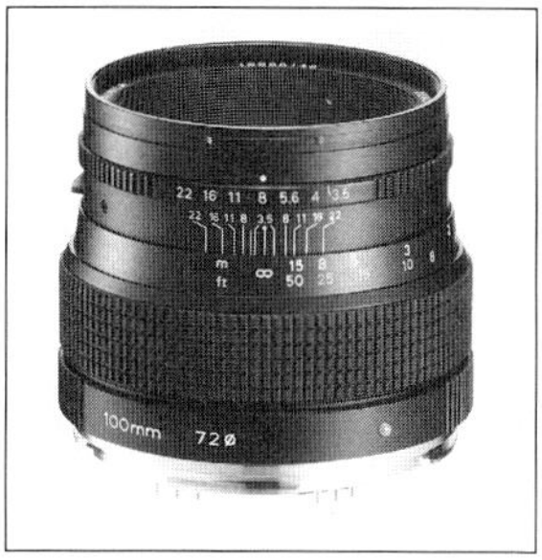

Zenzanon PG 100mm f3.5

With a field of view approximating to that of the human eye this is the standard lens of the Bronica GS-1 system. Its optical credentials are impressive and make it suitable for a wide variety of photographic subjects. Its comparatively fast maximum aperture can come in useful in less than perfect lighting conditions.

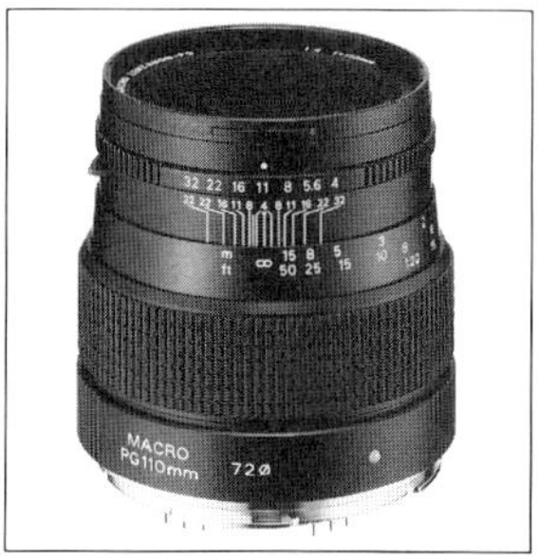

Macro Zenzanon PG 110mm f4

This lens has been designed specifically to perform best at close focusing distances but it can also be used as a general purpose optic. The minimum focusing distance of 0.66 metres gives a reproduction ratio of 1:4 and if greater magnification is required it can be combined with Auto Extension Tubes G or Auto Bellows Attachment G with minimal quality loss.

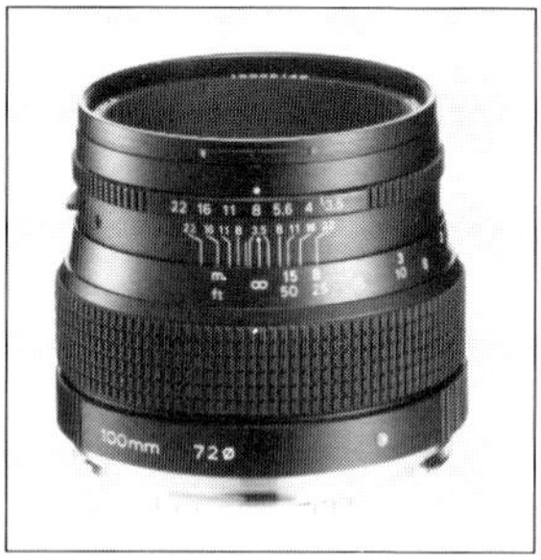

Zenzanon PG 150mm f4

This is an ideal portrait lens which allows the photographer to work at a distance comfortable to both him and the sitter. Its minimum focus of 1.5 metres means that it is possible to shoot frame-filling head-and-shoulders portraits. Of course, portrait work is not the only subject area that can be embraced with this high quality and compact optic.

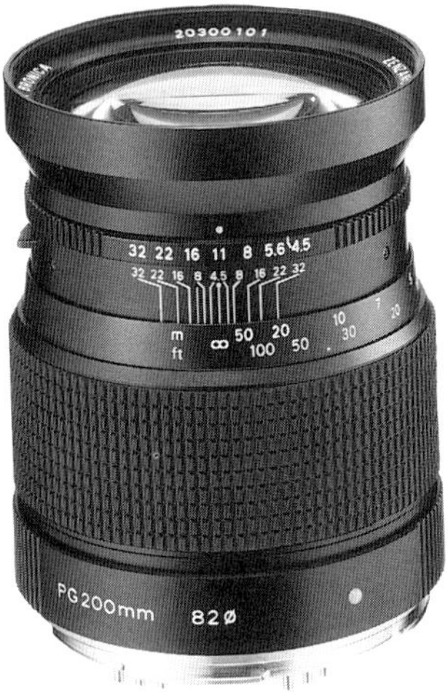

Zenzanon PG 200mm f4.5

With an optical construction of six elements in five groups this short-telephoto lens is compact and handles very well. It is equivalent to a 100mm telephoto in the 35mm format and so is a versatile short-telephoto lens which can be applied confidently to virtually any subject.

Zenzanon PG 250mm f5.6

This general purpose telephoto lens has a focal length equivalent to that of 125mm in the 35mm format. It has an optical configuration of six elements in five groups which ensures high resolution and accurate colour reproduction. All manner of photographic subjects fall within the compass of this telephoto lens: from portraits to sport, landscapes to still-life.

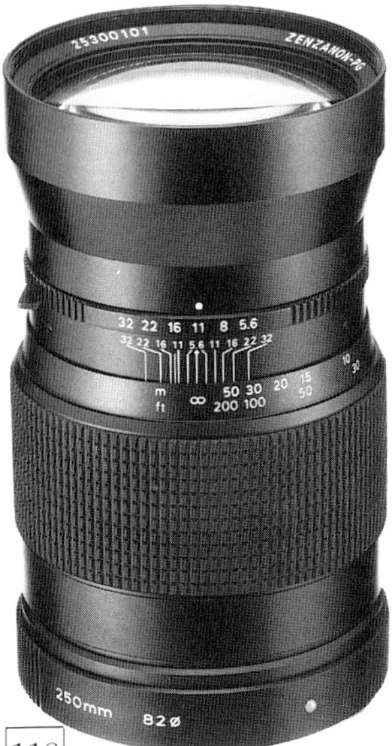

Specifications of Bronica GS-1 lenses

Lens description	Lens construction (elements/groups)	Angle of view	Apert rang
Zenzanon-PG 50mm f4.5	11/8	83°	f4.5/2
Zenzanon-PG 65mm f4	9/7	68°	f4-2
Zenzanon-PG 100mm f3.5	6/4	48°	f3.5-2
Macro Zenzanon-PG 110mm f4	6/4	44°	f4-3
Zenzanon-PG 150mm f4	5/5	33°	f4-2
Zenzanon-PG 200mm f4.5	6/5	25°	f4.5-3
Zenzanon-PG 250mm f5.6	6/5	20°	f5.6-3
Zenzanon-PG 500mm f8	11/10	10°	f8-6

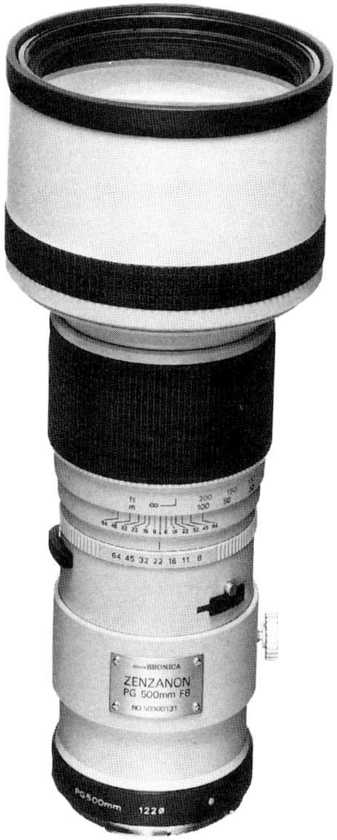

Zenzanon PG 500mm f8

By no means a lightweight, weighing in at 3.76kg, this lens has impressive telephoto qualities making it eminently suitable for sports and wildlife photographers. A rotating tripod mount is supplied.

Bitingly sharp, high contrast images are provided by this lens and chromatic aberration is minimised due to the use of low-reflective index and low-dispersion lens elements. A solid camera support is necessary to exploit this lens's true potential.

GS-1 Tele-converters

Two tele-converters are available in the Bronica GS-1 system. The G1.4X extends the focal length of the prime lens it is attached to by a factor of 1.4×; the G2X by two times. Both have been designed with full compatibility in mind and each contains all the necessary internal couplings to retain automatic diaphragm operation and, if a metering finder is used, full aperture through-the-lens exposure metering. Furthermore, because fitting a tele-converter does not alter the lens's minimum focusing distance a greater degree of magnification is possible.

Fitting and detaching a tele-converter to the camera is done in the same way as you would attach a

Shutter	Minimum focus distance	Macro magnification	Filter size	Size (length/ diameter)	Weight	Equivalent 35mm focal length
-1/500, T,B,A	0.5m	N/A	95mm	74 × 98mm	790 grams	25mm
-1/500, T,B,A	0.6m	N/A	72mm	71 × 87mm	715 grams	33mm
-1/500, T,B,A	0.75m	N/A	72mm	67 × 87mm	630 grams	50mm
-1/500, T,B,A	0.66m	1:4	72mm	78 × 87mm	725 grams	55mm
-1/500, T,B,A	1.5m	N/A	72mm	62 × 87mm	650 grams	75mm
-1/500, T,B,A	2.0m	N/A	82mm	97 × 87mm	970 grams	100mm
-1/500, T,B,A	3.0m	N/A	82mm	142 × 87mm	1200 grams	125mm
-1/500, T,B,A	8.0m	N/A	122mm	307 × 139mm	3700 grams	250mm

lens. You may fit the converter and lens together before attaching it to the camera body or, alternatively, fit the converter to the body first and then fit the lens.

Converters cannot be used in combination with each other nor should they be used with either the Auto Extension Tubes G or the Auto Bellows Attachment G.

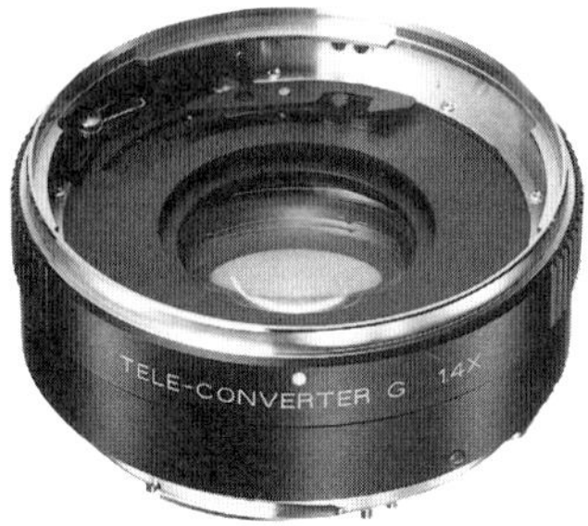

Tele-converter G1.4X

This compact five-element tele-converter is recommended for use with the following Zenzanon PG lenses: 100mm, 110mm, 150mm, 200mm, 250mm and 500mm. With a meter finder no exposure compensation is needed but, if a separate hand-held lightmeter is used, the exposure must be increased by a factor of 1.4× to compensate for light loss caused by the tele-converter.

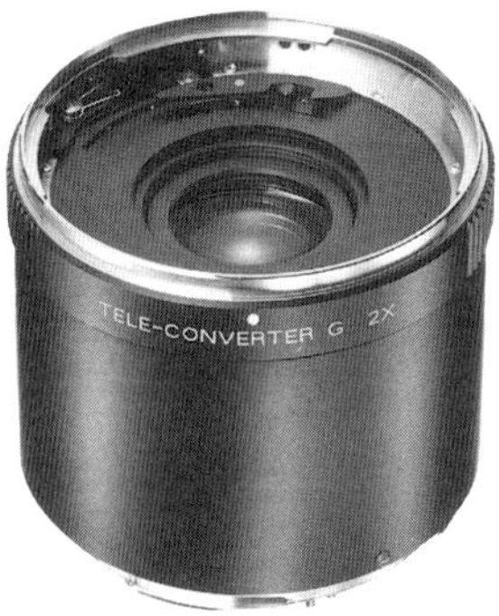

Tele-converter G2X

Basically identical to the 1.4X tele-converter except that it doubles the focal length of the lens it is fitted to and uses seven elements. The tele-converter is recommended for all Zenzanon PG lenses except the 50mm and 65mm. Fully coupled so there is no need for any exposure compensation if a metering finder is used. If a separate hand lightmeter is used to assess the light the exposure must be increased by two stops.

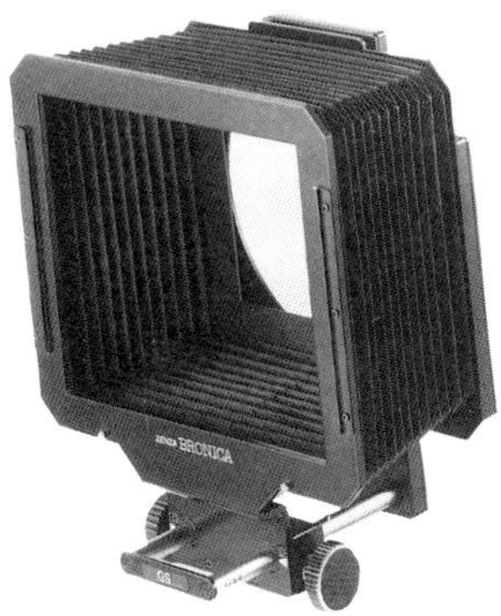

Professional Lens Hood G

To make the most of your lenses efficient protection from flare is important. This protection is offered by this extending bellows hood. Its rail-mounted bellows can be adjusted to suit whatever the focal length lens is in use at the time and has facility to accept gelatin and creative filters such as those from Hoyarex and Cokin.

It is suitable for focal length lenses from 65mm to 250mm and attaches to the lens via an adaptor ring. A mask insert is needed for focal lengths 150mm, 200mm and 250mm. Three adaptor ring sizes are available: 72mm, 82mm and 95mm.

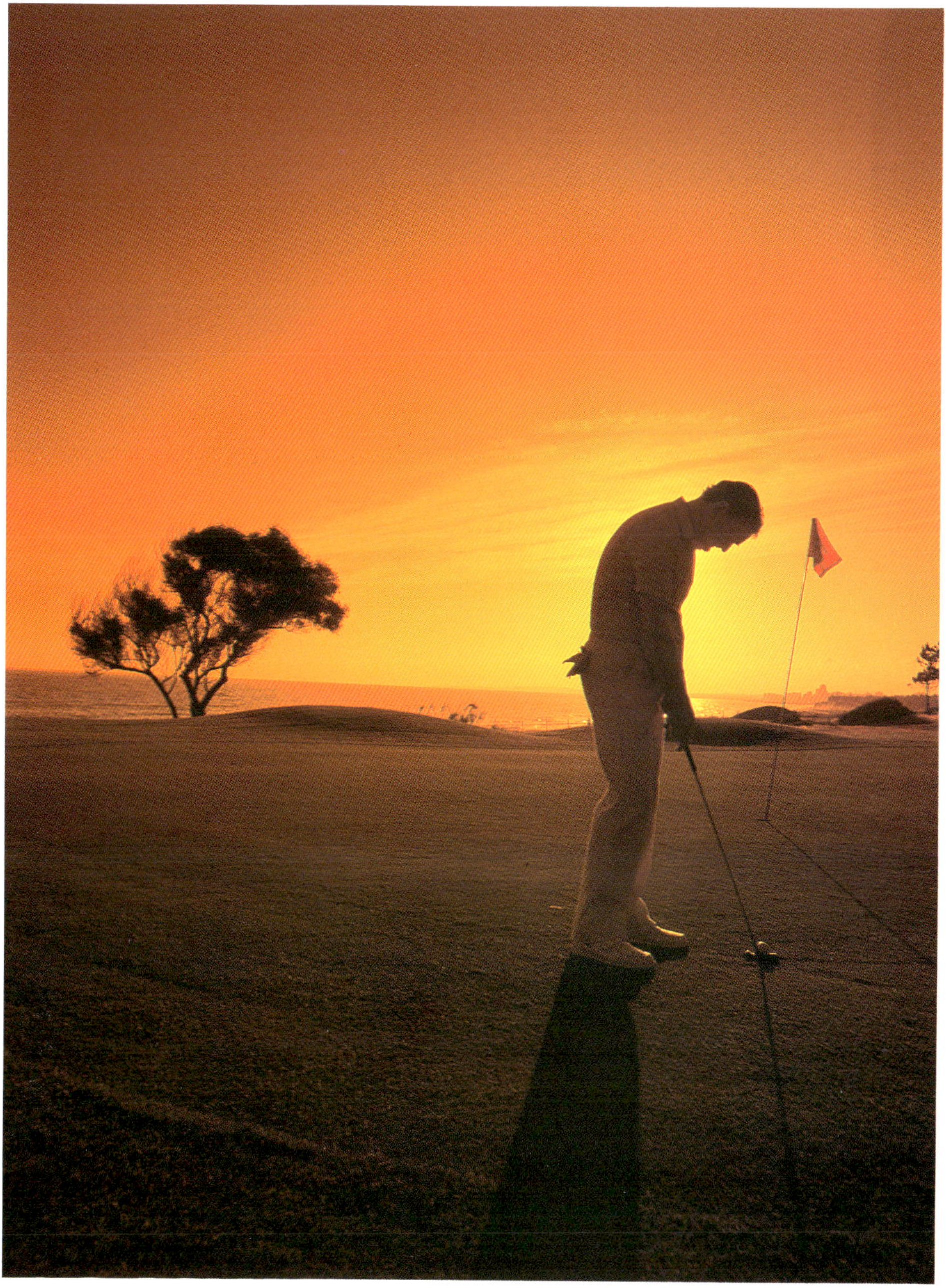

Golf Feature Shot, John Shire

Co Galway, John Freeman

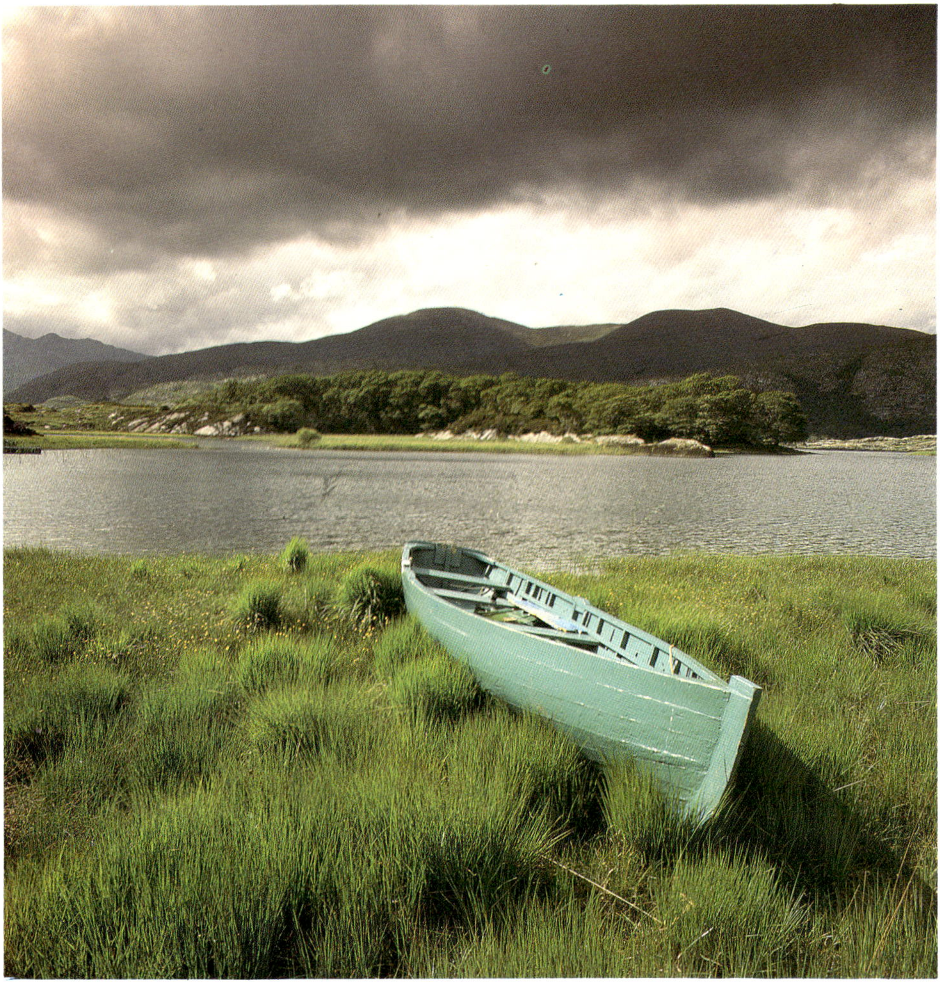

On Board, Kos Photos

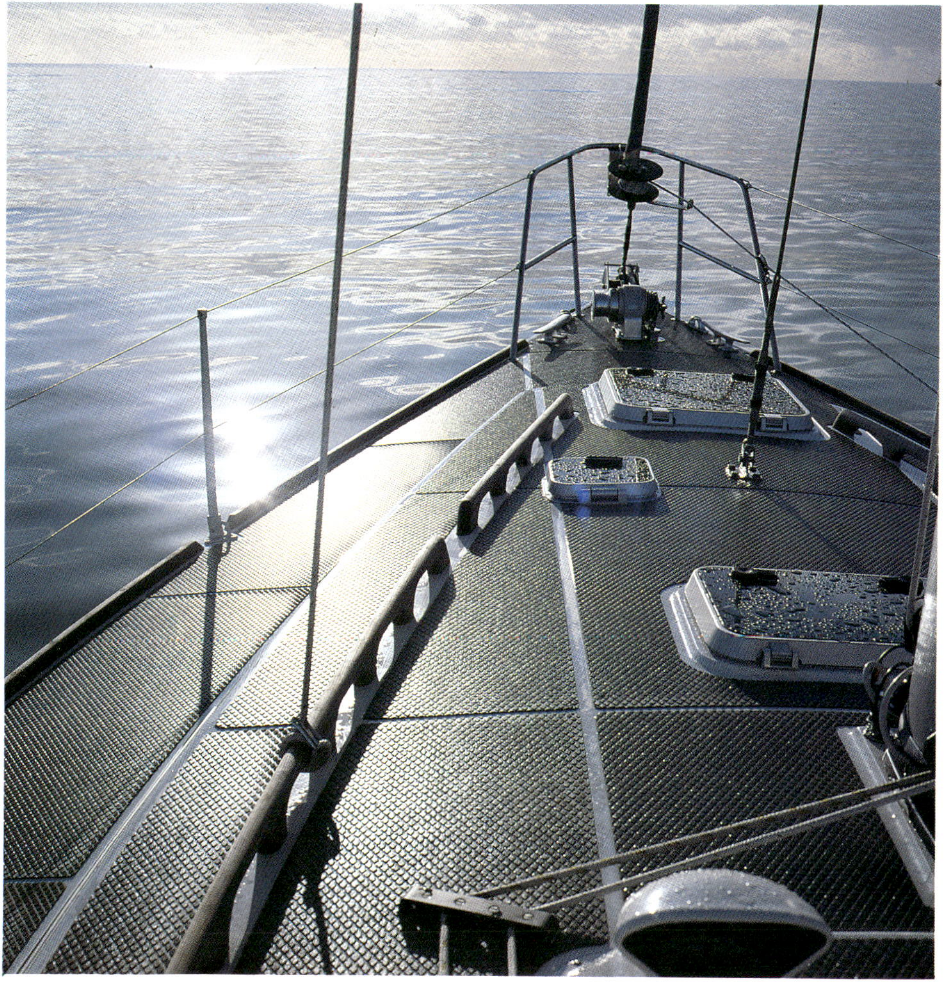

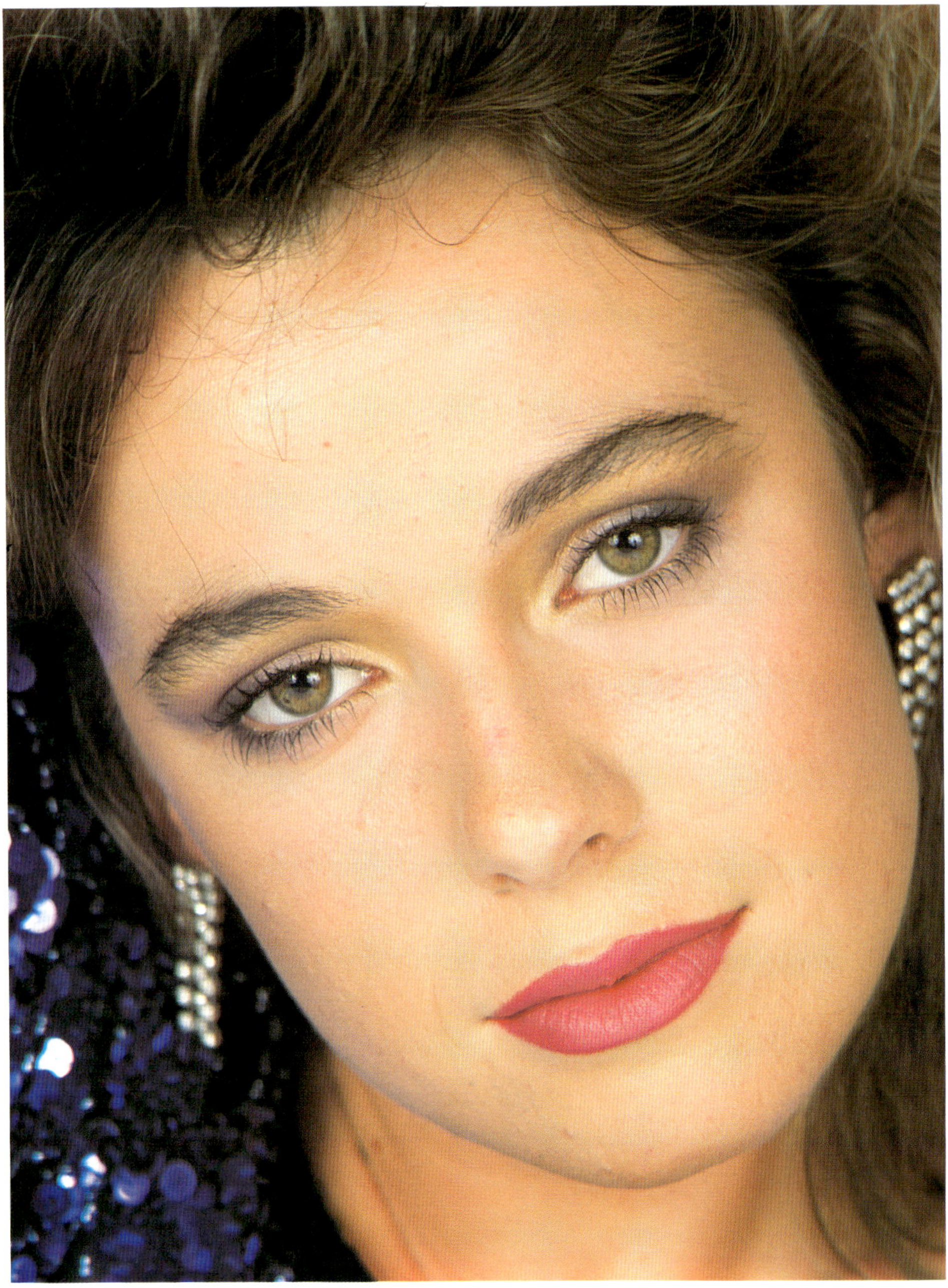

Portrait, Duncan Roe & Ashley Smith

Lens Hoods

Four fixed rubber lens hoods are available, suitable for 65mm, 100mm, 150mm and 200/250mm focal lengths respectively, and attach to the lens via a bayonet mount. Recommended when the Professional Lens Hood G would be too cumbersome for convenient camera operation.

Focus Lever G

Focusing efficiency is improved with the use of this accessory, which slips over the lens's rubberised focusing barrel and is held in position by tightening a screw. It is suitable for all Zenzanon G lenses except the 500mm f/8 telephoto.

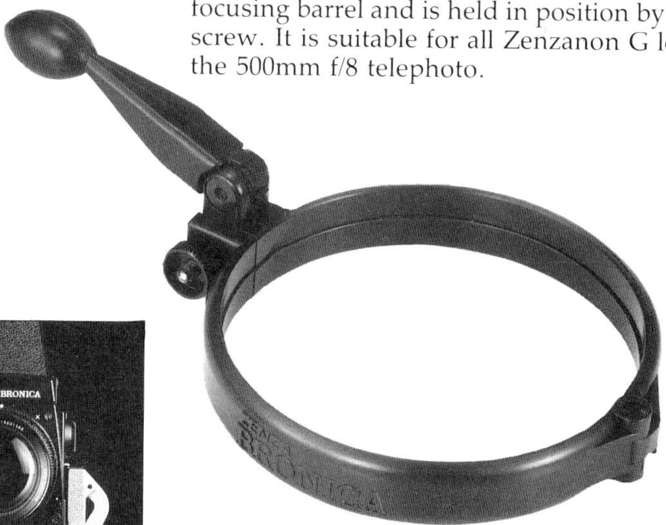

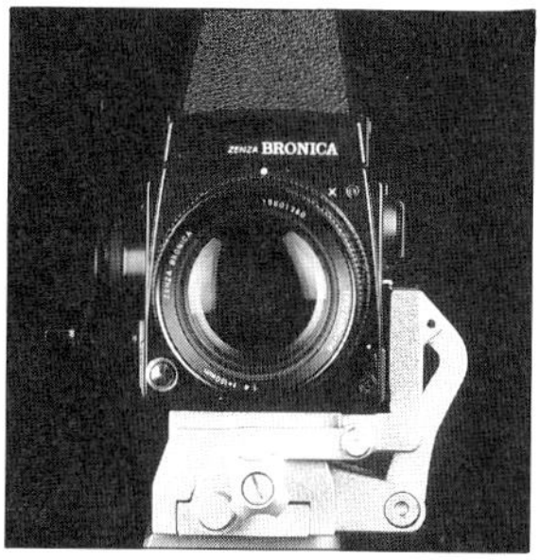

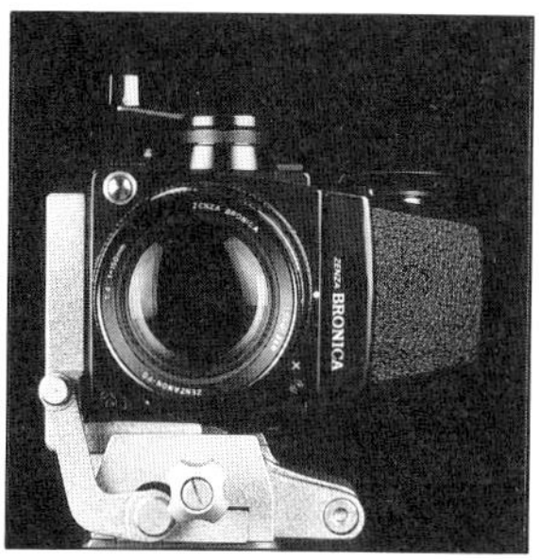

Revolving Tripod Adaptor

This cleverly designed gadget makes the task of shooting vertical or horizontal format pictures with a tripod-mounted Bronica GS-1 extremely straightforward. An ingenious cantilever mechanism enables smooth switching from horizontal to vertical, and vice versa, and, due to its very solid construction and efficient locking system, vibration is well damped.

Chapter Thirteen

Bronica GS-1 System Accessories

FINDERS

Waist Level Finder G

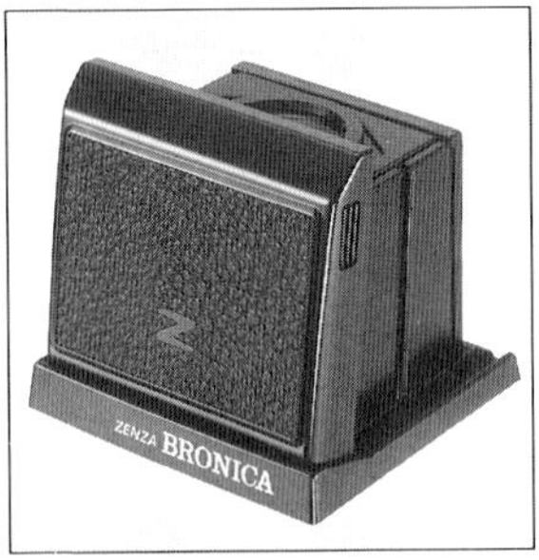

The non-metering Waist Level Finder G is the simplest of those available for the GS-1 and provides an upright, reversed viewing image. Correct shutter operation is confirmed by a red LED blinking briefly; no other readout is provided. A built-in spring-loaded magnifier eyepiece assists precise focusing. This has a diopter strength of −1.5; optional accessory eyepieces are available in strengths of −4.5, −3.5, −2.5, −0.5, +0.5 and +1.5. +2.5.

Prism Finder G

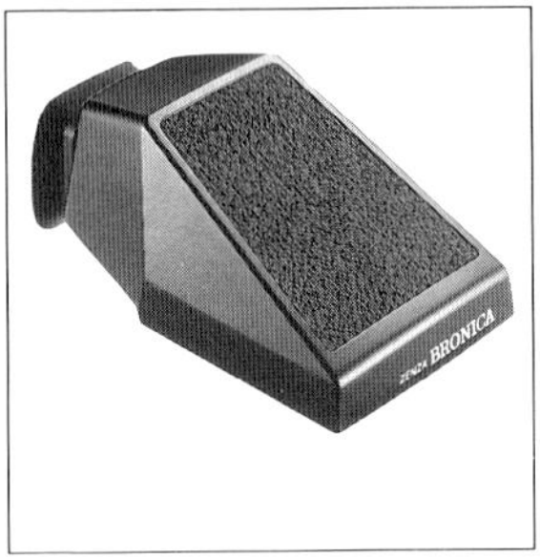

This streamlined, non-metering prism finder delivers a bright, upright, laterally-correct viewing image. When the shutter is partially depressed the chosen shutter speed is displayed on the LED panel and correct shutter operation is confirmed by an LED blinking briefly. The supplied eyepiece has a diopter value of −1.5. Optional eyepieces of the following strengths are available: −4.5, −3.5, −2.5, −0.5, +0.5 and +1.5. +2.5.

AE Prism Finder G

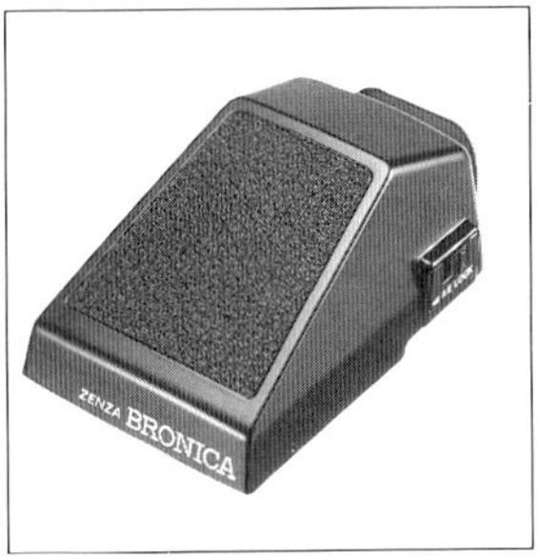

The option of full aperture manual metering or aperture-priority auto-exposure is provided with this finder. It is a compact unit which delivers a bright, upright, laterally-correct viewfinder image and shares the same system of diopter correction eyepieces as the Prism Finder G.

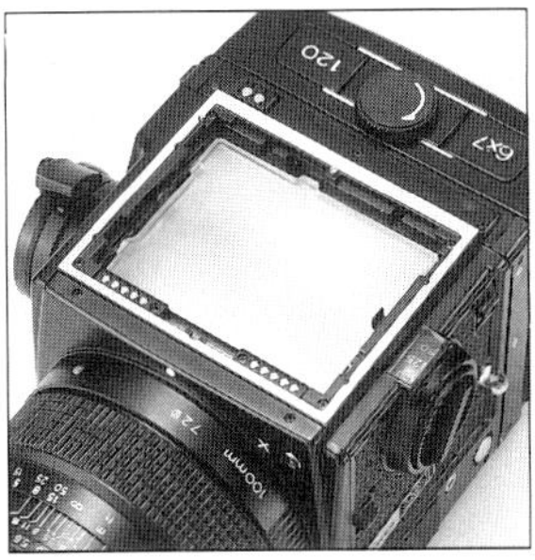

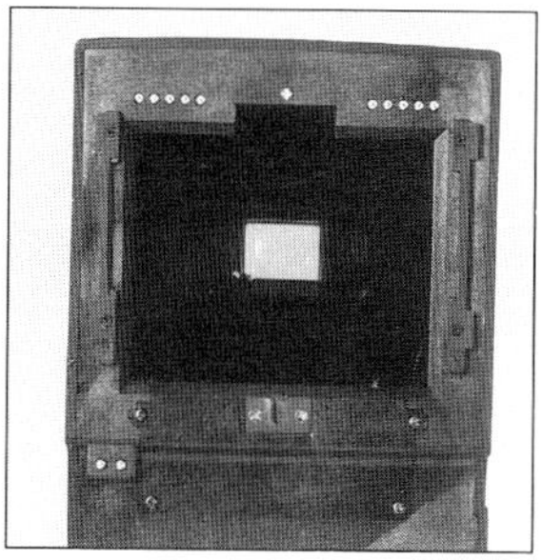

On the front of the finder's base are two sets of five gold contacts that relay information to and from the camera body. Power for the metering system is supplied by the camera battery via these contacts. The two contacts at the rear mesh with those on GS-1 film backs and collect film speed and exposure compensation details. It is important that the film's proper speed is selected on the ISO dial. Clean the contacts regularly with a soft, dry cloth to ensure proper functioning.

The two silicon photocells used for metering are positioned to give centre-weighted measurement regardless of what aperture is set on the lens. Their sensitivity range with ISO 100 film is EV 2-17.

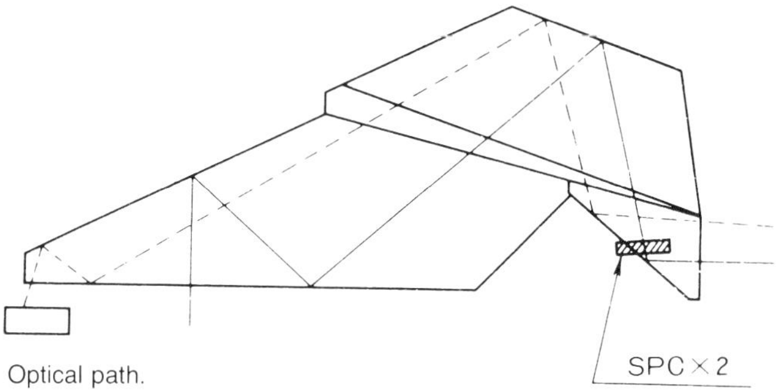

Optical path.

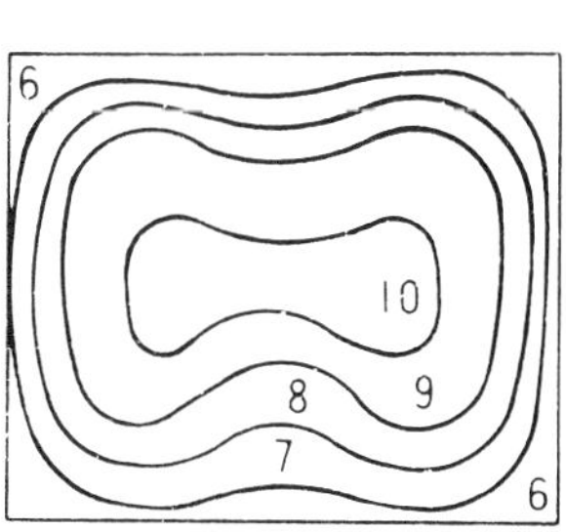

Meter sensitivity pattern of AE Prism Finder G.
The numbers indicate the sensitivity ratio for each zone.

Auto-exposure operation

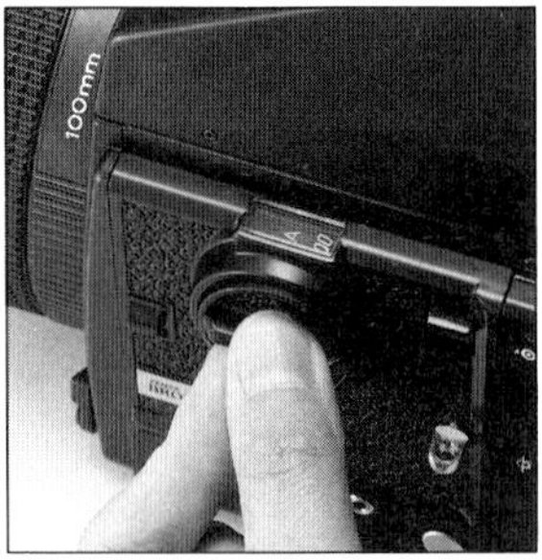

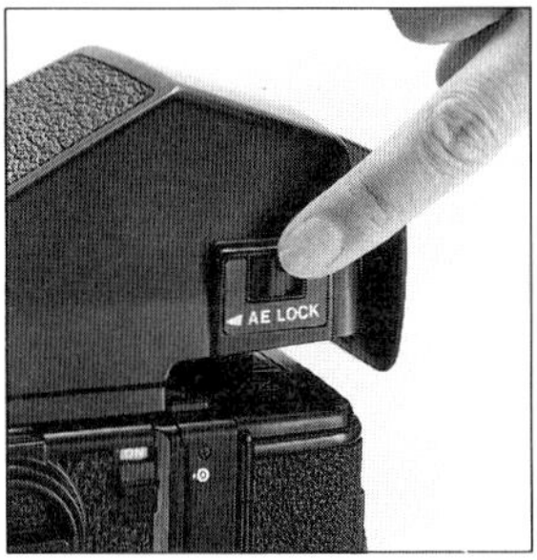

During AE operation the shutter is controlled by the finder in 1/8 stop steps within the speed range of 16 seconds to 1/500 sec. The camera's shutter dial must be set to 'A'; a locking button has to be pressed in before 'A' can be engaged or disengaged. At any setting apart from 'A' the finder will be in manual metering mode.

Partial depression of the shutter release will activate the viewfinder LED display and the nearest full shutter speed to that selected by the finder will light up. The LED panel stays on as long as the finger retains pressure on the shutter release except during AE lock operation. Over and under-exposure are indicated by the flickering LEDs 500 or 16″ respectively. Under such circumstances rotate the aperture ring until a suitable shutter speed is displayed.

An AE (auto-exposure) lock is provided. When selected, pressing the shutter release button will hold the exposure for 16 seconds and the viewfinder LED readout will remain lit; the AE lock cancels automatically after 16 seconds have elapsed or when the shutter has been triggered, whichever is the sooner. To cancel the lock return the AE control to its

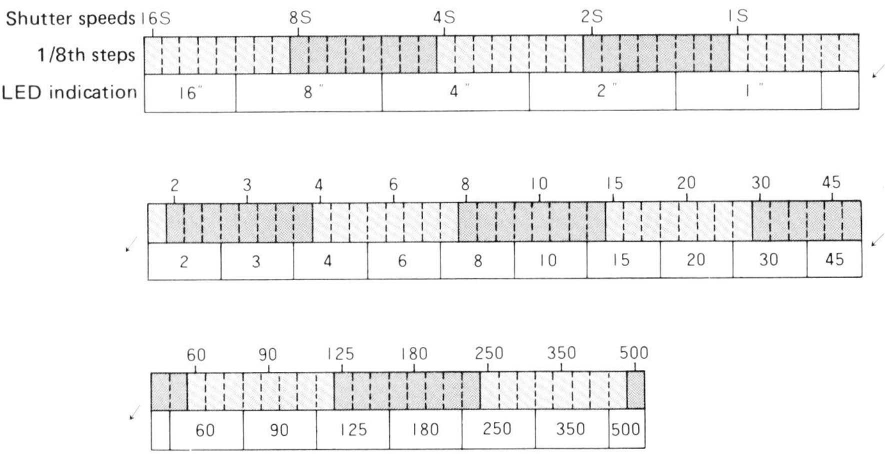

The above indications are automatically switched in brightness and become brighter at faste speeds than 1 second and become darker at slower speeds than 1 second.

Compensation / ASA/ISO	−3	−2	−1	0	+1	+2	+3
3					×	×	×
6						×	×
12							×
25							
50							
100							
200							
400							
800							
1600							
3200	×						
6400	×	×					

The range of exposure compensation available with the GS-1 during auto-exposure operation.

original position or turn the camera off at its main switch. During AE lock operation a yellow LED lights up in the viewfinder. Upon completing AE lock operations disengage the AE lock by returning the slider to its original position.

Exposure compensation up to ± three stops in 1/3 stop increments may be set by using the dial on GS-1 film backs. During normal operation the exposure compensation dial should be set to '0'. This position is the only one click-stopped and to move the dial off this setting the locking button must be depressed. Zero the dial after compensating for exposure and it will automatically lock into the '0' setting.

Manual exposure metering

The shutter dial can be set at any speed except 'A' and 'B' (Bulb) for manual through-the-lens exposure metering. All shutter dial settings are click-stopped and intermediate values should not be chosen.

Stroking the shutter button half-way will activate the viewfinder LED panel. Two readouts will be visible. On the left a blinking shutter speed is shown and its number corresponds with the speed set on the shutter dial. The LED on the right indicates the difference between the exposure set and the correct exposure within a range of ± three stops. Beyond ± three stops the '+3' or '−3' LED will flicker. To determine correct exposure adjust the aperture and/or shutter until an '0' LED is shown.

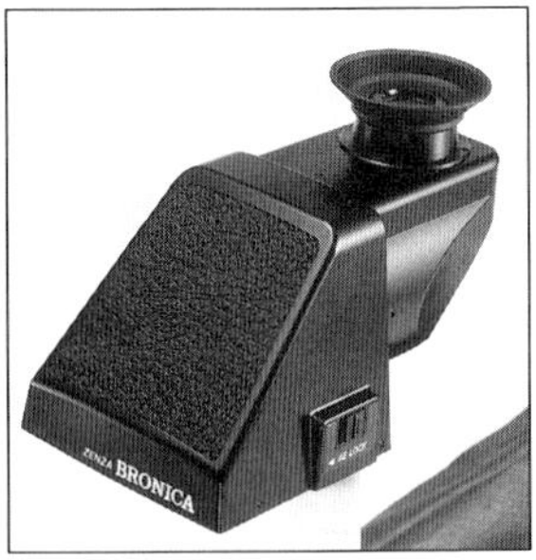

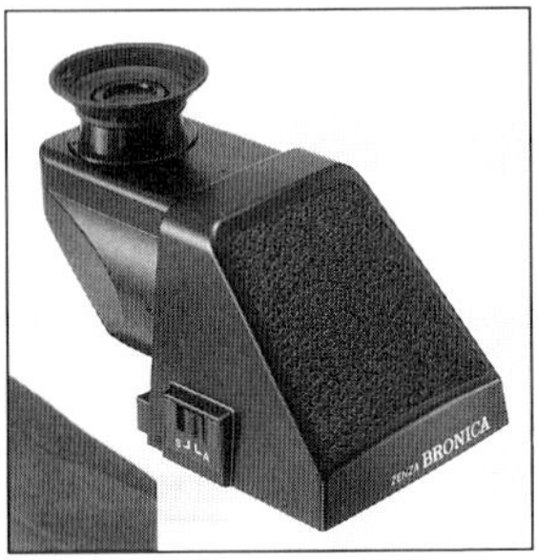

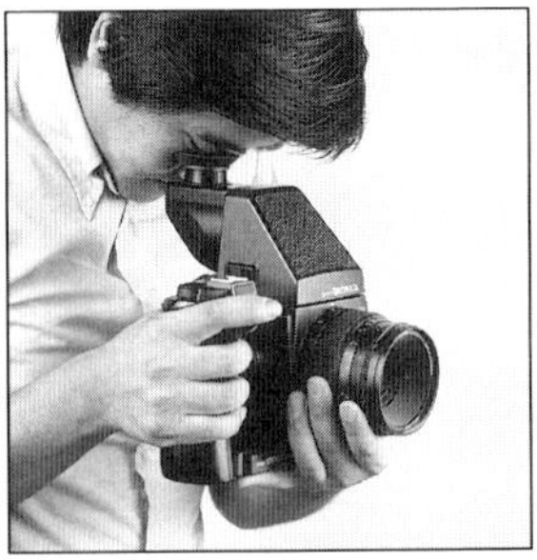

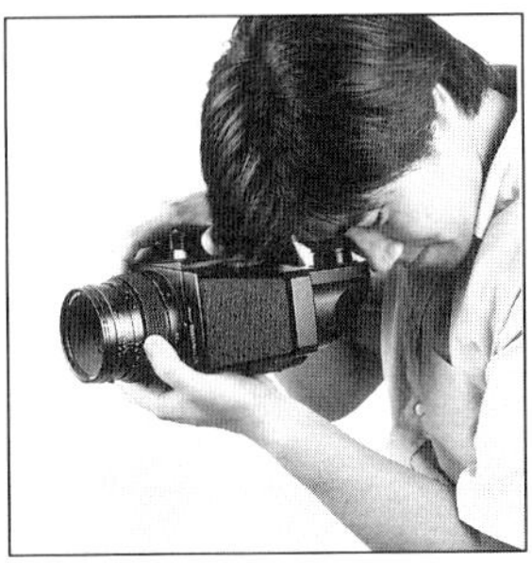

AE Rotary Finder G

This is the most sophisticated of the finders available for the GS-1 and its remarkable versatility makes it a worthwhile alternative to the AE Prism Finder G. Meter sensitivity is EV 4 to EV 17 with ISO 100 film.

The viewing image is bright, upright and laterally correct. Three click-stopped positions are available for shooting either horizontal or vertical format photographs although intermediate settings are possible so that the eyepiece can be tailored to suit specific shooting situations. This finder has, on the base, the same configuration of gold-plated contacts as the AE Prism Finder G. These contacts relay information from the body and film back to the finder as well as draw power from the camera battery.

Two metering modes are featured: manual and aperture-priority auto-exposure. Furthermore, with the standard matte focusing screen there is the option of spot metering; the meter's sensitivity being defined by the circle etched on the focusing screen. Engaging spot meter operation is achieved by sliding a switch on the right of the housing to the 'S' position; the 'A' setting is for average centre-weighted light measurement. When the shutter release is pressed half-way an 'S' LED in the viewfinder signifies that the spot meter is in operation. Selecting 'S' has no effect unless the standard matte screen is fitted.

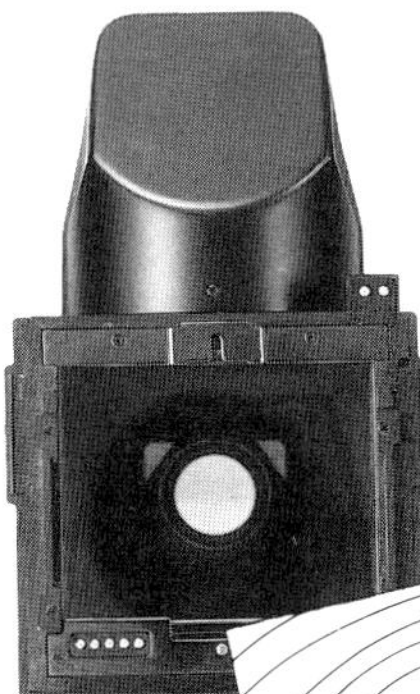

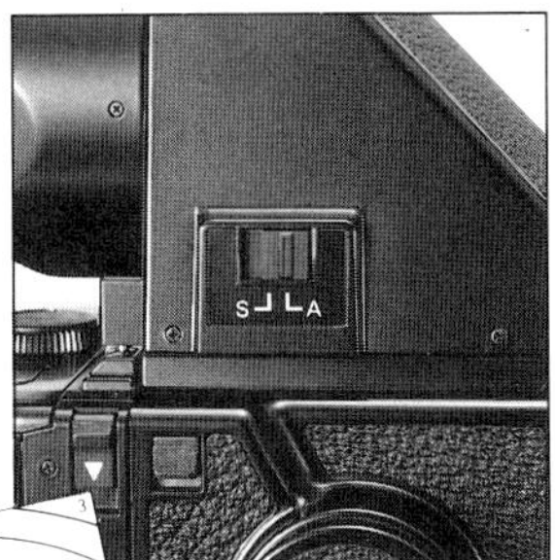

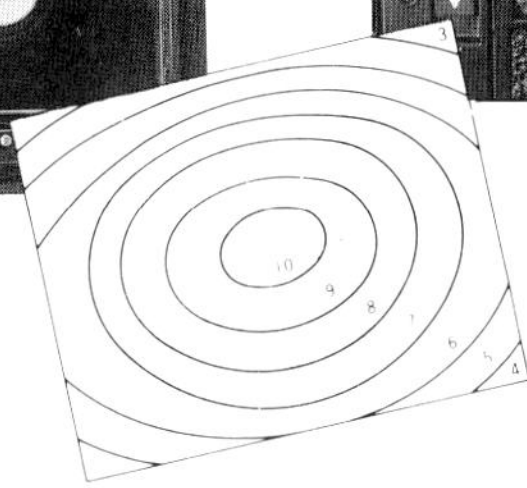

Automatic exposure operation

Choosing exposure mode is achieved by using the camera's shutter dial. Depress the small lock button and set the shutter dial to the 'A' position and aperture-priority AE mode is selected. Having the shutter dial set to any other speed — apart from 'B' (Bulb) — means that metered manual is in use. In either exposure mode aperture and shutter speed values, other than those click-stopped, should not be chosen as incorrect operation might result.

The viewfinder display varies according to which mode is in operation. During aperture-priority AE the nearest full shutter speed value will glow steadily when the shutter release is semi-depressed. Over and under-exposure warnings are provided.

In auto-exposure operation the GS-1's electronic shutter is controlled in 1/8 stop steps within the 16 seconds to 1/500 sec range. A memory lock, the control marked 'AE LOCK', is provided which enables the shutter value to be fixed during auto-exposure operation; this can be used in either average or spot metering modes.

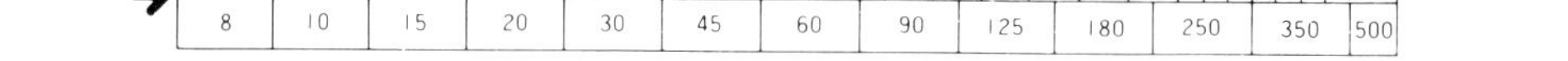

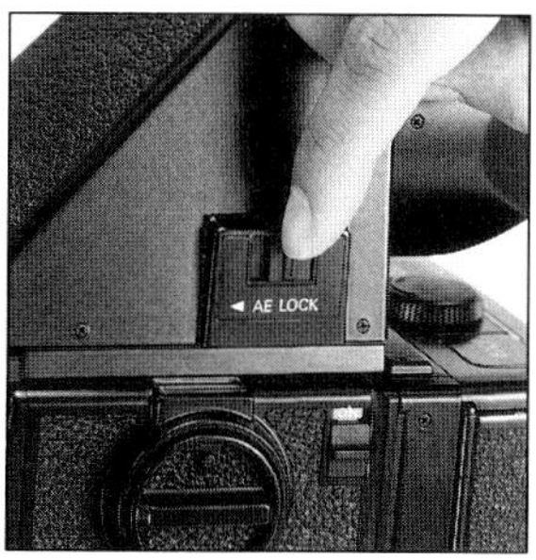

To utilise the AE lock slide the control in the arrow-indicated direction and partially depress the shutter release; a yellow coloured LED in the viewfinder will light up. The memorised reading is retained for 16 seconds after the finger is lifted from the shutter release before automatically cancelling itself. If the exposure is not made within this time it will be necessary to partially depress the shutter release to re-activate the lock. In low light it will be necessary to initiate meter operation before engaging the AE lock control. After you have finished with the AE lock return the switch to its original position.

There is also the option of using exposure compensation during auto-exposure operation using

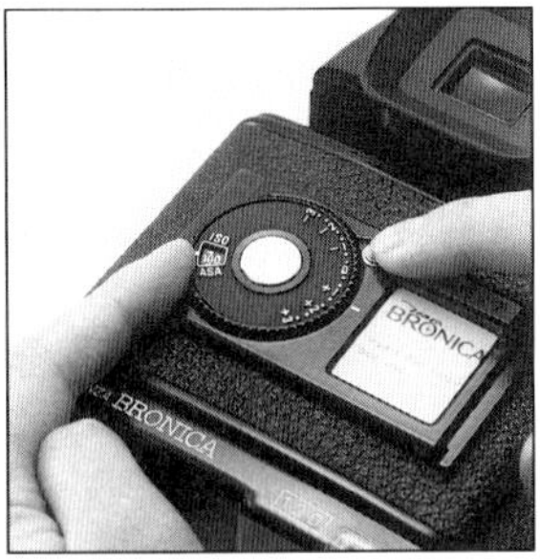

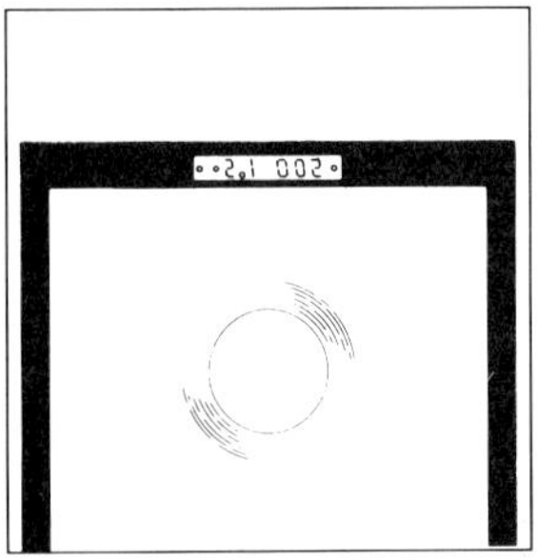

the control dial on the film back. This is click-stopped at the '0' position and the dial should be in this position during normal photography. To engage exposure compensation operate the locking lever and rotate the dial to the desired degree of compensation. The dial will automatically lock into the '0' setting as it is rotated back. The exposure compensation dial does not function during manual metering.

Manual exposure metering

Manual metering mode is engaged by selecting any setting apart from 'A' (auto-exposure mode) and 'B' (Bulb). Intermediate aperture and shutter settings should not be selected.

Partially depressing the shutter release will make the set shutter speed flicker on the LED panel. In addition, to the right of the shutter indication, a number will light up to show, within a range of ± three stops, how far you are from correct exposure. Adjust the aperture and/or shutter speed value until the '0' LED lights up. Beyond the range of ± three stops the '+3' or '−3' LED will blink steadily.

Practical hints for using the AE Prism Finder G and AE Rotary Finder G

- Clean the finder's base contacts regularly using a soft, dry cloth. Poor connections can interfere with correct operation.
- Save power by switching the camera off at the main switch when it is not in use.
- During long auto-exposures battery consumption is high. Use the 'T' (Time exposure) setting to conserve the battery.
- Aperture and shutter values other than those click-stopped should not be used.
- Make sure that the film's correct ISO rating is selected on the film back.
- Use a camera support if the indicated shutter speed is 1/30 sec or below.
- Zero the exposure compensation dial as soon as it is finished with. No warning is given that exposure compensation has been set.

- Cover the finder eyepiece with a piece of black cloth if you are not looking through the viewfinder during auto-exposure operation. Extraneous light entering the viewfinder eyepiece can affect the exposure.
- Keep your eye on the shutter closing confirmation LED in the viewfinder during long exposure operation. Wait until the shutter has closed before attempting to advance the film to the next frame. If the wind crank is operated before the shutter has closed the exposure will be terminated prematurely. Furthermore, because the film is advanced slightly as the crank is operated and before the shutter has closed, the frame might exhibit streaking. The following frame might also be partly exposed. Lastly, the next exposure will be made at 1/500 sec regardless.
- In auto-exposure mode winding on the film before the shutter closes will also mean that the shutter cannot be fired until the original set exposure time has elapsed.
- Do not operate the depth of field preview lever during exposure measurement because the photograph will be over-exposed by the difference between the indicated reading and the lens's full aperture.
- For flash photography select manual operation. In dim light using auto-exposure mode will result in long shutter speeds.
- Auto-exposure operation during single frame mirror lock-up operation is possible. However, if you require continuous mirror lock-up manual metering has to be used.

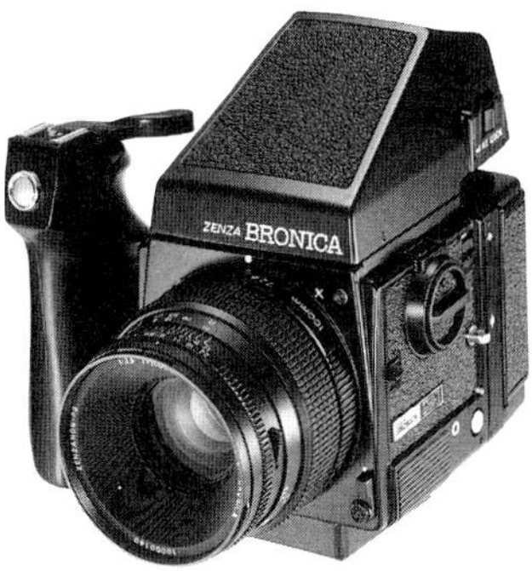

Speed Grip G

This anatomically designed hand grip promotes rapid handling when combined with the GS-1. The lever wind requires two full strokes to advance the film by one frame and cock the shutter. A shutter release is incorporated, as is a flash hot-shoe fitting, which has the necessary dedication contacts for automatic through-the-lens flash metering operation with the Speed-Light G-1.

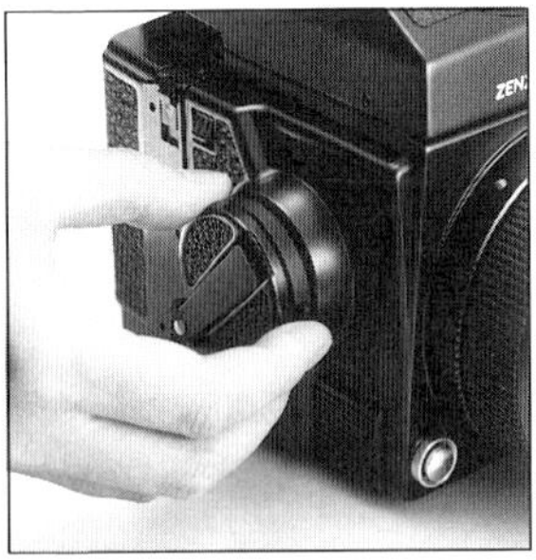

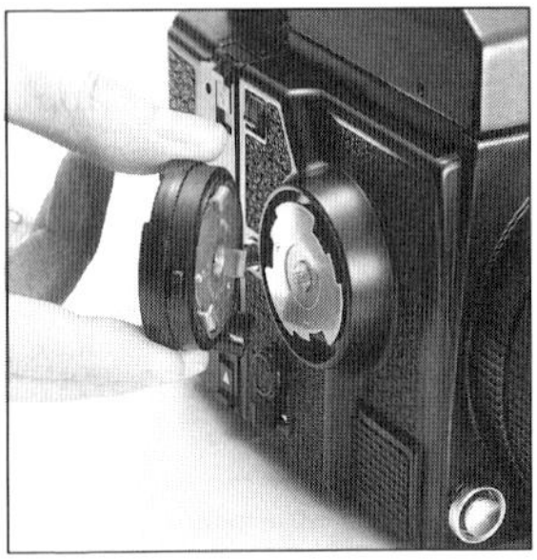

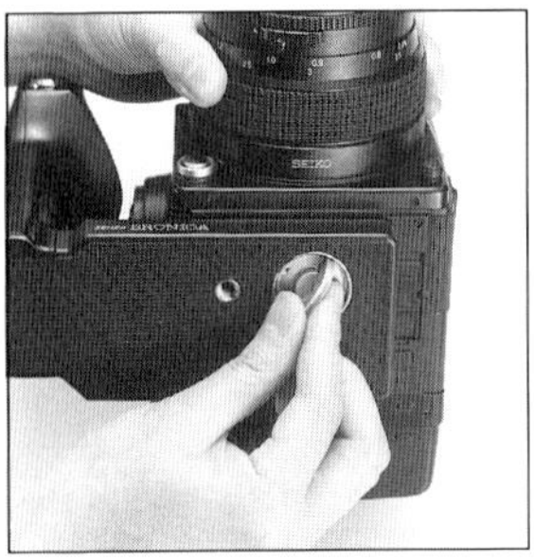

Fitting the Speed Grip G

1. First the film wind crank assembly must be removed. This is done by pulling the release lever outwards at the same time as rotating the crank assembly anti-clockwise. The cover supplied with the Speed Grip G should be fitted over the crank base to protect it from dust and grit.
2. The covers from the film winding coupler and the accessory contacts located in the camera base should be removed.
3. The Speed Grip G attaches to the camera via a locking screw. Operate the grip's wind lever to ensure full coupling.

CLOSE-UP ACCESSORIES

Close-up filters

Two 72mm screw-in close-up lenses are offered in the Bronica GS-1 system. Attached to the lens these provide a closer focusing distance than is normally possible, therefore giving greater image magnification; they may be used in combination and no exposure modification is necessary.

Table of Photographic Magnification of close-up filters

Lens type	Close-up filter No. 1	Close-up filter No. 2	Close-up filters No. 1 + No. 2
65mm f4	0.13-0.28	0.26-0.41	0.38-0.53
100mm f3.5	0.20-0.40	0.40-0.61	0.59-0.81
150mm f4	0.30-0.46	0.60-0.80	0.89-1.12
110mm f4	0.21-0.48	0.43-0.72	0.64-0.94

Automatic Extension Tubes G

Two fully automatic extension tubes are available for the GS-1, the G-18 and the G-36 giving 18mm and 36mm extension respectively, and they may be used in conjunction with all Zenzanon PG lenses. Both tubes contain the required internal linkages to retain fully automatic diaphragm operation.

Extending the lens from the film plane causes a light loss, so if a separate lightmeter is employed the appropriate exposure factor should be applied to give the correct exposure. When using the AE Prism Finder G or the AE Rotary Finder G through-the-lens metering automatically accounts for any necessary exposure correction. It is not possible to use more than one tube in combination and if greater image magnification is needed the Automatic Bellows Attachment G is required.

G-18 CLOSE-UP DATA

Lens type	Focusing ring setting	Magnification	Area photographed (cm)	Object-to-film plane (cm)	Object-to-front lens (cm)	Exposure factor
50mm	Infinity	0.36	15.4 × 19.2	30.5	12.8	1.4
	Maximum extension	0.51	10.9 × 13.5	27.2	8.7	1.6
65mm	Infinity	0.28	20.1 × 24.9	41.1	23.7	1.4
	Maximum extension	0.43	12.9 × 16.0	33.7	15.3	1.6
100mm	Infinity	0.18	30.9 × 38.3	76.5	59.5	1.4
	Maximum extension	0.37	15.1 × 18.7	50.0	31.0	1.8
Macro 110mm	Infinity	0.17	33.4 × 41.4	86.9	68.8	1.3
	Maximum extension	0.42	13.2 × 16.3	50.5	29.6	2.0
150mm	Infinity	0.12	46.3 × 57.5	157	140	1.4
	Maximum extension	0.25	22.2 × 27.6	93.5	75.1	1.9
200mm	Infinity	0.09	60.5 × 75.1	255	235	1.3
	Maximum extension	0.22	25.3 × 31.4	133	111	1.9
250mm	Infinity	0.07	75.7 × 93.9	385	361	1.3
	Maximum extension	0.18	31.6 × 39.2	194	167	1.7

G-36 CLOSE-UP DATA

Lens type	Focusing ring setting	Magnification	Area photographed (cm)	Object-to-film plane (cm)	Object-to-front lens (cm)	Exposure factor
50mm	Infinity	0.72	7.7 × 9.6	25.4	5.9	1.9
	Maximum extension	0.87	6.4 × 7.9	24.9	4.7	2.1
65mm	Infinity	0.55	10.0 × 12.5	31.2	12.0	1.8
	Maximum extension	0.71	7.8 × 9.7	29.6	9.4	2.0
100mm	Infinity	0.36	15.4 × 19.2	50.6	31.7	1.8
	Maximum extension	0.55	10.1 × 12.6	42.9	22.2	2.3
Macro 110mm	Infinity	0.33	16.7 × 20.7	56.3	36.4	1.7
	Maximum extension	0.59	9.4 × 11.7	45.0	22.3	2.4
150mm	Infinity	0.24	23.2 × 28.8	95.9	77.6	1.9
	Maximum extension	0.37	15.0 × 18.6	75.8	55.6	2.4
200mm	Infinity	0.18	30.3 × 37.6	150	128	1.7
	Maximum extension	0.31	17.8 × 22.1	109	84.4	2.3
250mm	Infinity	0.15	37.8 × 47.0	220	194	1.6
	Maximum extension	0.25	22.3 × 27.7	154	126	2.1

Using extension tubes

Fitting an extension tube to the camera is similar to mounting a lens. The shutter, tube and lens must all be cocked before they can be fitted together.

There are two methods: either pre-assemble the lens and tube before attaching the combination to the camera, or fit the tube to the camera body before fixing the lens to the tube.

Automatic Bellows Attachment G

This bellows unit houses the necessary contacts and linkages to enable fully automatic diaphragm operation and through-the-lens metering with the AE Prism Finder G and AE Rotary Finder G. The attached lens can be extended by between 53mm and 153mm; the bellows rail is marked with a scale of extension. Extension tubes G-18 and G-36 cannot be used in combination with this bellows unit.

Attaching the bellows unit

Mounting the bellows to the camera body is similar to fitting a lens. Firstly the various components — lens, shutter and bellows — must be cocked before proceeding. The correct assembly procedure is that the bellows should be fitted on to the camera before the lens is mounted on to the bellows.

Using the bellows

The bellows unit causes a light loss so an increase in exposure is required to compensate. The degree of exposure compensation varies depending on the extension of the lens from the film plane. See the table below. Because of the light loss, the viewfinder image is darkened and this, together with the limited depth of field available at close subject to lens distances, means that focusing should be conducted with care. Depth of field becomes more shallow as subject magnification increases so select the smallest aperture practicable to optimise image sharpness. Invariably, in ambient light, this will lead to a slow shutter speed. A tripod should be used and the shutter operated with a remote release. The GS-1's mirror lock-up feature will also help under such circumstances, keeping vibration to a minimum.

Flash offers a controlled lighting source. A co-axial flash socket is provided on the bellows lens plate and if flash is being used the flash lead should be plugged in here. The camera's own co-axial socket and, if attached, the Speed Grip's G's hot-shoe are inoperative when the bellows unit is in use.

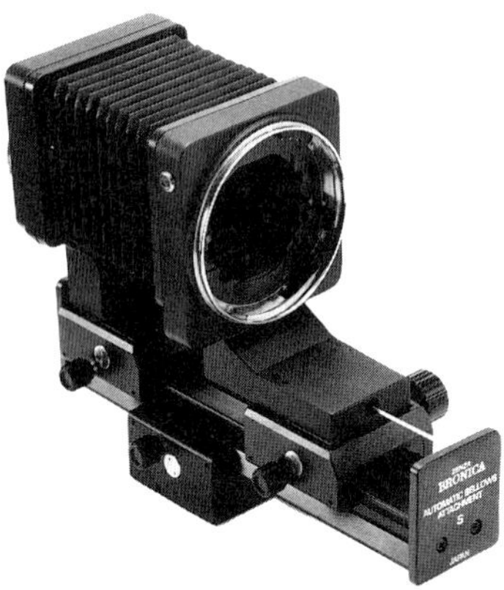

PG 100mm/Zenzanon-PG 100mm Lens

Bellows Extension	Magnification	Subject Area	Object-to-Film Plane Distance	Object-to-Front Lens Surface Distance	Exposure Factor	Extension Scale of Bellows	
mm		cm	cm	cm		cm	
53	0.53	10.5 × 13.0	43.4	22.8	2.2	0	With Focusing Ring of Lens at Infinity
63	0.63	8.82 × 11.0	41.4	19.8	2.5	1	
73	0.73	7.62 × 9.45	40.2	17.7	2.8	2	
83	0.83	6.70 × 8.31	39.6	16.0	3.1	3	
93	0.93	5.98 × 7.42	39.3	14.7	3.5	4	
103	1.03	5.40 × 6.70	39.2	13.7	3.8	5	
113	1.13	4.92 × 6.11	39.4	12.8	4.2	6	
123	1.23	4.52 × 5.61	39.6	12.1	4.6	7	
133	1.33	4.18 × 5.19	40.0	11.5	5.0	8	
143	1.43	3.89 × 4.82	40.5	11.0	5.4	9	
153	1.53	3.63 × 4.51	41.1	10.5	5.9	10	
171.9	1.72	3.23 × 4.01	42.2	9.8	6.7	10	

Note: (1) Values with maximum bellows extension plus maximum lens extension with helical focusing ring.
(2) Extension possible with helical focusing is 18.9mm with the 100mm lens.

Speed-Light G1

The Bronica GS-1 can be used in combination with any flashgun but for optimum versatility and exposure accuracy the Speed-Light G1 is recommended. This unit has been developed specifically as an integral part of the GS-1 system and, in conjunction with the Speed Grip G, through-the-lens automatic flash exposure is possible at all shutter speeds using a system called TTL Auto Film Plane Flash. A metering sensor located in the camera's mirror box and pointing at the film plane assesses the light as it is reflected off the film.

Used without the Speed Grip G or together with any Bronica camera non-TTL automatic flash operation is possible. Other facilities on offer include bounce flash illumination, manual control with fractional power settings and the option of an external auto-sensor.

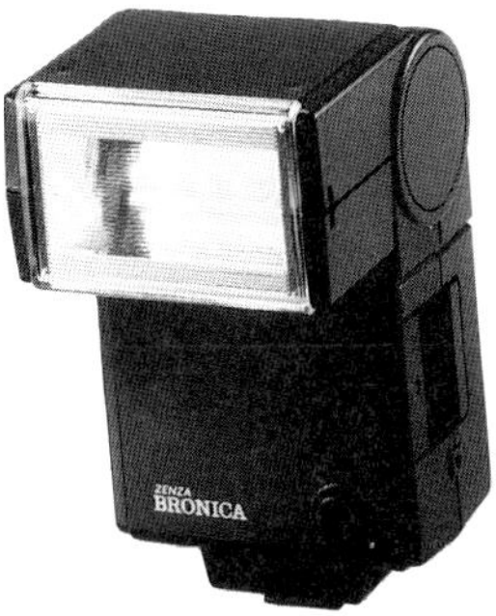

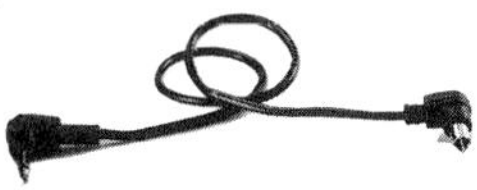

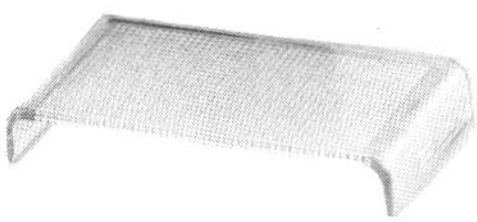

Number of flashes (approximate):

		Alkaline-manganese battery	Nickel-cadmium battery
TTL auto-flash		120 ~ 1,300	55 ~ 350
Non-TTL auto-flash		120 ~ 1,300	55 ~ 350
	FULL	120	55
	1/2	350	150
	1/4	600	200
	1/8	800	300

TTL auto-flash range (ASA/ISO 100/meter):

Aperture	Normal Panel	Wide Panel
F4	0.7 ~ 8 m	0.7 ~ 5.6m
F5.6	0.7 ~ 5.6m	0.7 ~ 4 m
F8	0.7 ~ 4 m	0.7 ~ 2.8m
F11	0.7 ~ 2.8m	0.7 ~ 2 m
F16	0.7 ~ 2 m	0.7 ~ 1.4m
F22	0.7 ~ 1.4m	0.7 ~ 1 m

Recycling time (approximate):

		Alkaline-manganese battery	Nickel-cadmium battery
TTL auto-flash		0.4 ~ 10sec.	0.4 ~ 7sec.
Non-TTL auto-flash		0.4 ~ 10sec.	0.4 ~ 7sec.
	FULL	10 sec.	7 sec.
	1/2	4.5sec.	3.5sec.
	1/4	3.5sec.	2 sec.
	1/8	2 sec.	1.5sec.

Non-TTL auto-flash range:

ASA/ISO	Orange Setting	Green Setting	Yellow Setting	Blue Setting
25	F 5.6	F 4	F 2.8	F 2
50	F 8	F 5.6	F 4	F 2.8
100	F11	F 8	F 5.6	F 4
200	F16	F11	F 8	F 5.6
400	F22	F16	F11	F 8
Normal	0.7 ~ 2.8m	0.7 ~ 4 m	1.0 ~ 5.6m	1.4 ~ 8 m
Wide	0.7 ~ 2 m	0.7 ~ 2.8m	1.0 ~ 4 m	1.4 ~ 5.6m

Guide numbers (ASA/ISO 100/meter):

Output setting	Normal Panel	Wide Panel
FULL	32	22
1/2	22	16
1/4	16	11
1/8	11	8

Specifications of the Bronica GS-1

Type	6 × 7cm format lens shutter single-lens-reflex camera with interchangeable lens, film back, finder and focusing screen.
Frame size	55.6mm × 69mm.
Film size	120 roll film (10 exposures); 220 roll film (20 exposures); and Polaroid Land. Exclusive film backs for each type.
Lens mount	Exclusive four-claw Bronica GS bayonet mount.
Shutter	Electronically controlled SEIKO #0 between-the-lens leaf shutter with speeds from 16 seconds to 1/500 sec; plus 'T' (Time exposure) and 'B' (Bulb). Mechanical speeds of 'T' and 1/500 sec only.
Flash synchronisation	Electronic X-flash synchronisation at all shutter speeds.
Depth of view preview	Every Zenzanon PG lens has a preview lever built-in.
Multiple exposure	Possible with lever on camera body.
Mirror lock-up	Single frame or continuous mirror lock-up capability with lever on camera body.
Finder system	Interchangeable with the choice of four: Waist Level Finder G; Prism Finder G; AE Prism Finder G; and AE Rotary Finder G.
Focus screen	Interchangeable with seven options. Full-area matte screen supplied as standard.
Battery	One six volt silver oxide (No 544, PX-28 or 4G13) or alkaline-manganese equivalent (A544 or 4LR44).
Battery check	Shutter speed LED lights up or flashes when shutter button is semi-depressed. Varies according to finder.
Dimensions	106.5mm wide × 117.7mm high × 196.5mm long (GS-1 main body with 100mm f3.5 lens, 120 film back and Waist Level Finder G.)
Weight	1830 grams (with above accessories but no battery).

Chapter Fourteen

Bronica 35mm and Polaroid Film Backs

Versatility is important to the discerning photographer and Bronica's appreciation of that fact manifests itself in the provision of a wide selection of interchangeable film backs for each of its cameras; Bronica cameras are truly multi-format.

What is on offer

Interchangeable film backs significantly widen a camera's appeal especially among professional photographers, and they invoke a dramatic improvement in handling. Film unloading and reloading can be achieved rapidly just by slipping off one back and replacing it with another already primed with film. More importantly, with a number of backs there is the possibility of shooting several film types including Polaroid with one camera body, and of switching from one film to another in mid-roll.

During the exchange of film backs always rotate the wind crank, or press the drive button in the case of the SQ-Am, to ensure that preparations for photography are complete. If the shutter is not cocked or an exposed frame is in the film gate the crank can be rotated and will stop automatically. Often you will find that the crank can be operated even if the shutter is cocked and the film wound on. In the latter instance there is no film wastage.

Loading the various 120 and 220 Bronica film backs is simple and with practice can be achieved

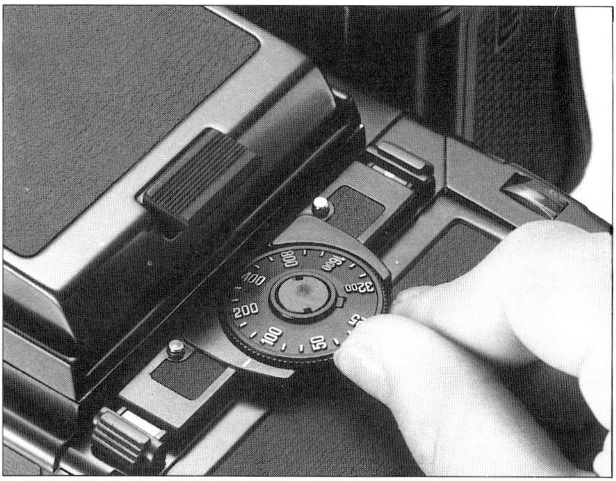

speedily. The procedure for loading each camera model is discussed in their respective chapters. Here we look at 35mm and Polaroid film backs.

35mm FILM BACKS

35mm film backs are available for both the ETR and the SQ systems. Two variants are offered in each system: 'N' backs give the standard 24 × 36mm format; and 'W' 24 × 54mm, a panoramic format which combines the height of the 35mm format with the width of the 6 × 6cm frame and is ideally suited to creative photography. In the case of the ETR the standard focusing screen has both 35mm frames etched on it for composition purposes.

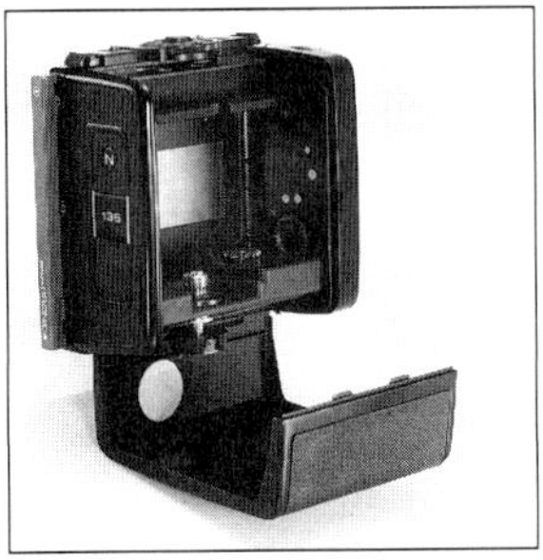

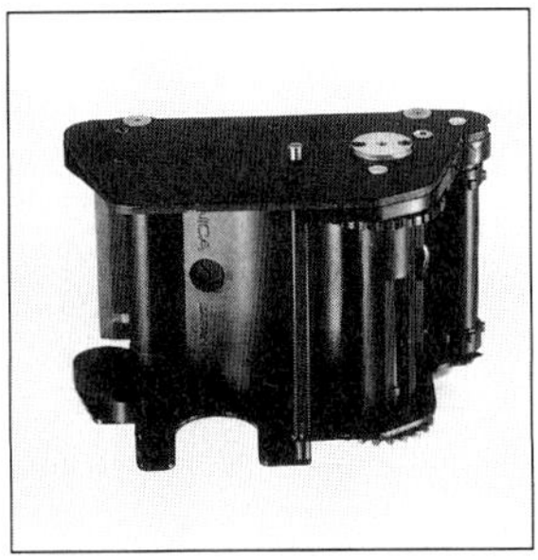

The components of a 35mm film back.

As far as many of the general points of handling are concerned 35mm and roll film backs are much the same. Important differences however concern loading and the film holder itself; obviously necessary because of the nature of 35mm cassette film.

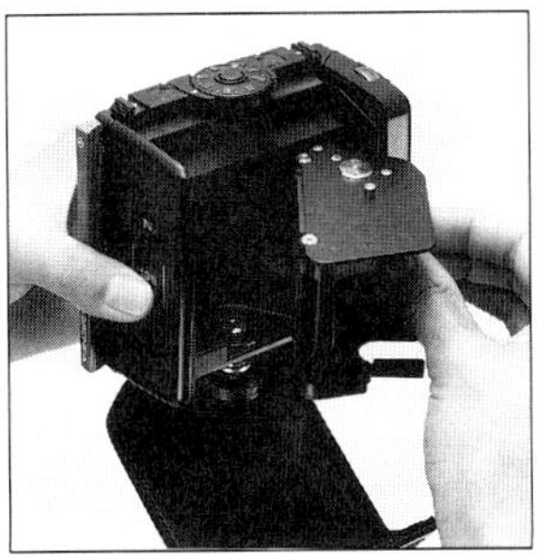

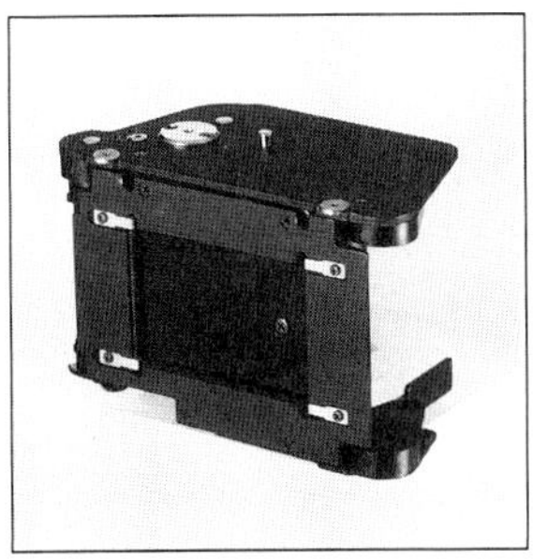

35mm film back loading

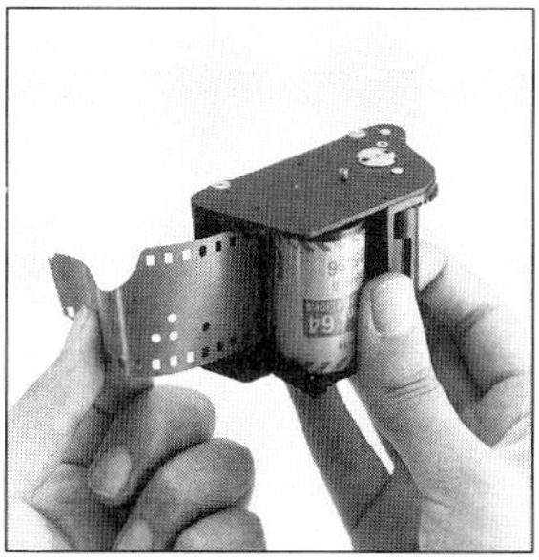

The loading and unloading procedures for both types of 35mm back are identical. Open the back cover by pushing in the two back release buttons and the film chamber is revealed. In order to extract the film holder the rewind crank must be pulled out and the insert gripped on the left side which will enable it to be withdrawn from the chamber. Loading can then take place. Drop the film cassette into position as indicated by the diagram on the insert casing, and pull out sufficient film leader to feed it, emulsion side out, between the spring loaded pressure plate and the masking plate and into the take-up spool, manually operating the drive cog to ensure that there is no slack film.

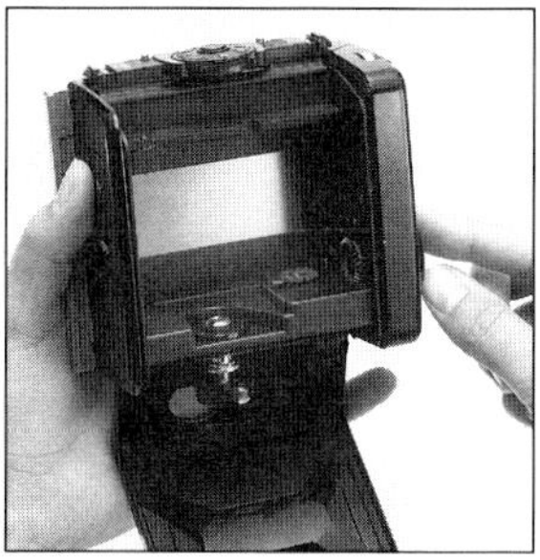

Before replacing the holder rotate the back's manual wind crank until the rewind button clicks and moves down. When the insert is in position push back the rewind crank engaging the film spool to hold it firmly in place. Gently rotate the manual film knob located on the left of the back to take up any slack and then close the back cover. Mount the back on to the camera, fire the shutter and wind-on. Repeat twice and you will be on the first frame.

On SQ film backs the film's correct ISO rating must be set on the back's film speed control if a meter finder is being used.

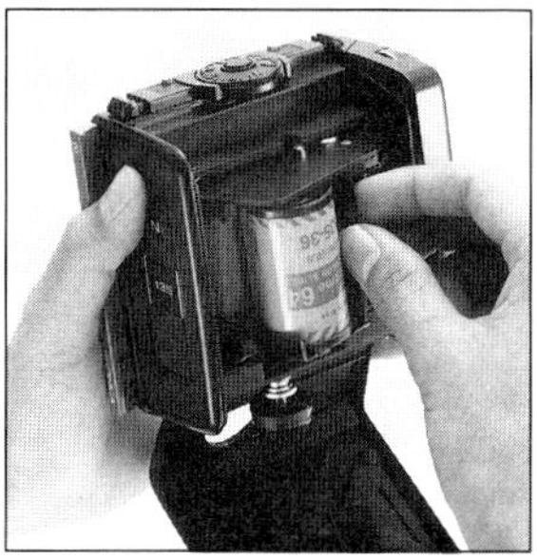

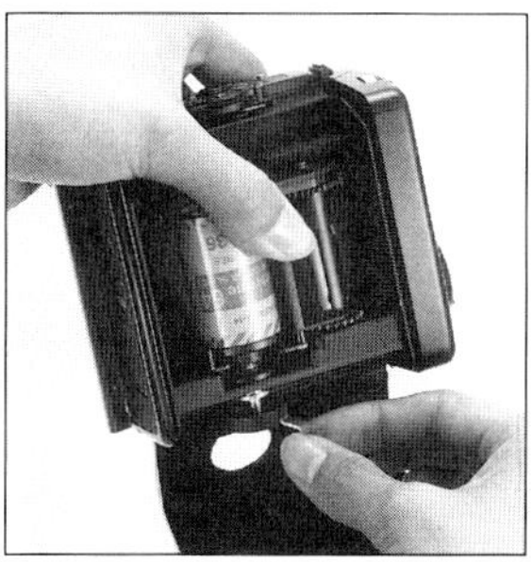

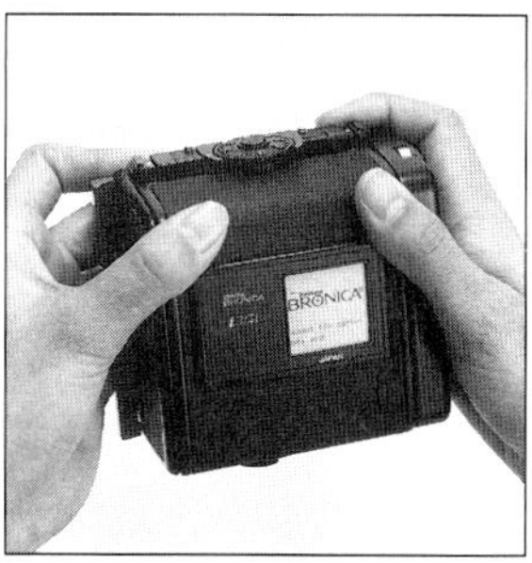

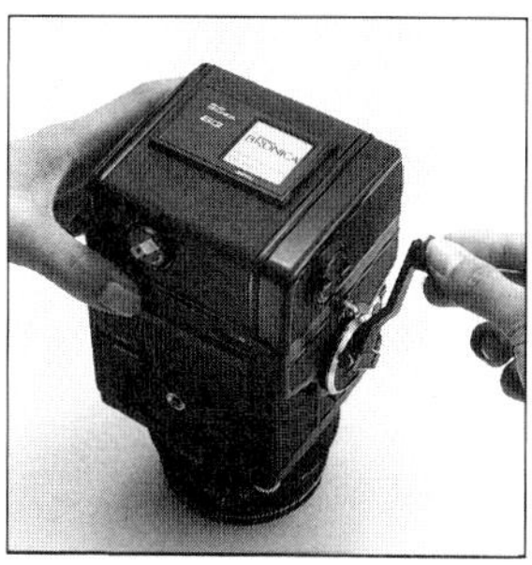

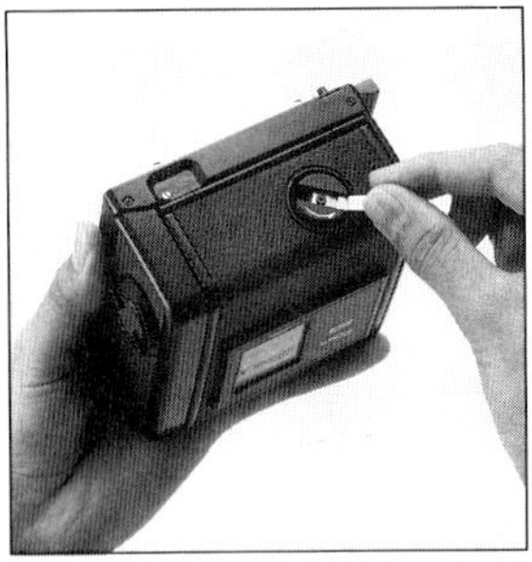

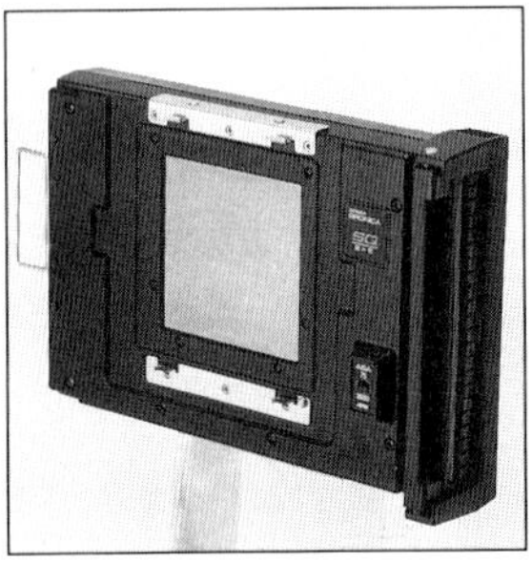

Unloading

After the last frame has been exposed you will find that the camera's wind crank will not rotate any further. Do not force it. Wind the exposed film back into the cassette by first pushing the film rewind button; if it pops out hold it in for a short while, as the film is being rewound, until it stays put. Unfold the rewind crank handle and rotate it in the direction of the arrow until the tension eases, which indicates that the film has been rewound. The back may now be opened and the exposed film removed.

POLAROID LAND FILM BACKS

Instant feedback is a facility that most professional photographers cannot do without and a Polaroid film back fulfils this need. Checking lighting, colour, composition and so on can save a great deal of time, effort and money.

Bronica Polaroid film backs share the mounting mechanism of other film backs though there are a

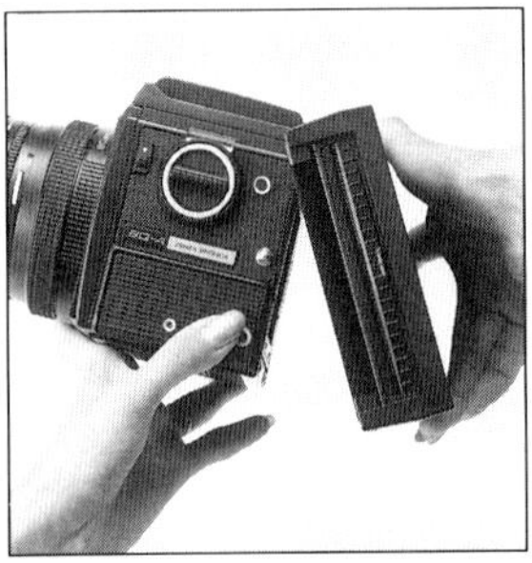

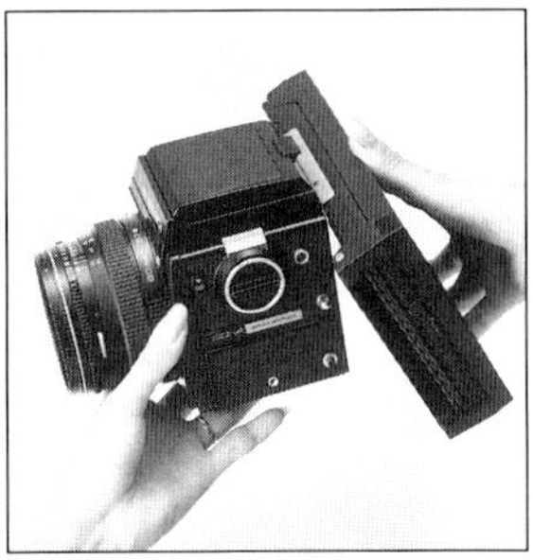

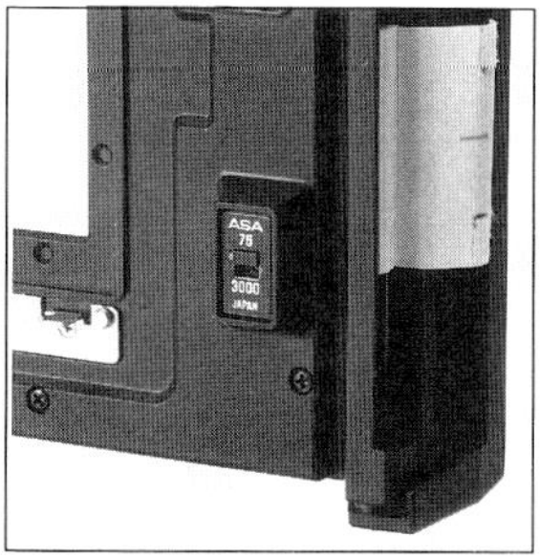

Polaroid backs for the SQ and GS-1 systems have an ISO selector switch.

couple of important points to bear in mind. Firstly, the shutter can be released with the dark slide fully inserted. Secondly, the film back can be taken off the camera while the dark slide is withdrawn.

Additionally, because the Polaroid film backs are not fully coupled to the camera body it is essential to set the camera to multiple exposure operation; this allows the shutter to be cocked after each exposure.

The Polaroid film back for the Bronica ETR system differs from those for the SQ and the GS-1 in that there is an absence of an ISO control. The film's ISO rating has to be transferred to the AE-II Prism Finder-E if it is fitted.

Bronica SQ and GS-1 Polaroid backs have a film speed selector with the choice of ISO 75 or ISO 3000. The set film speed is automatically transferred to the metering prism if one is fitted. When no meter finder is fitted the film speed selector has no effect.

Film loading

Polaroid Type 87 and 88 film packs are not sufficiently long to fully occupy the film chamber; a notch on the film pack must be placed to coincide with a gap in the side of the guide rail so that it will be held in the correct position. No such precautions are needed with Polaroid Type 665, 667, 668, 669 and 691 films which fit perfectly.

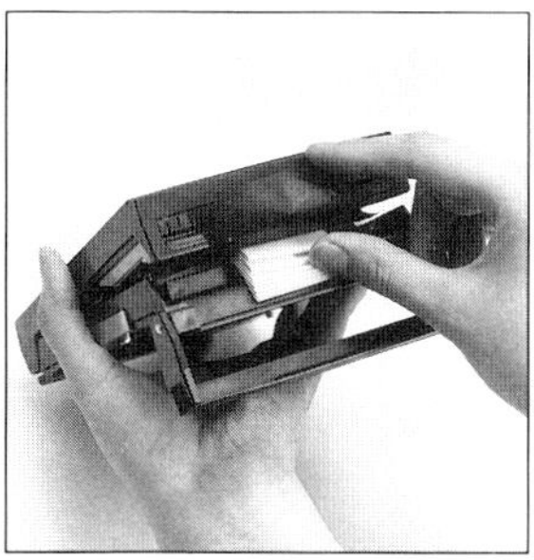

Release the back cover and position the film pack so that the white tabs under the black paper safety flap are free and not folded under the pack. Closing the back cover will leave the flap protruding. Grip this firmly and pull it all the way out, taking care not to rip it, and discard. This will bring the first white tab into place, and you are now ready to make a Polaroid exposure.

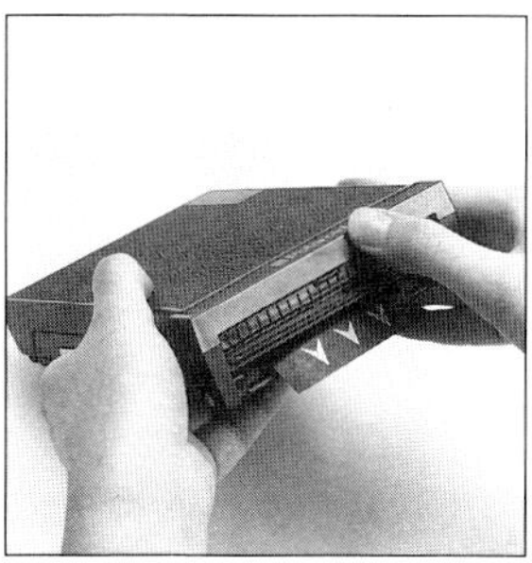

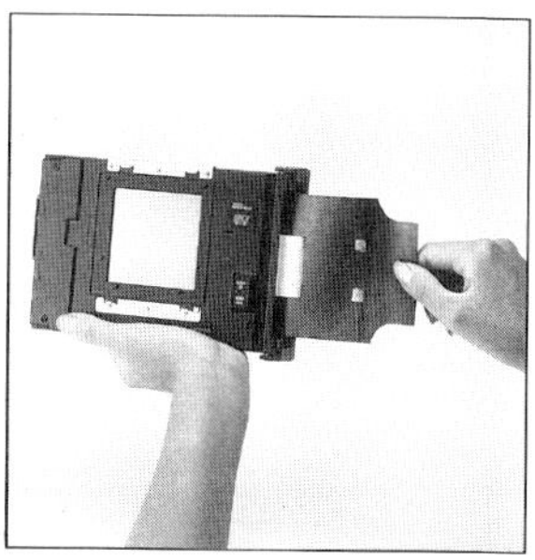

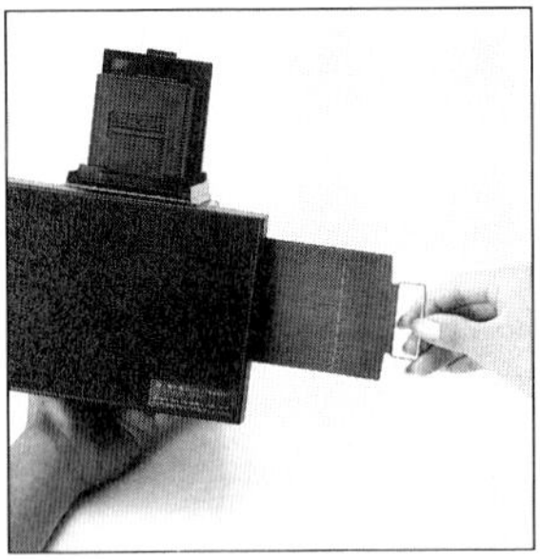

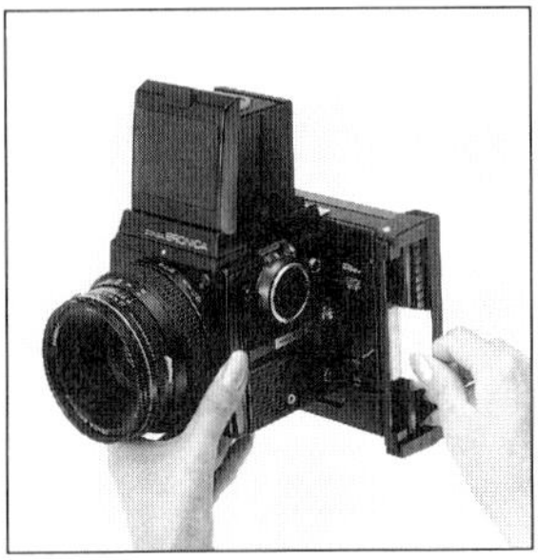

Polaroid film back in use

Pull out the dark slide. It is not necessary to withdraw the dark slide fully; an etched triangular mark indicates how far the slide needs be pulled out to be clear of the film.

After the exposure has been made the next stage is to process the film. Firmly pull out and discard the white tab. As this tab is pulled a yellow coloured tab appears in a spring loaded side flap. Grip the yellow tab and firmly and smoothly withdraw it in one uninterrupted motion. During this stage the chemical pods are broken open and the developer spread across the film surface. The timing of development should now begin. After the process time has elapsed peel the print off the black backing paper. If applicable coat the print with the supplied chemical. In the case of Type 665 film the backing sheet should be immersed in Sodium Sulphite solution if the negative image is required.

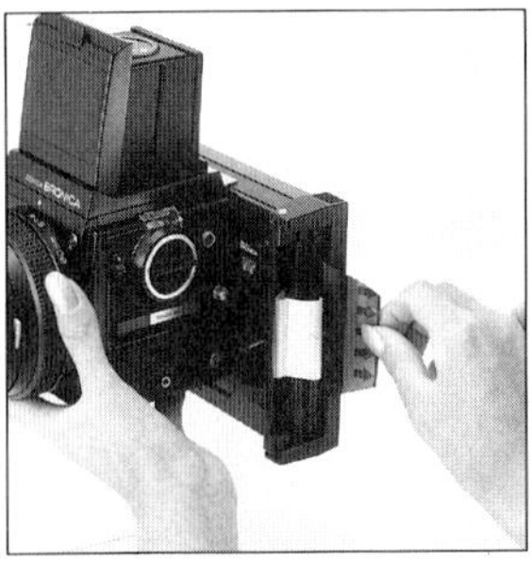

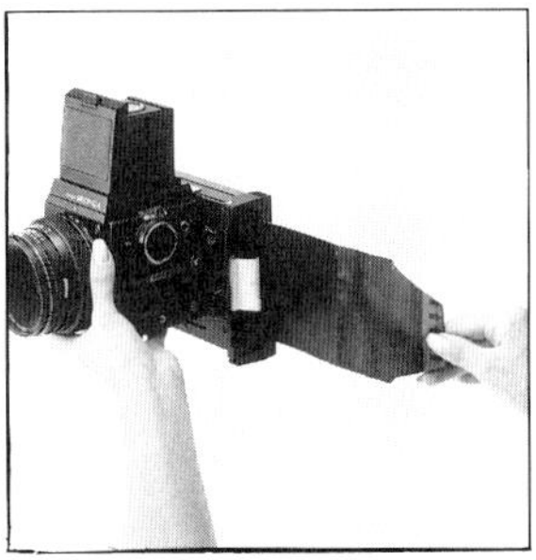

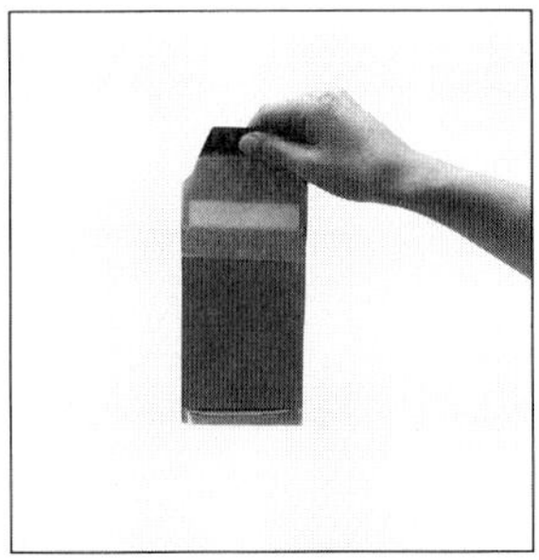

Making the most of the Polaroid film back

- Be precise about exposure. Polaroid films are reversal materials. Over-exposure gives unsaturated, very light prints or slides while under-exposure leads to dark, muddy results.
- Pull tabs smoothly yet firmly. Uneven development might be caused by stopping and starting as the yellow tab is pulled out.
- Time development carefully. Be accurate as well as consistent in your timing method.
- Check the ambient temperature. Chemical action is slower in colder temperatures and the process time will need extending.
- Keep the film back's roller scrupulously clean. Dirty rollers will cause uneven patches and white specks on the print or may even prevent the appearance of the yellow tab. Never scrape the metal rollers in case of possible damage but wipe with a soft, dry cloth.
- Prints change colour marginally as they dry so wait until they are dry before assessing them. Use a hair dryer to promote faster drying.
- In the case of Polaroid Type 667 and 87 films with speeds of ISO 3000 the use of neutral density filters may be necessary to bring their ISO down to manageable levels.

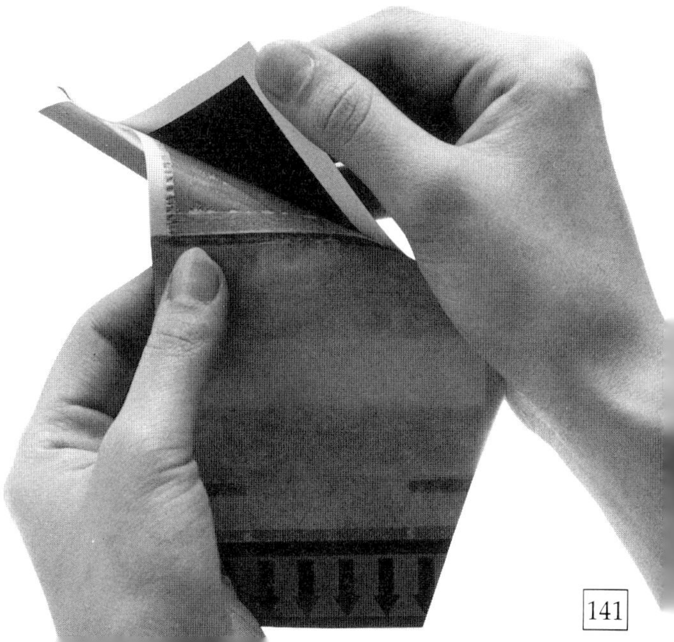

Chapter Fifteen

Exposure

Your photography will benefit greatly from an understanding of the principles of exposure and how lightmeters — integral and separate — should be applied to the best effect in practical situations. No current Bronica camera has an integral metering mechanism although each system has optional exposure finders available. For operational convenience Bronica metering finders can be highly recommended.

Whether the lightmeter is separate or integrated into the camera it has to be employed intelligently to exploit your equipment and materials to their utmost. This is true even though many modern films, especially negative types, have relatively wide exposure latitude and acceptable results may be obtained with the minimum of fuss. However, for optimum picture quality exposure should be as considered and as accurate as possible.

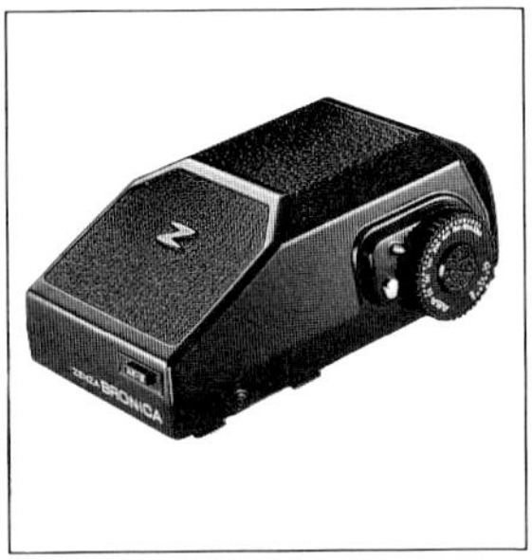

The AE-II Finder-E utilises fast reacting silicon photo cells.

Meter types

Exposure meters employ a variety of light sensitive cells. Selenium cells generate their own electric current when light falls on them and so have the advantage that they do not require any battery. They are, however, not very sensitive and have a limited response in poor-light. Nowadays this type of cell is only used in separate lightmeters; the most well known example is the Euromaster.

Cadmium Sulphide, or CdS, sensors require a battery to work from but are vastly more sensitive than selenium cells. Although in widespread use they do have disadvantages. They are slightly over-red sensitive, which means that under-exposure can be the result if a red filter is being used or if the subject is predominantly red and, they are relatively slow to react to changes of light intensity. When taking a light measurement from an average or low-light subject directly after taking a reading from strong sun, allow the meter to settle down first.

Most modern cameras and many separate lightmeters use silicon photo diodes. These are extremely sensitive and react almost instantaneously to lighting fluctuations. Also, unlike CdS cells the silicon sensor has an even spectral response.

Gallium photo diode or GPD cells are also used in modern cameras. However, although not as widely used as the silicon type, they offer a similar high standard of performance.

Through-the-lens exposure systems

Through-the-lens metering systems are incorporated into or are available optionally on the vast majority of modern cameras and they measure the amount of light actually entering through the lens. The various metering finders for Bronica cameras all have their sensor cells located in the finder and operate on this principle.

Light can be assessed in a number of ways, according to the meter's design. Average metering occurs when all of the light entering the lens is measured and integrated to give an exposure reading. The typical average metering system is reliable in most normal situations but it can be misled if there is something strongly bright or predominantly dark in the scene.

Centre-weighted systems have their meter sensitivity concentrated around the middle of the viewfinder although some of the surrounding area is taken into account. This type of system works on the principle that the subject is usually in the middle of the frame.

Selective metering systems measure the central 10% of the viewfinder image. The sensitivity area is usually defined on the focusing screen. The integral spot-meter is more highly selective and reads 2% or 3% of the picture area. Only light from the sensitivity zone is assessed. Of the metering finders available for Bronica cameras only the AE Rotary Finder G designed for GS-1 has the option of spot-metering. It should be noted that a true spot-meter, as discussed later, is a separate meter with an extremely narrow angle of view, usually one degree.

Separate lightmeters

Separate lightmeters are favoured by dedicated amateur and professional photographers and, used properly, they are the means to ultimate exposure control.

There are many brands and several types available. Most allow reflected and incident light measurements to be made and the more sophisticated models are usually supported by a system of attachments that enable the meter to be converted, for example, into a spot-meter or for darkroom use.

Separate spot-meters usually have an acceptance angle of one or two degrees and so are extremely selective, more so than spot-meters built into cameras. Typically, the separate spot-meter incorporates a mirror mechanism similar to that found on a single-lens-reflex camera and this allows the user to meter from the subject very precisely. Exposure details are usually conveyed by means of a viewfinder display.

Metering techniques

Average scenes comprise a complete range of tones, from deep shadows to bright highlights and every shade in between. Whatever the tonal characteristics of the subject, whether it is fully toned or predominantly white or black, the meter is calibrated to interpret it to give an aperture/shutter speed combination which will result in a negative density that will reproduce as 18% mid-grey on the final print.

In other words, the meter gives a compromise reading ensuring that the most crucial tone, the mid-tone, is represented correctly in the print leaving the highlight and shadow details to look after themselves.

In average situations the lightmeter's ability to reproduce an 18% grey tone is perfectly acceptable. However, it is in non-average situations that the lightmeter's reading has to be modified for correct tonal reproduction. For example, predominantly light or dark scenes will mislead the meter into under or over-exposure respectively. The Zone System, discussed later in this chapter, can be applied to effect here.

Light readings can be made by a number of methods. Reflected readings are taken with the meter aimed directly at the subject from the camera position. Self-evidently, through-the-lens metering systems provide reflected readings. The skill involved in taking such readings is to ensure that the meter is measuring the light being reflected off the most important aspect of the scene. This type of light reading is affected by strongly reflective subjects and bright backgrounds which can lead to severe under-exposure.

Realising when the meter is likely to be confounded and that exposure correction might be necessary is another aspect of taking meter readings. It is good technique to angle the meter or camera slightly downwards so that the sky is not over-influential; most hand-held lightmeters have an acceptable angle of 30 degrees. This will give a reading which will ensure sufficient exposure of foreground detail. Faced by a subject standing against a strongly-lit background a close-up meter reading of the subject will be necessary to guarantee adequate exposure.

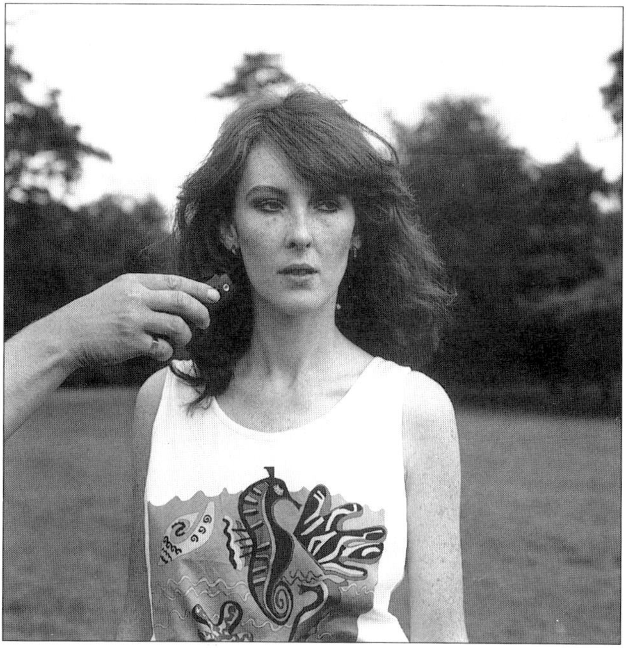

In tricky lighting situations move in close to the subject to take a meter reading. This guarantees that only the light being reflected from the subject is being measured.

As much depends on the effect envisaged, only general exposure guidelines can be given. For example, when shooting silhouettes and deliberate under-exposure to the foreground is required, the light reading should be taken from the highlights.

A variation of reflected light reading technique is to use a Kodak 18% grey card. By taking a reading directly from a grey card you are guaranteed a mid-tone regardless of the tonal qualities of the background or subject. To use a grey card, position it to receive the same light as the subject, angling it so that there is no glare and so that no shadows are falling across it. Move in close so that the meter's field of view is filled by the card.

Virtually all separate meters have the facility for incident light readings. A white diffuser dome or panel is placed over the light receptive window and the reading is taken from the subject with the meter

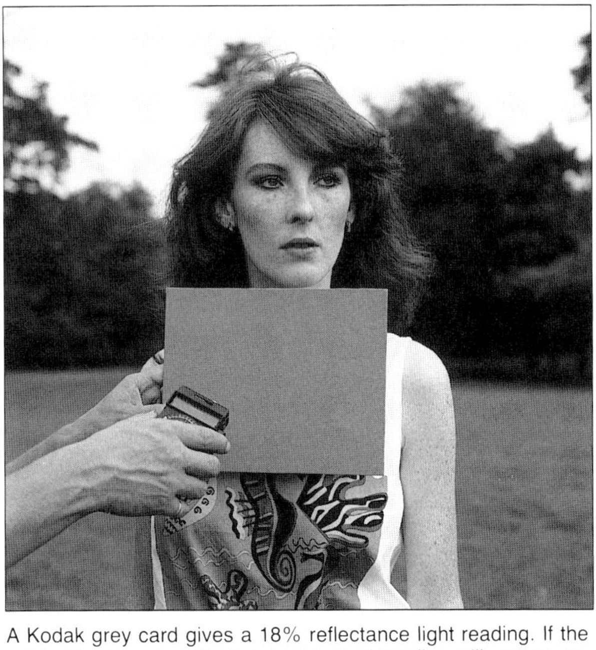

A Kodak grey card gives a 18% reflectance light reading. If the subject is strongly reflective a grey card reading will ensure an accurate meter reading.

aimed at the camera position. The advantage of incident readings is that they assess the light falling on the subject and so are independent of whatever is within the scene. They are not adversely affected by bright backgrounds or particularly reflective subjects and used without modification will reproduce an 18% mid-tone on film.

It is not always practical to walk up to the subject and take an incident reading so take a substitute incident reading by positioning the meter in an area which is receiving identical lighting.

The white diffuser can be separate from the lightmeter, as in the case of the Euromaster, or it might be integral, as in the meters from Gossen and Shepherd. In either case it should be kept clean and free from any dust that might affect the reading accuracy.

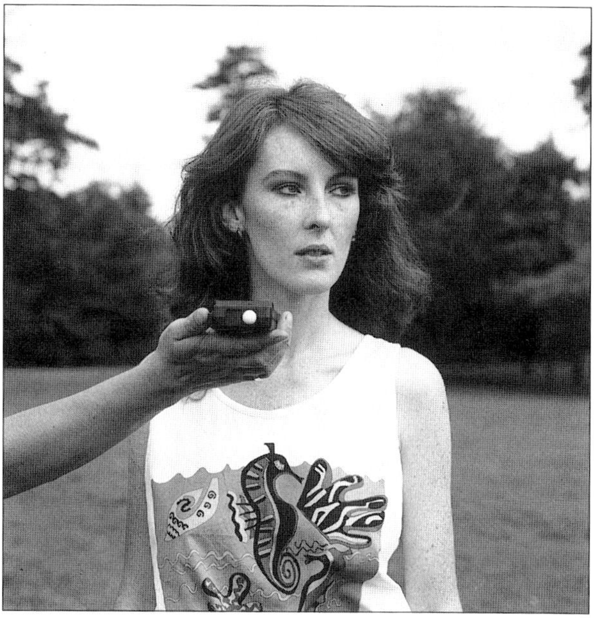

An incident reading measures the light falling on to the subject and is taken from the subject's position with the meter fitted with a diffuser and aimed towards the camera.

The Zone System

No discussion on exposure would be complete without reference to the Zone System, the ultimate in creative exposure control as developed by Ansel Adams and in which he applied the principles of sensitometry to photographic exposure.

The tones recorded by photographic film can be divided into ten distinct categories or 'zones', the exposure difference between each zone being equivalent to one complete f/stop. Zone 0 is pure detailless black (the film base plus fog on the negative), Zone 9 represents white tones with no detail (the paper's base) and in between are eight zones with Zone 5 representing 18% grey mid-tone. Clearly every time a light reading is made the subject, regardless of its true tonal value, is placed in Zone 5.

By placing the subject in the correct zone the photographer exercises his skill and judgement to directly affect the way in which the subject is reproduced on the finished print. To 'place' your subject in a particular zone is simple so long as you bear in mind that your lightmeter will automatically give Zone 5, which will print as 18% mid-tone on the final print without modification, and that the gap between each zone is exactly one stop. Therefore, if you estimate that your subject should be placed in Zone 6 and the lightmeter gives a reading of 1/125 second at f11, setting an aperture of f8, or a shutter of 1/60 second, will produce a tonally correct result. Similarly, if your subject is Zone 4, using the same exposure setting as above, an exposure of 1/125 second at f16 or 1/250 second at f11 will give correct tones.

It is important to appreciate that exposure modifications will affect the remainder of the tones present in the photograph and that deciding on the correct tone for one aspect of the scene might create problems elsewhere; filled-in shadows or burnt-out highlights for example. Using different paper grades will assist with the problem.

Although in its element when applied to black-and-white photography, colour transparency users can also benefit from the Zone System albeit in limited fashion: slides are originals and so do not undergo a second process, ie printing, and the exposure latitude of transparency film is limited.

A refinement of the Zone System is the individual development of each exposure. In the days when sheet film was in more common use treating each picture according to its individual needs was a straightforward process. However, for the modern photographers using 35mm or 120 roll film this is clearly impractical. But, because individual development is a refinement and not its principle, exposing your pictures according to the Zone System will still reward you with superb results.

The Zone System

Zone 9: Detailless white tones. Snow in strong sunlight. Paper base tone.

Zone 8: Whites with texture

Zone 7: Light grey subjects.

Zone 6: Caucasian skin tone in sunlight.

Zone 5: Middle grey. 18% reflectance

Zone 4: Average shadow tone on Caucasian skin.

Zone 3: Dark shadows with detail.

Zone 2: Slight tonality.

Zone 1: Almost black

Zone 0: Solid black

Chapter Sixteen Lenses

The lens is the camera eye through which your photographic vision becomes reality. But regardless of focal length, you will have probably realised that just one lens is likely to be insufficient to satiate your creative desires. Simply, some lenses are better disposed to some subjects than others.

Bronica has on offer for each of its camera systems an extensive range of focal length optics from extreme wide angle to long telephoto. Zenzanon lenses, computer-designed and using the highest quality optical glass, deliver superb resolution, biting sharpness and faithful colour reproduction throughout their aperture and focusing ranges. See the relevant chapter for what is available.

Assuming that you have purchased your Bronica camera with one lens, usually the standard lens, where next? Before proceeding it should be said that having several lenses is no guarantee of successful photographs. It is your 'seeing eye' that is all important and there is much that can be achieved even with something as seemingly humble as a standard lens.

Lenses of different focal length have different angles of view but there is a great deal more to be considered when choosing a lens than simply this; your own interests, for example. If sports photography appeals to you clearly a telephoto lens would be a more logical and suitable choice than a wide angle. Similarly, wide angles are eminently suited to photographing interiors and sweeping landscapes. But do not pigeon-hole lenses to specific photographic tasks. Who says that sports, for example, cannot be tackled with a wide angle lens or interiors with a telephoto?

Your photographic style has a big part to play. Confronted by a photographic opportunity one photographer might choose a telephoto while another would fit a wide angle lens yet both could come away with a brilliant picture.

Standard lenses

Normal or standard lenses have a field of view which approximates closely with that of the human eye. As a rough guide, the focal length of a standard lens is equal to the diagonal of the format frame. For example, 75mm in the case of the 6 × 4.5cm format,

85mm for the 6 × 6cm and 92mm for the 6 × 7cm format. The theoretical standard focal length for the 35mm format is 43.5mm but because, many years ago, lens manufacturers had problems producing sharp lenses of this focal length the longer 50mm lens was favoured.

Because of their normal perspective reproduction standard lenses can be deployed to great effect with an enormous range of subject matter. Generally, they have comparatively wide maximum apertures which means that they supply a crisp focusing image making them well suited to low-light photography.

Wide angle lenses

Once upon a time wide angle lenses were identified by their poor sharpness and susceptibility to flare and distortion. Optical design has vastly improved since those days and quality wide angle lenses are no longer dogged by such drawbacks. Typical modern wide angle lenses exhibit a very high level of sharpness throughout their aperture and focusing ranges, and are highly resistant to flare in contrasty lighting situations.

Pictorially, wide angle lenses are tremendously versatile. It is not just in cramped conditions that they come in useful. For portraying sweeping vistas, extreme depth of field effects and strong perspectives, the wide angle is out on its own. When the subject is some way from the camera the depth of field available with a wide angle lens is extensive and everything appears sharp. As the subject gets closer to the lens the quantity of available depth of field is reduced. However, by focusing using the hyperfocal distance (see page 155) it is possible to retain sharpness in both a near subject and a far background.

Telephoto lenses

All lenses with a focal length of longer than a standard lens are referred to as telephoto. These have the opposite effect to wide angles and their greater magnification 'compresses' the space in the picture. Used skilfully it appears that the distance between the subject and background is small when in reality it is great.

The effect of different focal lengths on the same subject.

40mm lens

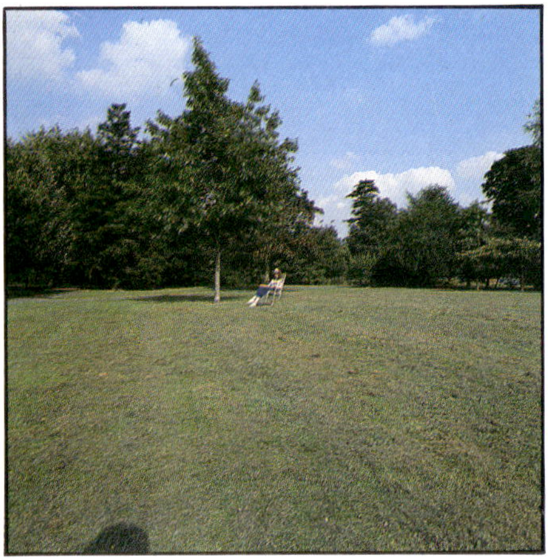

50mm lens

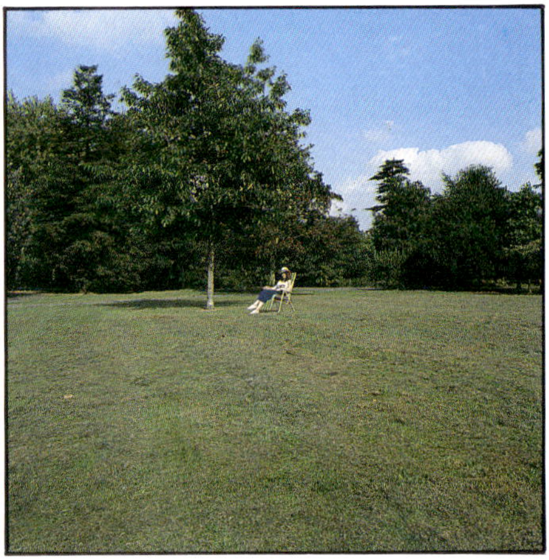

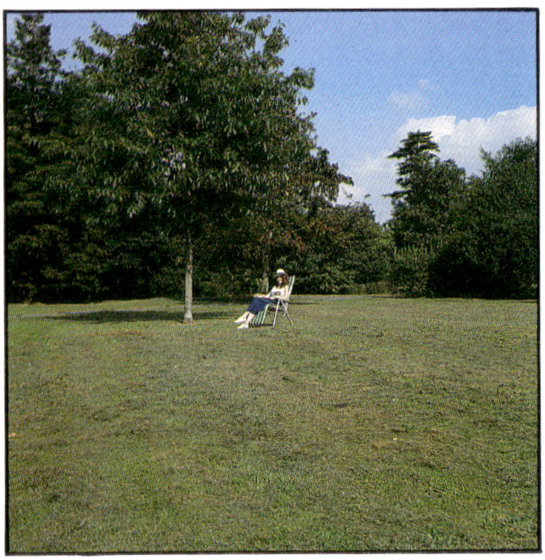

65mm lens

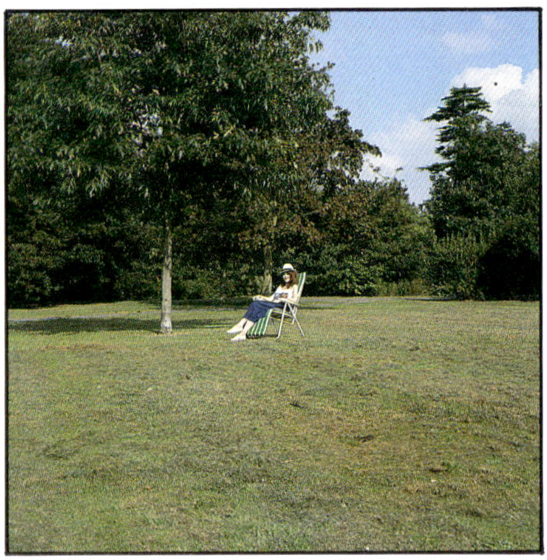

80mm lens

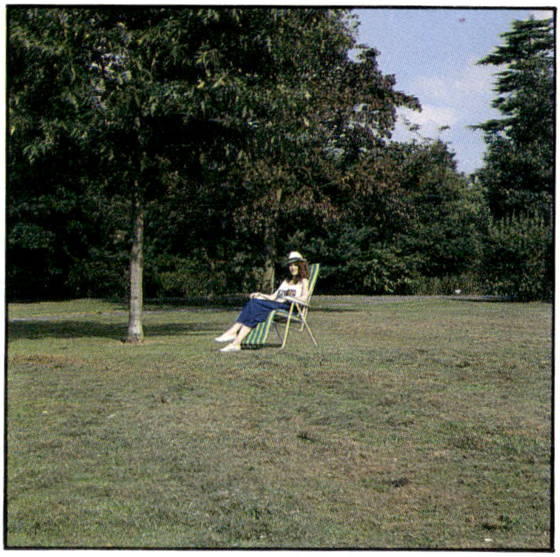

110mm lens

150mm lens

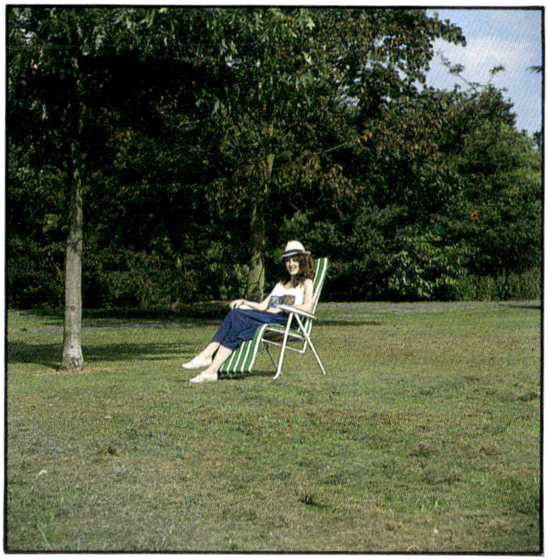

200mm lens

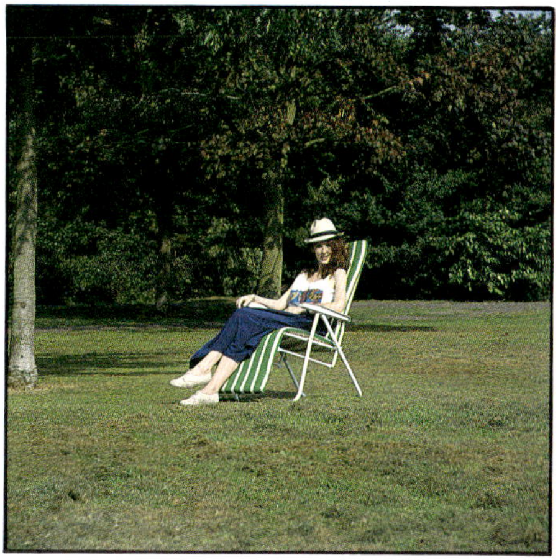

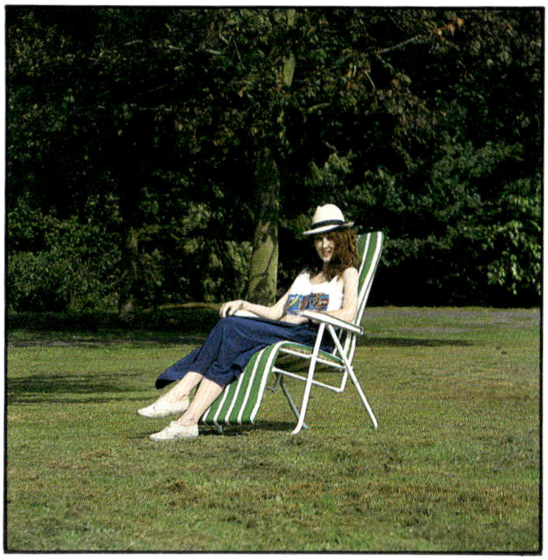

250mm lens

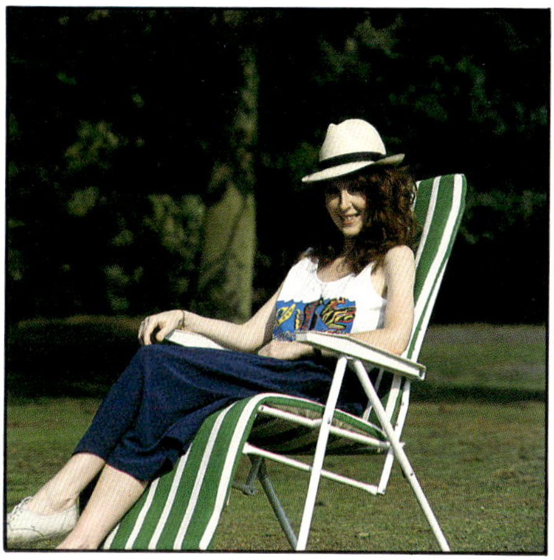

500mm lens

Longer focal length lenses have less depth of field than wide angles and consequently focusing has to be conducted with considerably more care. The effect of lesser depth of field can be used to advantage: select a wide lens aperture and the subject will stand out prominently from the background. Because of the greater magnification the problem of camera shake is more likely to surface so, if practical, use some form of camera support and select the highest shutter speed possible.

Depth of field

Depth of field can be defined as the zone of the subject, from foreground to background, in sharp focus. Learn to control depth of field and, to an extent, you will control the impact of your pictures. Too much depth of field can result in the background competing with the subject and distracting the viewer's eye from the main part of the photograph. Conversely, too little depth of field and the lack of sharpness might detract from a photograph's impact.

The amount of depth of field is dependent on a number of factors: the lens aperture, focal length and lens to subject distance.

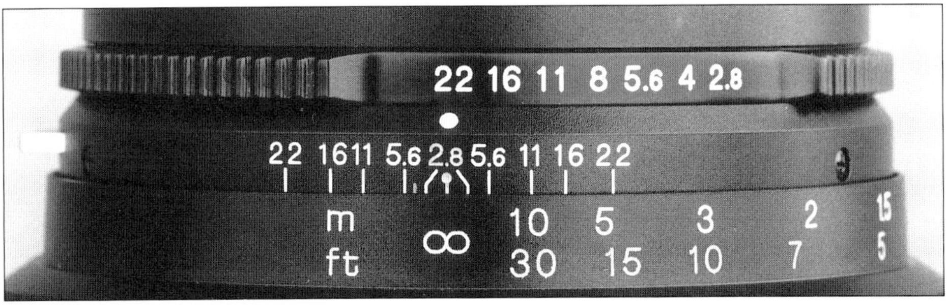

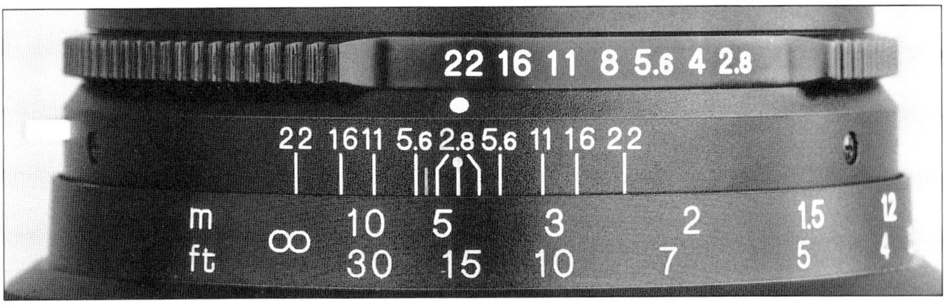

Depth of field is directly proportional to the f/number, ie double the f/stop number and depth of field is doubled. In other words the smaller the lens f/number the greater the depth of field. Conversely, the wider the lens aperture the shallower the depth of field.

Depth of field is greater with distant subjects. Double the subject to lens distance and depth of field is increased by a factor of four. With the subject at infinity therefore depth of field is enormous. At close focusing distances depth of field, even at small apertures, is minimal. The lack of depth of field is especially noticeable during macro photography when there can be insufficient sharpness for acceptable results.

As focal length increases so depth of field decreases. Wide angle lenses are ideal if you want extreme depth of field effects whereas, if you want to limit depth of field telephoto lenses are advised.

Obviously, the three factors discussed above should not be taken in isolation. They usually operate in conjunction with one another and this should be borne in mind whenever depth of field is considered.

Hyperfocal distance

The hyperfocal distance can be defined as the closest distance in sharp focus when the lens is focused on infinity. As an alternative explanation, it is the closest distance that can be focused on yet retain subject sharpness at infinity. The hyperfocal distance will vary depending on the aperture.

Focusing according to the hyperfocal distance will make the most of the depth of field available. Calculating the approximate hyperfocal distance is straightforward if the lens has a good, clear depth of field scale.

When the lens is focused on infinity depth of field extends from infinity to the hyperfocal distance. Take a look at the two pictures of the Zenzanon-E 75mm f2.8 lens barrel opposite. Let us assume a subject at infinity and a lens aperture of f22. With the lens focused at infinity, by reading off the scale we see that depth of field extends from infinity to a little under five metres (top picture). Note this distance and adjust the focus barrel so that it lies opposite the correct focus index (bottom picture). Reading off the scale notice now depth of field extends from infinity to approximately 2.5 metres. Therefore, by focusing hyperfocally the optimum amount of depth of field is obtained. Calculating the hyperfocal distance for any subject distance is done by using the same procedure; focus as normal on the subject and note the hyperfocal distance for the lens aperture in use. Then re-adjust the lens barrel to the noted distance.

Caring for your lenses

No matter how efficient the multi-layer coating, a lens's performance, particularly in rendering contrast, can suffer in certain lighting situations such as shooting into-the-light. For this reason a suitable lens hood should be used at all times to minimise flare and maximise contrast.

Dirt or grease on lens elements will degrade image quality. Carefully clean your lenses regularly using a soft camel hair blower brush or compressed air cleaner. Do not use a cloth which might be impregnated with grit, solvents or anything which can physically damage the sensitive lens surface. The front element can be protected by attaching a high quality ultra-violet or skylight filter; it is cheaper to replace a filter than it is a lens. While on the subject of looking after your lenses remember that vibration can harm them by actually shaking loose the internal elements. Carry your lenses around in a padded gadget bag or foam-lined case for the maximum protection and use lens caps regularly.

Chapter Seventeen

Film

Film technology has advanced considerably in recent years and it is an undeniable fact that the photographer has never had such a vast collection of materials available, catering for virtually every subject and lighting eventuality.

Generally speaking the slower the film the better the technical quality, with finer grain, richer colour and superior sharpness; even the differences between an ISO 50 and a medium speed ISO 100 film can be quite marked, although it might be the case that it is only with big enlargements that differences are discernible. However, such is the overall quality of modern products that ISO 400 or faster films are more than capable of fine results.

It is colour film that predominates although black-and-white photography has a strong following among both enthusiast and professional users. However, your choice of film will be greatly influenced by your interests and what you want to achieve with your photography.

Your film choice will also depend on how the individual film behaves in practice. No two are identical and, surprising though it might appear, there are substantial and very noticeable differences from film to film, especially regarding colour reproduction. Ideally, try as many products as possible before settling on one. Get to know the film as well as possible, discovering every foible. Only then can you predict with any accuracy how it will react in a particular situation.

Colour print film

The majority of colour film consumed is print material, which is suitable for everything from taking family snapshots on holiday to serious commercial work. This material is also often referred to as colour negative film and it provides the simplest and least expensive means to high quality prints.

The exposure latitude of colour print film is usually quite wide and so it is relatively tolerant to exposure error, particularly towards over-exposure. Under-exposure, however, is less well handled by colour print film and picture quality suffers as a consequence.

In obtaining prints colour negative film undergoes a two-stage process. First the exposed film is developed to give a negative; then the negative is enlarged to give a print. Virtually every print film is developed in Kodak C-41 or an equivalent process. A processed negative has a built-in orange mask and at this point the subject appears in its secondary colours — blue as yellow, green as magenta and red as cyan; it is not until the printing stage that colour correct prints are achieved. It is extremely difficult to perceive from the negative how colours will look on the final print, and as a consequence it is impossible to compare the print and negative.

Despite the enticements of convenience and quality offered by local processing laboratories, there are arguments in favour of developing and printing colour negative films at home. Having total creative control and being involved in producing your own work are just two inducements. There are, however, the investments in equipment, space and time to be considered.

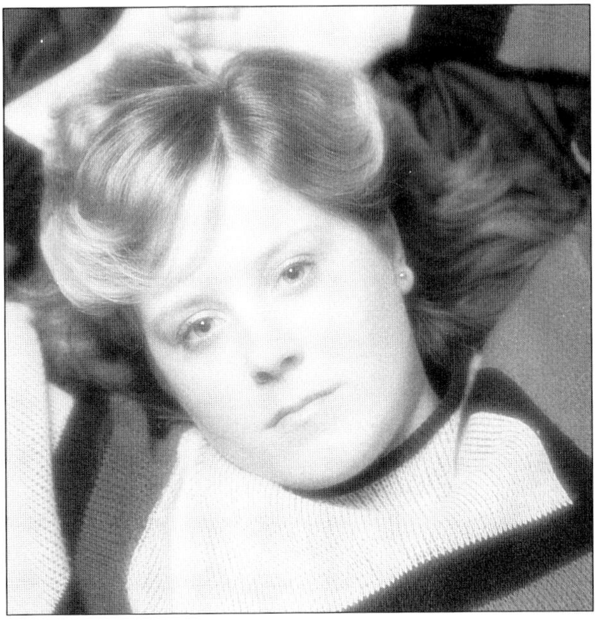

Colour transparency film

For the utmost in image quality, tonal range and colour fidelity, transparency — frequently known as reversal — material is the film to use; it is also the optimum material from which to reproduce or publish. Unlike negative films the processed transparency or slide is the finished product and it is therefore imperative to be as critical as possible during exposure, particularly in respect to composition. Furthermore, compared with negative film the exposure latitude of slide film is significantly tighter and so more care should be taken in this respect.

Slide films can be 'up-rated' to give a faster usable film speed. This means that the film is deliberately under-exposed and this under-exposure is then compensated for by extending the first development stage of the process — this is known as push-processing. Kodachrome slide films can also be push-processed (some laboratories in the USA offer such a service) but because of the very poor quality of the results obtained this is not recommended. Most E-6 type films respond favourably to being pushed. The majority can be exposed at up to two stops faster than their normal rating before there are any significant colour shifts and the grain becomes obtrusive.

Up-rating a film is an extremely useful technique. For example the light might be so poor that a faster film is needed to allow photography to be continued. Professional sports and press photographers frequently find themselves pushing film to enable them to obtain sharp pictures in the most atrocious light yet without any great sacrifices in image quality.

Most modern slide films are Kodak E-6 or compatible process, and can be either commercially or home-processed. Basic requirements for home-processing are a developing tank, chemicals and a supply of warm water, plus a few ancillaries such as measuring cylinders and a thermometer. The E-6 process comprises two basic stages: first the exposed film is developed as a black-and-white emulsion and then, after chemical reversal, the film's colour layers are processed. Older generation colour slide films necessitated physical exposure to light or 'reversal' after the black-and-white stage and before the colour developer. Nowadays the reversal stage is handled chemically.

Films bearing the name 'Kodachrome' undergo the complex K-14 process and can only be laboratory processed. Kodachrome was available only in 35mm format, but that changed with the introduction of Kodachrome 64 in 120 roll film size and the sparkling qualities of this film are now at the disposal of the medium-format photographer.

Prints can be made from slides if required; though in comparison with colour negative material the cost is greater. However, working from slides has the notable advantage that the print can be readily compared with the original transparency. Processes such as Ilford Cibachrome and Kodak Ektachrome R22 are ideally suited to the production of colour prints.

Colour temperature

While the human eye and brain can adjust for differences in colour temperature, a colour film cannot and it will record colours according to its spectral sensitivity. To us, under normal interior tungsten lighting conditions, the light appears to be perfectly natural and white but a daylight-balanced film will reproduce the scene with a strong orange colour cast. The cause is the difference in colour temperature between the light source and the film's colour balance. A typical daylight film is balanced for 5500 Kelvin; a typical tungsten 100 Watt lamp has a colour temperature of around 3200K. On the other hand, blue sky is about 12,000K.

Consequently, if you are shooting daylight-balanced film under tungsten lights a blue colour correction filter such as an 80A or 80B is necessary for the correct balance. Alternatively, use tungsten-balanced film. To use tungsten film in daylight an 85 series orange filter is required. The choice of tungsten-balanced films is limited and most are transparency films.

Monochrome

Black-and-white photography might not have the universal appeal of colour but for the keen photographer it offers an exciting and thought provoking medium. Moreover, the control it is possible to exercise over the finished print is considerable, giving black-and-white workers a creative flexibility not available to colour photographers.

As with colour print film, monochrome is a two stage process: develop first for a negative which is then enlarged for the print. Unlike colour slides or print films which undergo a standard process, the quality of your monochrome films can vary with your choice of film developer and there is a vast range of combinations.

Monochrome films can be up-rated for a higher effective speed by extending the development time. Depending on the film a one, two stops or even more push is permissible with the minimum deterioration in picture quality and the gain in speed usually more than offsets this factor. The quality obtainable from push-processing depends not only on the film but also on the developer employed.

During the past few years monochrome printing has been revolutionised. A giant leap was taken with the advent of resin-coated paper which enabled processing times to be reduced drastically, saving both time and water; a print can now be produced, dry to dry, in a matter of minutes and with a high degree of image stability. A more recent innovation is the availability of high quality variable-contrast, multigrade papers; material that has many contrast grades 'built-in' — each being selected by the use of coloured filters at the enlarging stage.

Ilford XP-1 deserves a special mention. It is a chromogenic film based on colour film technology: the processed negative has had its silver bleached out and replaced with dyes resulting in a less obvious grain structure compared with conventional monochrome films of the same ISO rating. This film can be developed in its own XP-1 process or put through the same C-41 process as colour print films.

Although Ilford XP-1 has a nominal speed of ISO 400 it does have a 'flexible' ISO rating, ie wide exposure latitude, and can be exposed within a range of ISO 50 to ISO 1600 for acceptable results and without recourse to processing modifications. In common with colour negative films under-exposure causes a noticeable falling off in picture quality. Conversely, slight over-exposure results in smoother grain although, because of the increase in negative density, enlarging times have to be suitably extended.

Monochrome negative films may be reversal processed with the appropriate chemistry to produce black-and-white slides. Generally it is best to use a slow film for the maximum contrast and the minimum grain. There is one specially designed monochrome slide film on the market: Agfa Dia-Direct, marketed in 35mm format only, which has an ISO speed of 12 and is sold process paid.

Polaroid Land

Instant feedback is the joy of Polaroid Land film and with its range of film backs Bronica has the facility to exploit its unique characteristics. Whether it is for examining colour, checking lighting arrangements or for allowing the client a glimpse of how the final result will look, Polaroid films are invaluable to the professional photographer. For more details on using Polaroid films see Chapter Thirteen.

Instant 35mm Polaroid films are also available and these can be loaded and used in Bronica 35mm film backs. Processing is performed in a portable processing unit using the chemical pack supplied with each film. For the best results follow the instructions supplied with the processor closely, particularly with regard to temperature.

Infrared films

Bronica lenses are designed to cope with the demands of infrared photography. Infrared radiation focuses at a point behind that of visible light and so a focus adjustment is necessary for pin-sharp pictures, though depending on the lens and aperture, depth of field can cover this discrepancy. To use the infrared focusing index, focus normally, note the distance and then adjust the lens barrel until the noted distance lies opposite the index.

Although used chiefly for medical and scientific purposes and produced in 35mm format only, Kodak Infrared Ektachrome can be employed creatively. Instead of being sensitive to blue, red and green visible light like conventional films it registers green, red and infrared radiation: because of this, colour reproduction is bizarre; orange foliage and green skies for example. It has an approximate ISO of 100 and has to be processed in E-4 chemistry. A yellow filter is advised. This film is predominantly sensitive to visible light so there is no need to use the infrared focusing index.

Kodak also has a monochrome infrared film available. It is called High-speed Infrared film and is sold in 35mm 36-exposure cassettes and in 4 × 5in sheets. Because this film is sensitive to all visible light as well as infrared radiation it must be handled in total darkness at all times until it is processed; this includes loading and unloading the camera. Exposure is best through a deep red or a special opaque infrared filter such as a Wratten 87 series and its ISO rating should be determined by experimentation.

Manufactured by Konica, there is an 120-size infrared film available which has similar properties to the Kodak emulsion.

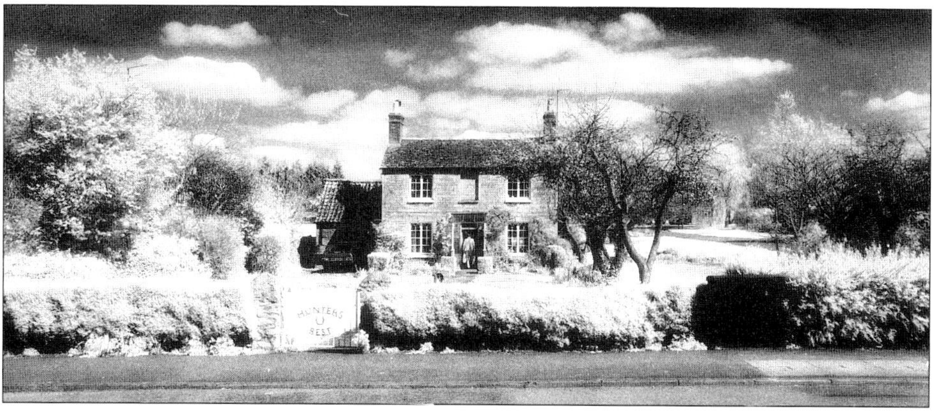

Kodak High-Speed Infrared film gives bizarre results. This shot was taken using a Bronica ETRS, Zenzanon 40mm lens, Hoya red filter and a 35W film back giving a 24 × 54mm negative.

Chapter Eighteen

Filters

Bronica has standardised as much as possible on filter sizes for each of its respective camera systems: ETRS lenses use 62mm filters; SQ-A and SQ-Am use 67mm; and the GS-1's standard is 72mm.

Zenzanon lenses have been formulated to deliver superb optical quality at all apertures throughout their focusing ranges and under the most flare inducing situations. Consequently, in order to optimise their potential it is a sound policy to use filters of the best possible optical quality, such as those available from Hoya.

Filter technique

More than half the secret of using filters successfully is knowing when they will enhance a photograph. With thoughtful application of filters an ordinary scene can be transformed into a photograph of extraordinary beauty and impact.

Filter facts

Most filters absorb light therefore exposure must be increased to compensate. Filter factors indicate by how much exposure has to be modified although they should be taken as a guide only because variables such as film type and lighting conditions can influence them. If you are using a separate hand meter any required exposure compensation has to be manually transferred to the camera. Through-the-lens metering systems automatically account for any light loss caused by the filter.

Filters for black-and-white photography

Most of the filters used in black-and-white photography alter tonal reproduction, either making the scene appear more natural or emphasising a particular aspect of the picture for impact.

A good example of what monochrome filters can do for your photography is their effect on the sky. Panchromatic films are over-sensitive to blue light, and without a filter if you take a landscape shot which includes a beautiful blue sky, it will appear white and detailless on the finished print. Fit a yellow or, for even greater effect, an orange filter and the sky will have an attractive tonal quality with white clouds contrasting strongly with the deeper sky tone. Use a red filter and the effect is even more pronounced.

Filters for colour photography

Unlike the human eye, colour film cannot adapt to various light sources and what we see as normal white light often appears entirely different on film. In tungsten lighting for instance the eye perceives the light as 'white'. Film, on the other hand can only respond according to its sensitivity and consequently a daylight-balanced film will record a tungsten-lit scene with a distinct orange colour cast. Conversely, a tungsten-balanced film will exhibit a pronounced overall blue colouring if exposed in daylight conditions. The need to correct colour is a major reason for the importance of filters in colour photography.

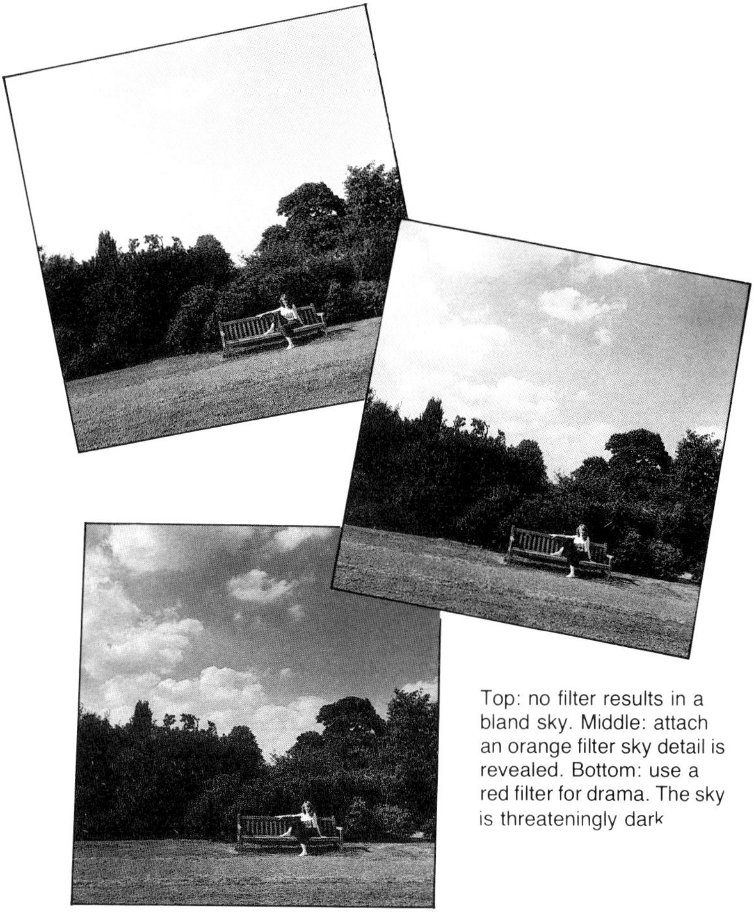

Top: no filter results in a bland sky. Middle: attach an orange filter sky detail is revealed. Bottom: use a red filter for drama. The sky is threateningly dark

The polariser

A polariser, under suitable conditions, can intensify colours, enrich blue skies and cut down reflections. In fact, such is the vast and unequalled potential of this filter that it deserves a section of its own.

Usually supplied in a rotating mount the polariser's effect can be studied in the camera viewfinder while the filter is adjusted. The degree of its effect varies because the amount of polarised light varies. Take the example of a clear, sunny day: face away from the sun and view the scene through the polariser rotating it for the optimum effect — its impact is minimal. Face towards the sun and the result is similar. However turn to face 90 degrees away from the sun, follow the same procedure, and the sky deepens significantly.

The polariser's performance with reflections is similar. Shoot a shop window straight on and any reflections are unaffected, but move round to face the window at an angle of 45 degrees and any reflections present can be effectively minimised.

If you are using a Bronica metering finder the polariser's filter factor is automatically taken care of. Of course, this is not the case with a manual light reading: the filter factor varies according to the situation but usually it is between ×3 to ×4, so bracket to make sure of a correct exposure.

Effects filters

A wide variety of creative effects filters are available, although many of the more outrageous filters should be used sparingly and reserved for special occasions. A selection of the most popular effects filters are described below.

Graduates: From transparent at one end of the filter to deep colour at the other, graduates are especially useful for adding colour to sky during pictorial photography.

While available in many colours, two in particular are strongly recommended as standard equipment: a grey graduate has the effect of a neutral density filter and can be positioned so that it cuts down light only from the sky, leaving the foreground unaffected; and a blue graduate which can be used to impart an attractive sky hue when it is dull and cloudy.

All Bronica Zenzanon lenses are equipped with depth of field preview capability and this is immensely practical with graduate filters for examining the effect at specific f/stops; wider apertures give smoother graduated effects than smaller apertures.

Starburst: Use a starburst on any scene including a few pin-point light sources, a night scene for example, and the effect can be dramatic. The number of points radiating out from the light source depends on the filter: 4, 8, 16-point starbursts are commonly available.

Soft focus and diffuser types: Modern lenses can be too critical and sharp and, in some circumstances, the application of a soft focus or diffuser filter can be desirable. Portraiture, for example, is a prime subject area for this filter type though they can also be deployed effectively for many other subjects. No exposure compensation required.

Close-up: Available in various strengths, and usually sold in sets of three, close-up filters fit on to the front of the lens and permit you to focus nearer than the lens's normal closest focusing distance. Bronica has close-up filters available in each of its camera systems. No exposure compensation necessary.

Filters for Monochrome Photography

Filter	Effect	Filter factor
UV (0)	In black-and-white photography this is chiefly a lens protection filter.	×1
Skylight 1B	Ideally suited for lens protection. Helps to cut-down haze.	×1
Yellow (K2)	Lightens yellow while darkens blue. Frequently used to induce contrast between sky and clouds without greatly affecting the tonal rendition of the remainder of the picture.	×2
Yellow Green (X0)	Greens appear lighter, reds darker. Has a similar effect on sky tone as the yellow filter but is stronger.	×2.5
Green (X1)	Lightens greens and darkens blue. Increases contrast if you are shooting foliage against a blue sky with the green tones recording relatively light against a darker sky background.	×4
Orange (G)	Lightens orange while darkening blues. Stronger than yellow/green, giving skies which can go quite dark with clouds standing out vividly. Useful contrast filter for architecture photography.	×2.5
Red (25A)	Gives powerful contrast effects. Lightens red and orange, darkens green and blue. A blue sky will appear dramatically dark on the final print with any white clouds standing out vividly. Caucasian skin tones appear unhealthy and pallid but tanned faces go slightly deeper. Also helps cuts through haze. Recommended for infrared photography.	×8
Polariser	Can be used to darken a blue sky, provided that the sun is in a suitable position, and has an effect similar to a yellow or orange filter but does not alter the tonal relationships of the subject. Extreme contrast effects in monochrome can be had by using a polariser in combination with a red filter. A polariser can eliminate reflections from glass, water, painted metal surfaces and so on. Its effect varies according to the angle of the lens to the subject. Can also be employed as a neutral density filter.	varies between ×3-4

Filters for Colour Photography

Filter	Effect	Filter factor
UV (0)	Absorbs ultra-violet light. Helps to reduce blueness in outdoor photographs. Also useful as a lens protector.	×1
Skylight 1B	Reduces excessive bluishness. For example outdoor photography under a strong blue sky, on the beach and in the mountains. Recommended as a constant companion on your lenses as protection against physical damage.	×1
Blue 80A	Colour correction filter for photography with daylight-balanced film under tungsten lighting conditions. Increases the colour temperature of tungsten light from 3200K to 5500K.	×2.4
Blue 80B	Similar to 80A except that this filter is for use with photoflood lamps. Changes colour temperature from 3400K to 5500K.	×2
Orange 81A	Faint orange colour filter which can be used to 'warm-up' a scene. Corrects tendency towards bluish tones. Ideal for healthy looking portraits and attractive landscapes. 81A is the weakest in the series.	×1.4
Blue 82A	Light balancing filter used to increase colour temperature giving a cooler rendering. Corrects tendency towards reddish tones. Can be used during early morning or late evening to give neutral skin tone. Weakest in the 82 series.	×1.3
Orange 85B	Decreases colour temperature from 5500K to 3200K. Allows correct colour reproduction with tungsten-balanced film in daylight. Can also be used to give a strong orange tinge to the scene.	×2.1
Polariser	Suitable for minimising distracting reflections from glass, painted metals, water and so on. Also eliminates glare and gives more saturated colour. With the sun in a suitable position blue skies are intensified and white clouds stand out; at wrong angle the effect is minimal. Also useful as a neutral density filter.	×3-4 approximately
Neutral Density	If you want to control the amount of light entering the lens without altering tones and colours neutral density filters are advised. Can be used for monochrome as well as colour. ND × 2 cuts down light by one stop; ND ×4 by two steps; and ND ×8 by three.	Various
FL-Day	For reducing the greenish colour cast which results when shooting daylight film under daylight-type fluorescent strip lighting.	×2
FL-W	Similar to FL-Day except that this filter is designed for use with warm white or white type fluorescent strip lighting.	×2

Chapter Nineteen

Camera care

Attaching the shoulder strap

The shoulder strap is designed to be extremely secure and the attaching procedure should be followed closely for maximum security.

- Prepare by unbuckling the strap to release the U-shaped eyelet from its plastic holder. Next insert the U-shaped ring into the camera body's neck strap eyelet, and then slide it back into the plastic holder ensuring that it is pushed fully home.
- Re-thread the strap, passing it through the U-shape eyelet, but before doubling it back through the plastic holder, adjust the strap's length to suit.
- Finally, weave the strap through the metal buckle and repeat the procedure on the other side of the camera body.

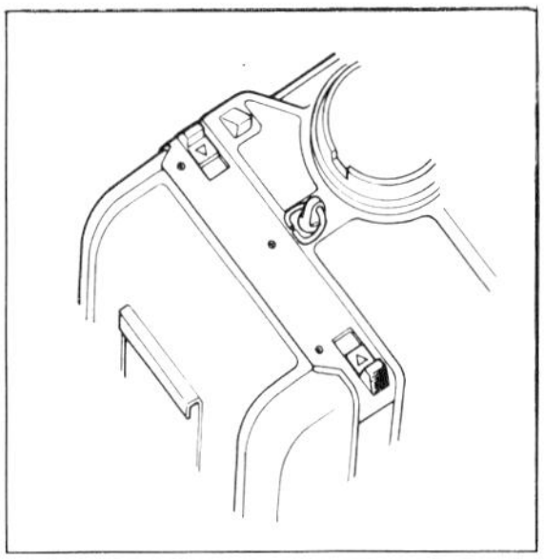

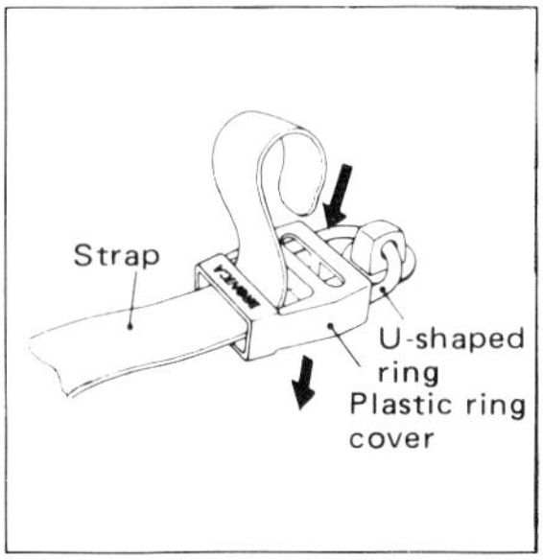

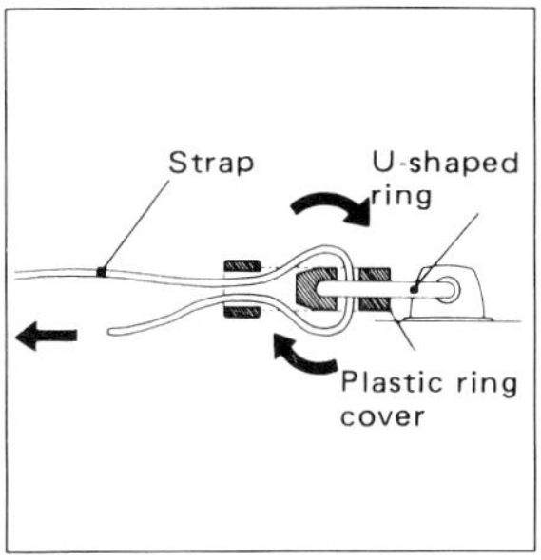

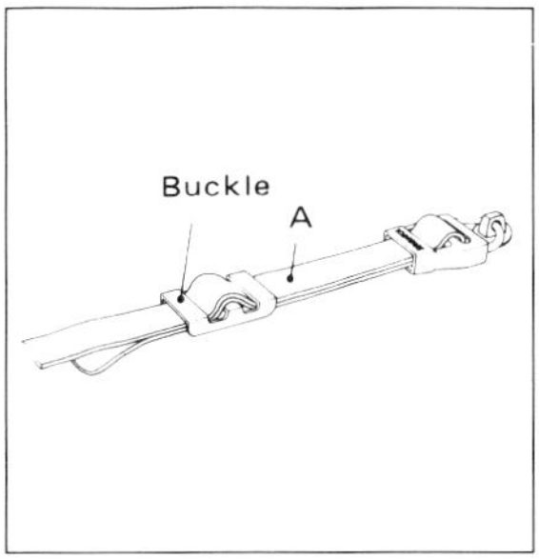

Caring tips

Your camera and lenses are precision instruments engineered to the tightest tolerances. Although they will withstand prolonged use under the most arduous situations they should be well looked after for maximum life.

- Never touch the reflex mirror or use a cloth to clean it. Restrict mirror cleaning to dusting lightly with a blower brush.
- Use lens tissues to clean the lens. First use a blower brush to dislodge any solid particles and then wipe very gently. Avoid silicon impregnated cloths because they can harm the lens coating.
- Protect the camera from vibration during transit. A high quality padded gadget bag, or better still, a foam-lined aluminium camera case will do the job admirably.
- Protect your equipment from dust and grit by using lens and body caps.
- If the camera gets wet then dry it carefully as soon as practicable. Separate the film back, finder and lens and leave them to dry overnight in a warm atmosphere.
- After using the camera in a salty environment wipe it with a moist cloth. Then wipe it dry with a soft, dry cloth.
- Be careful when attaching the camera to a tripod. Over-tightening the attachment screw can damage the body's internal mechanism.
- Remove the battery if the camera is not to be used for some time. Pack the camera in its original packaging with some silica gel desiccant. A battery left in the camera can leak and cause corrosion of the contacts.
- Periodically clean the contacts in the battery chamber using a soft cloth. Do not use sandpaper or emery cloth.
- Before fitting a metering finder to the camera give the electrical contacts a wipe down with a soft cloth.
- Do not clean camera equipment with solvents.
- Protect equipment from severe temperature fluctuations which might cause condensation to form inside the body. Do not leave the camera in direct sunlight or in a car glove compartment.
- Cover the camera's flash synchronisation socket and hot-shoe when not in operation.

INDEX

A

B

C

D

W

Z